Capital and Labour

Theo Nichols has taught sociology at the University of Bristol since 1969. He has written widely on issues related to the labour process and is the author of *Ownership, Control and Ideology* (1969) and co-author of *Safety or Profit* (1973), *Workers Divided* (1976) and *Living with Capitalism* (1977).

Capital and Labour: Studies in the Capitalist Labour Process

Edited by
Theo Nichols

FONTANA PAPERBACKS

First published by Fontana Paperbacks 1980
Copyright in selection and Introductions © Theo Nichols 1980

For further copyright details the reader is referred to pages 5, 6 & 7

Set in Linotype Times

Made and printed in Great Britain by
William Collins Sons & Co. Ltd, Glasgow

A hardback edition of this book is published by the Athlone Press

Contents

Contents

Part IV Management and its Relation to Capital and Labour

Part V The Labour Process and Class Struggle

Preface

Much of the material presented here will be familiar to former students – most of all to those who graduated in 1979. Many thanks are due to them because they taught me a lot. Even more thanks are due however to Mick Lineton, who has taught with me at Bristol, and to Huw Beynon, who used to do so, and with whom this book would have been a joint venture if only we could both have been free at the same time.

Helpful comments on what I've written below have been made among others by Huw Beynon, Christine Eden, Tony Elger, Mick Lineton, Dalbir Singh, Chris Smith and Jackie West. Once again I'm grateful to Doris Macey and Margaret Smith for their typing and good humour.

T.N.

Bristol, April 1979

Introduction

This book contains readings on the labour process that have been chosen from a Marxist perspective. Its publication now is due to three considerations: the state of those studies which we shall call 'industrial' and 'organizational'; the nature of economics; and certain features of contemporary Marxism. This Introduction comments briefly on each of these considerations. The Introduction to Part I then sketches some of the theoretical contours which shape such an approach to the labour process.

The first consideration. This relates to the state of that terminological welter of studies – 'industrial sociology', 'industrial social psychology', 'organization theory', 'occupational sociology', and 'industrial relations'. These studies 'industrial' and 'organizational' (and with them 'sciences' of the 'management' variety) have been responsible over the past decade for the dissemination of ideas about 'job enlargement', rotation and 'enrichment'; about 'participation' and 'industrial democracy'; 'socio-technical systems', 'semi-autonomous work groups'; and much else. But their record is a poor one. In 1978, for example, a working party report to the British Social Science Research Council noted that 'most research on new work organization has avoided consideration of the areas and problems of authority, control, power.' 'Most work is a-historical,' it added. And, as if these two characteristics did not sufficiently underline the slim possibility of such work relating in any meaningful way to the reality of people's lives or to an understanding of how these were formed and might be changed, it noted further that 'most of the research has had a ... consultancy basis with a bias towards particular interests, especially those of management.'[1]

Of course there is room for argument about whether academics who engage in consultancy discover more or less, or aid or hinder theoretical development, when compared to those who are 'pure'. And there is no denying, for instance, that so-to-say 'pure' (theoretically oriented) industrial sociologists exist, even if more so in the universities than in the business schools, polytechnics and the technical colleges, and more so in sociology departments than management ones. The plain fact is, however, that the *theorization* of 'industrial behaviour', as it is called, is itself in a poor state. Michael Rose's *Industrial Behaviour*[2] is now probably the most widely read text-book on the theory of industrial sociology. Yet it is remarkable for the negative way in which its author presents and evaluates the various twists and turns he sees to have characterized the subject's theoretical development. At the outset Rose makes it clear that he finds industrial sociology, and indeed sociology, of 'problematic value'. Throughout the book there is a marked lack of enthusiasm, even embarrassment, for his subject matter. And his conclusion is that 'any new approach to industrial behaviour must begin from an altogether different standpoint from that advanced, consciously or otherwise, to date.'[3]

The situation in 'industrial relations' is no better. In Britain, this area of study and practice grew up separately from industrial sociology, was in many respects pre-theoretical until the quite recent infusion of sociology,[4] and has a deserved reputation for being dull. The commonsensical definition of its subject matter is the study of the 'institutions of job regulation'. But this, as Richard Hyman has pointed out, diverts attention from the structures of power and interests, and the economic, technological and political dynamics of the broader society — factors which inevitably shape the character of relations between employers, workers and their organization. It also carries with it a danger of reification, so that it becomes easy to ignore the real, active men and women whose activities *are* industrial relations. Moreover, the very notion of regulation conceals the centrality of power, conflict and instability in the processes of industrial relations.[5] These are very basic criticisms. They echo some of those already introduced in relation to other 'industrial' and 'organizational' studies. Taken in conjunction with other remarks above they add up to saying that these studies are indeed in an uninspiring and flaccid state.

The second consideration. 'Organization theory' and the other subjects already mentioned really only emerged to their present level of prominence over the past decade. Economics is a relatively long-established discipline. But economics usually leaves the labour process out of account entirely. Inputs go in, outputs come out, but into and out of what it is that they come and go is, it seems, a little too vulgar to say. A deal of time is spent projecting the abstracted mental machinations of economic men whose place in society is socially unspecified. Just how real men in the real world actually produce the possibility of choosing to consume this or that is something which hardly figures at all. Here, then, in what economics does not do, is a second consideration that lies behind the appearance of this book.

But all this it not quite fair. There are indeed at least three quite different false impressions that may have been given so far.

One concerns the apparent lack of understanding of the world which may seem to have been imputed to certain academics. Any such impression must be qualified right away. Because at the top of the industrial relationists' and economists' professions the branches of these trees of knowledge intertwine with the apparatus of the state. And perched up there, and sometimes flitting between consultancy and academic work, are men who think and act as if to hold down wages is a difficult task with possible political implications; who are well aware that it could prove useful, for capital, if trade unions were more deeply incorporated; who are clear-headed about profit, and the contribution of workers to profit-making. The ideas they present in their academic works may conspire to obscure the basic facts, about power, about control, about inequality, in a word about capitalism. But their practice is a different thing.

Then again, it must be recognized that the above remarks have been of a general nature and there are exceptional cases. One such is Baldamus's book *Efficiency and Effort*.[6] First published in 1961, this broke sharply with what its author saw, correctly, to be a situation in which 'industrial sociologists and applied economists share an important postulate ... that the organization of industry as a whole reveals a natural harmony of interests between employers and employees.'[7] It is perhaps because Baldamus had himself worked on the shopfloor (and, as he put it, 'not as a participant observer') that he was so acutely aware, for example, that little was known about workers' experience of what he termed 'physical impairment'. And he was in no doubt why most researchers had neglected it (as they have largely continued to do): it was because 'the objective of past research has been confined to the efficiency of work – "efficiency" as conceived by the employer.'[8] *Efficiency and Effort* paid particular attention to the nature of 'efficiency' and to how 'effort' was related to it, and because it was grounded in experience and was also an explicitly theoretical work, it employed several categories that were, and still are, unfamiliar in what Baldamus called 'the analysis of industrial administration' (the sub-title of his own book). One such was 'the intensity of effort' (a reality very familiar to people who actually work, and a concept that has some parallel in the Marxist view of the labour process). Baldamus viewed 'the entire system of industrial production ... as a system of administrative controls which regulate the quantity, quality, and distribution of human effort.'[9] For him it was quite obvious that to ensure stability of effort and to intensify effort were central control problems for employers, and that competition between firms had a close bearing on the intensification of effort.

Baldamus made only the most fleeting reference to Marx in his whole book[10] but he had an eye for the same sort of thing. As we shall see in the Introduction to Part I, it was crucial to Marx's analysis of the capitalist labour process that what workers sell to capitalists is their labour-*power* or their *capacity* to labour. Baldamus gave the example of an agreement between employers and the national union in the boot and shoe industry to make just this point. He noted that it required employees 'to use their trade skill and productive ability to the best advantage and fullest capacity and with no restriction of output.' 'But who', asked Baldamus, 'can define ability, restricted output, capacity ("fullest" or otherwise)? If the intensity of effort expected from the worker is left undefined, then, surely, everything else that is stated about wages, hours, and method of payment is equally indeterminate ... the formal contract between employer and employee is *incomplete* in a very fundamental sense.' As far as he knew, he said, only one other writer had spotted this (the American organization theorist H. A. Simon). In practice, employers are sometimes much more specific than the example of the boot and shoe agreement suggests, but Baldamus (Marxist *manqué* or not) had here put his finger on an important point; on something of which it could be said that though it 'should be evident even to the casual observer it is very rarely admitted.'[11] A major problem with the studies 'industrial' and 'organizational' is precisely this: that a whole number of things that should be evident to even the casual observer are very rarely admitted.

There is, however, a third possible misunderstanding that may have been fostered. It concerns Marxism, which is itself, in relation to the labour process, the third major factor to lead to this book.

The third consideration. '*In Marxism*, the analysis of the labour process is integral to that of the capitalist mode of production itself.' '*In Marxism*, there is none of that reification according to which organizations take decisions. Men and women, as formed into social classes, are the centre of the historical stage.' '*In Marxism*, class boundaries are not slurred over to render one and all "employees".' The point about quoting these remarks here is to draw attention to the fact that they quite definitely do *not* hold true for the 'Marxism' of some modern Marxists.

In the higher reaches of contemporary Marxist theory, some parts of which bear the stamp of a rather brittle analytical philosophy, it is even charged – for this, note, is intended as a *criticism* – that 'a simple philosophical anthropology' lies at the bottom of any attempt to conceptualize the labour process as a theoretical unity and that 'the anthropology of humanism' is 'a theoretical element in the Marxist general concept of labour'.[12] Suffice to say that recent years have had more than their fair share of involuted philosophical games and to note that some Marxists now challenge the key assumptions ('gut assumptions' you might say) that underpinned Marx's own approach to the labour process.

Thankfully, however, the massive growth of interest in Marxism since the end of the 1960s has far from ignored the labour process. Indeed, since 1974, Harry Braverman's seminal work *Labour and Monopoly Capital*[13] has done a great deal to draw hitherto non-Marxist social scientists into its study. In Britain a number of academic economists who have turned Marxist have also become acquainted with this area through the Conference of Socialist Economists.[14] And in North America discussion about it now features not only in the journal *Monthly Review*, formerly edited by Braverman, but also in many others.[15] It is in the train of this welcome 're-discovery' of the labour process, as it might fairly be called, that this book has been put together. For, post-Braverman, there now exists an area of study which can be loosely indicated by this

15

term, which is the site of theoretical and of theoretically informed empirical work (though there is not yet anything like
enough of this), and which transcends the often rather tired,
narrow, and management-oriented concerns of organizational
and industrial studies. As a French writer has observed, Marxist theory between the wars almost entirely ignored the internal
evolution of the world of work.[16] But in neither Western
Europe nor North America can this be said today.

In short, then, the resurgence of Marxism has taken several
different directions, at least one of which has had the result
of restoring interest in the labour process. Indeed, it must be
admitted that in this connection, as in others, even that particular version of Marxist 'high theory' which disdains to
consider the labour process as a properly constituted 'theoretical object' has had some good effects too. Above all,
through its persistent questioning of the conditions necessary
for the existence of certain social relations, such theoretical
work alerts us to the possibility of variability within the capitalist (or any other) mode of production.[17] This Reader has in
fact been organized with a view to stressing such possible
variability.

Now to say something about the selection of readings in this
book, of which the first is that in taking a primary fix on the
labour process it is not possible to provide formally separate
and equivalent analyses and material on other related matters
as well, such as the state or, say, consumption rather than
production. Trade unionism is similarly denied any lengthy,
separate analysis, though it is obviously of great significance
for the form and intensity of the struggles that characterize
the labour process in the advanced, metropolitan centres of
capitalism upon which the book focuses. This, though, is to
avoid the repetition that would otherwise ensue, given that
Clarke and Clements have already done a useful job for the
Marxist and other literature on trade unions in their *Trade
Unions under Capitalism*.[18]

Certain other matters that are closely connected to the functioning of the labour process are also given relatively little
attention, unemployment and the role of unpaid housework,
for instance. However, an attempt has been made to write the
Introductions and to select the readings in such a way as to
indicate how these and other matters impinge on the labour
process and constitute necessary conditions (or not) of its

existence. No doubt it could be shown that everything which exists in a social formation that is dominated by a capitalist mode of production can be related in some way or other to the labour process. Here, such a logic has not been pursued to the absurd conclusion that to discuss anything it is necessary to examine everything at once. The thinking behind this project follows a different line: that there now exists much interesting and important material from several countries which is the more useful for being collected together in the one place. Centred on the labour process, the readings chosen fall into a pattern unlike that to be found in the traditional texts of industrial sociology. But they yield much that industrial sociologists and others might embrace should they wish to do so, for the major problem of compilation has not been what to put in, but what out of the whole range of writing that merits a wider audience to exclude.

Generally, the attempt has been made to select a few longish readings in each part. Also, as far as possible, those writers have been preferred who seek to make themselves understood, and who write as plainly as possible without undue complication. Regrettably, it is too often the case that Marxism proves itself to be a mystery, and it is not, as it should be, about the *de-mystification* of the world.

Even so, some Marxist concepts are far from universally familiar. It is for this reason that the Introduction to Part I appears in the form that it does. Rather than listing a sequence of overprecise definitions it seeks to use and interconnect various concepts simply introduced and, through their use in relation to the labour process, to break through the circle of mystification that much Marxism is. At the same time the rough sketching out of some of the conditions and inner processes of the capitalist labour process that is attempted there serves as an introduction to the structure of the book itself. For if there is an underlying rationale that gives the following Parts a unity it is only likely to emerge from a closer acquaintance with at least the rudiments of the theoretical perspective from which it stemmed.

Of course, Marxist work on the labour process touches areas that have always been of interest to industrial sociologists and others. In such cases it approaches them out of its primary concern with capital accumulation and class struggle. But sometimes it introduces new facts, or facts that lie outside the conventional boundaries of industrial sociology etc. Consider migrant labour, or shift-work or industrial injury, for instance. Industrial sociology has not paid anything like sufficient attention to any of these subjects, nor, collectively, do they belong to any one of the other subjects mentioned above. Several of the Introductions have been quite deliberately constructed to include information of this neglected type, and an attempt has been made to signpost further reading through the notes.

Just two further points. One, there is no separate Part to deal with 'worker resistance' or 'conflict'. In one form or another such conflict and resistance is integral to the capitalist labour process, and an attempt has therefore been made to deal with it as such throughout. Two, as for any suspicion that the very organization of these readings around the labour process suggests that, deep down, there lurks an 'anthropology of humanism' – well, that's right, there does.

NOTES AND REFERENCES

1 *Research Needs in Work Organisation*, Working Party Report to the Management and Industrial Relations Committee, Social Science Research Council, London, July 1978, p. 23.

2 M. Rose, *Industrial Behaviour: Theoretical Development Since Taylor*, London, Allen Lane, 1975.

3 ibid., pp. 9 and 227.

4 The work of Fox, Goldthorpe, and, from a Marxist perspective, Hyman, has probably been especially important: see, for example, Allan Flanders and Alan Fox, 'The Reform at Collective Bargaining: from Donovan to Durkheim', *British Journal of Industrial Relations*, vol. VII, 1969; John Goldthorpe, 'Industrial Relations in Great Britain: A Critique of Reformism', in *Politics and Society*, 1974; Richard Hyman, *Industrial Relations: A Marxist Introduction*, London, Macmillan, 1975.

5 R. Hyman, *Industrial Relations*, p. 31.

6 G. Baldamus, *Efficiency and Effort: An Analysis of Industrial Administration*, London, Tavistock, 1961. Baldamus is exceptional, though; so much so that, almost twenty years

after he wrote, the author of the most recent British book on organizations is able to claim that his very similar analysis constitutes, in the literature generally, a 'new approach'. See G. Salaman, *Work Organizations: Resistance and Control*, London, Longman, 1979, p. 25.

7 ibid., p. 6.
8 ibid., pp. 53–4.
9 ibid., p. 9.
10 ibid., p. 82.
11 ibid., pp. 90–1.
12 A. Cutler, 'The Romance of "Labour"', *Economy and Society*, vol. 7 (1), February 1978, pp. 77 and 78.
13 Harry Braverman, *Labour and Monopoly Capital: The Degradation of Work in the Twentieth Century*, New York and London, Monthly Review Press, 1974.
14 See, for example, Conference of Socialist Economists, *The Labour Process and Class Strategies*, Stage One, 1976; the related work by Andrew Friedman, *Industry and Labour: Class Struggle at Work and Monopoly Capitalism*, London, Macmillan, 1977; and various contributions (though often at a highly abstract level) to the CSE journal, *Capital and Class*.
15 Among others, URPE's *Review of Radical Political Economics; Politics and Society; The Insurgent Sociologist; Radical America; Socialist Revolution*.
16 See Serge Mallet, *The New Working Class*, Nottingham, Spokesman Books, 1975, p. 15.
17 Not that the authors of such theoretical work still use the term 'mode of production'. See A. Cutler, B. Hindess, P. Hirst and A. Hussain, *Marx's Capital and Capitalism Today*, 2 vols, London, Routledge and Kegan Paul, 1977 and 1978.
18 Tom Clarke and Laurie Clements, *Trade Unions under Capitalism*, London, Fontana/Harvester, 1977. (The work of the writers cited in note 4 can be consulted here.)

PART I

The Capitalist Labour Process

Introduction

Work has been part of human activity in all societies. Certainly this was Marx's view, insofar as work is defined somewhat abstractly as 'purposeful activity aimed at the production of use-values' and the 'appropriation of what exists in nature for the requirements of man'.[1] But *Capital*, even when it dealt directly with 'labour', was not about 'work' in the above sense – or was only partially about 'work'. Engels tried to put his finger on the nub of the matter when he noted: 'The English language has the advantage of possessing two separate words for these two different aspects of labour. Labour which creates use values and is qualitatively determined is called "work" as opposed to "labour"; labour which creates value and is only measured quantitatively is called "labour" as opposed to "work".'[2] If only English *did* correspond so neatly to Engels' distinction. But of course it doesn't, and as a consequence the double nature of what Marx claimed to be happening in the capitalist production process is more easily lost to sight. Similarly, and relatedly, the duality of the division of labour (the one aspect technical, the other social, though both existing in the same instant) is lost to those who believe that 'there has always been a division of labour'.

'Men have always worked.' 'There has always been a division of labour.' Both these statements are correct. Both also fail to account for why men work as they do today under a particular mode of production. Implicitly such statements deny that anything different is happening. And they conspire to hold back the suggestion that what is different stems from the dominance of the capitalist mode of production under which the organization of men's relations for the production of use values and the appropriation of natural substances to human requirements (the technical division of labour) is subject to a *particular* social division of labour (capitalist relations of ownership and non-ownership of the means of production). For to emphasize a favourite point of Marx: '*nature* does not produce on the one hand owners of money or commodities, and on the other hand men possessing nothing but their own labour power.'[3]

The first and the most basic understanding to be gained from a view of 'the labour process' derived from Marx is, therefore, that there is nothing 'natural' – or eternal – about the way it is organized under capitalism. Men were not always related to nature and to one another in this way and, unless we assume that history is now dead, we must not readily assume that they always will be. The wonder of societies dominated by the capitalist mode of production is indeed that they survive, not that one day they will disappear.

Marx frequently introduced two points of comparison to clarify the place occupied by workers in the capitalist mode of production. One concerned the difference between the place of the 'proletariat' in Ancient Greece and that occupied by its modern namesake. The other concerned differences between slavery, feudalism and capitalism. As to the two proletariats, in a few words the basic fact was that the proletariat of antiquity lived at the expense of society, whereas for the modern proletariat it was the opposite that was true. As to the place of the slave in slavery, the serf in feudalism and the worker in capitalism – again in a few words the slave worked for his master and was his property, this was clear enough; in the case of the serf subject to the corvée the *necessary labour* he performed on his own behalf could be distinctly marked off from the *surplus labour* that he performed for his lord, clear enough again; but with the free worker, surplus-labour and necessary labour were 'mingled together'.[4]

The importance of these brisk comparisons here is that they serve to introduce us to two important postulates: that the modern proletariat creates/produces a *surplus* upon which all of society lives, including non-producers (assuming here that there is no other mode of production present); and that it is 'not evident on the surface' how this surplus-producing process occurs, because this is masked by the wage form.

A pure capitalist mode of production is a system of generalized commodity production and exchange in which everything is a commodity, including, most importantly, the worker's labour-power (his capacity to labour). For their work the workers receive a wage; or rather, it appears as if workers receive a wage for their work but, in reality, for putting their capacity to work at the disposition of the capitalist for a limited period workers receive a wage upon which they can live, but which does not represent an equivalent exchange for what they have created. As Marx put it: 'the fact that half a day's labour is necessary to keep the worker alive during 24 hours does not in any way prevent him working a whole day.' So, in this example, labour for 24 hours, get paid for 12 (see page 57 below).

For Marx the capitalist process of production involved both a *labour process* (or, as Engels would perhaps have preferred, a 'work' process) and, at the same time, a *valorization process*; that is, a surplus-value-producing process in which the commodity labour-power was applied to other commodities – raw materials, instruments of production – to produce further commodities, the value of which was greater. But according to *the labour theory of value* only living labour-power (*'variable capital'*) could *create* value. Capital, with its 'one sole driving force ... to valorize itself' – being itself 'dead labour' – could therefore live 'only by sucking living labour'.[5] It paid workers at their historically relative costs of reproduction: that is, at the level considered necessary to maintain them in a given society, allowing for the costs involved in the reproduction of a future generation of workers.[6] But then, having made workers work enough to pay for their own wages, capital drove them to work longer still. Free wage labour indeed!

Workers – as opposed to serfs or slaves – are 'free' in two senses. They are free from any requirement to provide labour services for a particular lord or to labour forever for a slave-owner. They are free, too, in the sense that they are bereft of any means of subsistence other than that to be gained by selling their labour-power. Their labour-power is all that they have to exchange for the other commodities that have to be purchased in order to maintain themselves. 'Free' to enter the capitalist labour process, they are driven there by economic compulsion, not by enslavement or feudal obligation.

Free to choose which capitalist to work for, they are not, however, to be left free to work as they choose. Workers are organized at work by the capitalist or his agents to ensure that surplus is produced. 'Naturally,' Marx observed dryly, 'the consumption of labour-power by the capitalist is ... supervised and directed by him.'[7]

Some points implicit or explicit so far then: one, there is nothing 'natural' or eternal about the capitalist production process; two, it is the 'purpose' of the system – insofar as, of all systems, this anarchic system can be said to have a purpose – to produce a surplus, and it goes *from* labour *to* capital; three, and this is bound up with the last point about 'purpose', in a pure capitalist mode of production, where there is generalized commodity production, those who direct the capitalist enterprises of 'free enterprise' are about as free to choose not to accumulate (since they are separated from each other and are in competition) as the workers who constitute free wage labour are free not to sell their labour-power (since they are separated from the ownership of means of production). In short, 'the *differentia specifica* of capitalist production [is that] labour-power is not purchased under this system for the purpose of satisfying the personal needs of the buyer, either by its service or through its product. The aim of the buyer is the valorization of his capital, the production of commodities which contain more labour than he paid for, and therefore contain a portion of value which costs him nothing and is nevertheless realized [*realisiert*] through the sale of those commodities. The production of surplus-value, or the making of profits, is the absolute law of this mode of production.'[8]

We will return shortly to the matter of what is going on within the capitalist labour process. We will also attempt then to put forward an intelligible guide to the different forms in which Marx saw labour to be 'subsumed' under capital, and try in passing to introduce more fully some Marxist concepts which apply to the labour process.

The above remarks about the capitalist's direction and supervision of the labour process do, however, call for some comment here. At this early point it is also important to warn against a particular kind of tunnel vision that is sometimes associated with an interest in the labour process, and which relates to the concept of the *social relations of production*. So, two brief digressions.

First, this business about the capitalist 'naturally' intervening in the direction and supervision of the labour process. This may not, logically speaking, be a necessary feature of the capitalist mode. Clearly, experiments in worker 'participation', 'autonomous work groups' etc. do occur from time to time. But, as a matter of plain historical fact, very little control over the labour process has been relinquished voluntarily, and what element of control has been 'given' to workers has usually only been 'given' when compensated for by increased or stabilized production. Really, lack of 'progress' to 'industrial democracy' should cause no surprise, unless it is assumed that capitalists or their agents are blandly indifferent to future levels of profitability, and moreover, actually like taking 'risks' – with workers, and the rights of private property. Generally speaking one might suppose that they will not feel free to do this, so that it will indeed be the case that 'in the society where the capitalist mode of production prevails, anarchy in the social division of labour and despotism in the factory [will] mutually condition each other.'[9]

Second, about capitalist relations of production. The point about these is that they consist not only of intra-enterprise relations (capitalist/managers:workers) but also of inter-enterprise relations (that is, relations between private capitals, which are market-mediated and unplanned, as indicated by our earlier reference to the system's lack of 'purpose'). Because of this it is difficult, for example, for worker co-operatives to break away from capitalist principles of organization (hierarchy, wage differentials, minimization of 'wage costs' etc.). This is obvious enough perhaps in the case of the sole co-operative that seeks to stay afloat in a capitalist sea. But the same tendencies will assert themselves even if we consider the notional case of a society in which workers have appropriated *all* enterprises and seek to run them democratically and on the basis of equality – unless, that is, they have had the foresight to abolish the commodity relations which formerly entangled these enterprises. For if these co-operative enterprises had themselves been vested with ownership of their products and had been allowed to buy and sell them on the market, a definite tendency would sooner or later emerge towards accumulation for the sake of accumulation (for blind survival's sake). 'Takeovers' would soon occur, as would the strict organization of labour, and unemployment; and from the surplus population of non-owners now thrown out of work, labour-power would re-appear as a commodity to be bought and sold on the market like any other.[10]

Which is to say that if we restrict our concept of capitalist relations of production to what happens inside the enterprise/ factory, we will not only miss much, but fail to see why what happens does happen.

Capitalist relations of production, then, entail the existence of a class of workers who do not own the means of production; the (free) wage form; and the distribution of the product (including the means of production) through commodity exchange. The rise of 'the boss' and the detail factory labourer were for Marx all of a piece with this. But he distinguished two forms of '*the subsumption of labour under capital*' : the 'formal' and the 'real'.[11]

Viewed historically, it is with the first of these forms that capitalist production emerges from earlier modes of production. For such a *formal subsumption of labour under capital* involves changes in the method by which surplus has been extracted hitherto. Thus, the hierarchical order of guild production gives way to the straightforward distinction between capital and wage labour; the ex-slave-owner engages his former slaves as paid workers; the peasant becomes a farm labourer. There is no fixed political and social relationship of supremacy and subordination. Rather, a mode of compulsion comes into existence that is not based on personal relations of domination and dependency, but on differing economic functions, and the relation between the owners of the conditions of labour and the workers dissolves into a relationship of sale and purchase. It is now the case that before they enter the process of production, the former peasants and feudal lords, the slaves and slave-owners, the journeymen and masters etc, 'all confront each other as commodity owners and their relations involve nothing but *money*.' And within the process of production they meet as its components personified : the capitalist as 'capital', the immediate producers as 'labour'. In short, 'the process of exploitation is stripped of every patriarchal, political or even religious cloak.'

With the formal subsumption of labour under capital, labour itself has become more continuous. The independent artisan may be limited in his labours by the haphazard demands of his customers, but the wage labourer has a constant paymaster – or at least is impelled to seek one out, for unlike the unfree slave whose existence is guaranteed, his is not. The capitalist, for his part, intervenes to supervise the labour process himself. And though, technologically speaking, the labour process goes on much as before, he extends the *duration* of labour as far as possible, so as to increase the yield of surplus value.

By contrast, it is the advent of large-scale industry that marks *the real subsumption of labour under capital*. Its very scale overshadows what remains of the, by comparison, more or less isolated labour of individuals. *Socialized* (collective) *labour* comes into being as the product of co-operation, division of labour within the workshop, the use of machinery and the conscious application of scientific knowledge. And here – which is to say in the specifically capitalist mode of production – production techniques are subject to a constant revolution. 'Production for production's sake' – already on the scene with the formal subsumption of labour – now becomes an indispensable tendency. At this point we come also to the difference between *absolute and relative surplus value*. For if the capitalist does not keep up with the most productive techniques, his competitors will be able to sell their commodities cheaper. The preservation of capital thus requires its prodigious extension. New needs are created, new products, new techniques. Scientific discovery itself becomes a business incorporated into the body of capital, and the increased productivity of labour (*relative* surplus value) becomes the hallmark of real subsumption, just as prolongation of the working day (*absolute* surplus value) was of the formal.

In the English case it would seem that Marx saw the formal subsumption of labour under capital to be broadly coterminous with the period from the mid-sixteenth century up to the last third of the eighteenth. In this period there was simple co-operation between workers who performed the same task (as opposed to the separate production of individual handicraftsmen). There also came about the complex co-operation of the manufacturing division of labour which gave birth to the detail labourer and what Marx called 'manufacture'. However, it was in 'large scale industry' ('modern industry' in some translations of *Capital*) that the labour process was revolutionized. In this later period, the machine and 'science' confronted the worker as pre-existing material conditions of production. And with 'the factory proper' (as Marx called it) the strictest discipline was imposed through the dependence of the worker on the continuous and uniform motion of the machinery.

In this despotism of the factory, made possible by the production of machines by machines, it was the machine itself that had to be followed: 'In handicrafts and manufacture, the worker makes use of a tool, in the factory, the machine makes use of him. There the movements of the instrument of labour proceed from him, here it is the movements of the machine that he must follow. In manufacture the workers are the parts of a living mechanism. In the factory we have a lifeless mechanism which is independent of the workers, who are incorporated into it as living appendages.'[12] With the extraction of relative surplus value there was 'a heightened tension of labour power', 'a closer filling up of the pores of the working day', 'a condensation of labour'.[13]

'We saw', said Marx, looking back on his analysis of the production of relative surplus value, 'that within the capitalist system all methods for raising the social productivity of labour are put into effect at the cost of the individual worker; that all means for the development of production undergo a dialectical inversion so that they become means of domination and exploitation of the producers; they distort the worker into a fragment of a man, they degrade him to the level of an appendage of a machine, they destroy the actual content of his labour by turning it into a torment; they alienate [*entfremden*] from him the intellectual potentialities of the labour process in the same proportion as science is incorporated in it as an independent power; they deform the conditions under which he works, subject him during the labour process to a despotism the more hateful for its meanness; they transform his life-time into working-time, and drag his wife and child beneath the wheels of the juggernaut of capital.'[14] Marx's analysis of the production of relative surplus value was based on the historical case of England, it was analytically ('structurally') related to the distinction between formal and real subsumption, and, let it not be forgotten, it was imbued with a deep and abiding humanism. In Marx the historical, structural and humanist come together: to make exclusive claims for one *or* the other is not to follow the method of Marx.

What, though, of 'the juggernaut of capital' today? Clearly it has grown ever more massive. An unprecedented and international division of labour has been brought about. At the level of the particular company, capitalist investment, even, has become less an individual or family affair and has taken on a more collective, depersonalized form. Because of this both Marx's concept of the capitalist as a 'personification' of capital

– and his references to *'capitals'* rather than *'capitalists'* –
have a thoroughly modern ring.

This is not to say that the giant corporations that dominate
the economies of the metropolitan areas – and, of course,
beyond – are invincible. In the crisis of the last few years, not
least in Britain, the fate of some of the most prestigious of
them – Rolls-Royce for example – has left no room for doubt
on this score. True, the precise causes for the demise of large
corporations vary – the higher labour productivity of competitors can play a part, as can their technical superiority,
greater capital investment, longer production runs, bigger home
markets, the protection of their markets by one means or
another, their access to cheaper labour or greater benefits to
be had in the way of state support. Sometimes, too, just because they are gigantic, some of these corporations have been
propped up for the sake of socio-political stability, the state
being more apt to intervene in the present monopoly phase of
capitalism. Then again, the state has sometimes come to the
rescue for fear that the total demise of a corporation or industry might hinder further technical advance in other sectors,
this being indicative of the degree to which advanced economies
are inter-connected. But sometimes pretty well an entire
branch of production has collapsed, rapidly, as with British
motorcycles.

One way or another, then, not only is it the case that the big
fish still eat the little ones: they sometimes eat each other.
And they are big. According to the American economist, Heilbroner,[15] in 1968 the top 200 firms controlled as large a fraction
of total corporate assets as did the top 1000 in 1941. In Britain,
the largest 100 companies accounted for 15 per cent of manufacturing output in 1909, 20 per cent in 1950, nearly 50 per cent
in 1970 and on one estimate will account for nearly two-thirds
of this by 1980.[16] In 1958 just under 2000 businesses in manufacturing, employing 500 or more persons, accounted for 64
per cent of total manufacturing employment; less than a
quarter of a century earlier, in 1935, the proportion had been
more like 45 per cent.[17] Factory complexes with workforces
massed in their tens of thousands are of course still the exception, and likely to remain so for several reasons (one of
which may be that, whether small is beautiful or not, big, in
this context, is a political danger and employers know this).[18]
Small firms, although they most definitely persist – and indeed
have to be seen in relation to the big corporations for whom

29

they often do sub-contract work, with possible beneficial effects in terms of 'manpower flexibility' and innovatory services – are, however, relatively less important in Britain than in other advanced capitalist countries.

The big corporations are multinational. They dominate the home market and the export trade. For example, in 1972, seventy-five companies (fifty-five of them British, twenty the subsidiaries of foreign multinationals) were responsible for nearly half of British exports in manufacturing goods. The largest British companies derive at least one third of their profit, and sometimes over half, from production overseas, whereas approximately 16 per cent of net assets in manufacturing industry in Britain, and 15 per cent of net assets in all industries, were held by foreign companies in 1970.[19]

To some extent of course the big multinationals can play the market. Smaller suppliers can be played off, one against another. Through *multiple sourcing* (for example, producing the same motor car component, or the same motor car, in Britain and Germany) workers can be divided amongst themselves on a truly international scale. Even nation states can find themselves rivalling each other in their bids to attract capital. The case of Ford's changing relationship to Britain is illustrative here. Faced with a combative workforce at Halewood, Liverpool, Henry Ford once personally threatened to 'get out'. During the time that the Ford British labour force was a synonym for militancy it was in fact repeatedly threatened in this way. Yet in 1978, Ford announced a major new investment in Britain. A new labour force having been found that lacked a reputation for militancy – and the British government having in the meantime held down wages – the company was now happy to take advantage of the £145 million financial inducements offered and to invest £250 million in an engine plant at Bridgend, South Wales, rather than in Spain or Ireland.

Means of production that lie fallow represent a useless advance of capital, and the capital advanced in some quarters of the monopoly sector is very great. In some cases, notably in oil refining, labour is less than a fraction of one per cent of total costs for instance.[20] This makes shift-work very attractive; it is something that now structures millions of people's lives. And shift-work is on the increase. From 1954 to 1964 shift-work in British manufacturing rose from 12 per cent to 20 per cent.[21] On a later estimate, by 1968 more than 25 per cent of workers in manufacturing industry were on shifts, more than double the number in 1954.[22] Night-work has been increasing too. In all industrialized countries, between 8 and 15 per cent of those classified as economically active work nights, the numbers having doubled over the last twenty years and further accelerated over the last ten.[23]

As the Director-General of the International Labour Organization saw it in 1972: 'Shift-work, while no novelty, is increasing as a larger number of industries seek to take full advantage of greater mechanization and automation by the use on a twenty-four-hour basis of modern industrial equipment in a wider range of processes. Owing to the introduction of expensive data-processing equipment', he added, 'it is also being extended to many non-manual occupations where shift-work was previously unknown.'[24]

Despite the talk about directors and 'jet-lag' the real brunt of working shifts is felt elsewhere. According to a recent British survey about 15 per cent of white men work shifts, but the figure is a clear 30 per cent for all those of 'minority' origin and 38 per cent for Pakistanis and Bangladeshis. The figures for nights tell the same story: whites 9 per cent, minorities 19 per cent, Pakistanis and Bangladeshis 27 per cent. The author of these figures tells us that Asians are seeking these jobs in part because it allows them to form an ethnic workgroup which releases them from the need to speak English and allows them to continue in isolation from the white community;[25] in view of this, perhaps it really is necessary to stress that such work has disadvantageous consequences of a physical, psychological and social kind, for anyone, as well as having possible implications for working class organization.[26]

Capitalism in the monopoly phase is very evidently a highly interdependent system. Arguably, its complex, nationally and internationally interlinked production units have brought about a further integration, control and planning of the labour process, both within and between units.[27] Consequently, it now becomes even more apt to talk in terms of '*the collective worker*'. For inside the modern workplace, the individual labourer and the scientist alike tend to work as part of a team: and outside the workplace, the more the concentration and centralization of capital advances, the closer and closer become the bonds of objective co-operation between workers who live hundreds, if not thousands of miles apart. As Mandel has noted,[28] it is indeed one of the achievements of Marx's

Resultate. to have developed our understanding of the *objective socialization of labour by capitalism.* Yet there are no easy generalizations to be made about 'the labour process and monopoly capitalism'. For one thing, monopoly capitalism is a capitalist system dominated by monopoly capitals – not a macro system in which each capital is a microcosm of a monopoly. For another, the fact that the *Resultate.* was written some time between 1863 and 1866 – well over a century ago – must put us on our guard against exaggerating the significance of twentieth-century developments for the labour process. To take the example of shift-work: even in writing the first volume of *Capital* Marx was able to comment that it was 'well known' how this had 'predominated in the full-blooded springtime of the English cotton industry.'[29]

Then again, consider Taylorism and Fordism. It is now probably the generally accepted view that the scientific management of F. W. Taylor was more a systematic summation and formalization of many of the tendencies that Marx attributed to large-scale industry than a break from these. But it may also be in order to say something similar about Fordism, despite current claims that it constituted 'a real innovation',[30] or that it introduced 'a new epoch of the capitalist mode of production'.[31] Two principles claimed for Fordism, as distinct from scientific management, are that it introduced a new method of control over labour-power, and that it introduced the 'flow line'. The first of these, however, which refers to the introduction of a measured day work type system (see pages 267–9), has never been uniformally implemented, even throughout the car industry, though Henry Ford first introduced the 'Five Dollar Day' way back in 1914.[32] And the second – the flow line, with its objective 'to "fix" the worker to his work position so that he never has to step away from it'[33] – is simply an accentuation of, rather than a qualitative break from, how, in Marx's words, 'in the factory, the machine makes use of him ... it is the movements of the machine that he must follow ... In the factory we have a lifeless mechanism which is independent of the workers, who are incorporated into it as living appendages' (see page 68). In fact Marx was no stranger to the argument that high fixed (or 'overhead') costs – which are now associated with the flow line – pushed capital into continuous production (as is conceded by Sohn-Rethel, one of the modern Marxists who proposes a third, monopoly stage ['epoch'] of the capitalist labour process to follow manufacture and large-scale or 'modern' industry).[34]

Of course Ford's introduction of the flow-line principle (conveyors) in the concrete shape of the assembly line, had implications for the rate at which commodities could be produced, for the wages it was possible to pay workers (and for their physical and mental health). It had implications also for both the rate and mass of capital that could be accumulated and for the capital that then *had* to be accumulated to stay in the business of making profit (in this instance by making cars). But as has been seen, it was to just this sort of heightened intensity of the operation of the law of the capitalist mode of production and, with this, to the beginnings of the above effects on the labour process, that Marx referred by 'the real subsumption of labour under capital'. Much of what is all too familiar to millions of workers in factories, and increasingly today in offices, was captured already in what Marx had to say about 'The Factory' in 1867 (reproduced at pages 66–72 below).

'Men make their own history,' wrote Marx (adding, 'but they do not make it just as they please')[35] and he predicated his analysis of the capitalist production process on an equally animate and dynamic socio-historical theory, the labour theory of value.[36] There is a powerful affinity between these two views, about how history is made (and acts back upon men) and about how profit is made (and how the process of profit-making and the products of men's work act back on them). At the level of ideology, the *'fetishism of commodities'* lay in men's failure to recognize that what they saw as relations between things (commodities) were in fact the products of their own hands and brains and of a definite social relation between themselves. This fetishism was akin to the alienation of religion, whereby 'the products of the human brain appear as autonomous figures endowed with a life of their own, which enter into relations both with each other and with the human race.'[37] Capital, for Marx, was not therefore a thing but a social relationship within which men were treated as commodities (things). As with religion, the domination of capital was something that men produced, and re-produced, and, in certain circumstances, could alter. 'Capital', according to the labour theory of value, is 'objectified' labour; in the process of its reproduction workers reproduce the conditions of their own subservience – of their own alienation.

A further continuity to this theme – of agency, of potential, of relationship – is given in the way that Marx characterized what it is that the workers sell to capital in the capitalist labour process; it is of course their labour-*power*. 'Append-ages' to machines they might become – but '*living* appendages', with a potential to be otherwise than those who owned the means of production might want. Here, then, we come to two ideas that were central to the way that Marx looked at the capitalist labour process: one, that what workers sell to capital is their labour-*power* and, two, and related to this, the notion that labour-power is *variable capital*, this being a function also of the fact that capital is a relation.

'Instead of *labour*,' Marx remonstrated, 'Ricardo should have discussed labour-*power*' because then he would have had to reveal capital for what it is: 'as the material condition of labour, confronting the labourer as power that has acquired an independent existence ... as a *definite social relationship*.'[38] As a recent commentator[39] on the differences between Marx and Ricardo has put it, whereas for Ricardo and the neo-Ricardians capital is a social relationship only insofar as it represents a claim to part of the product, in the last analysis the distinction between Ricardo's labour and Marx's labour-power is that in purchasing labour-power, capital established its despotism *in the labour process*.

If one speaks only of the purchase of *labour*, there is noth-ing to distinguish the social relationship between an industrial capitalist and factory worker from that between a merchant capitalist and a petty commodity producer. The difference between different modes of production is therefore lost, and the slippery slide is on towards the ideas we mentioned at the outset: 'Men have always worked.' 'There has always been a division of labour.' At best, the labour process it taken to reflect an eternal/natural state of affairs; most likely it is ignored, a mysterious void between input and output.

'Labour-power', then, as a concept employed in the analysis of the capitalist mode of production, draws attention to the historical and comparative fact that capitalism is but *one* mode of production; it signposts the link between the class relations of the capitalist mode and the production process; and it reminds us that the working class, who sell their labour-power, are, in their massed potential, a danger to capital. Insofar as capitalist production rests on their imagination, their initiative, the acting out of their potential, it could not be otherwise. The major contradiction of the capitalist mode of production –

that between social production and private appropriation – can be traced back to just this fact. For capitalist accumulation requires *both* that this initiative and imagination be acted out – capitalism itself being, through the objective socialization of labour, a highly social, co-operative, mode of production – *and* that such initiatives be not unleashed, if they interfere with private appropriation.

'Value', said Joan Robinson, 'is just a word,'[40] and, sure enough, those who wish to test the labour theory of value as if it were a theory of prices may justifiably give assent to this. Leaving the value/price question aside here,[41] it has to be stressed however that just as labour-power is not just two words when one would do, so, awkward as it may sound at first, *'variable capital'* is not just two words of less than certain meaning either. In fact this concept constitutes a fine illustration of the way Marx thought in terms of relationships.[42] For variable *capital* (or labour-power) represented part of the (unequally founded) unity of capital *in toto*: the other part of which was constant *capital* (that which was advanced by the capitalist for buildings, machinery, raw materials, in short the physical means of production).

Why *'variable'* though? Is there anything to be learned from this further rudimentary component of Marx's analysis of the capitalist labour process? By calling labour-power *'variable* capital' Marx made it clear that surplus value – the value that was produced over and above that necessary to sustain and reproduce labour – was not determined in some mechanical, a-social way. For one thing it was affected by the duration of labour. The workers' fight *against* the extension of this restricted the extraction of absolute surplus value, just as much as the employers' extension increased it. For another thing, it was affected by the intensity of labour; the workers' fight *against* 'speed up', for example, could restrict an increase in the rate of surplus value just as the employer's successful implementation of this could increase it. (And, to give this term one final twist, for Marx of course the very value of labour-power was itself historically variable.) If powerful enough, then, employers can vary the surplus value created. And if they are strong enough, workers can vary this too. The term 'variable' draws attention to the fact that the surplus actually created varies according to the relative strength of the combatants within the production process;[43] a strength which will depend on many factors.

Of course, levels of unemployment, the availability of cheaper or dearer new means of production, the role the state plays in regard to wages and conditions of employment etc, can all have effects on what happens in actual capitalist labour processes, as can a host of other specifics. And always, in looking at labour processes, it is important to ask how far they match up to the features Marx held to characterize a pure capitalist mode of production. But taking the work of Marx as our starting point at least offers a general theory applicable to the labour process and its place in the capitalist mode of production, and an attempt has been made to structure the empirical and shorter-range theoretical contents of this Reader on this.

PART I   Following immediately below this Introduction, some of Marx's writing from *Capital* is presented that bears directly on the labour process and the valorization process, and on the factory.

PART II   Already it has been necessary to make references to a 'pure' capitalist mode of production. The idea that, in capitalism, the workers are 'free' to sell their labour-power has been put forward in this connection. Here therefore the subject matter is the freedom, or otherwise, of workers who work for capitalist enterprises in the world as it really is, and has been; which is to say, unevenly developed.

PART III   Again, it has been necessary already to introduce the concept of the 'reproduction of labour-power'. Here some of the recent literature on migrant labour is introduced in the context of an exploration of some of the different ways in which the labour force is reproduced. The family is also considered in relation to this, as, with reference to some of the ideological aspects of reproduction, is the educational system.

PART IV   The readings presented in this Part concern some of the questions that arise about the origins of management, and the present-day relations of managers to capital and to labour.

PART V The last few pages have stressed the importance of the concepts of 'variable capital' and 'labour-power'. Subsequent Parts, as can be seen above, consider aspects of forced and free labour (II) and the reproduction of the labour force (III). Through Part IV, however – which bears on the relation of management to the class structure – we come in Part V to a consideration of the labour process more narrowly defined. Given what has by now been indicated about the different economic, social and legal conditions that can form the context for particular capitalist labour processes, readings are presented here on different payment systems, productivity deals, scientific management, 'participation' and 'enrichment', and different balances of repression and incorporation as evidenced by studies of management strategies and techniques – on various techniques in fact that are used to intensify and stabilize labour productivity and to further the subsumption of labour under capital.

NOTES AND REFERENCES

1 *Capital*, vol. 1, Harmondsworth, Penguin, 1976, p. 290. Marx's writing on the capitalist labour process is to be found in the *Economic and Philosophical Manuscripts* in the *Grundrisse* and elsewhere. But the following account is mainly centred on his extensive analysis in *Capital*, vol. 1, especially in Part Three 'The Production of Absolute Surplus Value', Part Four 'The Production of Relative Surplus Value' and Part Five 'The Production of Absolute and Relative Surplus Value'. All references are to the Penguin edition. This is particularly useful to students of the labour process since it includes the first English translation of the so-called 'lost chapter': 'Results of the Immediate Process of Production' (the *Resultate*.).

2 Engels in *Capital*, vol. 1, p. 138n.

3 *Capital*, vol. 1, p. 273.

4 ibid., p. 346.

5 *Capital*, vol. 1, p. 342.

6 Thus: 'The value of labour-power was determined, not only by the labour-time necessary to maintain the individual adult worker, but also by that necessary to maintain his family.' *Capital*, vol. 1, p. 518. Marx went on to note – at a time when 'machinery, by throwing every member of that family on to the labour-market, spread(s) the value of the man's labour-power over his whole family' – that the mothers 'confiscated by capital' had to find substitutes for certain family functions, so that 'domestic work, such as sewing and mending must be replaced by the purchase of ready-made articles.' What this meant, as many a working mother knows today, is that 'the diminished expenditure of labour in the house is accompanied by an increased expenditure of money outside. The cost of production of the working-class family therefore increases, and balances its greater income.' (At the back of these developments lie questions about the necessity or otherwise of the nuclear family for the capitalist mode of production; this issue is taken up in Part III.)

7 *Capital*, vol. 1, p. 1026.

8 ibid., p. 769.

9 ibid., p. 477.

10 For the above example, which was originally applied in the context of a discussion about the USSR and state capitalism, see Ernest Mandel, 'The Nature of the USSR, Socialism, Democracy', *Inprecor*, 8 December 1977, pp. 5–6.

11 Marx's own discussion of the subsumption of labour under capital and of its 'formal' and 'real' forms is to be found in the *Resultate*.; see *Capital*, vol. 1, especially pp. 1019–38. A contemporary writer has put the difference between these forms as being that whereas the 'formal ... takes place through the market exchange of labour-power for a wage ... the real subjection ... takes place in the labour process itself.' See W. Lazonick, 'The Subjection of Labour to Capital: the Rise of the Capitalist System', *Review of Radical Political Economies*, 10, 1, 1978, p. 3.

12 *Capital*, vol. 1, p. 548.

13 ibid., p. 534.

14 ibid., p. 799.

15 R. L. Heilbroner, *Business Civilisation in Decline*, Harmondsworth, Penguin, 1977, p. 57.

16 *The Menace of the Multinationals*, London, Labour Research Department, 1974, p. 8.

17 G. C. Allen, *The Structures of British Industry*, London, Longman, 1970, p. 46.

18 At a 1977 SSRC Conference on Management and Industrial Relations an ex-industrial relations manager-cum-academic consultant stated that he knew of at least six companies that would never again build a factory for more than 2000 workers for this reason. He felt unable to name names. In 1979 an Engineering Employers' Federation inquiry into British machine tool companies reported that many of the companies interviewed kept themselves below a certain size to avoid 'industrial relations problems', even though this deprived them of economies of scale. See the *Observer*, 12 August 1979.

19 *The Menace of the Multinationals*, pp. 8, 9, 14.

20 Details of some startling cases of capital intensiveness are to be found in Charles Levinson, *Capital, Inflation and the Multinationals*, London, Allen and Unwin, 1971.

21 The 1964 figure was 18 per cent, for a more broadly defined group of industries. See *British Labour Statistics*: 1886–1968, London, HMSO, 1977, table 201.

22 *Employment: Working Conditions and Rewards*, IPC Sociological Monographs, 7, London, IPC Marketing Services, June 1975, pp. ii and 11.

23 J. Carpentier and P. Cazamina, *Night Work: Its Effects on the Health and Welfare of the Worker*, Geneva, ILO, 1977, p. 1.

24 Cited in A. A. Evans, *Hours of Work in Industrialised Countries*, Geneva, ILO, 1975, p. 94.

25 See David J. Smith, *Racial Disadvantage in Britain: The PEP Report*, Harmondsworth, Penguin, 1977, table A24, p. 81 and p. 82. This piece of sociological wisdom is repeated later on (p. 86) when, it being established that 'minority men' at 'the lowest job levels' have to do far more shift work to achieve equality of earnings with whites, he continues: 'It is therefore correct to describe the use of Asians and West Indians for unskilled and semi-skilled shift work as a form of exploitation, though this is part of a reciprocal system ... which ... offers social advantages ... to those who cannot speak English, whom shift work tends to insulate from the demands of English-speaking, white British society.' This is the kind of 'reciprocal system' in which

having only one arm is balanced by having only one leg.

26 For the effects of shiftwork see P. E. Mott *et al.*, *Shift Work: The Social, Psychological and Physical Conse-quences*, Ann Arbor, University of Michigan Press, 1965; with special reference to night-work see Carpentier and Cazamina. Further observations on the social, psychological and organizational effects of a 'continental' shift system are to be found in Nichols and Armstrong, *Workers Divided*, and Nichols and Beynon, *Living with Capitalism*. Industrial sociology has tended to ignore shiftwork (which, in British social sciences' division of labour belongs to industrial re-lations or social economics). The most exhaustive of in-dustrial sociology textbooks makes no mention of it, despite having a special part devoted to how 'Industry Influences the Community' (matched, of course, by 'The Community Influences Industry'!). What is less excusable is that, in Marxism, Marxist *theory* should have got to such a pitch that even when it bears on the labour process it, too, has paid scant attention to the hours people work – e.g. shift-work does not rate an entry in a recent book which *inter alia* actually predicates the rise of monopoly capitalism on 'the dominance of the overhead cost'. For the sociology see S. R. Parker *et al.*, *The Sociology of Industry*, London, Allen and Unwin, 3rd ed. 1977, pp. 65, 67; for the Marxism see Alfred Sohn-Rethel, *Intellectual and Manual Labour*, London, Macmillan, 1978, pp. 148–9.

27 Such, for example, would seem to be the view sketched by Poulantzas, see Nicos Poulantzas, *Classes in Contemporary Capitalism*, London, NLB, 1975, pp. 58, 116–30 and 134–5.

28 Ernest Mandel, Introduction to the *Resultate.* in *Capital*, vol. 1, pp. 945–6.

29 *Capital*, vol. 1, p. 367.

30 See for example Christian Palloix, 'The Labour Press: From Fordism to Neo-Fordism' in Conference of Socialist Economists, *The Labour Process and Class Strategies*, p. 59.

31 Sohn-Rethel, *Intellectual and Manual Labour*, p. 161.

32 On the 'Five Dollar Day' see Huw Beynon, *Working For Ford*, Harmondsworth, Penguin, 1973, pp. 20–5.

33 Palloix, 'The Labour Process', p. 59.

34 Sohn-Rethel, *Intellectual and Manual Labour*, pp. 140–3.

35 *The Eighteenth Brumaire of Louis Bonaparte*, in *Marx and Engels Selected Works*, London, Lawrence and Wishart, 1968, p. 96.

36 According to the labour theory of value the rate of surplus value is synonymous with the rate of exploitation (thus, where v=variable capital, s=surplus and e=exploitation, $e = \frac{s}{v}$).

Strictly speaking, 'exploitation' takes place in relation to the productive labour that alone produces surplus value. The term 'oppression' then refers to unproductive labour (which embraces, for instance, workers in insurance and banking; in commerce; various state employees in the social control and repressive apparatuses – social workers, soldiers etc.). Here, though, exploitation is used in its general sense throughout. The above hieroglyphic vein of Marxism is not followed either (though it does of course have authentic Marxian roots); nor is that kind of fatalistic economic Marxism embraced, which strains to argue everything back from the tendency of the rate of profit to fall. Marx's claim that capital buys labour-power in order to exploit it was at the bottom of his politics and, in so far as the organization of this book does loosely derive from the labour theory of value, it is what might be called its 'political' aspects that have been followed – that is, questions about how men are exploited, how they fight back, how this affects the techniques of exploitation, how and why power – including labour-power – works.

37 *Capital*, vol. 1, p. 165.

38 *Theories of Surplus Value*, part 2, London, Lawrence and Wishart, 1969, p. 400.

39 Bob Rowthorn, 'Neo-Classicism, New-Ricardianism and Marxism', *New Left Review*, 86, July–August 1974, p. 86.

40 Joan Robinson, *Economic Philosophy*, London, Watts & Co., 1962, p. 46.

41 For a recent contribution concerning the definition and status of certain value categories see Philip Armstrong, Andrew Glyn, John Harrison, 'In Defence of Value' (an extended review of Ian Steedman's *Marx After Sraffa*, London, NLB, 1977), *Capital and Class*, Summer 1978.

42 The general proposition about Marx and relationships is argued, though to excess, by Bertell Ollman, *Alienation*, London, Cambridge University Press, 1971.

43 See Rowthorn, p. 87.

1 Marx on the Labour Process

The Labour Process and the Valorization Process

Karl Marx

1. THE LABOUR PROCESS

The use of labour-power is labour itself. The purchaser of labour-power consumes it by setting the seller of it to work. By working, the latter becomes in actuality what previously he only was potentially, namely labour-power in action, a worker. In order to embody his labour in commodities, he must above all embody it in use-values, things which serve to satisfy needs of one kind or another. Hence what the capitalist sets the worker to produce is a particular use-value, a specific article. The fact that the production of use-values, or goods, is carried on under the control of a capitalist and on his behalf does not alter the general character of that production. We shall therefore, in the first place, have to consider the labour process independently of any specific social formation.

Labour is, first of all, a process between man and nature, a process by which man, through his own actions, mediates, regulates and controls the metabolism between himself and nature. He confronts the materials of nature as a force of nature. He sets in motion the natural forces which belong to his own body, his arms, legs, head and hands, in order to appropriate the materials of nature in a form adapted to his own needs. Through this movement he acts upon external nature and changes it, and in this way he simultaneously changes his own nature. He develops the potentialities slumbering within nature, and subjects the play of its forces to his own sovereign power. We are not dealing here with those first instinctive forms of labour which remain on the animal level. An immense interval of time separates the state of things in which a man brings his labour-power to market for sale as a commodity from the situation when human labour had not yet cast off its first instinctive form. We presuppose labour in a form in which it is an exclusively human characteristic. A spider conducts operations which resemble those of the weaver, and a bee would put many a human architect to shame by the construction of its honeycomb cells. But what distinguishes the worst architect from the best of bees is that the architect builds the cell in his mind, before he constructs it in wax. At the end of every labour process, a result emerges which had already been conceived by the worker at the beginning, hence already existed ideally. Man not only effects a change of form in the materials of nature; he also realizes [*verwirklicht*] his own purpose in those materials. And this is a purpose he is conscious of, it determines the mode of his activity with the rigidity of a law, and he must subordinate his will to it. This subordination is no mere momentary act. Apart from the exertion of the working organs, a purposeful will is required for the entire duration of the work. This means close attention. The less he is attracted by the nature of the work and the way in which it has to be accomplished, and the less, therefore, he enjoys it as the free play of his own physical and mental powers, the closer his attention is forced to be.

The simple elements of the labour process are (1) purposeful activity, that is work itself; (2) the object on which that work is performed; and (3) the instruments of that work.

The land (and this, economically speaking, includes water) in its original state in which it supplies[1] man with necessaries or means of subsistence ready to hand is available without any effort on his part as the universal material for human labour. All those things which labour merely separates from immediate connection with their environment are objects of labour spontaneously provided by nature, such as fish caught and separated from their natural element, namely water, timber felled in virgin forests, and ores extracted from their veins. If, on the other hand, the object of labour has, so to speak, been filtered through previous labour, we call it raw material. For example, ore already extracted and ready for washing. All raw material is an object of labour [*Arbeitsgegenstand*], but not every object of labour is raw material; the object of labour counts as raw material only when it has already undergone some alteration by means of labour.*

An instrument of labour is a thing, or a complex of things,

---

* Marx thus uses the term 'raw material' in a technical sense, narrower than that of standard English usage.

which the worker interposes between himself and the object of his labour and which serves as a conductor, directing his activity on to that object. He makes use of the mechanical, physical and chemical properties of some substances in order to set them to work on other substances as instruments of his power, and in accordance with his purposes.[2] Leaving out of consideration such ready-made means of subsistence as fruits, in gathering which a man's bodily organs alone serve as the instruments of his labour, the object the worker directly takes possession of is not the object of labour but its instrument. Thus nature becomes one of the organs of his activity, which he annexes to his own bodily organs, adding stature to himself in spite of the Bible. As the earth is his original larder, so too it is his original tool house. It supplies him, for instance, with stones for throwing, grinding, pressing, cutting, etc. The earth itself is an instrument of labour, but its use in this way, in agriculture, presupposes a whole series of other instruments and a comparatively high stage of development of labour-power.[3] As soon as the labour process has undergone the slightest development, it requires specially prepared instruments. Thus we find stone implements and weapons in the oldest caves. In the earliest period of human history, domesticated animals, i.e. animals that have undergone modification by means of labour, that have been bred specially, play the chief part as instruments of labour along with stones, wood, bones and shells, which have also had work done on them.[4] The use and construction of instruments of labour, although present in germ among certain species of animals, is characteristic of the specifically human labour process, and Franklin therefore defines man as 'a tool-making animal'. Relics of bygone instruments of labour possess the same importance for the investigation of extinct economic formations of society as do fossil bones for the determination of extinct species of animals. It is not what is made but how, and by what instruments of labour, that distinguishes different economic epochs.[5] Instruments of labour not only supply a standard of the degree of development which human labour has attained, but they also indicate the social relations within which men work. Among the instruments of labour, those of a mechanical kind, which, taken as a whole, we may call the bones and muscles of production, offer much more decisive evidence of the character of a given social epoch of production than those which, like pipes, tubs, baskets, jars, etc., serve only to hold the materials for labour, and may be given the general denotation of the vascular system of production. The latter first begins to play an important part in the chemical industries.[6]

In a wider sense we may include among the instruments of labour, in addition to things through which the impact of labour on its object is mediated, and which therefore, in one way or another, serve as conductors of activity, all the objective conditions necessary for carrying on the labour process. These do not enter directly into the process, but without them it is either impossible for it to take place, or possible only to a partial extent. Once again, the earth itself is a universal instrument of this kind, for it provides the worker with the ground beneath his feet and a 'field of employment' for his own particular process. Instruments of this kind, which have already been mediated through past labour, include workshops, canals, roads, etc.

In the labour process, therefore, man's activity, *via* the instruments of labour, effects an alteration in the object of labour which was intended from the outset. The process is extinguished in the product. The product of the process is a use-value, a piece of natural material adapted to human needs by means of a change in its form. Labour has become bound up in its object: labour has been objectified, the object has been worked on. What on the side of the worker appeared in the form of unrest [*Unruhe*] now appears, on the side of the product, in the form of being [*Sein*], as a fixed, immobile characteristic. The worker has spun, and the product is a spinning.*

If we look at the whole process from the point of view of its result, the product, it is plain that both the instruments and the object of labour are means of production[7] and that the labour itself is productive labour.[8]

Although a use-value emerges from the labour process, in the form of a product, other use-values, products of previous labour, enter into it as means of production. The same use-value is both the product of a previous process, and a means of production in a later process. Products are therefore not only results of labour, but also its essential conditions.

With the exception of the extractive industries, such as mining, hunting, fishing (and agriculture, but only in so far as it starts by breaking up virgin soil), where the material for labour is provided directly by nature, all branches of industry deal

---

* 'Spinning': a quantity of thread or spun yarn (*O.E.D.*).

with raw material, i.e. an object of labour which has already been filtered through labour, which is itself already a product of labour. An example is seed in agriculture. Animals and plants which we are accustomed to consider as products of nature, may be, in their present form, not only products of, say, last year's labour, but the result of a gradual transformation continued through many generations under human control, and through the agency of human labour. As regards the instruments of labour in particular, they show traces of the labour of past ages, even to the most superficial observer, in the great majority of cases.

Raw material may either form the principal substance of a product, or it may enter into its formation only as an accessory. An accessory may be consumed by the instruments of labour, such as coal by a steam-engine, oil by a wheel, hay by draft-horses, or it may be added to the raw material in order to produce some physical modification of it, as chlorine is added to unbleached linen, coal to iron, dye to wool, or again it may help to accomplish the work itself, as in the case of the materials used for heating and lighting workshops. The distinction between principal substance and accessory vanishes in the chemical industries proper, because there none of the raw material reappears, in its original composition, in the substance of the product.[9]

Every object possesses various properties, and is thus capable of being applied to different uses. The same product may therefore form the raw material for very different labour processes. Corn, for example, is a raw material for millers, starch-manufacturers, distillers and cattle-breeders. It also enters as raw material into its own production in the shape of seed; coal both emerges from the mining industry as a product and enters into it as a means of production.

Again, a particular product may be used as both instrument of labour and raw material in the same process. Take, for instance, the fattening of cattle, where the animal is the raw material, and at the same time an instrument for the production of manure.

A product, though ready for immediate consumption, may nevertheless serve as raw material for a further product, as grapes do when they become the raw material for wine. On the other hand, labour may release its product in such a form that it can only be used as raw material. Raw material in this con-

dition, such as cotton, thread and yarn, is called semi-manufac-
tured, but should rather be described as having been manufactured up to a certain level. Although itself already a product,
this raw material may have to go through a whole series of
different processes, and in each of these it serves as raw
material, changing its shape constantly, until it is precipitated
from the last process of the series in finished form, either as
means of subsistence or as instrument of labour.

Hence we see that whether a use-value is to be regarded as
raw material, as instrument of labour or as product is determined entirely by its specific function in the labour process, by
the position it occupies there: as its position changes, so do its
determining characteristics.

Therefore, whenever products enter as means of production
into new labour processes, they lose their character of being
products and function only as objective factors contributing to
living labour. A spinner treats spindles only as a means for
spinning, and flax as the material he spins. Of course it is impossible to spin without material and spindles; and therefore
the availability of these products is presupposed at the beginning of the spinning operation. But in the process itself, the fact
that they are the products of past labour is as irrelevant as, in
the case of the digestive process, the fact that bread is the product of the previous labour of the farmer, the miller and
the baker. On the contrary, it is by their imperfections that the
means of production in any process bring to our attention their
character of being the products of past labour. A knife which
fails to cut, a piece of thread which keeps on snapping, forcibly
remind us of Mr A, the cutler, or Mr B, the spinner. In a successful product, the role played by past labour in mediating its
useful properties has been extinguished.

A machine which is not active in the labour process is useless. In addition, it falls prey to the destructive power of natural
processes. Iron rusts; wood rots. Yarn with which we neither
weave nor knit is cotton wasted. Living labour must seize on
these things, awaken them from the dead, change them from
merely possible into real and effective use-values. Bathed in the
fire of labour, appropriated as part of its organism, and infused
with vital energy for the performance of the functions appropriate to their concept and to their vocation in the process, they
are indeed consumed, but to some purpose, as elements in the
formation of new use-values, new products, which are capable

of entering into individual consumption as means of subsistence or into a new labour process as means of production.

If then, on the one hand, finished products are not only results of the labour process, but also conditions of its existence, their induction into the process, their contact with living labour, is the sole means by which they can be made to retain their character of use-values, and be realized.

Labour uses up its material elements, its objects and its instruments. It consumes them, and is therefore a process of consumption. Such productive consumption is distinguished from individual consumption by this, that the latter uses up products as means of subsistence for the living individual; the former, as means of subsistence for labour, i.e. for the activity through which the living individual's labour-power manifests itself. Thus the product of individual consumption is the consumer himself; the result of productive consumption is a product distinct from the consumer.

In so far then as its instruments and its objects are themselves products, labour consumes products in order to create products, or in other words consumes one set of products by turning them into means of production for another set. But just as the labour process originally took place only between man and the earth (which was available independently of any human action), so even now we still employ in the process many means of production which are provided directly by nature and do not represent any combination of natural substances with human labour.

The labour process, as we have just presented it in its simple and abstract elements, is purposeful activity aimed at the production of use-values. It is an appropriation of what exists in nature for the requirements of man. It is the universal condition for the metabolic interaction [*Stoffwechsel*] between man and nature, the everlasting nature-imposed condition of human existence, and it is therefore independent of every form of that existence, or rather it is common to all forms of society in which human beings live. We did not, therefore, have to present the worker in his relationship with other workers; it was enough to present man and his labour on one side, nature and its materials on the other. The taste of porridge does not tell us who grew the oats, and the process we have presented does not reveal the conditions under which it takes place, whether it is happening under the slave-owner's brutal lash or the anxious eye of the capitalist, whether Cincinnatus undertakes it in tilling his couple of acres,* or a savage, when he lays low a wild beast with a stone.[10]

Let us now return to our would-be capitalist. We left him just after he had purchased, in the open market, all the necessary factors of the labour process; its objective factors, the means of production, as well as its personal factor, labour-power. With the keen eye of an expert, he has selected the means of production and the kind of labour-power best adapted to his particular trade, be it spinning, bootmaking or any other kind. He then proceeds to consume the commodity, the labour-power he has just bought, i.e. he causes the worker, the bearer of that labour-power, to consume the means of production by his labour. The general character of the labour process is evidently not changed by the fact that the worker works for the capitalist instead of for himself; moreover, the particular methods and operations employed in bootmaking or spinning are not immediately altered by the intervention of the capitalist. He must begin by taking the labour-power as he finds it in the market, and consequently he must be satisfied with the kind of labour which arose in a period when there were as yet no capitalists. The transformation of the mode of production itself which results from the subordination of labour to capital can only occur later on, and we shall therefore deal with it in a later chapter.

The labour process, when it is the process by which the capitalist consumes labour-power, exhibits two characteristic phenomena.

First, the worker works under the control of the capitalist to whom his labour belongs; the capitalist takes good care that the work is done in a proper manner, and the means of production are applied directly to the purpose, so that the raw material is not wasted, and the instruments of labour are spared, i.e. only worn to the extent necessitated by their use in the work.

Secondly, the product is the property of the capitalist and not that of the worker, its immediate producer. Suppose that a capitalist pays for a day's worth of labour-power; then the right to use that power for a day belongs to him, just as much as the right to use any other commodity, such as a horse he had hired for the day. The use of a commodity belongs to its purchaser, and the seller of labour-power, by giving his labour, does no

---

* The Roman patrician Lucius Quinctius Cincinnatus (dictator of Rome from 458 to 439 B.C.) was reputed to have lived a simple and exemplary life, cultivating his own small farm in person.

more, in reality, than part with the use-value he has sold. From the instant he steps into the workshop, the use-value of his labour-power and therefore also its use, which is labour, belongs to the capitalist. By the purchase of labour-power, the capitalist incorporates labour, as a living agent of fermentation, into the lifeless constituents of the product, which also belong to him. From his point of view, the labour process is nothing more than the consumption of the commodity purchased, i.e. of labour-power; but he can consume this labour-power only by adding the means of production to it. The labour process is a process between things the capitalist has purchased, things which belong to him. Thus the product of this process belongs to him just as much as the wine which is the product of the process of fermentation going on in his cellar.[11]

2. THE VALORIZATION PROCESS

The product – the property of the capitalist – is a use-value, as yarn, for example, or boots. But although boots are, to some extent, the basis of social progress, and our capitalist is decidedly in favour of progress, he does not manufacture boots for their own sake. Use-value is certainly not *la chose qu'on aime pour lui-même** in the production of commodities. Use-values are produced by capitalists only because and in so far as they form the material substratum of exchange-value, are the bearers of exchange-value. Our capitalist has two objectives: in the first place, he wants to produce a use-value which has exchange-value, i.e. an article destined to be sold, a commodity; and secondly he wants to produce a commodity greater in value than the sum of the values of the commodities used to produce it, namely the means of production and the labour-power he purchased with his good money on the open market. His aim is to produce not only a use-value, but a commodity; not only use-value, but value; and not just value, but also surplus-value.

It must be borne in mind that we are now dealing with the production of commodities, and that up to this point we have considered only one aspect of the process. Just as the commodity itself is a unity formed of use-value and value, so the process of production must be a unity, composed of the labour process and the process of creating value [*Wertbildungsprozess*].

* 'The thing desired for its own sake'.

50

Let us now examine production as a process of creating value.

We know that the value of each commodity is determined by the quantity of labour materialized in its use-value, by the labour-time socially necessary to produce it. This rule also holds good in the case of the product handed over to the capitalist as a result of the labour-process. Assuming this product to be yarn, our first step is to calculate the quantity of labour objectified in it.

For spinning the yarn, raw material is required; suppose in this case 10 lb. of cotton. We have no need at present to investigate the value of this cotton, for our capitalist has, we will assume, bought it at its full value, say 10 shillings. In this price the labour required for the production of the cotton is already expressed in terms of average social labour. We will further assume that the wear and tear of the spindle, which for our present purpose may represent all other instruments of labour employed, amounts to the value of 2 shillings. If then, twenty-four hours of labour, or two working days, are required to produce the quantity of gold represented by 12 shillings, it follows first of all that two days of labour are objectified in the yarn.

We should not let ourselves be misled by the circumstances that the cotton has changed its form and the worn-down portion of the spindle has entirely disappeared. According to the general law of value, if the value of 40 lb. of yarn = the value of 40 lb. of cotton + the value of a whole spindle, i.e. if the same amount of labour-time is required to produce the commodities on either side of this equation, then 10 lb. of yarn are an equivalent for 10 lb. of cotton, together with a quarter of a spindle. In the case we are considering, the same amount of labour-time is represented in the 10 lb. of yarn on the one hand, and in the 10 lb. of cotton and the fraction of a spindle on the other. It is therefore a matter of indifference whether value appears in cotton, in a spindle or in yarn : its amount remains the same. The spindle and cotton, instead of resting quietly side by side, join together in the process, their forms are altered, and they are turned into yarn; but their value is no more affected by this fact than it would be if they had been simply exchanged for their equivalent in yarn.

The labour-time required for the production of the cotton, the raw material of the yarn, is part of the labour necessary to produce the yarn, and is therefore contained in the yarn. The same applies to the labour embodied in the spindle. without whose wear and tear the cotton could not be spun.[12]

Hence in determining the value of the yarn, or the labour-time required for its production, all the special processes carried on at various times and in different places which were necessary, first to produce the cotton and the wasted portion of the spindle, and then with the cotton and the spindle to spin the yarn, may together be looked on as different and successive phases of the same labour process. All the labour contained in the yarn is past labour; and it is a matter of no importance that the labour expended to produce its constituent elements lies further back in the past than the labour expended on the final process, the spinning. The former stands, as it were, in the pluperfect, the latter in the perfect tense, but this does not matter. If a definite quantity of labour, say thirty days, is needed to build a house, the total amount of labour incorporated in the house is not altered by the fact that the work of the last day was done twenty-nine days later than that of the first. Therefore the labour contained in the raw material and instruments of labour can be treated just as if it were labour expended in an earlier stage of the spinning process, before the labour finally added in the form of actual spinning.

The values of the means of production which are expressed in the price of 12 shillings (the cotton and the spindle) are therefore constituent parts of the value of the yarn, i.e. of the value of the product.

Two conditions must nevertheless be fulfilled. First, the cotton and the spindle must genuinely have served to produce a use-value; they must in the present case become yarn. Value is independent of the particular use-value by which it is borne, but a use-value of some kind has to act as its bearer. Second, the labour-time expended must not exceed what is necessary under the given social conditions of production. Therefore, if no more than 1 lb. of cotton is needed to spin 1 lb. of yarn, no more than this weight of cotton may be consumed in the production of 1 lb. of yarn. The same is true of the spindle. If the capitalist has a foible for using golden spindles instead of steel ones, the only labour that counts for anything in the value of the yarn remains that which would be required to produce a steel spindle, because no more is necessary under the given social conditions.

We now know what part of the value of the yarn is formed by the means of production, namely the cotton and the spindle. It is 12 shillings, i.e. the materialization of two days of labour.

The next point to be considered is what part of the value of the yarn is added to the cotton by the labour of the spinner.

We have now to consider this labour from a standpoint quite different from that adopted for the labour process. There we viewed it solely as the activity which has the purpose of changing cotton into yarn; there, the more appropriate the work was to its purpose, the better the yarn, other circumstances remaining the same. In that case the labour of the spinner was specifically different from other kinds of productive labour, and this difference revealed itself both subjectively in the particular purpose of spinning, and objectively in the special character of its operations, the special nature of its means of production, and the special use-value of its product. For the operation of spinning, cotton and spindles are a necessity, but for making rifled cannon they would be of no use whatever. Here, on the contrary, where we consider the labour of the spinner only in so far as it creates value, i.e. is a source of value, that labour differs in no respect from the labour of the man who bores cannon, or (what concerns us more closely here) from the labour of the cotton-planter and the spindle-maker which is realized in the means of production of the yarn. It is solely by reason of this identity that cotton planting, spindle-making and spinning are capable of forming the component parts of one whole, namely the value of the yarn, differing only quantitatively from each other. Here we are no longer concerned with the quality, the character and the content of the labour, but merely with its quantity. And this simply requires to be calculated. We assume that spinning is simple labour, the average labour of a given society. Later it will be seen that the contrary assumption would make no difference.

During the labour process, the worker's labour constantly undergoes a transformation, from the form of unrest [*Unruhe*] into that of being [*Sein*], from the form of motion [*Bewegung*] into that of objectivity [*Gegenständlichkeit*]. At the end of one hour, the spinning motion is represented in a certain quantity of yarn; in other words, a definite quantity of labour, namely that of one hour, has been objectified in the cotton. We say labour, i.e. the expenditure of his vital force by the spinner, and not spinning labour, because the special work of spinning counts here only in so far as it is the expenditure of labour-power in general, and not the specific labour of the spinner.

In the process we are now considering it is of extreme importance that no more time be consumed in the work of transforming the cotton into yarn than is necessary under the given social conditions. If under normal, i.e. average social conditions of production, x pounds of cotton are made into y pounds of yarn by one hour's labour, then a day's labour does not count as 12 hours' labour unless $12x$ lb. of cotton have been made into $12y$ lb. of yarn; for only socially necessary labour-time counts towards the creation of value.

Not only the labour, but also the raw material and the product now appear in quite a new light, very different from that in which we viewed them in the labour process pure and simple. Now the raw material merely serves to absorb a definite quantity of labour. By being soaked in labour, the raw material is in fact changed into yarn, because labour-power is expended in the form of spinning and added to it; but the product, the yarn, is now nothing more than a measure of the labour absorbed by the cotton. If in one hour $1\frac{2}{3}$ lb. of cotton can be spun into $1\frac{2}{3}$ lb. of yarn, then 10 lb. of yarn indicate the absorption of 6 hours of labour. Definite quantities of product, quantities which are determined by experience, now represent nothing but definite quantities of labour, definite masses of crystallized labour-time. They are now simply the material shape taken by a given number of hours or days of social labour.

The fact that the labour is precisely the labour of spinning, that its material is cotton, its product yarn, is as irrelevant here as it is that the object of labour is itself already a product, hence already raw material. If the worker, instead of spinning, were to be employed in a coal-mine, the object on which he worked would be coal, which is present in nature; nevertheless, a definite quantity of coal, when extracted from its seam, would represent a definite quantity of absorbed labour.

We assumed, on the occasion of its sale, that the value of a day's labour-power was 3 shillings, and that 6 hours of labour was incorporated in that sum; and consequently that this amount of labour was needed to produce the worker's average daily means of subsistence. If now our spinner, by working for one hour, can convert $1\frac{2}{3}$ lb. of cotton into $1\frac{2}{3}$ lb. of yarn,[13] it follows that in 6 hours he will convert 10 lb. of cotton into 10 lb. of yarn. Hence, during the spinning process, the cotton absorbs 6 hours of labour. The same quantity of labour is also embodied in a piece of gold of the value of 3 shillings. A value of 3 shillings, therefore, is added to the cotton by the labour of spinning.

Let us now consider the total value of the product, the 10 lb. of yarn. Two and a half days of labour have been objectified in it. Out of this, two days were contained in the cotton and the worn-down portion of the spindle, and half a day was absorbed during the process of spinning. This two and a half days of labour is represented by a piece of gold of the value of 15 shillings. Hence 15 shillings is an adequate price for the 10 lb. of yarn, and the price of 1 lb. is 1s. 6d.

Our capitalist stares in astonishment. The value of the product is equal to the value of the capital advanced. The value advanced has not been valorized, no surplus-value has been created, and consequently money has not been transformed into capital. The price of the yarn is 15 shillings, and 15 shillings were spent in the open market on the constituent elements of the product or, what amounts to the same thing, on the factors of the labour process; 10 shillings were paid for the cotton, 2 shillings for the wear of the spindle and 3 shillings for the labour-power. The swollen value of the yarn is of no avail, for it is merely the sum of the values formerly existing in the cotton, the spindle and the labour-power: out of such a simple addition of existing values, no surplus-value can possibly arise.[14] These values are now all concentrated in one thing; but so they were in the sum of 15 shillings, before it was split up into three parts by the purchase of the commodities.

In itself this result is not particularly strange. The value of one pound of yarn is 1s. 6d., and our capitalist would therefore have to pay 15 shillings for 10 lb. of yarn on the open market. It is clear that whether a man buys his house ready built, or has it built for him, neither of these operations will increase the amount of money laid out on the house.

Our capitalist, who is at home in vulgar economics, may perhaps say that he advanced his money with the intention of making more money out of it. The road to hell is paved with good intentions, and he might just as well have intended to make money without producing at all.[15] He makes threats. He will not be caught napping again. In future he will buy the commodities in the market, instead of manufacturing them himself. But if all his brother capitalists were to do the same, where would he find his commodities on the market? And he cannot eat his money. He recites the catechism: 'Consider my abstinence. I might have squandered the 15 shillings, but instead I consumed it productively and made yarn with it.' Very true; and as a reward he is now in possession of good yarn instead of a bad conscience. As for playing the part of a miser, it would never do for him to relapse into such bad ways; we have already seen what such asceticism leads to. Besides, where there is nothing, the king has lost his rights; whatever the merits of his abstinence there is no money there to recompense him, because the value of the product is merely the sum of the values thrown into the process of production. Let him therefore console himself with the reflection that virtue is its own reward. But no, on the contrary, he becomes insistent. The yarn is of no use to him, he says. He produced it in order to sell it. In that case let him sell it, or, easier still, let him in future produce only things he needs himself, a remedy already prescribed by his personal physician MacCulloch as being of proven efficacy against an epidemic of over-production. Now our capitalist grows defiant. 'Can the worker produce commodities out of nothing, merely by using his arms and legs? Did I not provide him with the materials through which, and in which alone, his labour could be embodied? And as the greater part of society consists of such impecunious creatures, have I not rendered society an incalculable service by providing my instruments of production, my cotton and my spindle, and the worker too, for have I not provided him with the means of subsistence? Am I to be allowed nothing in return for all this service?' But has the worker not performed an equivalent service in return, by changing his cotton and his spindle into yarn? In any case, here the question of service does not arise.[16] A service is nothing other than the useful effect of a use-value, be it that of a commodity, or that of the labour.[17] But here we are dealing with exchange-value. The capitalist paid to the worker a value of 3 shillings, and the worker gave him back an exact equivalent in the value of 3 shillings he added to the cotton: he gave him value for value. Our friend, who has up till now displayed all the arrogance of capital, suddenly takes on the unassuming demeanour of one of his own workers, and exclaims: 'Have I myself not worked? Have I not performed the labour of super-intendence, of overseeing the spinner? And does not this labour, too, create value?' The capitalist's own overseer and manager shrug their shoulders. In the meantime, with a hearty laugh, he recovers his composure. The whole litany he has just recited was simply meant to pull the wool over our eyes. He himself does not care twopence for it. He leaves this and all similar subterfuges and conjuring tricks to the professors of political economy, who are paid for it. He himself is a practical man, and although he does not always consider what he says outside his business, within his business he knows what he is doing.

Let us examine the matter more closely. The value of a day's labour-power amounts to 3 shillings, because on our assumption half a day's labour is objectified in that quantity of labour-power, i.e. because the means of subsistence required every day for the production of labour-power cost half a day's labour. But the past labour embodied in the labour-power and the living labour it can perform, and the daily cost of maintaining labour-power and its daily expenditure in work, are two totally different things. The former determines the exchange-value of the labour-power, the latter is its use-value. The fact that half a day's labour is necessary to keep the worker alive during twenty-four hours does not in any way prevent him from working a whole day. Therefore the value of labour-power, and the value which that labour-power valorizes [*verwertet*] in the labour-process, are two entirely different magnitudes; and this difference was what the capitalist had in mind when he was purchasing the labour-power. The useful quality of labour-power, by virtue of which it makes yarn or boots, was to the capitalist merely the necessary condition for his activity; for in order to create value labour must be expended in a useful manner. What was really decisive for him was the specific use-value which this commodity possesses of being a source not only of value, but of more value than it has itself. This is the specific service the capitalist expects from labour-power, and in this transaction he acts in accordance with the eternal laws of commodity-exchange. In fact, the seller of labour-power, like the seller of any other commodity, realizes [*realisiert*] its exchange-value, and alienates [*veràussert*] its use-value. He cannot take the one without giving the other. The use-value of labour-power, in other words labour, belongs just as little to its seller as the use-value of oil after it has been sold belongs to the dealer who sold it. The owner of the money has paid the value of a day's labour-power; he therefore has the use of it for a day, a day's labour belongs to him. On the one hand the daily sustenance of labour-power costs only half a day's labour, while on the other hand the very same labour-power can remain effective, can work, during a whole day, and consequently the value which its use during one day creates is double what the capitalist pays for that use; this circumstance is a piece of good luck for the buyer, but by no means an injustice towards the seller.

Our capitalist foresaw this situation, and that was the cause of his laughter. The worker therefore finds, in the workshop, the means of production necessary for working not just six but twelve hours. If 10 lb. of cotton could absorb six hours' labour, and become 10 lb. of yarn, now 20 lb. of cotton will absorb twelve hours' labour and be changed into 20 lbs. of yarn. Let us examine the product of this extended labour-process. Now five days of labour are objectified in this 20 lb. of yarn; four days are due to the cotton and the lost steel of the spindle, the remaining day has been absorbed by the cotton during the spinning process. Expressed in gold, the labour of five days is 30 shillings. This is therefore the price of the 20 lb. of yarn, giving, as before, 1s. 6d. as the price of 1 lb. But the sum of the values of the commodities thrown into the process amounts to 27 shillings. The value of the yarn is 30 shillings. Therefore the value of the product is one-ninth greater than the value advanced to produce it; 27 shillings have turned into 30 shillings; a surplus-value of 3 shillings has been precipitated. The trick has at last worked: money has been transformed into capital.

Every condition of the problem is satisfied, while the laws governing the exchange of commodities have not been violated in any way. Equivalent has been exchanged for equivalent. For the capitalist as buyer paid the full value for each commodity, for the cotton, for the spindle and for the labour-power. He then did what is done by every purchaser of commodities: he consumed their use-value. The process of consuming labour-power, which was also the process of producing commodities, resulted in 20 lb. of yarn, with a value of 30 shillings. The capitalist, formerly a buyer, now returns to the market as a seller. He sells his yarn at 1s. 6d. a pound, which is its exact value. Yet for all that he withdraws 3 shillings more from circulation than he originally threw into it. This whole course of events, the transformation of money into capital, both takes place and does not take place in the sphere of circulation. It takes place through the mediation of circulation because it is conditioned by the purchase of the labour-power in the market; it does not take place in circulation because what happens there is only an introduction to the valorization process, which is entirely confined to the sphere of production. And so 'everything is for the best in the best of all possible worlds.'

By turning his money into commodities which serve as the building materials for a new product, and as factors in the labour process, by incorporating living labour into their lifeless objectivity, the capitalist simultaneously transforms value, i.e. past labour in its objectified and lifeless form, into capital, value which can perform its own valorization process, an animated monster which begins to 'work', 'as if its body were by love possessed'.*

If we now compare the process of creating value with the process of valorization, we see that the latter is nothing but the continuation of the former beyond a definite point. If the process is not carried beyond the point where the value paid by the capitalist for the labour-power is replaced by an exact equivalent, it is simply a process of creating value; but if it is continued beyond that point, it becomes a process of valorization.

If we proceed further, and compare the process of creating value with the labour process, we find that the latter consists in the useful labour which produces use-values. Here the movement of production is viewed qualitatively, with regard to the particular kind of article produced, and in accordance with the purpose and content of the movement. But if it is viewed as a value-creating process the same labour process appears only quantitatively. Here it is a question merely of the time needed to do the work, of the period, that is, during which the labour-power is usefully expended. Here the commodities which enter into the labour process no longer count as functionally determined and material elements on which labour-power acts with a given purpose. They count merely as definite quantities of objectified labour. Whether it was already contained in the means of production, or has just been added by the action of labour-power, that labour counts only according to its duration. It amounts to so many hours, or days, etc.

Moreover, the time spent in production counts only in so far as it is socially necessary for the production of a use-value. This has various consequences. First, the labour-power must be functioning under normal conditions. If a self-acting mule is the socially predominant instrument of labour for spinning, it would be impermissible to supply the spinner with a spinning-wheel. The cotton too must not be such rubbish as to tear at every other moment, but must be of suitable quality. Otherwise

* Goethe, *Faust*, Part I, Auerbach's Cellar in Leipzig, line 2141 ('*als hätt' es Lieb' im Leibe*').

the spinner would spend more time than socially necessary in producing his pound of yarn, and in this case the excess of time would create neither value nor money. But whether the objective factors of labour are normal or not does not depend on the worker, but rather on the capitalist. A further condition is that the labour-power itself must be of normal effectiveness. In the trade in which it is being employed, it must possess the average skill, dexterity and speed prevalent in that trade, and our capitalist took good care to buy labour-power of such normal quality. It must be expended with the average amount of exertion and the usual degree of intensity; and the capitalist is as careful to see that this is done, as he is to ensure that his workmen are not idle for a single moment. He has bought the use of the labour-power for a definite period, and he insists on his rights. He has no intention of being robbed. Lastly – and for this purpose our friend has a penal code of his own – all wasteful consumption of raw material or instruments of labour is strictly forbidden, because what is wasted in this way represents a superfluous expenditure of quantities of objectified labour, labour that does not count in the product or enter into its value.[18]

We now see that the difference between labour, considered on the one hand as producing utilities, and on the other hand as creating value, a difference which we discovered by our analysis of a commodity, resolves itself into a distinction between two aspects of the production process.

The production process, considered as the unity of the labour process and the process of creating value, is the process of production of commodities; considered as the unity of the labour process and the process of valorization, it is the capitalist process of production, or the capitalist form of the production of commodities.

NOTES AND REFERENCES

1 'The earth's spontaneous production being in small quantity, quite independent of man, appear, as it were, to be furnished by Nature, in the same way as a small sum is given to a young man, in order to put him in a way of in-

dustry, and of making his fortune.' James Steuart, *Principles of Political Economy*, Dublin, 1770, vol. 1, p. 116.

2 'Reason is as cunning as it is powerful. Cunning may be said to lie in the intermediate action which, while it permits the objects to follow their own bent and act upon one another till they waste away, and does not itself directly interfere in the process, is nevertheless only working out its own aims.' Hegel, *Enzyklopädie, Erster Theil, Die Logik*, Berlin, 1840, p. 382. [Para. 209, Addition. English translation: *Hegel's Logic*, tr. W. V. Wallace (revised by J. N. Findlay), Oxford, 1975, pp. 272–3].

3 In his otherwise miserable work *Théorie de l'économie politique*, Paris, 1815, Ganilh enumerates in a striking manner in opposition to the Physiocrats* the long series of labour processes which form the presupposition for agriculture properly so called.

4 In his *Réflexions sur la formation et la distribution des richesses* (1766), Turgot gives a good account of the importance of domesticated animals for the beginnings of civilization.

5 The least important commodities of all for the technological comparison of different epochs of production are articles of real luxury.

6 The writers of history have so far paid very little attention to the development of material production, which is the basis of all social life, and therefore of all real history. But prehistoric times at any rate have been classified on the basis of the investigations of natural science, rather than so-called historical research. Prehistory has been divided, according to the materials used to make tools and weapons, into the Stone Age, the Bronze Age and the Iron Age.

7 It appears paradoxical to asert that uncaught fish, for instance, are a means of production in the fishing industry. But hitherto no one has discovered the art of catching fish in waters that contain none.

8 This method of determining what is productive labour, from the standpoint of the simple labour process, is by no

* 'For the Physiocrats, the productivity of labour appeared as a *gift of nature, a productive power of nature* ... Surplus-value therefore appeared as a *gift of nature.*' *Theories of Surplus-Value*, part 1, pp. 49–51.

means sufficient to cover the capitalist process of production.

9 Storch distinguishes between raw material ('*matière*') and accessory materials ('*matériaux*'). Cherbuliez describes accessories as '*matières instrumentales*'.*

10 By a wonderful feat of logical acumen, Colonel Torrens has discovered, in this stone of the savage, the origin of capital. 'In the first stone which the savage flings at the wild animal he pursues, in the first stick that he seizes to strike down the fruit which hangs above his reach, we see the appropriation of one article for the purpose of aiding in the acquisition of another, and thus discover the origin of capital.' R. Torrens, *An Essays of the Production of Wealth, etc*, pp. 70–1. No doubt this 'first stick' [*Stock*] would also explain why 'stock' in English is synonymous with capital.

11 'Products are appropriated before they are transformed into capital; this transformation does not withdraw them from that appropriation.' Cherbuliez, *Richesse ou pauvreté*, Paris, 1841, p. 54. 'The proletarian, by selling his labour for a definite quantity of the means of subsistence (*approvisionnement*),† renounces all claim to a share in the product. The products continue to be appropriated as before; this is in no way altered by the bargain we have mentioned. The product belongs exclusively to the capitalist, who supplied the raw materials and the *approvisionnement*. This follows rigorously from the law of appropriation, a law whose fundamental principle was the exact opposite, namely that every worker has an exclusive right to the ownership of what he produces' (ibid., p. 58). 'When the labourers receive wages for their labour ... the capitalist is then the owner not of the capital only' (i.e. the means of production) 'but of the labour also. If what is paid as wages is included, as it commonly is, in the term capital,

---

* H. Storch, *Cours d'èconomie politique*, vol. 1, St Petersburg, 1815, p. 228; A. Cherbuliez, *Richesse ou pauvreté*, Paris, 1841, p. 14.
† See the discussion of Cherbuliez's notion of *approvisionnement in Grundrisse* (English edition), pp. 229–300: 'The economists, incidentally, introduce the *product* as third element of the substance of capital ... This is the product [as] ... immediate object of individual consumption; *approvisionnement*, as Cherbuliez calls it.'

it is absurd to talk of labour separately from capital. The word capital as thus employed includes labour and capital both.' James Mill, *Elements of Political Economy*, London, 1821, pp. 70–1.

12 'Not only the labour applied immediately to commodities affects their value, but the labour also which is bestowed on the implements, tools, and buildings with which such labour is assisted.' Ricardo, op. cit., p. 16.

13 These figures are entirely arbitrary.

14 This is the fundamental proposition which forms the basis of the doctrine of the Physiocrats that all non-agricultural labour is unproductive. For the professional economist it is irrefutable. 'This method of adding to one particular object the value of numerous others' (for example adding the living costs of the weaver to the flax) 'of as it were heaping up various values in layers on top of one single value, has the result that this value grows to the same extent ... The expression "addition" gives a very clear picture of the way in which the price of a manufactured product is formed; this price is only the sum of a number of values which have been consumed, and it is arrived at by adding them together; however, addition is not the same as multiplication.' Mercier de la Rivière, op. cit., p. 599.

15 Thus from 1844 to 1847 he withdrew part of his capital from productive employment in order to throw it away in railway speculations; and so also, during the American Civil War, he closed his factory and turned the workers on to the street in order to gamble on the Liverpool cotton exchange.

16 'Let whoever wants to do so extol himself, put on finery and adorn himself [but pay no heed and keep firmly to the scriptures] ... Whoever takes more or better than he gives, that is usury and does not signify a service but a wrong done to his neighbour, as when one steals and robs. Not everything described as a service and a benefit to one's neighbour is in fact a service and a benefit. An adulteress and an adulterer do each other a great service and pleasure. A horseman does great service to a robber by helping him to rob on the highway, and attack the people and the land. The papists do our people a great service in that they do not drown, burn, or murder them all, or let them rot in prison, but let some live and drive them out or take from them what they have. The devil himself does his servants a great, inestimable service ... To sum up: the world is full of great, excellent

daily services and good deeds. Martin Luther, *An die Pfarr-herrn, wider den Wucher zu predigen. Vermanung*, Wittenberg, 1540.

17 In *Zur Kritik der politischen Ökonomie*, p. 14 [English edition, p. 37], I make the following remark on this point: 'It is easy to understand what "service" the category "service" must render to economists like J. B. Say and F. Bastiat.'

18 This is one of the circumstances which make production based on slavery more expensive. Under slavery, according to the striking expression employed in antiquity, the worker is distinguishable only as *instrumentum vocale* from an animal, which is *instrumentum semi-vocale*, and from a lifeless implement, which is *instrumentum mutum*.* But he himself takes care to let both beast and implement feel that he is none of them, but rather a human being. He gives himself the satisfaction of knowing that he is different by treating the one with brutality and damaging the other *con amore*. Hence the economic principle, universally applied in this mode of production, of employing only the rudest and heaviest implements, which are difficult to damage owing to their very clumsiness. In the slave states bordering on the Gulf of Mexico, down to the date of the Civil War, the only ploughs to be found were those constructed on the old Chinese model, which turned up the earth like a pig or a mole, instead of making furrows. Cf. J. E. Cairnes, *The Slave Power*, London, 1862, pp. 46 ff. In his *Seaboard Slave States*, Olmsted says, among other things, 'I am here shown tools that no man in his senses, with us, would allow a labourer, for whom he was paying wages, to be encumbered with; and the excessive weight and clumsiness of which, I would judge, would make work at least ten per cent greater than with those ordinarily used with us. And I am assured that, with the careless and clumsy treatment they always must get from the slaves, anything lighter or less rude could not be furnished them with good economy, and that such tools as we constantly give our labourers and find our profit in giving them, would not last a day in a Virginia cornfield – much lighter and more free from stones

---

* The slave was the 'speaking implement', the animal the 'semi-mute implement' and the plough the 'mute implement' (Varro, *Rerum Rusticarum Libri Tres*, I, 17).

though it be than ours. So, too, when I ask why mules are so universally substituted for horses on the farm, the first reason given, and confessedly the most conclusive one, is that horses are always soon foundered or crippled by them, while mules will bear cudgelling, or lose a meal or two now and then, and not be materially injured, and they do not take cold or get sick, if neglected or overworked. But I do not need to go further than to the window of the room in which I am writing, to see at almost any time, treatment of cattle that would ensure the immediate discharge of the driver by almost any farmer owning them in the North.'*

* F. L. Olmsted, *A Journey in the Seaboard Slave States*, New York, 1856, pp. 46–7.

The Factory

Karl Marx

At the beginning of this chapter ['Machinery and Large-scale Industry'] we considered the physical constituents of the factory, the organization of the system of machinery. We saw there how machinery, by appropriating the labour of women and children, augments the quantity of human material for capital to exploit, how it confiscates the whole of the worker's lifetime by its immoderate extension of the working day, and finally how its progress, which permits an enormous increase in production within a shorter and shorter amount of time, serves as a means of systematically getting more work done within a given period of time, or, in other words, constantly exploiting labour-power more intensively. We now turn to the factory as a whole, and indeed in its most developed form.

Dr Ure, the Pindar of the automatic factory, describes it, on the one hand, as 'combined co-operation of many orders of work-people, adult and young, in tending with assiduous skill a system of productive machines continuously impelled by a central power' (the prime mover); and on the other hand as 'a vast automaton composed of various mechanical and intellectual organs, acting in uninterrupted concert for the production of a common object, all of them being subordinate to a self-regulated moving force'.* These two descriptions are far from being identical. In one, the combined collective worker appears as the dominant subject [*übergriefendes Subjekt*], and the mechanical automaton as the object; in the other, the automaton itself is the subject, and the workers are merely conscious organs, co-ordinated with the unconscious organs of the automaton, and together with the latter subordinated to the central moving force. The first description is applicable to every possible employment of machinery on a large scale, the second is characteristic of its use by capital, and therefore of the modern factory system. Ure therefore prefers to present the

* These quotations are from Ure, *Philosophy of Manufactures*, p. 13.

central machine from which the motion comes as not only an automaton but an autocrat. 'In these spacious halls the benignant power of steam summons around him his myriads of willing menials.'[1]

Along with the tool, the skill of the worker in handling it passes over to the machine. The capabilities of the tool are emancipated from the restraints inseparable from human labour-power. This destroys the technical foundation on which the division of labour in manufacture was based. Hence, in place of the hierarchy of specialized workers that characterizes manufacture, there appears, in the automatic factory, a tendency to equalize and reduce to an identical level every kind of work that has to be done by the minders of the machines;[2] in place of the artificially produced distinctions between the specialized workers, it is natural differences of age and sex that predominate.

Insofar as the division of labour re-appears in the factory, it takes the form primarily of a distribution of workers among the specialized machines, and of quantities of workers, who do not however form organized groups, among the various departments of the factory, in each of which they work at a number of similar machines placed together; only simple co-operation therefore takes place between them. The organized group peculiar to manufacture is replaced by the connection between the head worker and his few assistants. The essential division is that between workers who are actually employed on the machines (among whom are included a few who look after the engine) and those who merely attend them (almost exclusively children). More or less all the 'feeders' who supply the machines with the material which is to be worked up are counted as attendants. In addition to these two principal classes, there is a numerically unimportant group whose occupation it is to look after the whole of the machinery and repair it from time to time, composed of engineers, mechanics, joiners etc. This is a superior class of workers, in part scientifically educated, in part trained in a handicraft; they stand outside the realm of the factory workers, and are added to them only to make up an aggregate.[3] This division of labour is purely technical.

All work at a machine requires the worker to be taught from childhood upwards, in order that he may learn to adapt his own movements to the uniform and unceasing motion of an automaton. Since the machinery, taken as a whole, forms a system of machines of various kinds, working simultaneously and in combination, co-operation based upon it requires the distribution of various groups of workers among the different kinds of machine. But machine production abolishes the necessity of fixing this distribution in the manner of manufacture, i.e. by constantly appropriating the same worker to the same function.[4] Since the motion of the whole factory proceeds not from the worker but from the machinery, the working personnel can continually be replaced without any interruption in the labour process. The most striking proof of this is afforded by the *relay system*, put into operation by the manufacturers during their revolt of 1848 to 1850. Lastly, the speed with which machine work is learnt by young people does away with the need to bring up a special class of worker for exclusive employment by machinery.[5] The work of those people who are merely attendants can, to some extent, be replaced in the factory by the use of machines.[6] In addition to this, the very simplicity of the work allows a rapid and constant turnover of the individuals burdened with this drudgery.

Thus although, from a technical point of view, the old system of division of labour is thrown overboard by machinery, it hangs on in the factory as a tradition handed down from manufacture, and is then systematically reproduced and fixed in a more hideous form by capital as a means of exploiting labour-power. The lifelong speciality of handling the same tool now becomes the lifelong speciality of serving the same machine. Machinery is misused in order to transform the worker, from his very childhood, into a part of a specialized machine.[7] In this way, not only are the expenses necessary for his reproduction considerably lessened, but at the same time his helpless dependence upon the factory as a whole, and therefore upon the capitalist, is rendered complete. Here, as everywhere else, we must distinguish between the increased productivity which is due to the development of the social process of production, and that which is due to the exploitation by the capitalists of that development.

In handicrafts and manufacture, the worker makes use of a tool; in the factory, the machine makes use of him. There the movements of the instrument of labour proceed from him, here it is the movements of the machine that he must follow. In manufacture the workers are the parts of a living mechanism. In the factory we have a lifeless mechanism which is independent of the workers, who are incorporated into it as its living appendages. 'The wearisome routine of endless drudgery in which the same mechanical process is ever repeated, is like the torture of Sisyphus; the burden of toil, like the rock, is ever falling back upon the worn-out drudge.'[8]

Factory work exhausts the nervous system to the uttermost; at the same time, it does away with the many-sided play of the muscles, and confiscates every atom of freedom, both in bodily and in intellectual activity.[9] Even the lightening of the labour becomes an instrument of torture, since the machine does not free the worker from the work, but rather deprives the work itself of all content. Every kind of capitalist production, in so far as it is not only a labour process but also capital's process of valorization, has this in common, but it is not the worker who employs the conditions of his work, but rather the reverse, the conditions of work employ the worker. However, it is only with the coming of machinery that this inversion first acquires a technical and palpable reality. Owing to its conversion into an automaton, the instrument of labour confronts the worker during the labour process in the shape of capital, dead labour, which dominates and soaks up living labour-power. The separation of the intellectual faculties of the production process from manual labour, and the transformation of those faculties into powers exercised by capital over labour, is, as we have already shown, finally completed by large-scale industry erected on the foundation of machinery. The special skill of each individual machine-operator, who has now been deprived of all significance, vanishes as an infinitesimal quantity in the face of the science, the gigantic natural forces, and the mass of social labour embodied in the system of machinery, which, together with those three forces, constitutes the power of the 'master'. This 'master', therefore, in whose mind the machinery and his monopoly of it are inseparably united, contemptuously tells his 'hands', whenever he comes into conflict with them: 'The factory operatives should keep in wholesome remembrance the fact that theirs is really a low species of skilled labour; and that there is none which is more easily acquired, or of its quality more amply remunerated, or which by a short training of the least expert can be more quickly, as well as abundantly, acquired ... The master's machinery really plays a far more important part in the business of production than the labour and the skill of the operative, which six months' education can teach, and a common labourer can learn.'[10] The technical subordination of the worker to the uniform motion of the instruments of labour, and the peculiar composition of the working group, consisting as it does of individuals of both sexes and all ages, gives rise to a barrack-like discipline, which is elaborated into a complete system in the factory, and brings the previously mentioned labour of superintendence to its fullest development, thereby dividing the workers into manual labourers and overseers, into the private soldiers and the NCOs of an industrial army. 'The main difficulty' (in the automatic factory) 'lay ... above all in training human beings to renounce their desultory habits of work, and to identify themselves with the unvarying regularity of the complex automaton. To devise and administer a successful code of factory discipline, suited to the necessities of factory diligence, was the Herculean enterprise, the noble achievement of Arkwright! Even at the present day, when the system is perfectly organized and its labour lightened to the utmost, it is found nearly impossible to convert persons past the age of puberty into useful factory hands.'[11] In the factory code, the capitalist formulates his autocratic power over his workers like a private legislator, and purely as an emanation of his own will, unaccompanied by either that division of responsibility otherwise so much approved of by the bourgeoisie, or the still more approved representative system. This code is merely the capitalist caricature of the social regulation of the labour process which becomes necessary in co-operation on a large scale and in the employment in common of instruments of labour, and especially of machinery. The overseer's book of penalties replaces the slave-driver's lash.

NOTES AND REFERENCES

1 Ure, op. cit., p. 18.
2 ibid., p. 20. Cf. Karl Marx, *Misère de la philosophie*, pp. 140–1, [English edition, pp. 124–5].
3 It is characteristic of the English intention to deceive by use of statistics (and this is demonstrable in detail of other cases as well) that the English factory legislation expressly excludes from its area of competence, as being 'not factory workers', the class of workers last mentioned, while the 'Returns' published by Parliament just as expressly include in the category of factory workers not only engineers, mechanics, etc. but also managers, salesmen, messengers,

warehousemen, packers, etc., in short, everybody except the owner of the factory himself.

4 Ure concedes this. He says that 'in case of need' the workers can be moved at the will of the manager from one machine to another, and triumphantly exclaims: 'Such a change is in flat contradiction with the old routine, that divides the labour, and to one workman assigns the task of fashioning the head of a needle, to another the sharpening of the point.'* He ought rather to have asked himself why the 'old routine' is abandoned only 'in case of need' in the automatic factory.

5 When distress is very great, as for instance during the American Civil War, the factory worker is now and then, and by way of exception, employed by the bourgeois to do the roughest work, such as road-making, etc. The English *'ateliers nationaux'*† of 1862 and the following years, established for the unemployed cotton workers, differ from the French ones of 1848 in that in the latter the workers had to do unproductive work at the expense of the state, and in the former they had to do productive municipal work to the advantage of the bourgeois, and indeed more cheaply than the regular workers, with whom they were thus thrown into competition. 'The physical appearance of the cotton operatives is unquestionably improved. This I attribute ... as do the men, to outdoor labour on public works.' (*Reports of the Inspectors of Factories ... 31 October 1863*, p. 59). The reference here is to the factory workers of Preston, who were set to work on Preston Moor.

6 An example: the various pieces of mechanical apparatus introduced into woollen mills since the Act of 1844 in order to replace the labour of children. When the children of the manufacturers themselves have to go through a course of schooling as assistants in the factory, this hitherto almost unexplored area of mechanics will make remarkable progress. 'Of machinery, perhaps self-acting mules are as dangerous as any other kind. Most of the accidents from them happen to little children, from their creeping under the mules to sweep the floor whilst the mules are in motion. Several "minders" have been fined for this offence, but without much general benefit. If machine makers would only invent a self-sweeper, by whose use the necessity for these

* Ure, op. cit., p. 22.   † 'National workshops'.

little children to creep under the machinery might be prevented, it would be a happy addition to our protective measures' (*Reports of the Inspectors of Factories ... 31 October 1866*, p. 63).

7 So much then for Proudhon's wonderful idea: he 'construes' machinery not as a synthesis of instruments of labour, but as a synthesis of instruments of different partial operations for the benefit of the worker himself.*

8 F. Engels, *Lage etc.*, p. 217 [English edition, p. 205]† Even a very ordinary and optimistic free-trader like Molinari makes this remark: 'A man becomes exhausted more quickly when he watches over the uniform motion of a mechanism for fifteen hours a day, than when he applies his physical strength throughout the same period of time. This labour of surveillance, which might perhaps serve as a useful exercise for the mind, if it did not go on too long, destroys both the mind and the body in the long run through excessive application' (G. de Molinari, *Études économiques*, Paris, 1846 [p. 49]).

9 F. Engels, op. cit., p. 216 [English edition, p. 204].

10 *The Master Spinners' and Manufacturers' Defence Fund. Report of the Committee*, Manchester, 1854, p. 17. We shall see later that the 'master' can sing quite a different tune when he is threatened with the loss of his 'living' automaton.

11 Ure, op. cit., p. 15. Anyone who knows Arkwright's biography will be unlikely to apply the epithet 'noble' to this barber-genius.†† Of all the great inventors of the eighteenth century, he was unquestionably the greatest thief of other people's inventions and the meanest character.

* See Marx, *Poverty of Philosophy*, pp. 116–17.
† This is in fact a quotation from Engels' footnote reference to a book by Dr J. P. Kay, *The Moral and Physical Condition of the Working Classes Employed in the Cotton Manufacture in Manchester* (1832).
†† Sir Richard Arkwright (1732–92) started out as a barber, and gleaned such mechanical knowledge as he had from conversations with customers. Despite this, he patented a spinning-frame in 1769. It was later claimed that he had thereby stolen the invention of a certain Thomas Highs. Then, in 1775, he patented a whole series of other inventions, none of which he had invented himself. Though deprived of his patents in 1781, a decision which was confirmed after a court action in 1785, he continued to develop new factories, and died leaving £500,000.

PART II

Forced and Free Labour

Introduction

'This colony may prosper in the course of years,' wrote E. G.
Wakefield about Swan River in Western Australia in 1833, 'but
for the present it must be considered ... a decided failure.' Since
the colony had 'a fine climate, plenty of good land, plenty of
capital and enough labourers', this called for some explanation,
and the one that Wakefield provided introduces us directly to
the subject matter of the readings in this Part, which, as will be
seen, lies outside the capitalist labour process itself and in fact
concerns the conditions for its operation.

'The explanation', said Wakefield, 'is easy. In this colony,
there never has been a *class* of labourers.'[1] A student of the
political economy of England, of slavery in America and of
what he called 'the art of colonization', Wakefield thus laid
bare an important truth about capitalist relations of production. He provided a concrete illustration of what these
amounted to (or rather what their absence had meant in Swan
River) by means of a tale he recounted about a Mr Peel, a
founder colonialist who had gone there from England. Peel had
set out with 'capital of £50,000 and three hundred persons of
the labouring class, men, women and children' but, once arrived at Swan River, something went drastically wrong – his
labourers cleared off and took some of the good and plentiful
land for themselves. The goods that Peel had brought were left
to spoil and he found himself 'without a servant to make his
bed or fetch him water from the river.' Given access to an
abundance of good land, Peel's imported labourers had seen no
need to work for him. And sure enough, those colonialists who
remained in the area were soon begging the British government

for a supply of unfree convict labour. 'They want slaves,' Wakefield wrote. 'They want labour which shall be constant and liable to combination in particular works.' But he went on to console himself that the failure of Swan River would at least have one good effect 'if it help to teach the English and Americans, that the original and permanent cause of slavery in America is superabundance of good land.'[2]

Thirty years later it was Marx's turn to recount the tale of Mr Peel (though in *Capital* the story has improved a little, 300 labourers and their families now having grown to 3000). 'Unhappy Mr Peel', Marx mocked, he had the foresight to take with him means of subsistence, and physical means of production, and workers too – he had 'provided for everything except the export of English relations of production.'[3] What had been lacking in Swan River (in the absence of slavery, that is) was precisely 'a *class* of labourers' – a class of non-owners who had no choice but to labour for those who did own and control the means of production. Faced with what they saw as more of a real choice, Peel's labourers-to-be had chosen to work for themselves. Naturally enough perhaps. For, looked at in this context, what is 'unnatural' is the capitalist mode of production, which, formally speaking, requires certain property relations to come into existence before it can begin.

'Capital obtains ... surplus-labour without an equivalent, and in essence it always remains forced labour – no matter how much it may seem to result from free contractual agreement.' Terms like 'forced' and 'free' are powerful polemical tools, and Marx sometimes used them as such, as this quotation confirms.[4] Because of this, and because any real consideration of the labour process is likely to invite the analytical-cum-polemical use of such terms – and of others, like 'choice', 'unfree' and 'compulsion' – it may now be helpful to set down three brief comments. These concern the difference between forced and free labour; the relationship between free labour and economic compulsion and capitalism; and the freedom or otherwise of wage labour in the process of capitalist production.

First. The point about *free* as opposed to *forced labour* is that it is free at the level of *circulation*. Free wage labourers are free to sell their labour-power where they can. Chattel slaves, by contrast, being the property of slaveowners, are forced to labour for their slaveowner or for those to whom he assigns them.

Second. Class societies prior to capitalism extracted a surplus by means of *extra-economic* coercion. In capitalism, the surplus is pumped out through an *economic* relationship – one seemingly struck between free and equal agents in the form of the wage contract – not by legal or political sanctions. The absence of forced labour at the level of circulation is not however tantamount to the absence of *economic compulsion*.

To take the Swan River example again, it seems that some of those immigrants who fled from their employer soon proved anxious to return to him – 'having tried', in Wakefield's words, 'a life of complete independence *and felt the pains of hunger.*'[5] In short, the fact is that what people 'choose' is in part a function of what is otherwise available to them (like 'independence' *or* 'independence *and ... the pains of hunger*').

True, it has been frequently asserted on the political right that, today, workers in the 'advanced' capitalist nations do *not* have to face the choice: work or starve. But, then, the very absence of such a clear-cut choice is something that these ideologues see to constitute a *problem* for the capitalist system.[6] And much exaggerated as this 'problem' is, the very fact that it can be seen as a threat serves to remind us that free wage labourers are free only in the sense that they may choose to sell their labour-power to such-and-such capitalist or some other. 'Wage-slaves' is what Marx called them; 'slaves' to the *system* in which *labour-power* is a commodity, and which relies, in the 'pure' form, on *economic* compulsion.[7]

Third. Wage labour is not free in the process of *production*. Once labour-power becomes the property of capitalists, the labourers are subject to discipline and supervision.[8]

Amongst other things, the following extracts have been chosen to indicate how forced labour has occurred in the articulation of capitalism with other modes of production and how it can be important to locate free labour in an historical sequence that had free labour as its earlier moment, or *vice-versa*.

To introduce the readings in reverse order. The second, by Mandel, concerns Nazi Germany. It has been estimated that no less than seven and a half million prisoners of war and deportees from occupied countries were working in Germany by 1944 – but it is not to concentrate upon this narrower category of forced labour that this extract is reproduced here.[9] Rather, it is included to underline two things. One, that the degree of organization and fighting strength of the working class enters in to affect the degree to which free wage-labour can be said to be 'free'. Two, and more particularly, that there was a relationship between the unfreedom of labour under the Nazi dictatorship and the subsequent 'economic miracle' of Germany as a post-war 'free-world' capitalist power. For this is partly explicable in terms of the radical increase in the rate of surplus value, and the erosion of the value of labour-power that took place under Nazi rule – together with the smashing of trade unions and political organizations.[10] (Post-war Germany, as will be seen in Part III, was itself also to rely on a substantial supply of migrant labour – on a labour force that was to be less free than the indigenous population.)

As to '*Chibaro*'; this term, widely used by Africans at the time of which van Onselen writes, was synonymous with contract labour, forced labour and slavery. Quite whether *chibaro* technically amounted to slavery or not is rather beside the point of his analysis (indeed it is pertinent to remember a question asked by a *Rhodesian Herald* journalist in 1909: 'What is worse,' she asked, 'to be a slave and know, or to be told you are a free man, and treated like a slave?'[11]). What by contrast, is very much to the point of van Onselen's study of African labour in the gold mines of Southern Rhodesia is that a conjunction of particular geographical, historical, technical and economic realities (spelt out at a little length below, for here some 'background' is necessary) all contributed to a situation where, for the sake of profit and accumulation, it became desirable for mining capital to claw unto itself a labour force that was *unfree*. The compound system, a vehicle of such unfreedom, both maximized the employer's (sometimes brutal) control over labour and, together with the contract labour system and Pass Laws, denied Africans the right to sell their labour-power to whom they chose.[12]

Geologically, Southern Rhodesia, unlike the Rand, did not have a more or less continuous gold reef; certain economies of scale were therefore not possible. Moreover, the grade of ore was unreliable. Geographically, the country was land-locked and dependent on imported machinery and mining supplies. High rail tariffs meant that these cost more than they did in the Rand. Economically, the industry had to contend with the fact that for long periods the price of gold was fixed. Thus, if it was to be reconstructed and its long-term profitability assured – as it needed to be, after the failure of over-capitalized and largely speculative mining, and the collapse of the London market for Rhodesian mining stock in 1903 – strategies had to be devised both to increase production and to reduce costs.

An added constraint on the industry was that it had to operate within a regional economic system dominated by the Rand mines. 'Large' Rhodesian mines produced only one tenth of the 'average' mine in Witwatersrand. They had shorter working lives. Yet they had to compete for capital on the basis of the profits that shareholders expected to get from the Rand. The Rand's dominance had another consequence too. For Rand industry could pay higher wages and provide better living conditions. The Rhodesian gold-mine owners feared the recruiting potential of the Witwatersrand Native Labour Association (WNLA).

Central to the process of reconstruction was the need to reorganize the basis on which the industry was capitalized. The British South Africa Company (BSACo) made a contribution to overcoming this problem by waiving its requirement that companies be floated prior to any mining in Rhodesia (so encouraging individual small producers and syndicates, the so-called 'small workers'). It also dropped its requirement that it should have a 30 per cent shareholding in mining companies (a figure which had once been as high as 50 per cent) and thus made some contribution to lessening the over-capitalization problem.[13]

Increases in output occurred, largely through the emergence of the 'small workers'. But the minimization of costs was fundamentally to be achieved by reductions in labour costs. And the biggest contribution towards this was made by the exploitation of cheap African labour.

Within months of the collapse of the London market in 1903, the largest mines had joined together to form the Rhodesia (later Rhodesian) Native Labour Bureau (RNLB). By supplying cheap immigrant labour, drawn from the poor ranks of the peasantry, and based on long contracts, it assured the industry of its minimum labour requirements – and placed the employers in a position to reduce the wages of all black workers. This they did, general wage reductions taking place in 1906 and 1908.

However, it was difficult to recruit the indigenous peasantry because of the poor conditions in the compounds, the lowering of wages, and the fact that conditions and wages were worse than in the Witwatersrand.[14] The period of reconstruction –

which forms the subject matter of the following reading – therefore heralded what van Onselen calls 'the triumph of Chibaro', the RNLB sometimes providing over 50 per cent of the expanding labour force, and the length of the labour contract increasing to nearly a whole year by 1912.[15]

The reasons for the decline of the recruitment of *chibaro* labour also deserve a mention here. Although, of course, they resulted from the complex and particular situation which prevailed in Southern Rhodesia at this time, they are nevertheless of a type that is broadly familiar to us whether we are considering Southern Rhodesian mining post-1912, or the shift from field to factory that had earlier taken place in England, or the temporary failure of the process of making a class of labourers in Western Australia as described by Edward Wakefield. For basically, more than a quarter of a century of colonial presence in central Africa, and with this taxation, the decline of peasant markets, increases in population and restrictions on the amount of land available – all these had led an increasing number of Africans from the periphery of the regional economic system to 'choose' to offer themselves as wage-labour, at rates even *cheaper* than those paid under *chibaro*. What, in the period of reconstruction had been accomplished by *chibaro* was now being achieved by 'market forces'.[16]

NOTES AND REFERENCES

1 E. G. Wakefield, *England and America*, London, Richard Bentley, New Burlington Street, 1833, vol. 2, p. 33. My italics.
2 ibid., pp. 35–6.
3 *Capital*, vol. 1, p. 933.
4 *Capital*, vol. 3, London, Lawrence and Wishart, 1972, p. 819. Earlier, in the *Economic and Philosophical Manuscripts* 'forced labour' was directly linked to Marx's concept of alienation. Thus: 'work is not voluntary but imposed, *forced labour*. It is not the satisfaction of a need, but only a *means* for satisfying other needs. Its alien character is clearly shown by the fact that as soon as there is no physical or other compulsion it is avoided like the plague!' T. B.

Bottomore and M. Rubel (eds) *Karl Marx: Selected Writings in Sociology and Social Philosophy*, London, Watts and Co, 1956.

5 Wakefield, p. 34. My italics.

6 Incidentally, this 'problem' finds its counterpart on the Left in the view that provision of (some) redundancy pay has spiked demands like 'Work or Full Pay'. But in the 1960s to early 1970s the main talk was of course from managerially oriented circles; about a new young generation that lacked interest in (and by implication the necessity for) going to work. An example of such a view, which formed an aspect of the literature on 'job enrichment' and 'participation' (see Part V) is Judson Gooding's American piece, 'Blue Collar Blues', *Fortune*, July 1970. For some comments on the 'doley' myth in Britain and how it relates to 'sacrifice' in working-class ideology – and reality – see Theo Nichols and Huw Beynon, *Living with Capitalism*, pp. 193–8.

7 The concern here has been to make some brief, and necessarily quite abstract comments on economic compulsion and free wage labour in a capitalist mode of production. But it should be noted that the reality of 'economic compulsion' does not exist in an historical socio-cultural void. Notions of 'reasonable', 'proper', 'decent', and 'tolerable' conditions ('for people like us') can enter into concepts of 'need'. Some of the readings in Part III (the ones from Willis, and Bowles and Gintis) have been partly included to raise questions about how, and indeed whether, contemporary metropolitan educational systems enculture workers in such ways that, in striking bargains to meet their economic needs, they take for granted the despotism of the factory and its office and other equivalents.

The idea that economic compulsion is not, in practice, an entirely economic mechanism means of course that there are limitations to any theories of labour force reproduction that operate on an economic level only – workers-to-be as economic agents pure and simple on the one hand: empty, culturally transparent spaces in the economy on the other. Consider only the case of women: in reality, there are, on the one hand, their expectations (which can change of course) about jobs 'fit' for people like them; on the other, the jobs available to them ('women's work'). The danger of too much talk of 'spaces' etc is that, quite literally, it could itself prove empty, because these other matters have to be taken into account as well.

8 An argument about the role of the factory in securing this control is provided by Marglin at pages 237–54. His polemic against the bourgeois concept of 'choice' is also relevant to some of the above: 'it is a strange logic of choice that places its entire emphasis on the absence of legal compulsion' (page 248). A consideration of slavery is a mode of production is provided by Barry Hindess and Paul Q. Hirst, *Pre-Capitalist Modes of Production*, London, Routledge and Kegan Paul, 1975, Part 3; on industrial slavery see Robert S. Starobin, *Industrial Slavery in the Old South*, New York, Oxford University Press, 1970; for a welter of references on the question of 'unfree labour' see Philip Corrigan, 'Feudal Relics or Capitalist Monuments? Notes on the Sociology of Unfree Labour', *Sociology*, XI, 1977. Corrigan puts the stress on capitalism as a world system and on the articulation of unfree labour in relation to free labour.

9 See Pfahlmann, cited by Castles and Kosack, page 185. On foreign labour see J. H. E. Fried, *The Exploitation of Foreign Labour by Germany*, Montreal, ILO, 1945; E. L. Homze, *Foreign Labour in Nazi Germany*, Princeton, New Jersey, Princeton University Press, 1967. On control of hiring, release and compulsory mobility see L. Hamburger, *How Nazi Germany Has Controlled Business*, Washington, The Brookings Institution, 1943, pp. 38–43, and for a longer account the same author's *How Nazi Germany Has Mobilised and Controlled Labour*, Washington, The Brookings Institution, 1940.

10 A brittle logic would have it that since fascist states severely fetter free labour they are 'not capitalist'. To argue like this is usually to overlook, one, the political and economic origins of fascism; two, the question of its long-term stability; and, three, the twists and turns in which individual capitals and capitalist states engage for the sake of capital accumulation in their struggles against labour and each other.

11 See page 111 below.

12 The way that mining employers minimized costs through curtailing expenditure, among other things, on food, accommodation, hospitals and compensation for injury, and how this governed the living conditions of the black miners on

the compounds is described in gruesome detail in *Chibaro*, chapter 2, 'Conditions in the Mine Compounds'; the origin and functions of the compounds are explored in chapter 5, 'The Compound System'. For a description of the Rhodesian compound system in the mid-1960s, see E. Moyo, 'Shabani and the Outbreak of Violence' in S. Wilmer (ed.), *Zimbabwe Now*, London, 1973, pp. 106–15. For a general account from the 1930s, see A. T. Nzula, I. I. Potekhin and A. Z. Zusmanovich, *Forced Labour in Colonial Africa*, R. Cohen (ed.), London, Zed Press, 1979.

13 *Chibaro*, p. 33. For a detailed account of the above see chapter 1, 'The Growth and Development of the Rhodesian Mining Industry, 1900–1933', esp. pp. 11–26.

14 Prior to 1903, mining employers had flirted with the idea of obtaining West Indian, English, Italian, Indian or Chinese labour. These ideas seem not to have been pursued either because of the cost involved, or because it was felt it would be impossible to prevent a European class from organizing. In 1900 a labour recruiter had actually gone to the Red Sea, illegally bringing back Arabs, Somalis and others. These proved unsuitable, showing 'little or no respect for white gangers'. ibid., pp. 81, 85.

15 ibid., table D, p. 114.

16 ibid., pp. 116–17.

2 The Labour Contract

'Chibaro': Forced Mine Labour in Southern Rhodesia 1903–12

Charles van Onselen

The two fundamental objectives of the industry in this period came to be output maximization and cost minimization. The successful pursuit of these objectives, however, necessitated the resolution of new and serious contradictions in the different ways that African labour was to be mobilized.

The need to maximize production at the existing mines, and the labour demands of a new class of producer, the small worker, both necessitated an *expanded* labour force, so within Rhodesia the BSACo administration took steps to increase the supply. Essentially this involved restricting further African access to land during a period when the peasantry was expanding its production by the sale of agricultural produce; and increasing taxation and consequently the peasants' need for additional cash earnings.

The other requirement of the industry, however, the need to reduce costs, tended towards an opposite logic: reductions in African wages made the mines a less attractive labour market, so the peasantry, faced with increased cash demands, tried to expand the area it had under cultivation and increase the sale of crops – thus reducing the local labour supply.

Even acting alone, these two contradictory forces would have brought annual fluctuations in the labour supply – particularly between 1903 and 1908, when wages were constantly being adjusted downwards. But the fluctuations were made even more erratic by an additional seasonal element, and that was the fact that Ndebele and more particularly Shona tribesmen would consider work only in the agricultural off-season.

Such fluctuations, both seasonal and annual, could not however be reconciled with the requirements of an industry that desperately needed to demonstrate its profitability. As the Rhodesian Land & Mine Owners' Association explained:

As soon as a stamp battery or other extraction plant commences to run on a mine, the number of unskilled labourers is more than three times as great as the maximum that could be employed on preliminary development. *Unless the full number required can be constantly maintained the rate of extraction will invariably exceed the rate of advanced development and sooner or later production must cease.*

If then the Rhodesian industry was to regain any stability in its African labour force after 1903 it needed first to replace the semi-skilled Shangaan workers which it had lost to the south; and second, more importantly, it needed to recruit a constant supply of cheap unskilled underground labour which could augment the fluctuating local supplies.

These contradictions, by now essential to the Rhodesian mining industry's structure and policy, were in fact to be resolved by the RNLB, which set out to provide the constant pool of unskilled labour to enable uninterrupted production of gold. So while all African labour – local and foreign – was called upon to pay a price for the reconstruction of the Rhodesian industry after 1903, none paid a greater price than the RNLB workers.

In the years before 1903, and to a lesser but still significant extent in the years following, Shona and Ndebele workers constituted the poorest paid and most despised group of African miners. In part this dislike was the legacy of the two wars fought against them during the 1890s, but it derived also from the fact that the Ndebele and Shona remained relatively aloof from the unpopular industry which had transformed their country, and would consider only short periods of service on the mines during the agricultural off-season.

Mine managers disliked these short-term workers and the impunity with which they deserted to their adjacent farms and kinsmen when the work or the conditions were not to their liking. For these and other reasons, it was considered that 'the Mashona and Matabele are poor workers, far inferior to both Colonials, Zulus and Shangaans.' The numerically preponderant Shona were particularly disliked by mine managers who found them to be 'awkward and useless' workers, and in 1900 the Chief Native Commissioner was of the opinion that:

it will be some time before the Mashona natives can be of much use on the mines as they are the laziest, most ignorant, and unpromising material we have to deal with.

Settler stereotypes were combined with more objective considerations, such as the length of service offered by the worker, to produce a hierarchy of wage differentials on the mines ...

In general though, throughout the reconstruction period, Shona and Ndebele workers were consistently paid less than other workers for similar tasks. In addition each successive year between 1903 and 1912 saw a consistent decline in black wages in general. These factors, combined with the appalling health record of most mines in the country, reinforced the local tribesmen's preference for expanding their cash income by selling agricultural surplus, or working in other sectors of the economy, rather than go down a mine.

The fact that Ndebele and to a greater extent Shona peasants could largely ignore the mining industry between 1903 and 1912, and earn the bulk of their cash requirements from farming, was a cause of immense chagrin to the premier industry of the company-colony. Mine owners were constantly frustrated by the thought that they suffered from a shortage of cheap labour in the midst of an apparently abundant 'supply'. Shona and Ndebele peasants might have been willing to ignore the mines, but the mines were far from willing to ignore them.

Accordingly early in 1903 representatives of all employers of labour in Rhodesia, including the chairmen of the two Chambers of Mines, sent a deputation to Johannesburg. They hoped to put pressure on the visiting Secretary of State for the Colonies, Joseph Chamberlain, not only to speed up his approval of the Pass Laws, which would help control labour in Rhodesia, but also to sanction massive increases in tax on the peasantry. The employers urged his approval of a 'Labour Tax' of £4 for each African male who failed to work continuously for more than four months in the year. This tax, it was suggested, should be levied in addition to the annual Hut Tax of ten shillings already imposed on the African population.

Despite Administrator Milton's enthusiastic support for increased taxation, the Colonial Office was unwilling to sanction the enormous increases demanded by the employers and desired by the BSACo. The Secretary of State did, however, agree to raise the tax to £1 per annum, and to impose an extra levy on the peasants of ten shillings for each wife beyond the first. Despite the fact that this increase was exceptionally modest in comparison with what the mining industry had wanted, it produced a rate of taxation for the peasantry in Rhodesia 20 to 30 per cent higher than that for most Africans in the regional economic system.

Taxation alone did not, however, solve the mining industry's labour problem. The weakness in the use of taxation was that it did not discriminate between the state economy and the regional economic system; so while tax increases did improve the supply of labour locally, they also tended to push a significant number of local peasants further out into the regional economic system, benefiting the Transvaal mines. This was especially true of those peasants in Rhodesia who were already closest to the South African border: when tax was increased in 1901 many of the Ndebele in the southern province turned to the Rand to earn the necessary cash; and when the 1904 tax increases following the 1903 deputation to Johannesburg produced a seasonal glut of labour in Rhodesia, it was again reported that many hundreds of workers had turned to the Transvaal.

Throughout reconstruction the positive 'push' into the regional economic system from tax demands was reinforced by the decline in the attraction of the local labour market to Shona and Ndebele workers. As African mine-workers' wages fluctuated seasonally in Rhodesia, and cash income declined in successive years, so the offer by WNLA agents of guaranteed employment and a minimum wage became more attractive to peasants increasingly forced off the land. When co-ordinated employer action in Rhodesia produced the 1906 wage cuts, there resulted a 'stream of natives who wished to engage for work in the Transvaal' – a movement which surprised the Chamber of Mines, for they had assumed that local Africans would be put off by the 12-month WNLA contract.

The loss of labour to the Transvaal and the activities of WNLA were a constant irritant to the industry and the BSACo alike, who felt justified themselves in drawing on the labour supplies from territories further north but resented Africans within the areas under their jurisdiction continuing to move to better labour markets in the south. With financial resources strained it was impossible to establish police stations along the entire length of the Limpopo river, but 'Police and Native Commissioners patrolled the country as often as was feasible.' And it was specifically within this context that the Pass Law proved of such value to the company-colony. The wife of the British High Commissioner knew exactly how the system of Pass Law manipulation operated:

> The Southern Rhodesians are the only people who have a reasonable defence for it. 'Our mines' they say 'must have cheap labour, if it were not for the pass law our natives would be able to go to the Transvaal for the high wages there, but our officials are forbidden to give them passes outside Rhodesia, and our railways will not give them tickets unless they have passes.'

Many mine owners found the passage of WNLA workers drawn from central Africa through transit compounds in Rhodesia particularly disquieting. 'Gangs' bound for the Rand showed 'exuberant spirits', a description that could hardly be applied to the RNLB workers destined for the local mines. An official enquiry in 1906 came to the conclusion that:

> the practice of bringing gangs of labourers recruited by the Witwatersrand Native Labour Association in Northern Zambesia and the territories to the North, through Rhodesia, is detrimental to Rhodesian industries, and is calculated to spread discontent among the natives of Southern Rhodesia.

Members of the industry felt that the passage of such 'gangs' made the local peasants' heads turn south and that 'it were better to hamper the operations of the WNLA in every possible way.'

It is difficult to assess with any degree of precision the exact number of peasants drawn from Rhodesia to the Rand during the reconstruction period. What is clear however is that some hundreds of Shona and Ndebele peasants who were forced off the land during that time were willing to consider, and in increasing numbers, a year's service in the Rand mines before they would turn to the Rhodesian mines. At least some of the Rhodesian authorities' attempts to swell the local labour supply benefited the Transvaal instead. In 1910, a monthly average of 13,000 local tribesmen were working on Rhodesian mines, while in the same year there were over 1700 'Rhodesian boys' on twelve-month contracts in the Witwatersrand gold mines.

These figures reveal just how poorly the Rhodesian industry

was supplied with cheap local labour throughout reconstruction. In 1910, for example, the industry employed over 37,000 black workers, and local labour still provided less than 30 per cent of its annual requirements. Worse still from the mine owners' point of view were the severe seasonal fluctuations in the local labour supply at this time.

Such seasonal and annual fluctuations were never welcome, but they were particularly unwelcome when the industry was trying to attract capital, maximize production and demonstrate its profitability in the wake of the 1903 collapse. Short-term labour did not produce the productivity which the industry looked for, and as the 1906 Labour Enquiry Committee expressed it, 'frequent change of labourers is detrimental to the establishment, on a firm basis, of any continuous industry.' The uncertainty caused by the lack of an assured local labour supply had indeed been one of the central problems which had contributed to the 1903 collapse, and it continued to make foreign capital wary of investing during the first six years of reconstruction. In 1909 the industry spelt out the problem to the BSACo administration: what it required of the administration was to put still more pressure on the peasantry to ensure an even greater and steadier supply of local labour.

Attempts by employers to get longer periods of service from the local peasantry were made long before the years of reconstruction, but between 1903 and 1909 they assumed new urgency. The 1906 Native Labour Enquiry Committee noted its strong disapproval of the local peasants' practice of contracting for only one month's work at a time. The Committee explicitly suggested that measures be taken to discourage this practice, and the Rhodesia Chamber of Mines was quick to take up the suggestion with the administration – new legislation should impose longer contracts. The Executive Council of the BSACo, however, was probably aware that it would be difficult to get such legislation approved by the Colonial Office, and merely pointed out to the Chamber that the onus of extracting longer contracts from the peasantry really lay with the mine owners.

The 1906 Commission also suggested that tax collection should be arranged in such a way as to spread the flow of local labour to the agricultural and mining industries:

Southern Rhodesia should be divided into three different

districts for the purpose of collecting the native tax, and that it should be collected at different periods of the year in the various districts.

It was suggested in addition that local Africans who had been continuously employed for a period of twelve months should be exempted from the tax. These proposals too the BSACo felt unable to implement, and an annoyed industry reminded the administration of the fact in 1907 and 1909.

Through direct appeals to the BSACo, or through its representatives on commissions of inquiry, the mining industry continued trying to persuade the administration to take steps that would either lengthen the period of service of local labour, or spread the seasonal flow more evenly throughout the year. Where the BSACo could not succeed, individual mine owners and labour recruiters proved more successful. By employing a variety of techniques they managed to supplement the long-term structural developments in the economy (such as taxation or the growth of white agriculture) which were already indirectly tending to extract longer periods of service from local workers.

One of the favoured devices of labour recruiters and mine managers was to mislead Africans about the length of their contracted period. Consistent, and in many cases deliberate, confusions arose about whether a contract referred to a 'month' or a 'ticket': whereas the word 'month' referred simply to the elapse of a calendar month, the word 'ticket' referred to any period required for the worker satisfactorily to complete thirty working days. And a worker's 'ticket' would only be marked as having contributed to his contract if his day's task was approved by his supervisor at the conclusion of the shift. So while at first glance it would appear that a 'ticket' would take about a month to complete, in practice it could take substantially longer. Besides the more obvious and frequent abuse which arose through the white miner simply refusing to credit the labourer with his day's work, injury, illness or rest days could lengthen the period. In 1909, a thirty-day 'ticket' took on average forty-two days to complete and in 1911 it was estimated to take between thirty-five and forty-five days.

It was especially in the earliest years of the reconstruction period that this confusion was used by the less scrupulous to mislead Africans about periods of service. But the confusion occasionally worked to the detriment of the industry too. Mine managers were particularly frustrated when black workers gave only a month's notice rather than a 'ticket's'. This problem was serious enough by 1909 for 'Consolidated' Goldfields Ltd to bring a private prosecution against one of its employees as a test case. To the annoyance of the industry the magistrate upheld the worker's right to serve only a month's notice since the Masters and Servants Ordinance made no reference to the word 'ticket'.

In the wake of this setback the industry was quick to get the Legislative Council to pass the necessary amendment to the Masters and Servants Ordinance, but it was found that this simply created further ambiguities, and by 1911 the issue was still unsettled. In practice, however, the problem was being solved by the longer periods of service which workers contracted for as they became increasingly proletarianized. These longer contracts *were* enforced through the Masters and Servants Ordinance, which was uniformly hated by black mine workers: it relegated them to what they considered to be slave status and their derisive word *'chibaro'* or 'cibalo', used to describe the system of recruitment, referred as much to the contract system as it did to the RNLB.

Mine owners and managers also resorted to other less subtle methods of lengthening the period of service of workers. Here again the techniques were applied in some measure to all workers, but they were of special use in dealing with local labour. At the New Found Out mine, for example, the manager insisted on all workers agreeing to a six-month contract in the presence, moreover, of the compound 'police' of the mine. This practice must have produced at least a 50 per cent chance of there being an element of coercion in the 'bargaining' between employer and employee, since the oppressive role of the compound 'police' was well understood by most black workers. A more common ploy, however, was for mine managers simply to refuse to 'sign off' workers who had completed their contracts. Since a worker who did not have his pass 'signed off' was liable to be arrested as a 'deserter', this practice could be partially successful for some time with the more timid and vulnerable employees.

Less subtle still was the practice of keeping workers' wages in arrears – managers would simply keep back a month's earnings. With the worker consistently being owed a month's wages, the mine owner could reduce the risk of desertion, stretch the period of employment and obtain a month's free labour should the worker eventually abscond in desperation. Occasionally too, the under-capitalized small workers who were speculating in the industry withheld wages in the hope of an ultimate windfall. Not only would the workers' wages be at a considerable risk in such cases but they would also have to work lengthy periods in the hope of recovering some of their earnings.

The variety of devices and stratagems which mine managers were willing to employ indeed demonstrates the almost insatiable demand for labour in an industry whose black work force increased five-fold during the period. At a time of such demand Shona and Ndebele workers could no longer simply be shunned, hired last or fired first, so the industry was forced to readjust its stereotypes and make new assessments of its worth ...

Through changes in the structure of the political economy between 1903 and 1912 Ndebele and Shona tribesmen were becoming increasingly proletarianized. The structural determinants of the process of proletarianization, such as access to land, taxation and the inroads made by an increasingly competitive white commercial agricultural industry, were supplemented by the techniques used by mine managers to produce these features. The process revealed itself not only in the gradual increase in the number of local workers but also in the periods of service for which they engaged themselves. In 1909 the average number of local Africans employed monthly on the mines was 10,000. By 1910 it was up to 13,000 and in 1911 there was a further rise to 14,000. Whereas during the speculative years of the industry local labour had accounted for between 10 per cent and 15 per cent of the black work force on the mines, during reconstruction this average rose to between 20 per cent and 27 per cent annually. The average period of service on the mines rose from two months in 1901 to three months in 1909 and six months in 1912.

Although these figures testify to the growing contribution of local labour during reconstruction, they still represented a rate of 'progress' in labour supplies which was far too slow for the mining industry. Its labour requirements were expanding by as much as 9000 in a single year (such as 1906–7) and in comparison to this demand the Shona and Ndebele contribution was insignificant. Even in the best year for local labour, 1911, local labour only accounted for 14,000 relatively short-term workers of the industry's 38,000 black workers. Clearly, the success of reconstruction was not to be based on the contribution of local labour. The real solution was to be found further afield; and to depend upon the activities of the RNLB...

In a period of particularly rapid expansion of its labour requirements the mining industry could always turn to the specially created labour recruitment agency ...

As an RNLB Chairman at an Annual General Meeting of the organization put it in 1915:

> A nucleus of natives contracted to work for twelve months at a definite minimum wage has great advantages. They form the guarantee that certain work can be carried on. They tide employers over the wet season, when independent labour is scarce and they make employers to a large extent independent of the vagaries of the casual labourer.

In essence the task of the RNLB was to resolve the contradiction which arose from trying to expand the labour supply during the years when the industry was also cutting black wages.

The second function of the RNLB was to secure for the Rhodesian mining industry its share of African labour within the regional economic system. It had to try to ensure that labour from the northern territories made its way to the Rhodesian mines rather than to other labour markets, and that Africans did not proceed to the Witwatersrand after a short period of work. The Chairman of the Salisbury Chamber of Mines could thus look back and tell the Administrator what he considered to be the 'true' purpose of the RNLB:

> It was our policy to obstruct and discourage by any legitimate means in our power the exodus of our natives in search of work, because there is ample work for them here for their requirements ...

Seen in this way, the role of the RNLB was to frustrate the mobility of African labour which, under 'market conditions' would simply gravitate to the Rand and sell its labour in the relatively better paying South African mines and industries.

The third primary function of the RNLB developed as an outgrowth of the other two. It was to channel a supply of

African labour to mines within Rhodesia which, because of poor conditions or exploitative practices, could not normally secure 'voluntary' or, as it was sometimes called, 'independent' labour. Again the problem was well defined by the manager of the Bureau who told a commission of inquiry that 'if it was left to the natives they would not work at unpopular mines.'

It was in fact the task of the RNLB to supply the mining industry with a supply of cheap coerced labour between 1903 and 1912.

Given this role, it can readily be appreciated why it was that the Bureau was universally feared and hated by black workers. Throughout most of central Africa, work secured through the RNLB became known as *chibaro* – 'slavery' or 'forced labour'. So to secure *chibaro-labour* was neither a pleasant nor a simple task for some members of the Bureau. Manager Val Gielgud spoke plainly to the 1906 Labour Committee:

The labour business is not a particularly nice business at the best of times, there is always more or less underhand work.

To understand what this 'underhand work' meant it is necessary to examine how *chibaro-labour* was secured.

For hundreds, probably thousands, of black peasants in the territories in and around Rhodesia, *chibaro* meant exactly what they stated it to mean – 'forced labour'. In some districts of North-Western Rhodesia between 1904 and 1910, peasants were simply rounded up by the Native Commissioner's African messengers and sent to the *boma* [administrative centre] where they were handed over to the agents of the RNLB and their black assistants, and then marched to the Southern Rhodesian mines. Those peasants who refused to go were in some cases whipped by the Native Commissioner or his black assistant, or in others had their grain-stores burnt down.

From at least 1911 onwards, some supplies of forced labour were also obtained from within Mozambique – despite the fact that, officially, the RNLB was entitled to recruit only in Tete Province after 1914. The RNLB agent, Walkden, was based within Rhodesia at Mtoko, but he operated through a Portuguese middleman, Manuel Vira. Vira would obtain *chibaro-labour* from villages within Mozambique and would then escort his captives to the Rhodesian border, where he would hand them over to Walkden and receive his commission. The

Managing Director of the RNLB at the time, H. W. Kempster, valued the work of the Walkden-Vira combination and pointed out to the Administrator that

> Manuel Vira obtains natives who would otherwise, either not turn out at all, or proceed to the Rand, and thus legitimately increases the labour supply for Southern Rhodesia ...

The capacity of *chibaro-labour* to dry up the flow of voluntary labour from rural areas was ... evident in the Eldorado district of Mashonaland. This district for many years drew a supply of voluntary labour from Mozambique. When this supply was drastically reduced a local observer was not lost for an explanation:

> since the RNLB has acquired powers in that territory [Mozambique] it is with increasing difficulty that free labour even on a small scale can be obtained here.

Elsewhere in Mashonaland farmers found to their frustration that the flow of labour into the northern province was disrupted between 1910 and 1913 – and again the cause was in essence the same. Sleeping sickness was discovered in the Luapula and Kalungwisi districts of North-Eastern Rhodesia in 1910, so the RNLB acquired sole recruiting rights within the region on the grounds that it alone could ensure an adequate medical inspection of those workers going south. In theory, Africans who produced a certificate to indicate that they came from an infected area could still proceed south on a voluntary basis. In practice things worked out differently – virtually all workers from North-Eastern Rhodesia either had to engage for work through the RNLB or return to their homes. A Mount Darwin farmer pointed out how

> All north-eastern boys coming this way are caught and sent under police escort to be examined by the doctor at the Bureau station and are then handed over to them on the excuse that they may have sleeping sickness.

Once there, in the words this time of a member of the Legislative Council, 'All the boys required to do was to engage with the Bureau, and if they did that, that was sufficient to get rid of the suspicion of having sleeping sickness.'

Chibaro-labour from rural areas was also linked to the other mechanisms which were used to induce and channel the flow of black labour in settler economies – tax and passes. More especially, during the earliest years of reconstruction, the BSACo put severe pressure on the Northern Rhodesian peasantry to pay tax. In North-Western Rhodesia during 1904 the police raided the villages of 'tax defaulters', burning homes, crops and grain stores of those Africans who did not have the necessary cash. These harsh actions were designed to proletarianize the peasants rapidly and to force them to earn cash at the largest labour market close by – the Rhodesian mines. In the Guimbi sub-district, the Native Commissioner sent tax defaulters directly to the RNLB agent, while for other Africans even the fact that the tax had been paid offered no protection. In the same district, on instructions from the District Commissioner, passes for those wishing to travel south were only granted to those who would undertake to serve with the RNLB. It is very probable that a similar variation was employed within Southern Rhodesia itself, since RNLB agents there were also empowered as 'pass officers'.

Although much of this *chibaro-labour* was obtained from the more remote districts of the regional economic system to the north of Rhodesia, the Bureau did not always have to operate in the rural areas themselves. In very many cases RNLB agents allowed the labour to move in their direction rather than go out searching for it. In fact, the closer to the Rhodesian mines the labour could be procured the better for the Bureau, since it reduced the amount of money that had to be spent on workers in transit on items such as food, clothing or escorts.

The RNLB soon discovered that there was no need to rely exclusively on direct penetration into the rural areas. Once various other forces, such as taxation, had pushed the peasants off the land, they would move towards the labour markets of the system anyway. Secure in the knowledge that most peasants would have to move *south* to try to sell their labour, the *chibaro* agents could position themselves accordingly. To situate themselves on the main labour routes, however, was not enough, since 'boys were afraid to travel along the main routes for fear of being intercepted by the Bureau's agents.' Ideally, what the Bureau required was a set of barriers running at right angles (west to east) to the labour routes. In central Africa just such barriers existed in the form of the rivers which flowed eastwards towards the Indian Ocean.

From the earliest days of the industry in Rhodesia the mines had interested themselves in the ferries crossing the various larger rivers. Presumably it was the 'abuses' which arose from the private operation of the ferries and the need for reconstruction labour which, in 1908, prompted the BSACo administration to put the RNLB in sole charge of these 'free' ferries.

Certainly between 1908 and 1911, and possibly for some years thereafter, there was a campaign of well-organized recruiting by RNLB agents at the ferries crossing the Zambezi, Luangwa and Hunyani rivers. So successful was 'recruiting' at such points where 'free ferries' operated, that 'returns' were published showing specifically how many workers had been obtained there. In 1909, for example, at the Zambezi crossing of Kanyemba, the RNLB obtained the services of well over 2000 'independent natives' making their way south. There is no doubt that the 'recruiting' at the 'free ferries' left a deep impact on the workers of central Africa and that they regarded such contracts as *chibaro-labour*. When in 1928 new free ferries were opened in two places on rivers the responsible state official reported to the government that

For the first few months these facilities were very little used as natives were suspicious that there was some catch and that if they used the free ferries and accepted the free food they would find themselves bound to the Bureau or similar organisation.

Before 1912, the RNLB also recruited within Rhodesia itself, and this meant that in some cases *chibaro-labour* could be obtained even further south – and even more cheaply. The problem in obtaining such labour was that it was already close to the labour markets and this might, on occasion, disrupt a voluntary flow of labour to the mines. The Bureau manager was aware of this irritating problem but, as he told the 1906 commission of inquiry, 'if you put out agents they are bound to catch some boys who would otherwise apply to the mines.' Here again most of the RNLB effort was concentrated in the northern province of Mashonaland – a procedure which capitalized on the voluntary flow of labour southwards in the system.

Chibaro-labour for the mines during 1903–12 was thus obtained by outright coercion in two ways. First, labour was procured in the heart of the rural areas themselves. Most *chibaro-labour* of this type was probably obtained during the years between 1903 and 1910, that is, in the period when the industry's labour requirements were expanding most rapidly of all. In addition, it seems as if it was mostly obtained from North-Eastern and North-Western Rhodesia – that is from areas that were under the direct control of the BSACo.

Second, *chibaro-labour* for the RNLB was obtained by waiting for other economic forces to push the peasants off the land, and then claiming a percentage of this labour flow at suitable points on the routes south. The supplies of labour procured in these two ways, however, were still insufficient to meet all the demands, and *chibaro-labour* also had to be sought out in rural areas by making use of methods other than outright compulsion.

No central African peasant would, voluntarily, seek out conditions of employment where he was to be paid the lowest wages, obligated by the longest contracts and sent to the mines with the worst health and labour management records in Southern Rhodesia. To avoid that *chibaro-labour*, however, a peasant had to be fit to walk the hundreds of miles to the labour markets, have the necessary cash with which to provide himself with food and clothing for the journey, and not to have left home while he had important obligations to his kinsmen unfulfilled. The normal vicissitudes in agricultural cycles, sheer distance from the labour markets and new burdens such as tax all made inroads into the bargaining power of the 'independent' work seeker.

It was to those groups within the peasantry who had had their independence already undermined that the RNLB looked for many of its additional recruits. Operating in the more remote areas, where alternative solutions to these problems were few if they existed at all, the RNLB advanced supplies of cloth, grain or cash to the poorest members of traditional society. These men from the very periphery of the regional economic system thus started their RNLB contract with the added burden of indebtedness. This added load, when combined with the normally difficult lot of the *chibaro-labourer*, must have been manifest to some employers who complained of the 'discontent' of workers recruited in this way. The Bureau, however, explained:

... natives should pay their taxes and observe certain other obligations before leaving their homes and unless the Bureau met them in this respect it would be practically impossible for them to go to Southern Rhodesia.

Droughts, such as those of 1903, 1912 and 1918, could not only swell the number of 'voluntaries' or 'independents' seeking work, but it could also supplement the ranks of *chibaro*. In 1918 the RNLB agent in Mozambique noted that the peasants were only agreeing to contracts because they were starving and added that:

> as the Gangs get their issues of blankets, money and food on leaving Tete there are numbers of their friends and relations from their homes waiting for them to give them practically the whole of what they had received.

Here too it was obviously the plight of the peasant rather than the popularity of the proposed employment that assisted the RNLB in obtaining 'recruits'.

Whilst drought posed problems for entire families, individual Africans were always faced with the problem of food supplies for the long march south. The majority of the men setting out on that journey did not have the cash with which to purchase supplies along the way – indeed the shortage of cash was the major motivation for the journey – so these poverty-stricken migrants too became potential sources of RNLB recruits.

Bureau agents were fully aware that much of the 'independence' of the voluntary worker derived from his access to enough food to enable him to reach the labour market independently. Accordingly, it seems as if at least one stratagem employed by agents was to intercept 'independent' workers and then, under the guise of having greater powers than they really possessed, to order them to remain in one place until 'authorization' for the continuation of their journey had been received. Once the men had waited for a number of days and exhausted their food supplies, they would be forced to accept the RNLB 'offer' of further food in exchange for a contract with *chibaro*.

Workers from North-Eastern Rhodesia faced on average a 750-mile walk to the labour centres, and many must have walked even further. Not unreasonably, some were daunted by the time, effort and savings which such a journey would consume. In fact the journey south constituted an investment which had to be made even before their labour started to earn them cash. The less able the worker was to make this initial investment, the most likely he was to have to turn to *chibaro* for help. RNLB contracts thus also partly reflected the distance of the point of recruitment from the labour market. The closer to a labour market the worker had been, the more likely he was to have reached it 'independently' – consequently the greater his bargaining power and the shorter his RNLB contract. The Chairman of the Bureau made the point when he told members of the mining industry that: 'south of the river [the Zambezi] boys were seldom engaged for twelve months, but north of the river they were usually engaged for not less than six months.' It was also the sheer distance from the labour markets that made some workers willing to face the appalling RNLB rail journey. And it was for the same reason that the Bureau found it profitable to concentrate most of its recruiting drives in the remoter parts of central Africa.

Then there was a third category of RNLB workers – the 'orthodox recruits'. Occasionally the Bureau recruited labour by a method already familiar among some settler employers: that is, by advertising highly exaggerated conditions of employment. This technique, with its heavy reliance on dishonesty, was used for short periods in areas where, for any one of a number of reasons, African market intelligence had failed. However, once workers from such districts had experienced at first hand the disadvantages of *chibaro-labour,* they soon returned to spread the bad word amongst the remainder of their district's inhabitants. The Bureau itself expressed the position quite frankly in a circular to its agents: 'Marked success in Northern Rhodesia in one year is of course liable to diminish the chances of recruiting in the ensuing twelve months.' In other words, the successful 'orthodox recruiting' of one year tended to become the residual 'Hobson's choice' recruitment of subsequent years.

In theory, and in practice, this meant a continual exhaustion of recruiting grounds. As in some primitive rural robber-economy, the RNLB was always seeking out a potential new field to exploit briefly for a year before it passed on to the next ... The agents had to move far and fast indeed in order to keep ahead of *chibaro*'s reputation.

When one understands how the RNLB operated on the

fringes of the regional economic system, it becomes even clearer why Bureau recruiting within Rhodesia itself was such a dismal failure. For local Africans were both best informed about the terrors of *chibaro*, and in the best position to exploit alternatives to RNLB employment. Local peasants could go to the compounds to sell their produce rather than to the mine owners to sell their labour. The relative absence of rural poverty made the area south of the Zambezi in any case a comparatively poor recruiting field; and when Shona or Ndebele tribesmen did find it necessary to go to the mines they found themselves the best work conditions through a well developed system of local market intelligence. Further, when local peasants were recruited by force, they could desert the more easily because they could count on assistance and protection from local kinsmen along the path home. And their knowledge of local geography enabled them to avoid the more common labour traps at river crossings.

It was only two years after the second RNLB was formed in 1906 that the Chief Native Commissioner of the populous Mashonaland province reported that 'The efforts of the RNLB to obtain local natives for work have practically failed, and their agencies have been withdrawn except in the Victoria circle.' *Chibaro* recruitment became worse rather than better in subsequent years, and by 1912 the Attorney-General, who was a member of the Native Affairs Commission, noted that 'The Bureau had not recruited a single native in Southern Rhodesia.'

This failure of the RNLB effort within Rhodesia only exacerbated the need to look further afield, and this in turn involved greater movement of Africans over a larger area and movement cost money. Ferries, food, clothes and escorts for *chibaro* workers all added to the cost of labour and imposed a heavy burden on an industry trying to demonstrate its profitability. The Rhodesia Chamber of Mines was acutely aware that, 'The resources of the industry have always been strained in its efforts to afford to the labourer efficient and safe means of transport to and from the mines.' In part it was the attempt to recover this cost which forced the RNLB to extract lengthy periods of service from its 'recruits'.

The length of the contract, however, did little to directly recoup the cash outlay incurred in the provision of facilities to workers on the way south. In order to cover its expenses and running cost the RNLB therefore made a *per capita* charge to the employers. This charge involved the mine owner in a substantial cash outlay which he did not normally incur when he obtained the services of 'voluntary' or 'independent' workers, so he in turn sought to recover his cash expenditure from the workers of the RNLB he was provided with. In practice this meant working his RNLB workers to the limit (in some cases 'the limit' meant literally working Africans to death ...) and restricting, to an even greater extent than normal, direct and indirect expenditure on them. In short, RNLB workers were exploited more ruthlessly than any other African labour and the derogatory implications of the term *chibaro* reflected not only RNLB recruiting tactics, but the conditions of these workers in the compounds themselves.

They were forced to contribute towards the repayment of their capitation fees in a variety of ways. In a significant number of cases they received poorer rations than 'voluntary' workers. This, combined with the fact that they had a lower cash income and were forced to work for longer hours than other workers, produced a significantly higher death rate among them from scurvy and pneumonia. Moreover, Bureau workers were usually denied access to the better paid jobs and were paid the lowest wages possible for the entire duration of their contract. In addition it appears that in some cases they were the victims of harsher discipline even than was normal in the tightly regulated compound system.

Chibaro-labour formed the most exploited group of an exploited class. Recruited under strained circumstances, exploited in the work place, sent without choice to the most unpopular mines in Rhodesia and kept for long periods in a strange country, their lot was appalling. Indeed, if slavery be defined as, 'the bringing of strangers into a society for use in economic production and legally defining them in terms of the category of property', then *chibaro* was perilously close to the 'slavery' which Africans perceived it to be.

While black workers in Rhodesia were never legally defined 'in terms of the category of property', there is no doubt that they were perceived as commodities by their settler masters. In official circles, where terminology was usually more genteel than that of the mines, African workers were described as labour 'devices', labour 'units' or 'tax-paying units'. Employers were even less vague, and their thought patterns were revealed whenever they wrote about their black workers. A mine manager thus found nothing strange in writing of the amount of money 'spent on purchasing Kaffirs from labour agents,' and at least one RNLB employer claimed to have 'bought four boys' from the Bureau.

RNLB recruits themselves referred to the work as 'slavery'. The deprived socio-economic status of the *chibaro* workers was so apparent to all within the compounds that fellow black 'voluntary' workers also referred to RNLB employees as 'slaves': the rivalry involved divided the black labourers and was, at least on occasion, encouraged by the management. Nor was the *chibaro* status of the RNLB workers lost on the compound managers: the compound manager at the Yankee Doodle mine welcomed the new RNLB arrivals at the mine with the comment 'look at the slaves coming in.' And at least one perceptive journalist in Rhodesia, Gertrude Page, wrote about the lot of black miners in the *Rhodesia Herald* under the title 'Rhodesian Slavery', asking: 'Which is worse, I wonder, to be a slave and know, or be told you are a free man, and treated like a slave?'

In an economy where the system of control over African labour was so extensive, employers held powers which placed them on a footing remarkably close to that of the slaveowners of the nineteenth century. Control over African labour was so effectively ensured through the Masters and Servants Ordinance, the Pass Laws, the Native Regulations Ordinance and the compound system that some settlers actually were in a position to 'sell' black workers to other employers. The combined hold of legislation, fear of settler employers, and the remoteness of a legal system controlled by a colonial power, all inhibited the African's ability to resist. In the mining district of Selukwe in 1911 it was reported that labour agents 'had been peddling in boys and making a living out of them in that way'. When a mine was bought or sold, employers took for granted the fact that African labour formed part of the deal and an inspector of compounds noted that 'the custom of selling the mine and the labour together is open to abuse.' The workers for their part also felt that they had been 'sold' in such deals, and *chibaro* workers particularly claimed that they were 'sold' by the RNLB contracts with unpopular mines.

So it was that what an illegal and largely unsuccessful campaign of forced labour had failed to achieve in the speculative years, the legal, systematic and organized activities of *chibaro* succeeded in achieving over the decade of reconstruction. It was the RNLB that ensured the industry its share of labour drawn from within a regional economic system in which it could not offer competitive wages. It was the supply of *chibaro-labour* that ensured that mines which could not attract a supply of 'voluntary' labour remained in continuous production. It was the Bureau that systematically extracted the longest contracts from the poorest peasants, which in turn ensured that the mines could develop ore reserves and continue milling during the Rhodesian wet season. Above all, it was *chibaro* that bridged the gap between labour supply and demand during the years when the industry's requirements for black workers expanded while at the same time it reduced wages for African miners.

Labour and the State in Nazi Germany

Ernest Mandel

If the fighting strength and degree of organization of the working class are high, even a fall in real wages as a result of heavy unemployment will only be transient in nature and will be made good once again by a rapid rise in wages in the subsequent phase of industrial upswing ...

If, on the other hand, capital succeeds in decisively weakening, or even smashing, the trade unions and all other organizations of the working-class – including their political organization; if it succeeds in atomizing and intimidating the proletariat to such an extent that any form of collective defence becomes impossible and workers are once more relegated to the point from which they started – in other words, the 'ideal' situation, from the point of view of capital, of universal competition of worker against worker, then it is quite possible (1) to use the pressure of unemployment to bring about a significant reduction in real wages; (2) to prevent wages returning to their previous level even in the phase of upswing following a crisis, i.e., to lower the value of the commodity of labour-power in the long term; (3) to force the price of the commodity of labour-power down, by means of manipulations, deductions and various swindles, even below this already diminished value; (4) simultaneously to achieve a significant increase in the average social intensity of labour and even to attempt, in tendency, to prolong the working day. The outcome of all these changes can only be a rapid and massive rise in the rate of surplus-value.

This is exactly what occurred in Germany following the victory of fascism under Hitler. The pressure of mass unemployment had forced German workers to bear with significant wage reductions in the years 1929–32. These were less catastrophic in *real* than in *nominal* terms, for there was a simultaneous fall in the price of consumer goods – but they were nonetheless considerable. The average gross hourly wage fell from the index figure of 129·5 in 1929 to 94·6 in 1932, i.e.,

103

by more than 35 per cent. The average hourly wage of skilled workers in seventeen branches of industry dropped from 95·9 pfennigs in 1929 to 70·5 pfennigs, i.e., by 27 per cent; in the case of unskilled workers the drop was less severe : from 75·2 to 62·8 pfennigs, or only 17 per cent. These percentages must be multiplied by the fall-back in the hours worked. However, since the price of foodstuffs declined by nearly 20 per cent in the same period, and the price of industrial goods fell by a similarly high percentage, the decline in real wages was not as steep as would appear from the abrupt plunge of nominal wages. At any rate, it was not as grave as might have been assumed with unemployment near the 6,000,000 mark and a catastrophic collapse in profits.[1] The rate of surplus-value fell – as it mostly does in severe economic crises – partly because of the devalorization of the commodities embodying surplus-value, and partly because a portion of the surplus-value produced could not be realized, but most of all because the production of surplus-value was itself declining due to part-time work and the decrease in the number of hours worked, since it is not possible to reduce the number of working hours necessary to reproduce labour-power exactly as much as the length of the total working day.[2]

What, then, occurred after the Nazis' seizure of power? The average gross hourly wage increased from the index figure of 94·6 in the year 1933 to 100 in 1936 and 108·6 in 1939. Despite full employment, therefore, the average gross hourly wage in 1939 was far below the level of 1929, when it had reached 129·5. The total mass of wages and salaries paid out in 1938 was still less than in 1929 (RM 42.7 billion as against RM 43 billion in 1929), while at the same time the total number of wage-earners had risen from 17·6 million in 1929 to 20·4 million in 1938.[3] Taking into account the lowering of the value of the commodity of labour-power, while simultaneously forcing the price of labour-power down even below its value in spite of full employment.

It is not difficult to locate the social and political secret behind this 'success'. The smashing of trade unions and all other workers' organizations, and the resultant atomization, intimidation and demoralization, condemned a whole generation of workers to loss of their capacity for self-defence. In the 'incessant struggle between capital and labour' one of the contending parties had its hands tied and its head stunned. The 'respective powers of the combatants' had been tilted decisively towards capital.

Even under conditions where the working class is completely atomized, however, the laws of the market which determine short-term fluctuations in the price of the commodity of labour-power do not disappear. As soon as the industrial reserve army contracted in the Third Reich, workers were able to try, by means of rapid job mobility – for instance into the spheres of heavy industry and armaments which paid higher wage-rates and overtime – to achieve at least a modest improvement in their wages, even without trade union action. Only a violent intervention by the Nazi state to sustain the rate of surplus-value and the rate of profit, in the form of the legal *prohibition* of job changes, and the *compulsory tying* of worker to their jobs, was able to prevent the working class from utilizing more propitious conditions on the labour market.[4] This abolition of the freedom of movement of the German proletariat was one of the most striking demonstrations of the capitalist class nature of the National Socialist State.[5]

NOTES AND REFERENCES

1 Charles Bettelheim, *L'Economie Allemande Sous le Nazisme*, Paris, 1946, pp. 152, 210, 211.

2 Kuczynski calculates that gross money wages in the metal industry plunged from an index figure of 184 in 1929 to 150 in 1930, in the chemical industry from 247 to 203, and in the whole of industry from 215 to 177. By contrast, the index of wages actually paid out is said to have fallen by half, and the index of net real wages from 100 in 1928 to 64 in 1932, hence by a full third. This last figure ought to be examined critically. Jurgen Kuczynski, *Die Geschichte der Lage der Arbeiter in Deutschland*, Berlin, 1941, vol. I, pp. 325–6, 329–30.

3 Bettelheim, op. cit., pp. 210–22.

4 On the restriction of the freedom of movement of wage-earners in the Third Reich as from 1936, see, among others, Kuczynski, op. cit., vol. II, pp. 119–21, 195–8; Neumann,

op. cit., pp. 341–2, 619.
5 See Neumann, op. cit., pp. 344–8, for cases in which wage-earners reacted to some of the most severe coercive measures of the Third Reich by slowing down their work and met with partial success; for example, such action led to the reversal of the decision to abolish special pay for overtime or work on Sundays.

PART III

The Reproduction of the Labour Force

Introduction

In Part II the readings focused on *chibaro* labour in Southern Rhodesia almost three-quarters of a century ago, and on the case of Nazi Germany, a regime brought down in 1945. The sites of such super-exploitation in no way justify complacency in Western Europe today. For now, instead for instance of British capital benefiting from the exploitation of labour in the colonies (together of course with a supply of raw materials from the same source) it benefits, at home, from the exploitation of workers from the former colonies. In this sense, the object of exploitation, labour-power, can be said to have been transferred into the metropolis itself. More accurately, metropolitan capital now either produces abroad and/or in the absence of a significant, job-producing 'outward' international movement of capital, pressures are set up towards an 'inward' international mobility of labour power.[1]

The mass movement into Western Europe of labour-power from Italy, Spain, Portugal, Greece, Yugoslavia, Turkey, Morocco (as well, of course, in the British case, from the West Indies and the Indian sub-continent) can be partly understood in terms of the attempt by immigrants to improve their material condition in a world that is manifestly unevenly developed. To take but one example, it has been estimated that throughout the 1950s and 1960s real wages in Yugoslavia were five times lower than in West Germany.[2]

About eleven million migrant workers have made the move to Western Europe in recent years – the largest number going to France (over three million), West Germany (just under three million) and Great Britain (2.6 million). But such raw numbers mask the different proportions of the labour force that migrants represent in different countries – in Belgium/Holland/Luxembourg, and in Sweden, Britain, France, and West Germany between four to nine per cent – but a remarkable thirty per cent in Switzerland. They also obscure the fact that the migrants are mainly young men who are active in the labour force to an extent that is not true for the native population, with its higher proportions of children, women and old people.[3]

This brings us to the other side of the coin: the advantages, to metropolitan capital, of importing such labour-power. That there can be such benefits is not difficult to see. Castells, for example, has argued that when considered from the standpoint of capital as a whole, one of the 'essential effects of immigration is to enable considerable savings to be made in the costs of the social reproduction of the labour force ... thereby raising correspondingly the overall average rate of profit.'[4] He sees this to be accomplished in three ways. First, as noted already, by recruiting immigrants primarily from among the young and productive. In this way it is possible to avoid paying the costs of 'rearing' workers and, he adds, the maintenance costs after their working lives have ended. Second, given the restrictive measures governing immigration and the conditions in which immigrants live and work, the majority are unmarried or 'forced' bachelors, and the costs of reproduction of families are not borne by capital, which thereby saves on the cost of facilities such as public housing, schools, hospital beds, welfare benefits etc. Third, the conditions of reproduction of the immigrants themselves, as well as of the families who succeed in accompanying them, are below the average standards of indigenous workers.

Some of the above points, and even more so Castells's argument that the vulnerability to repression of immigrants is brought about by their 'legal-political status as foreigners', might suggest that he has in mind migrant labour systems that differ in significant respects from the immigration that characterizes Britain. After all, so it is argued, in Britain there is 'immigration', not 'migrant labour'. But to the extent that there is something in this view, and the British case *is* a distinctive one, it has become less so over the last decade and a half. The fact is that the control of immigration and the status of immigrants has been altered by a succession of legislative changes: to tie the entry of Commonwealth workers to vouchers (the 1962 Immigration Act); to remove the right of entry to British passport holders unless they had at least one grandparent born here (the 1968 Act); to make the status of most Commonwealth immigrants that of aliens, at least in the first instance (the 1971 Act). According to the latter, non-patrial Commonwealth citizens have no right to settle or to bring dependants; they need work permits for specific jobs in specific places for specific periods (usually twelve months). Although they can vote (and hold trade union office etc., which is not always the case with migrant labour in other parts of Europe), they, like aliens, need permission to change jobs, have to register with the Department of Employment, and may only apply to register as British citizens free of conditions after four years, provided they are of 'good character' (as defined by the Home Office). As Robert Moore points out, because of all this the non-patrial (that is, in effect, *black*) migrant is put at the mercy of the employer, the police and the Home Office. It is not difficult to see that the powers of the Home Secretary to deport those whose presence is 'not conducive to the public good' could deter civil rights and trade union activism among future immigrant workers.[5] Britain, then, has moved closer to a 'European' form of contract migrant labour system, even though it has not gone the whole way. Many migrant workers will now have a different relationship to the state, compared both to contemporary indigenous workers and those who migrated before them twenty or so years ago.

Integral to the analysis of Castles and Kosack are what ought perhaps to be regarded as the two classic Marxist lines on labour immigration – those which derive from notions about *the reserve army of labour* and *the labour aristocracy*. These author's work, though now somewhat dated, has done much to rescue the study of important modern developments in this area from the often anodyne and subjectivist treatment they have received in much so-called 'race relations'. However, Marxist analyses are not free from differences of interpretation. Thus whereas Castles and Kosack's argument about migrants being a 'structural necessity' for Western European capitalism rests in part on the use of such labour to overcome *shortages*, a quite different case is advanced by Castells to seek to justify his view that migrant labour is 'not a conjunctural phenomenon ... but a structural tendency ... of monopoly capitalism'.

Crucial to Castells's view is that it is the inflationary crises to which monopoly capitalism is subject that make immigrants the 'ideal worker-consumer'.[6] This follows since, aside from being both highly productive *and* disposable, they consume relatively little in expansionary periods – presumably living at or near subsistence and sending money home, thereby not fuelling inflationary tendencies – and because when not at work (i.e. when expelled from the economy) the absence of their purchasing power has a corresponding, relatively low impact on the overall level of effective demand. This argument may be rather intricate (more so in fact than Burawoy concedes, see pages 151–2), but it stands in some need of empirical substantiation. Moreover, and no less important, though one can quite see the economic logic of an argument that migrant labour meets the requirements of monopoly capitalism for stabilized production and the cushioning of inflationary oscillations, a limitation here is that this argument is only an *economic* one.[7] It would be impossible to understand the development of immigration policy in Britain, for instance, without considering its *political* nature; and this whatever theories were advanced to explain what was in the interest of capital in general, *economically* defined.

As to the question of the *substitutability* of migrant and other sources of labour-power, there are of course cases where particular areas in an economy have successively employed children, then women, then immigrants. Examples of this are afforded by the British textile industry (which we have come across before in connection with Pakistani and Bangladeshi work and shift-work [pages 30–1]). Interchangeability is not something that can be assumed, however. It remains a matter for concrete historical analysis to establish which sources are drawn upon by capital in particular situations. As Beechey has noted, this is determined by the availability of various sources of reserve labour and by political expediency, as well as by the relative economic advantages offered by different groups of labour such as married women and migrant workers, who are partially dependent upon sources other than their own wages for the costs of reproducing their labour-power.[8]

To turn to Burawoy. It is a strength of his analysis, as it is of Marxist analyses in this area generally, that it breaks from the perspective of the individual migrant. Studies of labour migration have traditionally tended to adopt this, for they have generally involved the examination of two questions: the reasons for migration, and its consequences at the level of the individual or group. In answer to the first question, it has generally been assumed that individuals respond to the 'push' and 'pull' factors associated with the market. As to the second question, attention has been directed towards problems of the adaptation, assimilation and acculturation of the newly arrived migrant. Such approaches have failed to clarify the functioning of a *system* of migrant labour either in its broader social, political and economic contexts or where the flow of labour is regulated to a greater or lesser extent to suit dominant political and economic interests. The analysis of such systems of migrant labour, Burawoy argues, requires a different perspective: one which focuses on the nature of external coercive institutions and their mode of organization. He seeks to provide this by means of a comparison of migrant labour outside the European context, in modern-day California and South Africa, the latter providing him with a 'transparent' case of the state organization of the separation of what he terms the *'maintenance'* and *'renewal'* aspects of the reproduction of a system of migrant labour. He avoids unsituated analyses of highly abstract questions about the relation between monopoly capitalism and migrant labour etc., and his work has the virtue that it deals quite directly with specific political as well as economic considerations.

Migrant labour is only one mechanism by which the labour force can be replenished or enlarged. As noted above, it is only one source of the reserve army of labour, albeit one that in the pure case is marked out from indigenous labour by the distinctive relation that it has to *the state* – a relationship that involves the denial of civil, political rights. But in most capitalist societies, and certainly in Britain, the wage labour of women is statistically more important. And the very existence of such female wage labour poses questions about the significance of 'domestic labour' – the work which, at certain times of day, certain weeks, months, decades, may be all the work a woman does and which at other times, for the same woman, may have to dovetail with paid labour.

Would it not make economic sense, in a capitalist society, for women's work in the family – the domestic labour that provides for both the maintenance and renewal needs of the labour force – to be socialized? This is the sort of issue that Jackie West looks at below. In joining what is often called the 'domestic labour debate',[9] her contribution thus differs from some recent writers who, for example, stress the ideological and political significance of the family in such a way as to focus on and even celebrate its non-commoditized, allegedly 'non-alienated' nature.[10]

The rekindling of interest in the relation of the family to capitalism has of course led to a mounting theoretical literature. This is to be welcomed since the family has figured in only a trivial way in bourgeois economics and at least until the last few years, has been a tired, dull subject in sociology. But much of the new discussion about capitalism and the family has been conducted at a very high level of abstraction, with little actual regard for historical evidence (indeed, this same point has recently been made by Middleton with particular reference to the treatment of evidence about, and variation within, pre-capitalist social formations).[11] Moreover, as is indicated by Jackie West's piece many of the theoretical propositions currently advanced still stand in need of close scrutiny.

Family activities that contribute to the maintenance and renewal of the labour force are often carried out simultaneously: in many instances food is prepared for the worker-husband *and* for the children; house cleaning, washing etc, cannot be neatly apportioned to one function rather than the other. By contrast, educational institutions are concerned with renewal only.

Education is, as we know it today, a differential process. It confers different competences and different badges of competence (certificates, diplomas, degrees) upon those who attend different institutions and even sometimes different parts of the same institution. Such a system has its 'success' stories. However, given the actual distribution of jobs in the economy, its supreme achievement might be thought to be the systematic production of 'failure'. This brings us to the matter of how the disadvantage that goes with this is mediated to the mass of the population.

Unlike many economists, Bowles and Gintis do not simply assume that the education system is such that it reproduces the labour force replete with the requisite technical skills and knowledge. Such is their way of presenting their argument indeed, that it serves to deflect attention from the possibility that this is at least one of the system's purposes. For looking to form rather than content, they argue that education (specifically 'schooling') contributes to the reproduction of the *social* relations of production; more particularly, that it serves as a mechanism of social control, inculcating a familiarity with, and acceptance of, authority. Clearly, it is not part of their argument that *all* schooling has this consequence. Some minority sectors of the educational system do of course have the opposite effect. They inculcate and further familiarize styles for the performance of professional and, in the widest sense, management work. And they provide the future incumbents of such positions with qualifications that in turn can serve as devices for cultural exclusion. These people, who so often inhabit the world of the office, are imbued with complex cultural effects (as is the office itself). They are not confined to Britain, unique though the British variant may be. Thus, writing from France about the cultural symbolism that encases mental labour, Poulantzas tells us that it 'extends from the traditional esteem given to "paper work" and "clerical workers" in general (to know how to write and to present ideas), to a certain use of "speech" (one must know how to "speak well" in order to sell products and make business deals – the "art of salesmanship"), and finally includes ideological differentiations between general culture and savoire-faire on the one hand, and technical skills (manual labour) on the other. All these things, of course, require a certain training: learning to write in a certain way, to speak in a certain way, to dress in a certain way for work, to take part in certain customs and usages.' But, he adds: 'this "certain way" is always the other way, opposed to that of the working class. Everything that needs to be known in this respect is that which the others (the working class) do not know, or even cannot know (through original sin); this is the knowledge that matters, genuine knowledge. "Brain workers" are defined in relation to others (the working class). The main thing in fact is to know how to "intellectualize" oneself in relation to the working class; to know in these practices that one is more "intelligent", that one has more "personality" than the working class, which for its part, can at most be "capable". And to have the monopoly and the secrecy of this "knowledge".'[12]

Now this wrong-footing of workers quite definitely takes place. Very frequently they find that the right way is the other way, '*their* way'; that 'our way' is the wrong way. Are things quite this straightforward though? Aren't there different segments of the working class across which generalization of this type is not possible? Do many working class children really believe that formal qualifications are of real value, for instance, and are they really socialized into compliance through familiarity with structures of authority? Is their precious confidence even sapped?

One of the strengths of Paul Willis's *Learning to Labour* is that it begins to open up some of these questions. For their part, Bowles and Gintis concede that the educational system may not accomplish its objectives, but Willis's analysis is altogether more complex and, a certain romanticism aside, more challenging. For in the school's failure to wrong-foot (at least some) working-class kids, and to inculcate in them mindfuls of other-given values, in this failure he sees to reside – for the kids – a kind of success. Only a *kind* of success because the counter-school culture with its distinctive forms and vitality is, in the end, linked to a celebration of going to work. And whereas the counter-school culture and the culture of the shop-floor 'are not simply layers of padding between human beings and unpleasantness [but] ... appropriations in their own right, exercises of skill', it still remains the case that Willis's lads go freely to sell their labour-power.

Joyfully or not, many, many others have not only had to learn to labour but have had to labour to earn. Furthermore, they often do so under circumstances when the opportunities for informal control over the labour process (to which Paul Willis refers) can be easily exaggerated. But even in 'getting by' – minor sabotage, piss-takes and the rest – even in resisting in a culturally creative way – and indeed by virtue of their largely subterranean form of struggle – workers like the young ones Willis describes leave the primary relation of exploitation intact; in fact reproduce it.

This relation does not *have* to be reproduced any more than educational systems have to be 'successful', or women accept their oppression in the family, or the political conditions survive for the operation of a migrant labour system. But it is to be hoped that in future years the precise and complex ways that it *is* and *has been* reproduced, and with it, for it, the labour force, will receive increased attention.

NOTES AND REFERENCES

1 See Marios Nikolinakos, 'A General Theory of Migration in Late Capitalism', in Ayse Kudat and Yibuaz Özkan (eds), *International Conference on Migrant Workers*, International Institute for Comparative Social Studies, Berlin, June 1975, p. 11; Ernest Mandel, *Late Capitalism*, p. 325.

2 James Bellini, 'European Migrant Labour: Present and Future Conditions', *New Community*, 4, 1, Winter/Spring 1974–5, p. 7.

3 See Robert Moore, *Racism and Black Resistance in Britain*, London, Pluto, 1975, esp. pp. 5–7. On Switzerland, see John Berger and Jean Mohr, *A Seventh Man*, Harmondsworth, Penguin 1975; for a similar analysis of migrant *women*, see Jean Guyot *et al.*, *Migrant Women Speak*, London, Search Press/Geneva, World Council of Churches, 1977. For an aptly entitled account of the Ugandan Asians driven from Uganda by Amin, see Mahmood Mamdani, *From Citizen to Refugee*, London, Frances Pinter, 1973.

4 Manuel Castells, 'Immigrant Workers and Class Struggle in Advanced Capitalism: The Western European Experience', *Politics and Society*, 5, 1, 1975.

5 Robert Moore, *Racism and Black Resistance in Britain*, p. 34; see also his work with Tina Wallace, *Slamming the Door: The Administration of Immigration Control*, London, Martin Robertson, 1975.

6 'Immigrant Workers and Class Struggle', p. 56.

7 A related limitation in the sense that this too concerns an aspect of the political applies to 'dual labour market' theories in which migrant labour and female labour are categorized together as falling into a disadvantaged 'secondary' sector, despite possible important differences of political status. See R. D. Barron and G. M. Norris, 'Sexual Divisions and the Dual Labour Market', in Diana Barker and Sheila Allen (eds), *Dependence and Exploitation in Work and Marriage*, London and New York, Longman, 1976.

8 Veronica Beechey, 'Critical Analysis of Some Sociological Theories of Women's Work', in Annette Kuhn and Ann-Marie Wolpe, *Feminism and Materialism: Women and*

Modes of Production, London, Routledge and Kegan Paul, 1978, p. 191.

9 For most of the major contributions, see her references to 'Political Economy of the Family' at p. 185.

10 Eli Zaretsky might be considered in this light. Of course such ideas have also been at the bottom of much orthodox sociology. See *Capitalism and the Family and Personal Life*, London, Pluto, 1976.

11 Christopher Middleton, 'The Sexual Division of Labour in Feudal England', *New Left Review*, January/April 1979, pp. 13–14; see also Jackie West 'Some Notes on the Changing Relationship of Domestic Labour to the Reproduction of Labour Power', Bristol, 1979 (mimeo).

12 Nicos Poulantzas, *Classes in Contemporary Capitalism*, London, NLB, 1975, p. 258.

3 Migrant Labour

The Function of Labour Immigration in Western European Capitalism

Stephen Castles and Godula Kosack

The domination of the working masses by a small capitalist ruling class has never been based on violence alone. Capitalist rule is based on a range of mechanisms, some objective products of the economic process, others subjective phenomena arising through manipulation of attitudes. Two such mechanisms, which received considerable attention from the founders of scientific socialism, are the industrial reserve army, which belongs to the first category, and the labour aristocracy, which belongs to the second. These two mechanisms are closely related, as are the objective and subjective factors which give rise to them.

Engels pointed out that 'English manufacture must have, at all times save the brief periods of highest prosperity, an unemployed reserve army of workers, in order to produce the masses of goods required by the market in the liveliest months.'[1] Marx showed that the industrial reserve army or surplus working population is not only the necessary product of capital accumulation and the associated increase in labour productivity, but at the same time 'the lever of capitalist accumulation', 'a condition of existence of the capitalist mode of production'.[2] Only by bringing ever more workers into the production process can the capitalist accumulate capital, which is the precondition for extending production and applying new techniques. These new techniques throw out of work the very men whose labour allowed their application. They are set free to provide a labour reserve which is available to be thrown into other sectors as the interests of the capitalist require. 'The whole form of the movement of modern industry depends, therefore, upon the constant transformation of a part of the labouring population into unemployed or half-employed hands.'[3] The pressure of the industrial reserve army forces those workers who are employed to accept long hours and poor conditions. Above all: 'Taking them as a whole, the general movements of wages are exclusively regulated by the expansion and contraction of the industrial reserve army.'[4] If employment grows and the reserve army contracts, workers are in a better position to demand higher wages. When this happens, profits and capital accumulation diminish, investment falls and men are thrown out of work, leading to a growth of the reserve army and a fall in wages. This is the basis of the capitalist economic cycle. Marx mentions the possibility of the workers seeing through the seemingly natural law of relative over-population, and undermining its effectiveness through trade-union activity directed towards co-operation between the employed and the unemployed.[5]

The labour aristocracy is also described by Engels and Marx. By conceding privileges to certain well-organized sectors of labour, above all to craftsmen (who by virtue of their training could not be readily replaced by members of the industrial reserve army), the capitalists were able to undermine class consciousness and secure an opportunist non-revolutionary leadership for these sectors.[6] Special advantages, sometimes taking the form of symbols of higher status (different clothing, salary instead of wages, etc.) rather than higher material rewards, were also conferred upon foremen and non-manual workers, with the aim of distinguishing them from other workers and causing them to identify their interests with those of the capitalists. Engels pointed out that the privileges given to some British workers were possible because of the vast profits made by the capitalists through domination of the world market and imperialist exploitation of labour in other countries.[7] Lenin emphasized the effects of imperialism on class consciousness: 'Imperialism ... makes it economically possible to bribe the upper strata of the proletariat, and thereby fosters, gives shape to, and strengthens opportunism.'[8] '... A section of the proletariat allows itself to be led by men bought by, or at least paid by, the bourgeoisie' and the result is a split among the workers and 'temporary decay in the working-class movement'.[9]

The industrial reserve army and the labour aristocracy have not lost their importance as mechanisms of domination in the current phase of organized monopoly capitalism. However, the way in which they function has undergone important changes. In particular the maintenance of an industrial reserve army within the developed capitalist countries of West Europe ha become increasingly difficult. With the growth of the labour movement after the First World War, economic crises and unemployment began to lead to political tensions which threatened the existence of the capitalist system. Capitalism responded by setting up fascist regimes in the areas where it was most threatened, in order to suppress social conflict through violence. The failure of this strategy, culminating in the defeat of fascism in 1945, was accompanied by the reinforcement of the non-capitalist bloc in East Europe and by a further strengthening of the labour movement in West Europe. In order to survive, the capitalist system had to aim for continuous expansion and full employment at any price. But full employment strikes at a basic principle of the capitalist economy : the use of the industrial reserve army to keep wages down and profits up. A substitute for the traditional form of reserve army had to be found, for without it capitalist accumulation is impossible. Moreover, despite Keynesian economics, it is not possible completely to avoid the cyclical development of the capitalist economy. It was therefore necessary to find a way of cushioning the effects of crises, so as to hinder the development of dangerous social tensions.

IMMIGRANTS AS THE NEW INDUSTRIAL RESERVE ARMY

The solution to these problems adopted by West European capitalism has been the employment of immigrant workers from under-developed areas of Southern Europe or from the Third World.[10] Today, the unemployed masses of these areas form a 'latent surplus-population'[11] or reserve army, which can be imported into the developed countries as the interests of the capitalist class dictate. In addition to this economic function, the employment of immigrant workers has an important socio-political function for capitalism : by creating a split between immigrant and indigenous workers along national and racial lines and offering better conditions and status to indigenous workers, it is possible to give large sections of the working class the consciousness of a labour aristocracy.

The employment of immigrant workers in the capitalist production process is not a new phenomenon. The Irish played a vital part in British industrialization. Not only did they provide a special form of labour for heavy work of a temporary nature on railways, canals and roads;[12] their competition also forced down wages and conditions for other workers. Engels described Irish immigration as a 'cause of abasement to which the English worker is exposed, a cause permanently active in forcing the whole class downwards.'[13] Marx described the antagonism between British and Irish workers, artificially created by the mass media of the ruling class, as 'the secret of the impotence of the English working class, despite their organization'.[14] As industrialization got under way in France, Germany and Switzerland in the latter half of the nineteenth century, these countries too brought in foreign labour: from Poland, Italy and Spain There were 800,000 foreign workers in the German Reich in 1907. More than a third of the Ruhr miners were Poles Switzerland had half a million foreigners in 1910 – 15 per cent of her total population. French heavy industry was highly dependent on immigrant labour right up to the Second World War. According to Lenin, one of the special features of imperialism was 'the decline in emigration from imperialist countries and the increase in immigration into these countries from the more backward countries where lower wages are paid.'[15] This was a main cause of the division of the working class. The fascist form of capitalism also developed its own specific form of exploiting immigrant workers: the use of forced labour. No less than $7\frac{1}{2}$ million deportees from occupied countries and prisoners of war were working in Germany by 1944, replacing the men recruited for the army. About a quarter of German munitions production was carried out by foreign labour.[16]

Compared with early patterns, immigration of workers to contemporary West Europe has two new features. The first is its character as a permanent part of the economic structure Previously, immigrant labour was used more or less temporarily when the domestic industrial reserve army was inadequate for some special reason, like war or unusually fast expansion; since 1945, however, large numbers of immigrant workers have taken up key positions in the productive process, so that even in the case of recession their labour cannot be dispensed with. The second is its importance as the basis of the modern industrial reserve army. Other groups which might conceivably fulfil the same function – non-working women, the disabled and the chronic sick, members of the lumpenproletariat whose conditions prevent them from working,[17] have already been integrated into the production process to the extent to which this is profitable for the capitalist system. The use of further reserves of this type would require costly social measures (e.g. adequate kindergartens). The main traditional form of the industrial reserve army – men thrown out of work by rationalization and cyclical crises – is hardly available today, for reasons already mentioned. Thus immigration is of key importance for the capitalist system.

THE DEVELOPMENT OF IMMIGRATION SINCE 1945

There are around 11 million immigrants[18] living in West Europe, making up about 5 per cent of total population. Relatively few have gone to industrially less developed countries like Norway, Austria and Denmark, while large concentrations are to be found in highly industrialized countries like Belgium, Sweden, West Germany, France, Switzerland and Britain. Our analysis concentrates on the four last-named which have about 90 per cent of all immigrants in West Europe between them.

Immigrants in West Germany, France, Switzerland and Britain[19]

	Immigrants (thousands)	Immigrants as percentage of total population	Date of figures (latest available)
West Germany	2,977	4·8	September 1970
France	3,177	6·4	December 1969
Switzerland	972	16·0	December 1969
Britain	2,603	5·0	1966

Most immigrants in Germany and Switzerland come from Southern Europe. The main groups in Germany are Italians (574,000 in 1970), Yugoslavs (515,000), Turks (469,000), Greeks (343,000) and Spaniards (246,000). In Switzerland, the Italians are by far the largest group (532,000 in 1969) followed by Germans (116,000) and Spaniards (98,000). France and Britain also have considerable numbers of European immigrants, but in addition large contingents from former colonies in Africa, Asia and the Caribbean. France has 617,000 Spaniards, 612,000 Italians, 480,000 Portuguese, as well as 608,000 Algerians,

143,000 Moroccans, 89,000 Tunisians, about 55,000 black Africans and an unknown number (probably about 200,000) from the remaining colonies (euphemistically referred to as Overseas Departments) in the West Indies and the African island of Réunion. The largest immigrant group in Britain comes from the Irish Republic (739,000 in 1966). Most of the other Europeans were displaced persons and the like who came during and after the war: Germans (142,000), Poles (118,000). Cypriots number 60,000. There are also an increasing number of South Europeans, often allowed in on a short-term basis for work in catering and domestic service. Coloured immigrants comprise about one third of the total, the largest groups coming from the West Indies (269,000 in 1966), India (240,000) and Pakistan (75,000).[20]

The migratory movements and the government policies which direct them reflect the growing importance and changing function of immigrant labour in West Europe. Immediately after the Second World War, Switzerland, Britain and France recruited foreign workers. Switzerland needed extra labour for the export boom permitted by her intact industry in the middle of war-torn Europe. The 'European Voluntary Workers' in Britain (initially displaced persons, later Italians) were assigned to specific jobs connected with industrial reconstruction. The reconstruction boom was not expected to last. Both Switzerland and Britain imposed severe restrictions on foreign workers, designed to stop them from settling and bringing in their families, so that they could be dismissed and deported at the least sign of recession. France was something of an exception: her immigration policy was concerned not only with labour needs for reconstruction, but also with permanent immigration to counteract the demographic effects of the low birth-rate.

When West German industry got under way again after the 1949 Currency Reform there was at first no need for immigrants from Southern Europe. An excellent industrial reserve army was provided by the seven million expellees from the former Eastern provinces of the Reich and by the 3 million refugees from East Germany, many of whom were skilled workers. Throughout the 1950s, the presence of these reserves kept wage-growth slow and hence provided the basis for the 'economic miracle'. By the mid-1950s, however, special labour shortages were appearing, first in agriculture and building. It was then that recruitment of foreign workers (initially on a seasonal basis[21]) was started. Here too, an extremely restrictive policy was followed with regard to family entry and long-term settlement. 'Rotation' of the foreign labour force was encouraged. In this stage, the use of immigrants in the countries mentioned followed the pre-war pattern: they were brought in to satisfy special and, it was thought, temporary labour needs in certain sectors. They were, as an official of the German employers' association put it, 'a mobile labour potential'.[22]

By the 1960s, the situation was changing. Despite mild cyclical tendencies it was clear that there was not going to be a sudden return to the pre-war boom-slump pattern. The number of immigrant workers grew extremely rapidly in the late 1950s and early 1960s. Between 1956 and 1965 nearly 1 million new workers entered France. The number of foreign workers in West Germany increased from 279,000 in 1960 to over 1·3 million in 1966. In Switzerland there were 326,000 immigrant workers (including seasonals) in 1956, and 721,000 in 1964. This was also the period of mass immigration to Britain from the Commonwealth.[23] The change was not merely quantitative: immigrants were moving into and becoming indispensable in ever more sectors of the economy. They were no longer filling gaps in peripheral branches like agriculture and building but were becoming a vital part of the labour force in key industries like engineering and chemicals. Moreover, there was growing competition between the different countries to obtain the 'most desirable' immigrants, i.e. those with the best education and the least cultural distance from the receiving countries. The growing need for labour was forcing the recruiters to go further and further afield: Turkey and Yugoslavia were replacing Italy as Germany's main labour source. Portugal and North Africa were replacing Italy and Spain in the case of France.

As a result, new policies intended to attract and integrate immigrant workers, but also to control them better, were introduced. One such measure was the free labour movement policy of the EEC, designed to increase the availability of the rural proletariat of Sicily and the Mezzogiorno to West European capital.[24] Germany and Switzerland liberalized the conditions for family entry and long-term settlement, while at the same time tightening political control through measures such as the German 1965 Foreigners Law. France tried to increase control over entries, in order to prevent the large-scale clandestine immigration which had taken place throughout the 1950s and 1960s (and still does, despite the new policy). At the same time restrictions were made on the permanent settlement of non-

Europeans – officially because of their 'greater difficulties in integrating'. In Britain, racialist campaigns led to the stopping of unrestricted Commonwealth immigration in 1962. By limiting the labour supply, this measure contradicted the economic interests of the ruling class. The new Immigration Act of 1971, which could provide the basis for organized and controlled labour recruitment on the German and French pattern, is a corrective, although its application for this purpose is not at present required, since the ruling class has created an internal industrial reserve army through unemployment.

In view of the stagnant domestic labour force potential and the long-term growth trend of the economy, immigrant labour has become a structural necessity for West European capitalism.[25] It has a dual function today.[26] One section is maintained as a mobile fluctuating labour force, which can be moved from factory to factory or branch to branch as required by the development of the means of production and which can be thrown out of work and deported as required without causing social tensions. This function was shown clearly by the West German recession of 1966–7, when the foreign labour force dropped by 400,000, although there were never more than 29,000 receiving unemployment benefit. As a United Nations study pointed out, West Germany was able to export unemployment to the home countries of the migrants.[27] The other section is required for permanent employment throughout the economy. They are offered better conditions and the chance of long-term settlement.[28] Despite this they still fulfil the function of an industrial reserve army, for they are given inferior jobs, have no political rights and may be used as a constant threat to the wages and conditions of the local labour force.

OCCUPATIONAL POSITION

The immigrant percentage of the population given in the table above in no way reflects the contribution of immigrants to the economy. They are mainly young men, whose dependants are sent for later if at all. Many of them remain only a few years, and are then replaced by others, so that there are hardly any retired immigrants. Immigrants therefore have higher than average rates of economic activity, and make contributions to health, unemployment and pension insurance far in excess of their demands on such schemes.[29] Particularly high rates of activity are to be found among recently arrived groups, or among those who for social and cultural reasons tend not to bring dependants with them: Portuguese and North Africans in France, Turks in Germany and Pakistanis in Britain. Immigrant workers are about 6·5 per cent of the labour force in Britain, 7–8 per cent in France, 10 per cent in West Germany and 30 per cent in Switzerland. Even these figures do not show adequately the structural importance of immigrant labour, which is concentrated in certain areas and types of work.

The overwhelming majority of immigrants live in highly industrialized and fast-growing urban areas like Paris, the Lyon region, the Ruhr, Baden-Württemberg, London and the West Midlands. For example 31·2 per cent of all immigrants in France live in the Paris region, compared with only 19·2 per cent of the total population. 9·5 per cent of the inhabitants of the Paris region are immigrants.[30] In Britain more than one third of all immigrants are to be found in Greater London compared with one sixth of the total population. Immigrants make up 12 per cent of London's population.[31]

More important still is the concentration in certain industries. Switzerland is the extreme case: the whole industrial sector is dominated by foreign workers who make up more than 40 per cent of the factory labour force. In many branches – for instance textiles, clothing, building and catering – they outnumber Swiss employees.[32] Of the nearly 2 million foreign workers in Germany in September 1970, 38·5 per cent were in the metal-producing and engineering industry, 24·2 in other manufacturing branches and 16·7 per cent in building. Foreign workers accounted for 13·7 per cent of total employment in metal producing and engineering. The proportion was even higher in some industries with particularly bad working conditions, like plastic, rubber and asbestos manufacture (18·4 per cent). In building, foreign workers were 17·5 per cent of the labour force. On the other hand they made up only 3·4 per cent of all employees in the services, although their share was much higher in catering (14·8 per cent).[33] Similar concentrations were revealed by the 1968 Census in France: 35·6 per cent of immigrant men were employed in building and 13·5 per cent in engineering and electrical goods. 28·8 per cent of foreign women were domestic servants. In Britain the concentration of immigrants in certain industries is less marked, and different immigrant groups have varying patterns. The Irish are concentrated in construction, while Commonwealth immigrants are over-represented in metal manufacture and transport. Pakistani men are mainly to be found in the textile industry and Cypriots in clothing and footwear and in distribution. European immigrants are frequently in the service sector. Immigrant women of all nationalities tend to work in services, although some groups (Cypriots, West Indians) also often work in manufacturing.[34]

In general immigrants are concentrated in certain basic industries, where they form a high proportion of the labour force. Together with their geographical concentration this means that immigrant workers are of great importance in the very type of enterprise and area which used to be regarded as the strongholds of the class-conscious proletariat. The real concentration is even greater than the figures show, for within each industry the immigrants tend to have become predominant in certain departments and occupations. There can be hardly a foundry in West Europe in which immigrants do not form a majority, or at least a high proportion, of the labour force. The same applies to monotonous production line work, such as car-assembly. Renault, Citroën, Volkswagen, Ford of Cologne and Opel all have mainly foreign workers on the assembly line (the British motor industry is an exception in this respect).

Perhaps the best indication of the occupational concentration of the immigrant labour force is given by their socio-economic distribution. For instance a survey carried out in 1968 in Germany showed that virtually no Southern Europeans are in non-manual employment. Only between 7 per cent and 16 per cent of the various nationalities were skilled workers while between 80 per cent and 90 per cent were either semi-skilled or un-skilled.[35] By comparison about a third of German workers are non-manual, and among manual workers between one third and one half are in the skilled category in the various industries. In France a survey carried out at Lyon in 1967 found that where they worked in the same industry, the French were mainly in managerial, non-manual or skilled occupations, while the immigrants were concentrated in manual occupations, particularly semi-skilled and unskilled ones. The relegation to unskilled jobs is particularly marked for North Africans and Portuguese.[36] In Britain, only about 26 per cent of the total labour force fall into the unskilled and semi-skilled manual categories, but the figure is 42 per cent for the Irish, 50 per cent for the Jamaicans, 65 per cent for the Pakistanis and 55 per cent for the Italians.[37]

Immigrants form the lowest stratum of the working class

carrying out unskilled and semi-skilled work in those industrial sectors with the worst working conditions and/or the lowest pay.[38] The entry of immigrants at the bottom of the labour market has made possible the release of many indigenous workers from such employment and their promotion to jobs with better conditions and higher status, i.e. skilled, supervisory or white-collar employment. Apart from the economic effects, this process has a profound impact on the class consciousness of the indigenous workers concerned. This will be discussed in more detail below.

SOCIAL POSITION

The division of the working class within the production process is duplicated by a division in other spheres of society. The poor living conditions of immigrants have attracted too much liberal indignation and welfare zeal to need much description here. Immigrants get the worst types of housing: in Britain slums and run-down lodging houses, in France *bidonvilles* (shanty-towns) and over-crowded hostels, in Germany and Switzerland camps of wooden huts belonging to the employers and attics in the cities. It is rare for immigrants to get council houses. Immigrants are discriminated against by many landlords, so that those who do specialize in housing them can charge extortionate rents for inadequate facilities. In Germany and France, official programmes have been established to provide hostel accommodation for single immigrant workers. These hostels do provide somewhat better material conditions. On the other hand they increase the segregation of immigrant workers from the rest of the working class, deny them any private life, and above all put them under the control of the employers twenty-four hours a day.[39] In Germany the employers have repeatedly attempted to use control over immigrants' accommodation to force them to act as strike-breakers.

Language and vocational training courses for immigrant workers are generally provided only when it is absolutely necessary for the production process, as in mines for example. Immigrant children are also at a disadvantage: they tend to live in run-down overcrowded areas where school facilities are poorest. No adequate measures are taken to deal with their special educational problems (e.g. language difficulties), so that

127

their educational performance is usually below-average. As a result of their bad working and living conditions, immigrants have serious health problems. For instance they have much higher tuberculosis rates than the rest of the population virtually everywhere.[40] As there are health controls at the borders, it is clear that such illnesses have been contracted in West Europe rather than being brought in by the immigrants.

The inferior work-situation and living conditions of immigrants have caused some bourgeois sociologists to define them as a 'lumpenproletariat' or a 'marginal group'. This is clearly incorrect. A group which makes up 10, 20 or 30 per cent of the industrial labour force cannot be regarded as marginal to society. Others speak of a 'new proletariat' or a 'sub-proletariat'. Such terms are also wrong. The first implies that the indigenous workers have ceased to be proletarians and have been replaced by the immigrants in this social position. The second postulates that immigrant workers have a different relationship to the means of production than that traditionally characteristic of the proletariat. In reality both indigenous and immigrant workers share the same relationship to the means of production: they are excluded from ownership or control; they are forced to sell their labour power in order to survive; they work under the direction and in the interests of others. In the sphere of consumption both categories of workers are subject to the laws of the commodity market, where the supply and price of goods is determined not by their use value but by their profitability for capitalists; both are victims of landlords, retail monopolists and similar bloodsuckers and manipulators of the consumption-terror. These are the characteristics typical of the proletariat ever since the industrial revolution, and on this basis immigrant and indigenous workers must be regarded as members of the same class: the proletariat. But it is a divided class: the marginal privileges conceded to indigenous workers and the particularly intensive exploitation of immigrants combine to create a barrier between the two groups, which appear as distinct strata within the class. The division is deepened by certain legal, political and psychological factors, which will be discussed below.

16

DISCRIMINATION

Upon arrival in West Europe, immigrants from under-developed areas have little basic education or vocational training and are usually ignorant of the language. They know nothing of prevailing market conditions or prices. In capitalist society, these characteristics are sufficient to ensure that immigrants get poor jobs and social conditions. After a period of adaptation to industrial work and urban life, the prevailing ideology would lead one to expect many immigrants to obtain better jobs, housing, etc. Special mechanisms ensure that this does not happen in the majority of cases. On the one hand there is institutionalized discrimination in the form of legislation which restricts immigrants' civic and labour market rights. On the other hand there are informal discriminatory practices based on racialism or xenophobia.

In nearly all West European countries, labour market legislation discriminates against foreigners. They are granted labour permits for a specific job in a certain firm for a limited period. They do not have the right to move to better-paid or more highly qualified positions, at least for some years. Workers who change jobs without permission are often deported. Administrative practices in this respect have been liberalized to some extent in Germany and Switzerland in recent years, due to the need for immigrant labour in a wider range of occupations, but the basic restrictiveness of the system remains. In Britain, Commonwealth immigrants (once admitted to the country) and the Irish had equal rights with local workers until the 1971 Immigration Act. Now Commonwealth immigrants will have the same labour market situation as aliens. The threat of deportation if an immigrant loses his job is a very powerful weapon for the employer. Immigrants who demand better conditions can be sacked for indiscipline and the police will do the rest.[41] Regulations which restrict family entry and permanent settlement also keep immigrants in inferior positions. If a man may stay only for a few years, it is not worth his while to learn the language and take vocational training courses.

Informal discrimination is well known in Britain, where it takes the form of the colour bar. The PEP study,[42] as well as many other investigations, has shown that coloured immigrants encounter discrimination with regard to employment, housing and the provision of services such as mortgages and insurance.

The more qualified a coloured man is, the more likely he is to encounter discrimination. This mechanism keeps immigrants in 'their place', i.e. doing the dirty, unpleasant jobs. Immigrants in other European countries also encounter informal discrimination. Immigrants rarely get promotion to supervisory or non-manual jobs, even when they are well-qualified. Discrimination in housing is widespread. In Britain, adverts specifying 'no coloured' are forbidden, but in Germany or Switzerland one still frequently sees 'no foreigners'.

The most serious form of discrimination against immigrant workers is their deprivation of political rights. Foreigners may not vote in local or national elections. Nor may they hold public office, which in France is defined so widely as to include trade-union posts. Foreigners do not generally have the same rights as local workers with regard to eligibility for works councils and similar representative bodies. The main exception to this formal exclusion from political participation concerns Irish and Commonwealth immigrants in Britain, who do have the right to vote ... But the Mangrove case shows the type of repression which may be expected by any immigrants who dare to organize themselves. Close police control over the political activities of immigrants is the rule throughout Europe, and deportations of political and trade-union militants are common. After the May Events in France, hundreds of foreign workers were deported.[43] Foreign language newspapers of the CGT labour federation have been repeatedly forbidden. The German Foreigners Law of 1965 lays down that the political activity of foreigners can be forbidden if 'important interests of the German Federal Republic require this' – a provision so flexible that the police can prevent any activity they choose. Even this is not regarded as sufficient. When Federal Chancellor Willy Brandt visited Iran in March 1972 to do an oil deal, the Shah complained strongly about Iranian students being allowed to criticize him in Germany. The Greek and Yugoslav ambassadors have also protested about the activities of their citizens. Now the German Government is working on a new law which would go so far as to make police permission necessary even for private meetings of foreigners in closed rooms ...[44]

Discrimination against immigrants is a reflection of widespread hostility towards them ...

It is feared that they will take away the jobs of local labour, that they will be used by the employers to force down wages and to break strikes.[45] Whatever the behaviour of the immigrant workers – and in fact they almost invariably show solidarity with their indigenous colleagues – such fears are not without a basis. It is indeed the strategy of the employers to use immigration to put pressure on wages and to weaken the labour movement.[46] The very social and legal weakness of the immigrants is a weapon in the hands of the employers. Other points of competition are to be found outside work, particularly on the housing market. The presence of immigrants is often regarded as the cause of rising rents and increased overcrowding in the cities. By making immigrants the scapegoats for the insecurity and inadequate conditions which the capitalist system inevitably provides for workers, attention is diverted from the real causes ...

IMMIGRATION AND SOCIETY

The impact of immigration on contemporary West European society may now be summarized.

Economic effects: the new industrial reserve army of immigrant workers is a major stabilizing factor of the capitalist economy. By restraining wage increases, immigration is a vital precondition for capital accumulation and hence for growth. In the long run, wages may grow more in a country which has large-scale immigration than in one which does not, because of the dynamic effect of increased capital accumulation on productivity. However, wages are a smaller share, and profits a larger share of national income than would have been the case without immigration.[47] The best illustration of this effect is obtained by comparing the German and the British economies since 1945. Germany has had large and continuous increases in labour force due to immigration. At first wages were held back. The resulting capital accumulation allowed fast growth and continuous rationalization. Britain has had virtually no growth in labour force due to migration (immigration has been cancelled out by emigration of British people to Australia etc.). Every phase of expansion has collapsed rapidly as wages rose due to labour shortages. The long-term effect has been stagnation. By the 1960s, German wages overtook those of Britain, while economic growth and rationalization continued at an almost undiminished rate.

Social effects: the inferior position of immigrant workers with regard to employment and social conditions has led to a division of the working class into two strata. The split is maintained by various forms of discrimination and is reinforced by racialist and xenophobic ideologies, which the ruling class can disseminate widely through its hegemony over the means of socialization and communication. Large sections of the indigenous workers take the position of a labour aristocracy, which objectively participates in the exploitation of another group of workers.

Political effects: the decline of class consciousness weakens the working-class movement. In addition, the denial of political rights to immigrants excludes a large section of the working class from political activity, and hence weakens the class as a whole. The most exploited section of the working class is rendered voiceless and powerless. Special forms of repression are designed to keep it that way.

NOTES AND REFERENCES

1 Engels, 'The Condition of the Working Class in England' in Marx and Engels, *On Britain*, Moscow, 1962, p. 119.

2 Marx, *Capital*, vol. I, Moscow, 1961, p. 632.

3 ibid., p. 633.

4 ibid., p. 637.

5 ibid., p. 640.

6 Engels, Preface to the English edition of 'The Condition of the Working Class in England', op. cit., p. 28.

7 Engels, 'The English Elections' in *On Britain*, op. cit., p. 505.

8 Lenin, *Imperialism – the Highest Stage of Capitalism*, Moscow, 1966, pp. 96–7.

9 ibid., pp. 99–100.

10 In this article we examine the function of labour migration only for the countries of immigration. Migration also plays an important stabilizing role for the reactionary regimes of the countries of origin – a role which is understood and to some extent planned by the ruling class in West Europe. Although we are concerned only with West Europe in this article, it is important to note that the use of certain special

categories of workers, who can be discriminated against without arousing general solidarity from other workers, is a general feature of modern capitalism. The blacks and chicanos are the industrial reserve army of the USA, the Africans of white-dominated Southern Africa. Current attempts by 'liberal' capitalists to relax the colour bar to allow blacks into certain skilled and white-collar jobs, both in the USA and South Africa, however estimable in humanitarian terms, are designed mainly to weaken the unions and put pressure on wages in these sectors.

11 Marx mentions several forms taken by the industrial reserve army. One is the 'latent' surplus-population of agricultural labourers, whose wages and conditions have been depressed to such an extent that they are merely waiting for a favourable opportunity to move into industry and join the urban proletariat. (*Capital*, vol. I., op. cit., p. 642.) Although these workers are not yet in industry, the possibility that they may at any time join the industrial labour force increases the capitalist's ability to resist wage increases. The latent industrial reserve army has the same effect as the urban unemployed. Unemployed workers in other countries, insofar as they may be brought into the industrial labour force whenever required, clearly form a latent industrial reserve army in the same way as rural unemployment within the country.

12 See E. P. Thompson, *The Making of the English Working Class*, Harmondsworth, 1968, pp. 469–85.

13 'The Condition of the Working Class in England', op. cit., p. 123.

14 Letter to S. Meyer and A. Vogt, 9 April 1870, in *On Britain*, op. cit., p. 552.

15 *Imperialism*, op. cit., p. 98.

16 Hans Pfahlmann, *Fremdarbeiter und Kriegsgefangene in der deutschen Kriegswirtschaft, 1939–1945*, Darmstadt, 1968, p. 232.

17 For the role of the lumpenproletariat in the industrial reserve army, see *Capital*, vol. I, op. cit., p. 643.

18 We use 'immigrants' in a broad sense to include all persons living in a West European country which is not their country of birth. Much migration is of a temporary nature, for a period of 3–10 years. But such temporary migration has effects similar to permanent migration when the returning migrant is replaced by a countryman with similar character-

istics. Such migrants may be regarded as a permanent social group with rotating membership.

19 For sources, as well as a detailed analysis of social conditions of immigrants, see Stephen Castles and Godula Kosack, *Immigrant Workers and Class Structure in Western Europe*, London, Oxford University Press for Institute of Race Relations' 1972.

20 The 1966 census figures are at present the most recent ones available. It should, however, be noted that, for technical reasons, they seriously under-enumerate the Commonwealth immigrants in Britain. Moreover, the number has grown considerably since 1966, particularly if we look at the whole community including children born to Commonwealth immigrants in Britain, who were not counted by the census. We shall have to wait for the results of the 1971 census to obtain a more accurate picture of the immigrant population in Britain.

21 Many foreign workers are still employed on a seasonal basis in building, agriculture and catering in France and Switzerland. This is a special form of exploitation. The worker has no income in the off-season and is therefore forced to work very long hours for the 9–10 months when he does have work. He cannot bring his family with him, he has even more limited civic rights than other immigrants, and he has absolutely no security, for there is no guarantee that his employment will be continued from year to year.

22 Ulrich Freiherr von Gienanth, in *Der Arbeitgeber*, vol. 18, 20 March 1966, p. 153.

23 For Commonwealth immigration see E. J. B. Rose *et al.*, *Colour and Citizenship*, London, 1969.

24 Eurocrats refer to the free movement policy as the beginning of a 'European labour market'. But although EEC citizens have the right to choose which country to be exploited in, they lack any civic or political rights once there. Moreover, the Southern Italian labour reserves are being absorbed by the monopolies of Turin and Milan, so that intra-EEC migration is steadily declining in volume, while migration from outside the EEC increases.

25 Where formalized economic planning exists, this necessity has been publicly formulated. Prognoses on the contribution of immigrants to the labour force were included in the Fourth and Fifth Five-Year Plans in France and play an even more prominent part in the current Sixth Plan. See

Le VIe plan et les travailleurs étrangers, Paris, 1971.

26 Cf. Ruth Becker, Gerhard Dörr, K. H. Tjaden, 'Fremdar-
beiterbeschäftigung im deutschen Kapitalismus', *Das Argument*, December 1971, p. 753.

27 United Nations Economic Commission for Europe, *Economic Survey of Europe 1967*, Geneva, 1968, chap. I, p. 49.

28 The distinction between the two sections of the immigrant
labour force is formalized in the new French immigration
policy introduced in 1968. There are separate regulations
for South Europeans, who are encouraged to bring in their
families and settle permanently, and Africans (particularly
Algerians) who are meant to come for a limited period only,
without dependants.

29 It is estimated that foreign workers in Germany are at
present paying about 17 per cent of all contributions to
pension insurance, but that foreigners are receiving only 0·5
per cent of the total benefits. Heinz Salowsky 'Sozial-
politische Aspekte der Auslanderbeschaftigung', *Berichte
des Deutschen Industrie instituts zur Sozialpolitik*, vol. 6 (S),
no. 2, February 1972, pp. 16–22.

30 Calculated from: 'Statistiques du Ministère de l'Intérieur',
Hommes et Migrations: Documents, no. 788, 15 May 1970;
and *Annuaire Statistique de la France 1968*.

31 1966 Census.

32 *Statistisches Jahrbuch der Schweiz 1967*, pp. 140–1.

33 *Ausländische Arbeitnehmer 1970*, Nürnberg, 1971.

34 1966 Census. For a detailed analysis of immigrants' employment see K. Jones and A. D. Smith, *The Economic Impact
of Commonwealth Immigration*, Cambridge, 1970. Also
Immigrant Workers and Class Structure in Western Europe,
op. cit., chap. III.

35 *Ausländische Arbeitnehmer 1969*, Nürnberg 1970, p. 86.

36 'L'insertion sociale des étrangers dans l'aire métropolitaine
Lyon-Saint-Étienne', *Hommes et Migrations*, no. 113, 1969,
p. 112.

37 1966 Census.

38 Some employers – particularly small inefficient ones –
specialize in the exploitation of immigrants. For instance
they employ illegal immigrants, who can be forced to work
for very low wages and cannot complain to the authorities
for fear of deportation. Such cases often cause much indignation in the liberal and social-democratic press. But, in
fact, it is the big efficient firms exploiting immigrants in a

legal and relatively humane way which make the biggest profits out of them. The function of immigration in West European capitalism is created not by the malpractices of backward firms (many of whom incidentally could not survive without immigrant labour), but by the most advanced sectors of big industry which plan and utilize the position of immigrant workers to their own advantage.

39 'So far as we are concerned, hostel and works represent parts of a single whole. The hostels belong to the mines, so the foreign workers are in our charge from start to finish,' stated a representative of the German mining employers proudly. *Magnet Bundesrepublik*, Informationstagung der Bundesvereinigung Deutscher Arbeitgeberverbände, Bonn 1966, p. 81.

40 A group of French doctors found that the TB rate for black Africans in the Paris suburb of Montreuil was 156 times greater than that of the rest of the local population. R. D. Nicoladze, C. Rendu, G. Millet, 'Coupable d'être malades', *Droit et Liberté*, No. 280, March 1969, p. 8. For further examples see *Immigrant Workers and Class Structure in Western Europe*, op. cit., chap. VIII.

41 For a description of how a strike of Spanish workers in a steel-works was broken by the threat of deportation, see P. Gavi, *Les Ouvriers*, Paris 1970, pp. 225–6.

42 W. W. Daniels, *Racial Discrimination in England*, based on the PEP Report, Harmondsworth, 1968.

43 See *Review of the International Commission of Jurists*, no. 3, September 1969 and *Migration Today*, no. 13, Autumn 1969.

44 Cf. *Der Spiegel*, no. 7, 7 February 1972.

45 Surveys carried out in Germany in 1966 show a growth of hostility towards immigrants. This was directly related to the impending recession and local labour's fear of unemployment.

46 Historically, the best example of this strategy was the use of successive waves of immigrants to break the nascent labour movement in the USA and to follow extremely rapid capital accumulation. *The Jungle* by Upton Sinclair gives an excellent account of this. Similar was the use of internal migrants (the 'Okies') in California in the 1930s – see John Steinbeck, *The Grapes of Wrath*.

47 Many bourgeois economists and some *soi-disant* Marxists think that immigration hinders growth because cheap labour

reduces the incentive for rationalization. Bourgeois economists may be excused for not knowing (or not admitting) that cheap labour must be the source for the capital which makes rationalization possible. Marxists ought to know it. A good study on the economic impact of immigration is: C. P. Kindleberger, *Europe's Postwar Growth – the Role of Labour Supply*, Cambridge (Mass.), 1967.

Migrant Labour in South Africa and the United States

Michael Burawoy

THEORETICAL INTRODUCTION

For an economy to function, a labour force has to be maintained and renewed. In other words, workers have to subsist from day to day and vacancies created by their departure from or by the expansion of the labour force must be filled by new recruits. Under capitalism the distinction between these two elements of the reproduction of labour-power is normally concealed. The same institutions simultaneously perform both renewal and maintenance functions. For example, the distinction between the rearing of children and the day-to-day sustenance of the productive worker is not normally inscribed in the organization of the family. On the contrary, domestic work simultaneously provides for both maintenance and renewal requirements of the labour force ...

By contrast, the organization of migrant labour not only makes the distinction apparent but is even defined by the separation of the processes of maintenance from those of renewal. How does this separation manifest itself? First, the two processes take place in geographically separate locations. Second, at the level of the institutions of reproduction, the institutions of maintenance may be very different from those of renewal, or a single institution may continue to engage in both processes. To take the family as an example of the latter possibility, geographical separation of the two processes is reflected in a corresponding division of labour and internal differentiation of the family unit. Thus, for Mexican migrants, processes of renewal are organized under the Mexican state in the Mexican economy and those of maintenance in the United States. Yet the kinship group remains a single cohesive unit despite its internal differentiation. What is important for this paper is that the activities of maintenance and renewal are separated.

They remain, however, indissolubly interdependent, as reflected in the oscillatory movement of migrants between work and home. Under capitalism the binding of production and reproduction is achieved through economic necessity: for the labouring population, work is necessary for survival; under feudalism the unification is achieved through coercive regulation. A system of migrant labour contains elements of each. On the one hand, renewal processes are dependent on income left over from maintenance, which is remitted home by the productive workers. On the other hand, productive workers require continued support from their families engaged in renewal at home, because they have no permanent legal or political status at the place of work. In other words, the state organizes the dependence of the productive worker on the reproductive worker, while the economy organizes the dependence of the reproductive worker on the productive worker. The interdependence establishes the cohesion of the family. Similar ties link the state supplying labour and the state employing labour: the former requires revenue and employment for its population, the latter requires labour at low wage rates.

In the following sections, I explore two implications of the separation of the maintenance and renewal processes. The first concerns the functions of migrant labour. Under such a system costs of renewal, normally borne by the employing state and economy, are to a considerable degree borne by another economy or another state or a combination of the two. Furthermore, the employer of migrant labour is neither responsible politically nor accountable financially to the external political and economic systems. In other words, a proportion of the costs of renewal is externalized to an alternate economy and/or state. The second implication concerns the conditions for the reproduction of a system of migrant labour – namely, the reproduction of its defining characteristic, the separation of maintenance and renewal processes ....

MINE WORKERS IN SOUTH AFRICA

The South African gold mines, first commercially exploited in the last decade of the nineteenth century, have relied on two types of migrant labour. On the one hand, unskilled tasks have been and continue to be performed by African labour recruited from the rural hinterland and surrounding territories (see Wilson 1972*a*, p. 70, for exact distribution by geographic location). Once cajoled into selling their labour power by expropriation of land, imposition of taxation, and similar non-market inducements, African workers became attracted to wage employment as a way of making up or supplementing their means of subsistence (Horwitz, 1967, chap. 2). On the other hand, white labour, initially recruited from Britain, was employed in skilled and supervisory positions. Just as craft unions at that time had a powerful monopoly of a sector of the British labour market, so the white workers of South Africa, in part influenced by their experience at home, formed a union to protect their positions from competition from black labour (Simons and Simons 1969, chap. 3). Although mine owners wished to advance blacks into more skilled occupations, their efforts were obstructed as early as 1893 by the legal enforcement of the colour bar which reserved a range of jobs for white workers. As the mining industry expanded, the colour bar became an entrenched feature of the occupational structure, barring blacks from advancement into skilled and even semi-skilled jobs and stipulating an upper limit to the employment ratio of blacks to whites (Wilson 1972a, pp. 110–19). On a number of occasions, most notably during the Rand Revolt of 1922, management attempted to breach the colour bar, but the power and determination of white workers to protect their monopolistic position proved insurmountable.

Once the colour bar was accepted as irrevocable, management sought to offset the costly protection of white labour by externalizing the costs of renewal of a black labour force. This process was made possible by the reproduction of the system of migrant labour. Initially a response to the insecurity of employment in industry and the lack of provision for permanent settlement near the place of work under colonial rule, migrant labour continues to be an institutionalized feature of the mining industry. Just how the system has been perpetuated and how certain labour costs are reduced under it will be examined in subsequent sections.

The Economic Functions of Migrant Labour

Earlier I was careful to define a system of migrant labour in institutional terms. Others have defined it in economic terms, and I now propose to consider some of the difficulties of these formulations. Wolpe (1972), Castells (1975), and, with some qualifications, Castles and Kosack (1973, chap. 9) all assert that a system of migrant labour lowers the cost of the reproduction of labour power; Wolpe goes so far as to claim that it constitutes a system of cheap labour power. However, the assessment of the costs and benefits of migrant labour and of its effects on the rate of profit is far more complicated than even Castles and Kosack (pp. 374–5, 422) indicate and requires considerably more substantiation than any of the writers provide. First, they fail to distinguish among the institutions whose costs are reduced, pre-eminently between the state and the employer – though, of course, the two sets of costs are not unrelated. In other words, they do not address the question, Cheap for whom? (Castles and Kosack, however, do discuss the implications for domestic labour.) Second, they do not adequately examine which aspects of the costs of the reproduction of labour power – maintenance or renewal – are reduced. Third, while it is true that migrant labour does lead to some economic savings for employer and state, the reproduction of a *system* of migrant labour in itself represents a cost which may outweigh the economic benefits based on the externalization of renewal. None of these writers considers the costs (political as well as economic) of the reproduction of a system of migrant labour. ...

While the extraction of produce from a pre-capitalist mode of production redounds to the benefit of the employer of migrant labour, reliance on an alternate state or its functional equivalent redounds to the benefit of the South African state. Functions normally performed by the state, such as provision of welfare facilities, education, and social security, are transferred to the communal context of the pre-capitalist economy. The provision of urban amenities is therefore limited to those necessary for the single productive worker.

But pointing to the existence of 'excessive exploitation' and the externalization of costs of labour-force renewal is not the same as demonstrating the existence of cheap labour. In one sense all labour is cheap simply because it is exploited. In another sense, it is a more difficult concept to grapple with. *Cheap with respect to what?* It is conceivable, for example, that the reduction in the costs of reproducing labour power through access to a subsistence economy would be outweighed by the latter's replacement by a capital-intensive agricultural economy. (In fact, given the state of soil erosion in the reserves, this is unlikely, but it is the sort of question involved in examining whether a particular system of labour is cheap.) So far, I have highlighted the *economic* benefits for state and capital of a system of migrant labour, but there are also political benefits.

A series of political costs are externalized to the reserves, costs associated with the residence of a large, stable black population under a white supremacist state. Indeed, the system of migrant labour is often perceived in political terms.

We cannot, however, ignore the *costs* associated with migrant labour, such as high rates of turnover, recruitment expenses, and the more general set of costs experienced by the state and arising from the political and legal conditions for the reproduction of a system of migrant labour. When all these are introduced, many of them intangible, the balance sheet becomes so complex that the notion of cheap labour, in practice if not in principle, may become impossible to handle.

One way of circumventing the problem is to dispense with the notion of cheap labour altogether. An alternative approach is to adopt the tautological argument that migrant labour exists because it is cheap and it is cheap because it exists. This is not as unenlightening as it might appear, for tautologies are useful if they lead to the formulation of important questions. For example, we may be led to ask what is cheap about migrant labour and thus to generate new insights.

Finally, it may be that 'Cheap with respect to what?' is less appropriate than *'Cheap for whom?'* While migrant labour may be cheap for industries that rely extensively on unskilled labour and have facilities for the recruitment of migrant labourers, the smaller industry which uses skilled labour and has little access to isolated labour supplies finds a system of migrant labour more expensive. If industry bears a small minority and the state the majority of the costs of organizing a system of migrant labour, the former may find it cheap compared with other systems of labour, while the latter may find it more expensive than systems relying more on market institutions for the regulation of labour supplies. Yet at the same time, one must not forget that the state does not finance itself but relies on industry to support its activities. Thus the question of whether migrant labour is cheap for a particular industry involves not only an examination of the direct costs experienced by that industry but also secondary costs, such as taxation appropriated by the state. While 'Cheap for whom?' may appear to simplify the problem, it still remains inordinately complex, and the problems of comparison – that is, cheap for whom with respect to what and under what conditions? – are still with us.

I have argued elsewhere (Burawoy 1974) that the appearance

of migrant labour in South Africa must be sought, not in its specific or general cheapness, but in the historically concrete circumstances of the articulation of different modes of production and the corresponding superstructures. At the level of function, there is nothing necessary about the system of migrant labour. It is not what Castells (1975) refers to as an 'organic' part of capitalism at a particular stage in its development. Instead, it is a conjunctural feature which acts as a functional substitute for other modes of organizing labour under capitalism.

Dependence on a Capitalist Economy

I turn now to examine the conditions for the reproduction of a system of migrant labour. They naturally revolve around the separation of the means of renewal from the means of maintenance of a labour force. Two aspects of the reproduction of this separation can be delineated. First, there is the reproduction of a twin dependency upon the capitalist economy on the one hand and upon a subsistence economy and/or alternate state on the other. Second, there is the (coercive) separation of the family from the worker (in such a manner as to preserve their mutual dependence) through a series of legal and political measures and institutions.

What is the basis of a dependence on the capitalist economy, and how is it reproduced? Originally, the imposition of taxes upon the Africans living in the rural areas dislocated them from their subsistence livelihood and required them to seek employment in the emerging extractive industries. This was so, for example, for Malawians who trekked to the South African gold mines and the Zambian copper mines. In South Africa, the movement of blacks to the towns was further compounded by the state's expropriation of land, making subsistence existence increasingly difficult and reliance on an additional source of income increasingly necessary. With regard to Mozambique, Harris (1959) shows how the colonial administration forced able-bodied males into the system of migrant labour by conscription, where necessary. Even where subsistence livelihood could still be eked out, Africans have supplemented it with income from employment in the urban areas. Arrighi (1973) shows how Africans who began to respond to the demand for agriculture produce with the development of Southern Rhodesia at the beginning of this century were priced out of the market through discriminatory subsidies favouring the Euro-

143

pean farmer. Accordingly, the rewards of remaining in the rural areas and accumulating surplus produce were arranged to be less than those of entering wage employment. In this way, the colonial administration managed to generate a commitment to and, to a certain degree (taxes still had to be paid in cash), a dependence on the capitalist economy. In all these cases, Africans who engaged in productive activities in the towns were able to send home a portion of their income out of which taxes could be paid and on occasion 'luxury' items bought. The broadening commitment to the South African wage economy and in particular the gold mines stems largely from the inability of the reserves in South Africa and, to a lesser extent, the rural areas of Malawi and Mozambique to support the reproduction of a labour force.

Dependence on a Subsistence Economy

Wages earned by African mine workers on the Rand are calculated on the assumption that they supplement the produce of a subsistence economy (Bettison 1960; Harris 1959). To provide some material basis for such an assumption and to ensure continuing dependence on a subsistence economy, the economy must be capable of providing for some needs. It must be continually re-created in the face of the eroding tendency of capitalism (Lenin 1960, pp. 40-1). It is necessary in this discussion, therefore, to examine the impact of an industrial economy upon the subsistence economy in the surrounding rural areas.

The rural economy in the South African reserves has been under continual decay, as soil erosion and overpopulation make the extraction of a viable existence there increasingly difficult. The South African government's recognition of this fact and its desire to prevent the further decline of the rural black economy lead Wolpe (1972) to interpret the policy of 'separate development' as an endeavour to re-create the subsistence base of the migrant labour force. So far, the actual resources invested in the Bantustans are meagre compared with what will be necessary to reverse the trend. One factor in the slowing down of the accumulation of land in the hands of a few Africans in the reserves and the dispossession of the majority has been the government's active policy of reproducing a system of communal land tenure and the corresponding pre-capitalist relations of production. How much the reserves are able to produce is a matter for some debate. In any event, the numerous prosecutions under the pass laws suggest that the dependence is more an artifact of the legal and political institutions forcing Africans back into the reserves than a result of a commitment to a viable economy.

The situation in surrounding black territories like Malawi is somewhat different. While the impact of migrant labour in some areas has contributed to the erosion of the subsistence economy, in others it has reinforced that economy. The crucial variable would appear to be the reliance of the subsistence economy on able-bodied males. Where the economy is such that the absence of males does not prevent the cultivation of crops, the earnings remitted by those absent serve to bolster the rural political economy (van Velsen 1961; Harris 1959; Watson 1958). By contrast, those economies relying on male labour for cultivation, as in 'slash and burn' techniques, have tended to be adversely affected by the system of migrant labour (Richards 1939).

The Regulation of Circulation

The twin dependency on two modes of production does not reproduce itself without recourse to non-economic institutions. We have already noted how attachment to the capitalist economy was generated by the intervention of colonial administrations in the subsistence economies and how dependency on the latter is perpetuated by preventing their erosion through supra-market intervention. The thesis I am about to outline is that the twin dependency can be better seen as a *reflection* of a set of political and legal arrangements designed to separate the means of renewal from those of maintenance and at the same time to ensure a continued connection between the two.

The separation of family from worker is organized through a set of laws restricting urban residence, with few exceptions, to those who are gainfully employed. The enforcement of pass laws externalizes the supplies of unemployed labour and the processes of labour-force renewal to areas where those not gainfully employed are legally permitted to reside – namely, the reserves or Bantustans and the surrounding black territories. Influx control and pass laws also ensure that, on termination of a contract with an employer, a worker returns to the 'home' area before being allowed to gain further employment in the urban area. Should a worker become unemployed owing to retirement, physical disability, or simply scarcity of opportunity, he can have no legal residence outside the reserves or wherever his home may be. Such arrangements compel the

145

worker to maintain close ties with the remainder of the family in the reserves or surrounding territories. Equally, these measures lead to the remittance of a proportion of wages earned in town and thereby supply the domestic unit with necessary commodities for the renewal of the labour force. In other words, influx control and pass laws preserve the separation of renewal and maintenance functions, prevent the stabilization of families in the urban areas and the surrender of subsistence existence in the reserves, uphold the continued interdependence of worker and family, and, finally, regulate the circulation of labour between the place of work and 'home'.

Restrictions on Occupational Mobility

Participation in a system of migrant labour has tended to be incompatible with employment in skilled positions (Arrighi 1973, pp. 216–18) for at least two reasons. First, for jobs requiring both training and experience for their effective performance, high rates of labour turnover could be prohibitively costly. Second, entry into the more skilled occupations in any considerable numbers could result in the development of power based on the possession of a relatively scarce resource. We may conclude, therefore, that the preservation of the colour bar is not merely a matter of safeguarding the interests of white workers but also represents a major factor in the reproduction of a system of migrant labour.

In this condition, we have the possible seeds of the erosion of a system of migrant labour. With its superior recruitment facilities and extensive use of unskilled labour, the mining industry has successfully adapted itself to the exigencies of a system of migrant labour. However, as manufacturing assumes an increasingly important role in the South African economy, and as the colour bar is removed from increasingly higher skill levels, a greater number of Africans will be engaged in skilled and supervisory positions. This is perhaps the major contradiction between the reproduction of a system of migrant labour and the development of the South African economy.

Migrant Labour Powerlessness

The reproduction of a system of migrant labour hinges on the inability of the migrants, as individuals or as a group, to influence the institutions that subordinate them to the other fractions of the labour force as well as to the employer. Domination of the migrant force takes place in three arenas:

the labour market, the industrial organization, and the state.

I shall deal with the state first. Under the capitalist state, the migrant is treated as an alien without rights of citizenship. In the South African colonial superstructure, the differential incorporation of races leaves the subordinate race with no formal power to modify fundamental institutions. The migrant has no significant political rights and only limited legal rights in the urban areas. Only in the Bantustans or reserves can Africans exercise rights of citizenship, and because of their very limited resources such participation is unable to affect their lives materially. Protest by blacks directed at the South African state has been dealt with violently, and the rise of a police state makes combination almost impossible (see, e.g., Simons and Simons 1969; Roux 1964; Kuper 1957).

In cementing the system of migrant labour, the role of ideology is not unimportant. The coincidence of racial characteristics and participation in a system of migrant labour has a number of consequences. All dominant ideologies under capitalism tend to conceal the underlying class structure; if an ideology has a strong component of racial supremacy, class differentiation is masked by the prevailing racial perspectives. This remark applies equally to the consciousness of the dominant and the dominated classes. As a result, the dominant ideology pays little attention to the economic role of migrant labour and the manner in which its exploitation is organized. Behavioural characteristics due to participation in a system of migrant labour are portrayed by the dominant ideology as racial characteristics. Migrant labour is seen as a voluntaristic form of participation in the South African economy, upholding the integrity and indigenous culture of the African people. It is considered the natural and inevitable form of black labour. It purportedly reflects the strength of tradition pulling the African from the foreign and corrosive urban area to his natural environment and thereby solidifying his so-called tribal allegiances. Instead of there being an inherent conflict between the dominant ideology and the system of migrant labour, the former reinforces and legitimates the coexistence of two structurally different modes of organization of labour distributed according to racial characteristics.

Domination within industry is enforced with the cooperation of the state, as when strike action is suppressed. Though not actually illegal, trade union organization among blacks has been thwarted through 'racial discrimination in the law and in

147

labour practices; government obstruction and intimidation; and colour prejudice among white workers' (Hepple 1971, p. 72). Only 2 per cent of black workers in South Africa are organized into trade unions. The structural conflict between migrant labour and organized non-migrant white workers redounds to the advantage of the employer. The conflict is based on competition over the distribution of income *within* the working class. Concessions extracted from the mine owners by one group are granted, to a considerable extent, at the expense of the other group. For example, the restrictive practices and development of a strong white trade union led to the institutionalization of a system of migrant labour incorporating an ever-increasing earnings gap between black and white workers (Wilson 1972*a*, p. 46). Not surprisingly, white workers have assisted management in the subordination of black workers within industry, for example, through the breaking of strikes. Equally, white workers are ever conscious of management's interest in breaching the colour bar and advancing black workers into more skilled positions. This reinforces divisions within the working class. In addition, the black labour force has been the victim of collusion among the different mining companies in wage fixing. With the development of the Chamber of Mines to coordinate policies of the industry in areas of common interest to the various companies, there arose a common wage policy based on the principle of 'maximum average' (Horwitz 1967, p. 27). Such industry-wide policies prevented competition for labour redounding to the advantage of the black migrant workers.

Finally, I turn to the domination of black workers in the labour market. The superior recruitment organizations of the mining industry give it monopolistic access to such labour reservoirs as Malawi and Mozambique and even more distant territories. In 1973 foreign labour accounted for 80 per cent of the blacks employed. Since pass laws preclude the development of a labour reservoir within the urban areas, they favour industries with effective recruitment organizations which employ black labour in primarily unskilled occupations. With a weaker recruitment capacity, manufacturing industry has to restrict itself to a labour supply from the reserves, for which it competes with all other employers of black labour. Overpopulation in the reserves and diminishing subsistence levels have led to increases in earnings necessary to supplement rural incomes. Being less dependent on South African labour and drawing extensively on foreign labour reservoirs where subsistence levels have not declined, the mining industry has managed to maintain the real earnings of its black workers at approximately the same level over the past 60 years (Wilson 1972a, table 5).

A System of Migrant Labour which Failed to Reproduce Itself

So far I have argued that the distinguishing feature of a system of migrant labour is the separation of processes of renewal from those of maintenance. Further, this separation is not a natural or voluntaristic phenomenon but must be enforced through a set of political and legal mechanisms which presuppose that the migrant is without citizenship rights and has only limited power in the state of employment. Therefore, when the specific mechanisms that enforce the circulation of labour, restrict its upward mobility, and establish the migrant's powerlessness are relaxed or disappear, if my thesis is correct, we should then expect the system to fail to reproduce itself. In this context the decline of migrant labour in Zambia is pertinent.

Prior to the Labour Government's assumption of power in Britain after the Second World War, the pattern of migrant labour between the Northern Rhodesian (now Zambian) copper mines and the rural hinterland followed that just described for South Africa. Until the postwar period, the colonial administration actively organized the political and legal mechanisms that separated the worker from his family. Subsequently, the administration retreated from the performance of these functions for reasons related to Zambia's status as a British protectorate. First, Africans were not merely allowed to organize trade unions but in some instances were actively encouraged to do so. Later in the 1950s, political parties representing the African population began to appear. At the same time, the colonial government became less resolute in defending the colour bar in industry (particularly the copper industry). Without support from the colonial administration, white workers were unable to prevent the removal of the colour bar from jobs which they had previously monopolized. As restrictions on African advancement were being relaxed, regulations on the geographical movement of black workers began to disappear also. Significantly, in the early 1950s the mining companies began to dispense with their 'pole-and-dagga' huts and to build family accommodations for their black employees. Thus, the separation of renewal and maintenance functions was being slowly and even deliberately undermined. Finally, shifts in ideology from white supremacy to evolutionary movement to African self-determination further weakened the legitimacy of migrant labour and the regulatory mechanisms necessary for its reproduction. Therefore, we may tentatively conclude that, unless separated by a specific set of political and legal institutions, the processes of maintenance and renewal tend to coalesce. In other words, economic factors by themselves cannot enforce the separation of worker from family but must be supplemented by structures of coercion.

Systems of migrant labour, as they have existed or continue to exist in southern Africa, may be regarded as 'pure' types. State organization of the separation of maintenance from renewal is transparent. Further, I have shown how a system of migrant labour dissolves when the state no longer performs this function. But the framework developed is of limited interest if it can be applied only to southern Africa. The question before us now is: Can the framework be extended to shed light on the nature of migrant labour in other, radically different countries?

FARM LABOUR IN CALIFORNIA

The discussion here is complicated by the more variegated history of seasonal agricultural labour in California. I will endeavour to highlight the aspects most relevant to comparison with South African mine workers and to the development of a more general framework for the analysis of systems of migrant labour in capitalist societies.

Because California is the United States's largest agricultural producer, farm labour has assumed a critical role in its development. The history of farm labour is the history of a succession of labour reservoirs. Each group entered as a domestic migratory or alien migrant labour force, but, before stabilizing, voluntarily left agriculture for employment in other sectors of the economy or was removed forcibly and succeeded by a new group of migrants.

The Chinese were the first immigrant group to respond to the seasonal demands of California agriculture. They were rendered occupationally immobile by discriminatory practices, and their stabilization coincided with increasing demands for Chinese exclusion by domestic labour during the last two decades of the nineteenth century (McWilliams 1964, chap. 2). With the eclipse of Chinese labour, whites affected by the depression of the 1890s were recruited for work in the fields; but with the return of economic prosperity, a new reservoir was tapped – the Japanese (ibid., chap. 4). By the end of the first decade of this century, the Japanese had superseded every other group, only to lose their dominance to Mexicans by 1915. After the First World War and increasingly until the Second, white domestic labour was again recruited for farm work. Although attempts to settle the dust bowl migratory workers of the 1930s into camps were made, they were never very successful (McWilliams 1971, chap. 16). Many labourers were recruited from the skid rows of California cities for temporary jobs in agriculture (Fisher 1953, pp. 51–7; Anderson 1923; Parker 1920).

The wartime demand for labour outside agriculture threatened the supply of domestic labour. The governments of Mexico and the United States signed an agreement providing for the use of Mexican labour under contract in farm employment. Known as the bracero programme, this was the first governmentally administered system of migrant labour in agriculture. At the same time as braceros entered legally under contract, illegal migrants, referred to as 'wetbacks', were also crossing the border from Mexico in search of employment. Their numbers have varied according to such factors as the state of the Mexican economy (Gamio 1930, chaps. 1, 12), the stringency of border controls (Samora 1971), and the availability of jobs in the United States (see Frisbie [1975] for a statistical analysis of economic push and pull factors). Although the actual number of illegal Mexican entrants is not known, the number apprehended annually rose steadily from the early 1940s to a peak of over a million in 1954 (Galarza 1964, chap. 8). Recent studies indicate that with the termination of the bracero programme in 1965 the number of illegal entrants has again risen, while commuters who live in Mexico and work in the United States have assumed a new prominence in the border states (North 1970, chaps. 1, 3). Meanwhile, domestic labour has organized itself in an attempt to prevent competition from labour recruited legally or illegally from foreign labour pools.

The Economic Functions of Migrant Labour

Castells (1975) indicates that, in addition to suffering excessive exploitation, migrant labour functions as a regulator of capitalist crises, cushioning the impact of the expansion and contraction of capital. When industry faces a recession, for example, migrant workers are particularly easy to lay off. The nature of agricultural production, rather than capitalist crises, gives rise to fluctuations in the demand for farm labour. Nonetheless, migrant labour performs the same 'regulatory' function in California agribusiness, providing for seasonal labour requirements.

> The basic dilemma faced by farm employers, particularly those with farm operations requiring seasonal hands in large numbers, is this: They want a labour supply which, on the one hand, is ready and willing to meet the short-term work requirements and which, on the other hand, will not impose social and economic problems on them or on the community when work is finished. This is what is expected of migratory workers. The demand for migratory workers is thus twofold: To be ready to go to work when needed; to be gone when not needed. [U.S. President's Commission on Migratory Labor 1951, p. 16]

The more generic function of a system of migrant labour – namely, the externalization of the costs of labour force renewal and low wage labour – is complicated by the coexistence of three different labour systems in California. First, there are migrants who circulate between Mexico and California. They constitute a system of external migrant labour. Second, there are aliens who reside in California throughout the year. They constitute a system of internal migrant labour. Finally, there is a domestic labour force which migrates from place to place in search of employment. It does not constitute a system of migrant labour as defined here. I shall refer to this fraction of the labour force as migratory labour. At different periods in the history of California agriculture, different systems have been dominant.

The migrants from Mexico bear the closest resemblance to Africans from Malawi or the reserves working in the South African mining industry. In both cases the system of migrant labour facilitates the externalization of the costs of renewal and the provision of earnings at a level commensurable with the day-to-day existence of the farm labourer. A system of internal migration has no obvious parallel with the South African situation. Japanese, Chinese, and many Mexican aliens who worked in the fields during the harvest period did not return 'home' in the off-season but eked out an existence in California towns. As a result, they became a potential burden upon the state where they were employed. At the same time, because they were mainly single, able-bodied men, the processes of maintenance were separated from those of renewal, which took place in their country of origin (see, e.g., Fuller 1940, p. 19824).

Domestic migratory labour distinguishes itself from migrant labour by the fusion of the functions of labour-force renewal and maintenance. The employer and/or state must bear all the costs of reproducing labour power. Other techniques are adapted to compensate for the inability to externalize costs in the case of domestic migratory workers. The prevailing adaptation has been the exploitation of family labour in picking crops, so that earnings of the *individual* can be maintained at inordinately low levels. If we look upon wages as the costs of maintaining and renewing the family, the greater the number employed within each family, the less each individual member has to be paid. In this way, the earnings of domestic labour are kept at the level paid to internal and external migrants. However, with domestic labour the state of employment has to bear a set of costs, such as welfare for the old and young and education, even though these may be small as compared with costs for other sectors of the national labour force.

Although there is evidence to suggest that growers prefer a system of migrant labour to a system of migratory labour (U.S. President's Commission on Migratory Labor 1951, p. 16), there have been periods in California history, particularly during economic depressions, when migrant labour barely existed. More recently, the organization of migratory labour in the United Farm Workers Union and the eclipse of the bracero programme have led to an increase in the use of domestic labour. Clearly the interests of the state, as defined by such factors as the level of employment and the political power of domestic groups, interact with the interests of the growers to determine the relative importance of each system of labour.

The issue of cheap labour arises in the California context, just as it did for South Africa. The immediate economic gains to growers from the use of migrant labour may be more apparent in the case of farm labour. First, migrant labour is a common form of adaptation to seasonal fluctuations in the demand for unskilled work. For example, in the first half of the nineteenth century, Irish migrants travelled to England to work as farm labourers during harvest periods and returned to Ireland during the slack seasons (Redford 1926, pp. 122–29). They were also paid less than domestic labour. Second, the system of migrant labour is not such a 'total' institution in California as it is in South Africa, and it may require fewer resources for its reproduction. It appears to be less a response to government intervention than a direct reflection of the economic interests of the growers. It may be argued that in South Africa political costs as well as economic costs are being externalized, whereas in California the economic costs are paramount. So long as migrant labour was readily available, the need for capital substitution was not urgently felt. But with moves in the direction of effective union organization of domestic migratory workers and the dissolution of the bracero programme, growers have turned increasingly to picking by mechanization.

Twin Dependency

In discussing South Africa, I noted that a system of migrant labour involved a twin dependency on two separated economies. This is also true, but in a weaker sense, in California. External migrants – essentially Mexicans – depend on their own state and to a lesser extent on employment in the United States. In the case of internal migrants, there is an overriding dependency on employment in the United States; and, like external migrants, they have tended to be restricted to such marginal occupations as farm labour. In both instances, there is a separation of the processes of labour-force maintenance from those of renewal, but the connection between the two is stronger for external migrants.

With respect to the migrant's dependency on employment in the South African economy, I noted the deliberate policies of the colonial administration to force the African population off the land and into the labour market to create an industrial work force and also remove competition with white farmers in the commodity market for agricultural products. These goals were achieved through the expropriation of land and the levying of taxes. The dependency of Mexicans on the United States economy cannot be reduced to such terms. The availability of Mexican labour has been contingent upon such factors as the state of the Mexican economy and political change, as in the revolutionary period between 1910 and 1930 which led to the release of many Mexicans from peonage in the haciendas.

However, at a more general level the proximity of the United States has been a factor in the persistent underdevelopment of Mexico, making it difficult for that nation to absorb the full potential of its labour force or to compete with wages available in the United States. Furthermore, the very sale of labour-power by an underdeveloped country, such as Malawi or Mexico, to an economically advanced nation serves only to reinforce the relations of economic subjugation and domination. This is so despite protestations by the South African and United States governments that in employing nationals of underdeveloped countries they are doing these countries a service. In a narrow sense, they are doing just that by absorbing surplus labour that could present a political threat to the underdeveloped nation and by providing rural workers with 'their only real opportunity for economic self improvement' and the possibility of remitting income home (Hancock 1959, p. 122). In a broader context, however, migrant labour exists only because of the uneven development of capitalism and reflects the economic dependence of Mexico on the United States and Malawi on South Africa.

It should be noted that some Mexicans who cross the border to work do not in fact return to Mexico on the termination of their employment, just as there are many Malawians residing illegally in South Africa. Many Mexicans attempt to find jobs elsewhere in the United States. Being illegal residents in the United States makes them much more vulnerable to arbitrary exploitation by employers. In many respects their position is akin to that of the internal migrant who faces limited employment opportunity and discriminatory practices. The Chinese and Japanese during those periods when they dominated farm labour were dependent on finding employment in marginal occupations. Unlike Mexicans, they could not easily return home and become the responsibility of another state. However, because they are single, internal migrants can subsist on relatively small incomes.

Finally, brief mention should be made of attempts to establish a system of migrant labour among domestic workers when they dominated the farm-labour force in the interwar period. Apart from increasing exploitation through the employment of family labour, there were moves among growers to create subsistence economies so as to reduce the burden of the work force on the state and to stabilize its movement. Such programmes

155

for 'land colonization' stemmed from the potential shortage of labour and the costs of armies of unemployed during the slack season, but they achieved little success before growers discovered alternative external labour reservoirs (McWilliams 1971, pp. 92–6, 200–10; U.S. Congress 1940, pp. 230–1, 240, 250). In effect, the programmes were efforts to set up a system of 'reserves' as in South Africa or a system of workhouses like those which provided a pool of labour for English employers in agriculture and industry during the eighteenth century (Redford 1926, pp. 21–3).

More common has been the technique of engendering dependence through the distribution of relief. Unemployed domestic labour is maintained during the slack season by the judicious provision of relief immediately suspended when openings appear in the fields. This ensures the availability of labour in the busy season (McWilliams 1971, pp. 285–96). Similar mechanisms for the distribution of relief appeared in England at the end of the eighteenth century: '... the perpetuation of the Speenhamland and "roundsman" systems, in all their variety, was ensured by the demand of the larger farmers – in an industry which has exceptional requirements for occasional or casual labour – for a permanent cheap labour reserve' (Thompson 1968, p. 244). As the study of Piven and Cloward (1971, chaps. 1, 4) suggests, the distribution of poor relief is designed to meet the conditions for dual dependency upon the state on the one hand and the employer on the other, so that labour may be mobilized and distributed to accommodate the changing demands of the economy. Poor relief, therefore, may be regarded as a functional equivalent of migrant labour, in that both perform the same regulatory function, cushioning the seasonal labour requirements of the agricultural industry.

The Regulation of Circulation

Poor relief and land colonization are designed to control the movement of *domestic* labour, so that it is available where and when it is needed and does not constitute a liability where and when it is not needed. What mechanisms are available to control the movement of external migrants such as those from Mexico? The work contract, defining the relationship between migrant workers and growers or intermediaries, is by its very nature only for temporary employment; after it has expired, the workers have no alternative but to leave the agricultural areas. They may leave for their homes across the border, move into a

California town, or migrate to some other part of the United States.

Just as influx control enforces the separation of maintenance and renewal functions while regulating the return of labour to its home, similar mechanisms operate to regulate the movement of Mexican migrants. Thus, border patrol (Samora 1971, chaps. 1, 2) attempts to restrict illegal immigration into the United States. Immigration laws are designed to separate workers from their families, so that the costs of labour-force renewal are borne in Mexico while the United States employer and government, either at the federal or regional level, are responsible only for maintaining workers during the period of employment (North 1970, pp. 92–3).

Immigration laws and their enforcement by border patrol and other government agencies aim to prevent the emergence of pools of unemployed Mexicans liable to become public charges. At the same time, they provide growers and other employers with adequate supplies of labour. The consolidation of the bracero programme in the 1950s was accompanied by more stringent policies of influx control. During this period, immigration authorities attempted to restrict migration across the border to workers contracted for agricultural employment by agencies established in Mexico. At the same time, legislative measures in the United States were introduced to prevent braceros from 'escaping' from farm employment and seeking jobs elsewhere. Accordingly, each worker was given a card bearing a contract number, an employer's name, and the names of counties in which it was valid (Galarza 1964, p. 83). In other words, it was a species of the notorious South African pass. These types of restriction on migrant employment in the United States and the removal of migrants from the country when the contract expired ensured their continuing reliance on Mexico and a binding connection to the processes of labour-force renewal.

Restrictions on Occupational Mobility

The return of migrants to their homes after the termination of the employment contract serves to restrict them to unskilled occupations in particular sectors of employment. Under the system of migrant labour found in South Africa, the colour bar broadly defines the boundaries between jobs monopolized by migrants and those held as the preserve of domestic white labour. Structural conflict within the working class of the

157

mining industry occurs in a vertical dimension between a white labour aristocracy and black migrant labour. By contrast, within California there is no need for the counterpart of a colour bar, because virtually all jobs are unskilled. At the same time, the equivalent of a colour bar does operate to prevent mobility out of agricultural employment.

The result is that conspicuous conflicts have occurred in the horizontal dimension between migrant workers (Chinese, Japanese, Mexicans, etc.) and domestic workers (white depression victims, Chicanos, etc.). Differing relations to the means of production have not been the axis of manifest conflict; on the contrary, the working class has been internally divided as a result of differing relations to superstructural elements – that is, differences of legal and political status in the place of employment. Though weak in comparison with organized labour, domestic farm labour is potentially more powerful than are migrant workers. Thus, during the last decade of the nineteenth century, domestic labour successfully resisted displacement by Chinese labour. Growers continued to employ Chinese labour after legislation had been passed to provide for the exclusion from employment of Chinese not legally resident in the country. The refusal of growers to bow before pressure from labour organizations led to riots throughout the state between 1893 and 1896, eventually forcing the removal of Chinese from the fields (McWilliams 1971, pp. 74–80; Fuller 1940, pp. 19814–15). Since then, domestic labour has had only limited success in establishing itself as a permanent farm-labour force, reflecting its vulnerability to the political power of agribusiness.

The Vulnerability of Farm Labour

In discussing the reproduction of the system of migrant labour in South Africa, I contrasted the strength of the domestic white workers with the powerlessness of black migrants who confront a state organized for their repression. The perpetuation of the system turns on the ability of white workers to maintain the colour bar at a skill level consistent with migrant labour. In California, the situation is reversed. There the reproduction of the system of migrant labour rests, not on the strength, but on the weakness of domestic labour, its inability to prevent growers from drawing upon foreign supplies of labour. We take it for granted that the migrant – internal or external – has little or no power, few if any rights, and virtually no means of appealing against infringements of his labour contract. Therefore, what is of interest is the manner in which *domestic* labourers have been systematically prevented from forcing the growers to employ them and them alone, under minimum wage conditions.

Farm labour has traditionally been excluded from labour legislation (Briggs 1973, chap. 5; Myers 1959). For example, the National Labour Relations Act of 1964 excluded farm workers from unemployment compensation. From 1910 to 1956, farm wages ranged from 40 per cent to 75 per cent below factory wages (Hancock 1959, p. 25). In 1966 farm wages were half the average of those in industrial employment as a whole. When domestic labour has threatened to organize, it has been either displaced by migrant labour – external or internal – or violently repressed. Thus, Galarza (1964, pt. 4) describes in detail how the bracero programme fostered the replacement of domestic labour with Mexican labour paid at prevailing rates, ones which domestic workers found unacceptable since they were based on labour-force maintenance rather than maintenance and renewal. In this way the braceros came to dominate the picking of a number of crops. The segmentation of the farm-labour force into migrants (legal or illegal) and domestics has obstructed the development of effective union organization. As recently as 1973, strike activity by the United Farm Workers Union was unable to prevent the gathering of the harvest crop by labour recruited from foreign countries.

In other words, the ability of domestic labour to organize itself is severely circumscribed by the power of the growers, who have gained monopolistic access to external labour reservoirs. In achieving these ends, there has been a long history of collaboration between farmers and immigration authorities (Greene 1969) and of collusion between farmers and state police in suppressing labour organizations and labour protest. Where police efforts have been inadequate or ineffectual, growers have shown no hesitation in recruiting 'citizen armies' and vigilante groups to combat resistance from farm labour (see, e.g., McWilliams 1971, chaps. 14, 15; U.S. Congress 1940, which was devoted to these issues). While the federal government has been aware of the collaboration of the rich and powerful in California and of the use of the state as an instrument for protecting the economic interests of large-scale farmers, the strength of the farm lobby in Washington has managed to prevent any effective intervention (Galarza 1970). As recently as 1974, despite opposition from organized labour, the Supreme Court sanctioned the use of foreign migrants on the basis of the administrative fiction that they are legal residents of the United States.

The power of the growers is reflected in their ability to establish common wage rates, and even in times of labour scarcity, these have prevented competition from redounding to the advantage of farm labour. Fisher (1953), McWilliams (1971), Galarza (1964) and other have documented the collaboration of growers in employer associations to define what is in effect a 'maximum average', though it is referred to as the 'prevailing wage'. In theory, the prevailing rates are to be fixed by the free play of the market. In fact, they are established unilaterally by the growers according to the same criteria followed by the South African Chamber of Mines: '... a wage which is fair to one's neighbour in that it is no higher, and a wage which is fair to oneself in that it is no lower' (Fisher 1953, p. 110).

Unilateral wage fixing, monopolistic recruitment, militant anti-unionism, and powerful lobbies in central government imply an inordinate concentration of power. For some time commentators have viewed the low wage levels and unhealthy working conditions of farm labour as a consequence of the concentration of land ownership and the vertical integration with the cannery industry, which has engaged in price fixing (McWilliams, 1971, pp. 279–80). With the concentration of ownership and the absorption of agriculture into a national food industry, recent years have witnessed the entry of large corporations and industrial conglomerates into large-scale farming. Thus, one discovers that the four leading private owners of agricultural land are Southern Pacific Company, Tenneco Incorporated (the large oil and chemical conglomerate), Tejon Ranch Company (half owned by the *Los Angeles Times Mirror* Corporation) and Standard Oil of California (see Fellmeth 1971, vol. 1, chap. 1; vol. 2, appendix 1B; Agribusiness Accountability Project 1972). If this were not enough, the problems facing the United Farm Workers Union have been compounded by the intervention of the International Brotherhood of Teamsters, which has signed 'sweetheart' contracts with many of the growers.

Does the dominant ideology exercise a moderating influence on the arbitrary use of this power and in particular on the reproduction of the system of migrant labour? Whereas the South African ideology of white supremacy legitimates the colonial superstructure (Burawoy 1974) that organizes the conditions

of reproduction of the system of migrant labour and insti-
tutionalizes migrant powerlessness, the dominant ideology
in the United States is conditioned by notions of 'equality',
'justice', and 'citizenship'. Accordingly, the United States government has frequently appeared to resist the use of migrant
labour in agriculture, particularly when subjected to pressures
from organized labour concerned to protect domestic farm
workers (Hawley 1966; Scruggs 1960). The various bracero programmes since 1942 have required growers to provide evidence
of a shortage of domestic labour and to make visible attempts
to recruit such labour. The agreement between the United
States and Mexico also stipulated that braceros had to be paid
at prevailing rates, and employers were required to make contributions to insurance schemes, housing, and non-profit canteen facilities and to offer each worker a minimum number of
hours of work every week (see, e.g., Galarza 1964, pts. 2, 3).

While these provisions are to be found in the agreements
signed between the governments of the United States and
Mexico, their execution has been quite a different matter. To
supervise the scheme, the United States government appointed
bodies sympathetic to the interests of the growers. Together
with associations of farm employers, these bodies worked out
ways to circumvent the provisions (Fisher 1953, chaps. 4, 5;
Galarza 1964, pts. 4, 5). It was in the administration of the
programme that the government was able to conciliate the
powerful growers opposed to restrictions imposed on their
employment practices.

If the dominant ideology does not exercise much constraint
over the practices of growers, it does tend to conceal those
practices. First, it presents United States agriculture as composed of a large number of small-scale independent farmers
who work on their own land. This hides the decline in the
numbers of such independent farmers and the fact, particularly
significant in California, that the overwhelming proportion of
land is owned by industrial consortiums and worked by a
migrant or migratory labour force. Second, the dominant ideology tends to obscure the typical conditions of migrant-labour
exploitation. Just as in South Africa the racial perspectives of
separate development have tended to conceal the position of
particular groups with respect to the means of production, in
the United States the combination of an ideology which stresses
ethnic pluralism with the coincidence of ethnicity and occupa-

tion has had a similar effect. Whereas in South Africa conflict between migrants and non-migrants is highlighted but seen in racial terms, in California conflict between migrant and domestic labour is masked by their common Mexican heritage.

CONCLUSION

We have learned that one condition for the separation of maintenance and renewal processes lies in the political status of migrant labourers. It is their relation to the state – the denial of legal, political, and civil rights – that distinguishes migrant workers from domestic workers. The distinction holds for both mine workers on the Rand and farm labourers in California. At the same time, we have observed a marked contrast in relations between domestic and migrant workers in the two areas. In South Africa a caste division in the form of a colour bar separates the two sectors of the labour force, while in the United States competition between domestic and migrant labour prevails. In the former country, domestic labour has access to considerable resources of political power, while in the latter it appears relatively weak. What does this discrepancy signify?

The State and Its Bearing on the Reproduction of Migrant Labour

The fact that unbridled competition between migrant and domestic labour is as ubiquitous in the United States as it is restricted and regulated in South Africa, *irrespective* of the particular industry, indicates that the skill differentials found in the mining industry and absent in agriculture cannot explain the different patterns of relations between migrant and domestic workers in our two case studies. On the contrary, it suggests that we must turn to broader characteristics of the two societies in order to understand the differences alluded to in the previous paragraph.

First, there is the simple demographic fact that migrant labour, legal and illegal, is *relatively* insignificant in the United States (though not as insignificant as is commonly supposed) as compared with its central role in the South African labour system. Second, domestic labour in South Africa constitutes a minority segment of the total labour force and as a result is *relatively* undifferentiated as compared with the domestic labour force in the United States. The simple dichotomy between domestic workers with rights to citizenship and migrants with no rights may be a useful simplification in the South African context, but it is too crude for the United States, where such marginal fractions of the domestic labour force as migratory farm workers are incomparably weaker than organized labour in other sectors of the economy.

At the same time, the numerical and functional significance of migrant labour is contingent upon the state's capacity to reproduce a system of migrant labour. I have emphasized repeatedly that the volume of migrant labour is not something to be taken as given but is *created and re-created by the state*. Within a single nation, the *state* determines the relative importance of migrant and domestic labour. Accordingly, changes in the organization of the state, as in Zambia, can go so far as to transform a numerically dominant sector of the labour force from migrant to domestic status and at the same time deny a minority sector its domestic status. Similarly, in contrast to other European countries, Britain has until recently awarded full citizenship rights to immigrants from other parts of the Commonwealth. Whereas immigrants to France, Germany, and Switzerland have tended to assume the status of migrants, in Britain they became part of the domestic labour force (Castles and Kosack 1973, chap. 11). To what extent the political status of immigrants actually affects their economic status has been an issue for debate, with some playing down the importance of differences (Castles and Kosack 1973) and others giving them greater emphasis (Rex 1974). The point is, however, that the state determines whether an immigrant is to be a migrant or a domestic worker. Therefore, the first two factors considered above – the demographic importance of migrant labour and the differentiation of the domestic labour force – are contingent upon a third: the nature of the state, its organization and in particular the relative autonomy of the economy with respect to the political system.

In South Africa a dual labour market is organized by a monolithic state, so that one sector is largely composed of migrant workers and the other of domestic workers. In the United States, on the other hand, with its less centralized state apparatus, the dual labour market is defined in terms of relation to the economic structure. Low-profit service and competitive industries with an unstable non-unionized or weakly unionized labour force produce the lower income strata of the working class, while high-profit monopoly industry with stable unionized labour accounts for the higher income strata (O'Connor 1973, chap. 1; Harrison 1972). The dominant division in the South African labour market is based on relation to the state, whereas that in the United States is based on industry of employment, that is, relation to the economy. In one instance, migrant labour constitutes the basis of an entire segment of the labour force; in the other, it forms but a fraction of a segment. Yet in both instances, although for different reasons, the reproduction of migrant labour deepens the division between the two segments. We may conclude, therefore, that the relevant differences between South Africa and the United States turn on the relative autonomy of the economy with respect to the state. In South Africa an overarching state intervenes in the organization of productive and market relations, whereas in the United States productive and market relations are reproduced with significantly less intervention from the state.

What, then, has this analysis of reproduction requirements accomplished? I have assumed that, although the conditions of reproduction may vary over time and between societies, what is being reproduced is defined by certain invariant structures. In the case of migrant labour, the invariant structure was found to be the separation of maintenance and renewal processes. Furthermore, the unique characteristics and consequences of a given system of migrant labour emerge out of the interplay between the invariant structure and a specific economic and political context. In other words the marked dissimilarity of the systems of migrant labour in South Africa and the United States may be attributed to the differing political, ideological, and economic situations in which the separation of maintenance and renewal process is organized. Thus, reproduction analysis is a powerful tool in comparative analysis, between societies and over time, because it accounts simultaneously for similarity and diversity. Yet the very strength of such analysis is also its major weakness, as is apparent in my treatment of labour power. Throughout, I have assumed that labour power itself is invariant. This is implied by limiting the reproduction of labour power to two processes – maintenance and renewal. The treatment ignored the possibility that labour-power, like machinery, may be adapted to the changing demands of capital and technological innovation. In my examples of migrant labour, adaptation is not a significant factor, because the jobs performed remain the same over time. But extending the analysis of reproduction of labour-power to an entire labour force over a long period shows that requisite skills, education, and socialization in the broadest sense, that is, the content of labour-power, undergo considerable change (Braverman 1974). Changes in the structure of capitalism, such as the consolidation of the dual economy, have repercussions for processes of labour force adaptation (Bowles 1972). In other words, a diachronic rather than synchronic analysis of the reproduction of labour power cannot, in general, restrict itself to the process of maintenance and renewal but must be extended to include processes of adaptation.

The Rise and Fall of Systems of Migrant Labour

So far, I have established the conditions for the reproduction of a system of migrant labour, but a complete theory of reproduction should embrace a characteristic dynamics (Cortés, Przeworski and Sprague 1974, pp. 279–80). The reproduction of any system in and of itself creates tendencies towards its change and persistence. Moreover, these tendencies can be deduced from the 'laws' or conditions of reproduction. Are there any rudimentary processes which might constitute a theory of the dynamics of a system of migrant labour? Or are the changes brought about by the internal structure of the system, that is, by its dynamics, swamped by external exigencies which impinge in an unpredictable fashion upon the system?

I noted that the system of migrant labour in Zambia dissolved primarily because the colonial state disengaged itself from the organization of the separation of maintenance and renewal processes. To what extent was this the product of a dynamics immanent in the structure of the system of migrant labour and its reproduction? To what extent was it the result of external forces? The expansion of the Northern Rhodesian (Zambian) economy required the expansion of the system of migrant labour. The increased involvement of Africans in wage employment led to their organization initially into tribal associations but also into embryonic and, later, strong trade unions. Organized economic class struggles inevitably led to increased remuneration and consequently undermined the foundations of the system of migrant labour and precipitated its dissolution. Advancing with economic struggles, political struggles eroded another central requirement of the reproduction of a system of migrant labour – migrant-labour powerlessness. In other words, the expansion of the system of migrant labour stimulated and structured class struggles which ultimately forced the breakdown of the system itself. At the same time, however, intertwined with such a 'bottom up' view of the dynamics of the system of migrant labour are the 'top down' concessions by the colonial government prompted by political changes in Britain and by the general climate in the colonized world. To disentangle the intricate interaction of concessions and struggles in the decline of the system of migrant labour in Zambia would be a worthwhile and challenging task. Suffice it to say here that internal dynamics are but a partial explanation of the dissolution of the system in Zambia.

Nonetheless, Zambia does illustrate dynamics arising in the place of employment – namely, the weakening of the colonial state and the advance of the political and economic status of the migrant worker. By contrast, for South Africa we stressed the dynamics of the interaction of capitalist and pre-capitalist economies and the way in which the expansion of the former tended to erode the latter. In its reproductive role, the South African state organizes counteracting influences to re-create the pre-capitalist mode of production. But it is becoming increasingly apparent that, although the system of migrant labour contains its own contradictions that continually threaten to undermine the system, the major threat to the system, particularly as it affects the gold mines, is from relatively autonomous external sources.

Prior to 1950, southern Africa constituted a relatively coherent political unit bound together by various forms of colonial rule and organized around certain focal points of industrial development. The peripheral areas served as labour reservoirs and were made subservient to the economic interests of the extractive industries, most notably the copper mines of Northern Rhodesia, the coal mines of Southern Rhodesia, and the gold mines of South Africa, as well as agriculture in all these territories. Struggles for political independence in Malawi, Tanzania, and Zambia led to the 'autonomization' of the foreign reservoirs that supplied labour for the gold mines. The ban on recruitment for South African industry imposed by the Zambian and Tanzanian governments meant that South Africa would have to become increasingly reliant on its own internal system of migrant labour. Hence there emerged renewed interest in the reserve areas and the creation of Bantustans. With no major industry of its own, Malawi continued to serve as a major foreign labour reservoir for South African industry, particularly the gold mines, reinforcing its own underdevelopment and its dependency on South Africa.

The sporadic but very definite success of guerrilla movements in Portuguese Africa led to a coup d'état in the metropolitan country and to the demise of Portuguese colonialism in Africa, precipitating disturbances throughout southern Africa. The white minority regime of Southern Rhodesia is now under pressure to negotiate with black nationalist leaders, and in 1974 Malawi declared a ban on the supply of migrant labour to South Africa. With the independence of Mozambique, there is the possibility of another major source of labour withdrawing its supply to South Africa. The reaction of the South African Chamber of Mines has been as follows:

'Energetic steps have been taken to attract South Africans and the proportion has increased from 22 per cent at 31st March, 1974 to 32 per cent at 30th April, 1975. It is hoped that it will be possible to increase this proportion even further, and it will therefore be necessary to compete for labour with other sectors of the economy and to provide more housing accommodations for South African workers. Inevitably the bulk of mining labour will remain migratory for many years to come but it is hoped that a core of stable South African employees can be built up on longer-life mines. . . .' [South African Chamber of Mines 1975]

The South African state is now faced with the dilemma of choosing either the expanded reproduction of the system of migrant labour within its own boundaries or the dissolution of the system. (For further details, see South African Institute of Race Relations 1975, pp. 281–8; Leys 1975.)

The South African example demonstrates that a system of migrant labour is placed in jeopardy as soon as the external labour reservoir gains political autonomy. The study of Mexican migrant workers in the United States lends some support to such a conclusion. The utilization of Mexican labour to bolster the United States economy has been the subject of considerable political debate within Mexico, from time to time leading the Mexican government to impose controls and conditions on the use of such labour. The bracero programme, with its elaborate although rarely entirely enforced system of regulations, reflected just such a concern for the treatment of Mexican nationals. In practice, however, political control over the supply of labour is only a minor factor in the determination of the ebb and flow of migrant labour across the border. Indeed, it may be argued that in this instance it is unrealistic to speak of a system of migrant labour at all, because any characteristic dynamics of the system are overwhelmed by a wide range of external factors, such as the state of the economy on either side of the border ....

Beyond Migrant Labour

What light does our conceptual distinction between maintenance and renewal shed on systems of labour that are not migrant and in which internal differentiation of the domestic labour is prominent? One approach to these broader issues is a reformulation of our analysis of the costs of reproduction of labour power. Earlier, the savings generated by a system of migrant labour were expressed in terms of the *externalization* of certain costs. That is, certain processes normally financed by the employer and the state of employment are externalized so that the employer and the employing state assume no responsibility. However, such savings could be viewed in terms of the *reduction* of certain renewal costs rather than their externalization. That is, it is cheaper to educate and bring up a family, and so forth, in a Bantustan or a Mexican shantytown than in Johannesburg or California, where the reproduction of labour power is organized for higher-income groups and where, as a result, lower-income groups are penalized. Luxuries superfluous to the basic processes of renewal in the Bantustan or Mexican town or village bcome necessities in Johannesburg or California. In other words, the requirements for a minimal standard of living vary from place to place, according to the level of industrial development. Increases in the level of consumption or, more broadly, the rise of the cost of reproduction of labour-power, is a consequence of and a condition for the economic expansion of capitalist societies (Gorz 1967, chap. 4).

Against this background, the significance of migrant labour lies in the separation of the processes of maintenance and renewal, so that renewal takes place where living standards are low and maintenance takes place within easy access of employment. Thus, wages earned by migrant workers are lower than those of domestic workers, because the former require fewer resources to sustain the renewal process than the latter. Where a supply of migrant labour is not available, industry itself may migrate to areas where the costs of reproduction of labour-power are lower. Indeed, the migration of industry may be a more attractive proposition for capitalists, as it relieves them of responsibility for the social and political costs of the maintenance of migrant labour. On the other hand, when a host country assumes responsibility for the regulation and domination of the labour force, the capitalist enterprise is frequently subjected to political and economic uncertainties beyond its control.

REFERENCES

Agribusiness Accountability Project 1972. *A Profile of California Agribusiness.* Washington, D.C.: Government Printing Office.

Anderson, N. 1923. *The Hobo.* Chicago: University of Chicago Press.

Arrighi, G. 1973. 'Labour Supplies in Historical Perspective: A Study of the Proletarianization of the African Peasantry in Rhodesia.' Pp. 180–234 in *Essays on the Political Economy of Africa,* by G. Arrighi and J. Saul. New York: Monthly Review Press.

Baerresen, D. W. 1971. *The Border Industrialization Program of Mexico.* Lexington, Mass.: Heath-Lexington.

Balibar, E. 1970. 'The Basic Concepts of Historical Materialism.' Pp. 201–308 in *Reading Capital,* by L. Althusser and E. Balibar. New York: Pantheon.

Baron, H. M., and B. Hymer 1968. 'The Negro Worker in the Chicago Labor Market.' Pp. 232–85 in *The Negro and the American Labor Movement,* edited by J. Jacobson. New York: Anchor.

Bell, T. 1973. *Industrial Decentralisation in South Africa.* London: Oxford University Press.

Bettison, D. G. 1960. 'Factors in the Determination of Wage Rates in Central Africa.' *Human Problems in British Central Africa,* no. 28 (December), pp. 22–46.

Blauner, R. 1972. *Racial Oppression in America.* New York: Harper & Row.

Bluestone, B. 1972. 'Capitalism and Poverty in America: A Discussion.' *Monthly Review* 24 (2): 65–71.

Bowles, S. 1972. 'Unequal Education and the Reproduction of

the Hierarchical Division of Labor.' Pp. 218–28 in *The Capitalist System*, edited by R. C. Edwards, M. Reich and T. E. Weisskopf. Englewood Cliffs, N.J.: Prentice-Hall.

Braverman, H. 1974. *Labor and Monopoly Capital*. New York: Monthly Review Press.

Briggs, V. M. 1973. *Chicanos and Rural Poverty*. Baltimore: John Hopkins University Press.

Burawoy, M. 1972. *The Colour of Class on the Copper Mines: From African Advancement to Zambianization*. Zambian Papers, no. 7, Manchester: Manchester University Press, for the Institute of African Studies, Zambia.

—— 1974. 'Race, Class and Colonialism.' *Social and Economic Studies* 23 (4): 521–50.

Castells, M. 1975. 'Immigrant Workers and Class Struggles in Advanced Capitalism: The Western European Experience.' *Politics and Society* 5 (1), 33–66.

Castles, S., and G. Kosack 1973. *Immigrant Workers and Class Structure in Western Europe*. London: Oxford University Press, for the Institute of Race Relations.

Cortés, F., A. Przeworski, and J. Sprague 1974. *Systems Analysis for Social Sciences*. New York: Wiley.

Epstein, A. L. 1958. *Politics in an Urban African Community*. Manchester: Manchester University Press.

Fellmeth, R. C., ed. 1971. *Power and Land in California*. Washington, D. C.: Center for the Study of Responsive Law.

Fisher, L. H. 1953. *The Harvest Labor Market in California*. Cambridge, Mass.: Harvard University Press.

Fogel, R. W., and S. L. Engerman 1974. *Time on the Cross: The Economics of American Negro Slavery*. Boston: Little, Brown.

Frisbie, P. 1975. 'Illegal Migration from Mexico to the United States: A Longitudinal Analysis.' *International Migration Review* 9 (1): 3–14.

Fuchs, V. R. 1968. *The Service Economy*. New York: National Bureau of Economic Research.

Fuller, V. 1940. 'The Supply of Agricultural Labor as a Factor in the Evolution of Farm Organization in California.' Part 54 in U.S. Congress, Senate, Committee on Violations of Free Speech and Rights of Labor, *Hearings before a Subcommittee of the Committee on Education and Labor, United States Senate*. Washington, D.C.: Government Printing Office.

Galarza, E. 1964. *Merchants of Labor.* Santa Barbara, Calif.: McNally & Loftin.

——— 1970. *Spiders in the House and Workers in the Field*, Notre Dame, Ind.: University of Notre Dame Press.

Gamio, M. 1930. *Mexican Immigration to the United States.* Chicago: University of Chicago Press.

Genovese, E. 1974. *Roll, Jordan, Roll: The World the Slaves Made.* New York: Pantheon.

Gorz, A. 1976. *Strategy for Labor.* Boston: Beacon.

Gramsci, A. 1971. *Prison Notebooks.* New York: International.

Greene, S. 1969. 'Immigration and Rural Poverty – the Problems of the Illegal Entrant.' *Duke Law Journal* 69 (3): 475–94.

Hancock, R. H. 1959. *The Role of the Bracero in the Economic and Cultural Dynamics of Mexico.* Stanford, Calif.: Stanford University Hispanic American Society.

Harris, M. 1959. 'Labor Migration among the Mozambique Thonga: Cultural and Political Factors.' *Africa* 29 (1): 50–64.

Harrison, B. 1972. 'Public Employment and the Theory of the Dual Economy.' Pp. 41–76 in *The Political Economy of Public Service Employment*, by H. L. Sheppard, B. Harrison and W. J. Spring. Lexington, Mass.: Heath-Lexington.

Hawley, E. W. 1966. 'The Politics of the Mexican Labor Issue, 1950–1965.' *Agricultural History* 40 (3): 157–76.

Hepple, A. 1971. *South Africa: Workers under Apartheid.* London: Christian Action Publications, for the International Defence and Aid Fund.

Hobsbawm, E. J. 1964. *Labouring Men: Studies in the History of Labour.* London: Weidenfeld & Nicolson.

Horwitz, R. 1967. *The Political Economy of South Africa.* New York: Praeger.

Jones, L. 1965. 'Mexican-American Labor Problems in Texas.' Ph.D. dissertation, University of Texas.

Kleinberg, J. 1974. 'Public Child Care: Our Hidden History.' Pp. 27–36 in *The Day Care Book*, edited by V. Breitburt. New York: Knopf.

Kuper, L. 1957. *Passive Resistance in South Africa.* New Haven, Conn.: Yale University Press.

Lenin, V. I. 1960. *Collected Works.* Vol. 3, *The Development of Capitalism in Russia.* Moscow: Foreign Languages Publishing House.

Leys, R. 1975. 'South African Gold Mining in 1974: "The Gold of Migrant Labour." ' *African Affairs* 74 (295): 196–208.

Liebow, E. 1967. *Tally's Corner*. Boston: Little, Brown.

McWilliams, C. 1964. *Brothers under the Skin*. Boston: Little, Brown.

———— 1971. *Factories in the Field*. Santa Barbara, Calif.: Peregrine.

Mayer, P. 1971. *Townsmen or Tribesmen*. London: Oxford University Press.

Myers, R. 1959. *The Position of Farm Workers in Federal and State Legislation*. New York: National Advisory Committee on Farm Labor.

North, D. S. 1970. *The Border Crossers: People Who Live in Mexico and Work in the United States*. Washington, D.C.: Trans-Century Corp.

O'Connor, J. 1973. *The Fiscal Crisis of the State*. New York: St. Martin's.

Parker, C. 1920. *The Casual Laborer and Other Essays*. New York: Russell & Russell.

Piven, F. F., and R. A. Cloward 1971. *Regulating the Poor: The Functions of Public Welfare*. New York: Random House.

Poulantzas, N. 1973. *Political Power and Social Classes*. London: New Left.

Redford, A. 1926. *Labour Migration in England: 1800–1850*. Manchester: Manchester University Press.

Rex, J. 1974. 'Ethnic and Class Stratification: Their Interrelation and Political Consequences – Europe.' Paper delivered to the International Sociological Association, Toronto, August 19.

Richards, A. 1939. *Land, Labour and Diet in Northern Rhodesia*. London: Oxford University Press.

Roux, E. 1964. *Time Longer than a Rope: A History of the Black Man's Struggle for Freedom in South Africa*. Madison: University of Wisconsin Press.

Samora, J. 1971. *Los Mojados: The Wetback Story*. Notre Dame, Ind.: University of Notre Dame Press.

Scruggs, O. M. 1960. 'Evolution of the Mexican Farm Labor Agreement of 1942.' *Agricultural History* 34 (3): 140–49.

———— 1963. 'Texas and the Bracero Program, 1942–1947.' *Pacific Historical Review* 32 (3): 251–82.

Simons, H. J., and R. E. Simons 1969. *Class and Colour in*

South Africa: 1850–1950. Harmondsworth: Penguin.

Smith, R. T. 1956. *The Negro Family in British Guiana*. London: Routledge & Kegan Paul.

South African Chamber of Mines 1975. *Presidential Address*. Advertisement in *Wall Street Journal*.

Supreme Court Reporter 1974. Vol. 95, no. 4 (December 15).

Survey of Race Relations in South Africa 1974, A 1975. Johannesburg: South African Institute of Race Relations.

Thompson, E. P. 1968. *The Making of the English Working Class*. Harmondsworth: Penguin.

U.S. Congress, Senate. Committee on Education and Labor 1940. *Report on Violations of Free Speech and Rights of Labor*. 77th Cong. 2d Sess. Washington, D.C.: Government Printing Office.

U.S. President's Commission on Migratory Labor 1951. *Migratory Labor in American Agriculture*. Washington, D.C.: Government Printing Office.

van den Berghe, P. L. 1967. *Race and Racism*. New York: Wiley.

van Velsen, J. 1961. 'Labour Migration as a Positive Factor in the Continuity of Tonga Tribal Society.' Pp. 230–41 in *Social Change in Modern Africa*, edited by A. Southall. London: Oxford University Press, for the International African Institute.

Wallerstein, I. 1976. 'American Slavery and the Capitalist World-Economy.' *American Journal of Sociology* 81 (March): 1199–1213.

Watson, W. 1958. *Tribal Cohesion in a Money Economy*. Manchester: Manchester University Press, for the Rhodes-Livingstone Institute.

Wilson, F. 1972a. *Labour in the South African Gold Mines 1911–1969*. Cambridge: Cambridge University Press.

——— 1972b. *Migrant Labour in South Africa*. Johannesburg: South African Council of Churches and SPRO-CAS (Study Project on Christianity in Apartheid Society).

Wilson, W. J. 1973. *Power, Racism and Privilege*. New York: Macmillan.

Wolpe, H. 1972. 'Capitalism and Cheap Labour-Power in South Africa: From Segregation to Apartheid.' *Economy and Society* 1 (4): 425–55.

4 The Family

A Political Economy of the Family in Capitalism: Women, Reproduction and Wage Labour

Jackie West

Labour-power, which must be regenerated in any society, acquires a special significance in capitalism since labour-power is the source of surplus value. It is not therefore surprising to find Marx observing that 'the individual consumption of the working class is ... the production and reproduction of that means of production so indispensable to the capitalist: the labourer himself.'[1] Marx was however little concerned with this process as such and indeed went on to make the now famous remark that 'The maintenance and reproduction of the working class is and ever must be a necessary condition for the reproduction of capital. But the capitalist may safely leave its fulfilment to the labourer's instinct of self-preservation and of propagation.' While domestic labour in the family may be involved in maintaining and renewing labourers, their substitutes and labourpower as such (the qualitative reproduction of labour-power), surplus value arises in the appropriation of that labour-power once it has been exchanged with capital. Thus capital's twin concern only to reduce the value of labour-power – or what is the same thing 'to reduce the individual consumption of the labourer to what is strictly necessary' – and to maximize the employment of wage labourers.

We might suppose then, that whereas the labourer is indispensable the family as a means to 'his' reproduction is not, particularly given the transformation of women's work into wage labour and the fact that consumption is increasingly achieved through wage goods purchased on the market. After all the proletarianization of women (meaning here simply their becoming waged workers), together with some degree of socialization in the reproduction of labour-power, must surely increase the production of surplus value rather than impair it. In considering these questions however a number of others are raised – about the economic significance of domestic labour, about the likely requirements of the entry of women into full-time employment, about the economic, not just political and ideological, significance of the family in contemporary capitalism. Child care is far from being the only remaining obstacle to socialized reproduction.

This paper is an examination of these issues. Its focus on the specific connection between domestic labour, reproduction and women's wage labour derives essentially from two observations. First, despite the tendency in capitalism towards proletarianization, women's wage labour has not been developed on the same 'free' basis as that of men (part-time work being the clearest contemporary illustration of this). Second, the family has persisted as the site for the basic reproduction of labour-power. It is the institution within which most commodities and services are consumed, which provides for the mediation of the wage, and whose material responsibilities and relations of dependency and support are reinforced by the state.

Domestic Labour and Reproduction

What kind of contribution does domestic labour make to the reproduction of labour-power? One suggestion has been that it is actually productive of value, and for some this means it thus provides a hidden source of surplus labour appropriated by capital. This position is in fact untenable, but it is worth outlining why this is the case as a means of introducing, albeit at first rather technically, the characteristics of domestic labour which distinguish it from wage labour.

Domestic labour creates use values, for example by transforming wage goods or other products into directly consumable items like meals. Although it is involved in the qualitative reproduction of labour-power and its product is sold as a commodity, domestic labour itself is not economically productive. It does not engage the housewife in the production of surplus value.[2] But nor does it permit domestic labour a part in reproducing the exchange value of the commodity labour power since that value can only be established through the mechanisms of commodity production.[3] Domestic labour is private and there are no means of establishing the socially necessary domestic labour time that might enter into the value of its product, in contrast to the labour time embodied in wage goods (the means of subsistence). Aside from whether eating, dressing, sleeping and sexual services should be included in necessary domestic labour time (which, significantly, is just what is claimed by the political demand for wages for housework), the value of labour-power cannot be related to the average level of productivity of domestic labour. There is no way of competition between domestic units minimizing the labour time embodied, and no tendency towards the equalization of working conditions among housewives compensated or matched by differences in their 'pay' (their part of the wage).[4]

We cannot say anything about domestic labour's relation to the value of labour-power on the basis of the distribution of the wage. For if domestic labour created value it must be reflected in wages as long as wages are determined by the value of labour-power, and this would still obtain in principle even if in practice wives did not receive a portion equivalent to their domestic labour time. However on the one hand this would mean that only married men, not capital, could benefit from appropriating their wives' labour, by determining their wives' share of the wage.[5] On the other hand the fact that there are no forces inherent in family structure to equalize the division of resources as between husbands and wives is of crucial importance if we wish to understand the forces that do actually operate on the performance of domestic labour.

First, then, and in an immediate sense, there is marriage. Wages earned in production are seen as the breadwinner's property and the claim of the full-time housewife on the wage packet to purchase means of subsistence (or labour-saving devices) can only result from a personal bargain struck with her husband, on how much he is willing, or can be persuaded or coerced into giving her. The obligation on husbands to maintain wives is unenforceable until divorce, and even then practically so. Indeed, even with rising wages, it is not uncommon for wives to receive a less than proportional increase of housekeeping, if any at all, out of the larger wage packet.[6] The more or less binding, personal and servant relationship of wives to husbands and of mothers to children decrees that housework and child care are labours of love. It is the private and personal relations of the family that provide domestic labour with considerable elasticity, a kind of flexibility which would be inconceivable were it mediated directly through the market. It is this in particular which accounts for the possibility of married women's wage labour in the context of inadequately provided or insufficient substitutes for domestic labour.[7]

Second, although the law of value does not *allocate* domestic labour, this far from prevents its influence. The relationship between capital accumulation and domestic labour is a complex one. Moreover, while domestic labour (privatized reproduction) is neither productive nor unproductive[8] this does not at all rule out its economic significance in advanced capitalism. But since it is more conventional to argue that the family's material basis is being or has been eroded, it is this position which is first addressed in the discussion below.

The Case for Socialized Reproduction

This case it put most forcefully by Mandel who suggests that the family is being displaced not only as a unit of production but of consumption too : 'Since the reproduction of the commodity of labour-power is increasingly achieved by means of capitalistically produced commodities and capitalistically organized and supplied services, the material basis of the individual family disappears in the sphere of consumption as well.'[9]

This tendency corresponds to what is now a familiar twofold problem of valorization in advanced capitalism : the difficulties of securing an adequate rate of profit in industry proper and of realizing what surplus value there is at all. Capital's entry into new spheres of commodity production (consumer goods) and services permits new sources of surplus value or at least an average rate of profit for service capital. This, in combination with ever cheapened commodities, offsets the rise in wages necessary both to replace domestic labour and bring all women into social production and to provide the basis for the increased consumption of wage-earners which expands markets or the sphere of exchange and thus the realization of surplus value. In addition there are tendencies towards the socialization of child care which correspond to the need for an adequate labour force (schooling) and, as Gardiner has emphasized, to the need to increase women's labour time or the numbers in employment.[10]

A great deal of substitution for domestic labour certainly permits capital accumulation through the direct extraction of surplus value. For as Mandel emphasizes 'the production of vacuum cleaners, central heating systems, electricity for private consumption and industrially pre-cooked meals' is 'capitalist production of commodities and surplus value', unlike the

177

housemaid or private cook, and the same can of course be said of electrical household appliances, tinned, frozen and convenience foods and ready-made clothes. Since, furthermore, some of these new commodities are bought with women's additional wages to replace their formerly unpaid services, the transformation of housewives into wage workers also 'facilitates profit realization and expanded reproduction.'[11] What more could capital want?

There are, however, problems with this sort of approach. Such an argument takes insufficient account of, on the one hand, the relationship between surplus value and the cheap labour-power and dual role of women as paid and unpaid labourers, and, on the other, the nature of conditions required by or resulting from the full proletarianization of women.

The economic limits to the socialization of reproduction can only be explored by first considering the positive material benefits of domestic labour.[12] Domestic labour creates use values only, but in doing so it secures the qualitative reproduction of labour-power at a level unmet by the wage or wage goods alone. This much is acknowledged even by those who, like Mandel, ignore domestic labour as such in their concern with socialization, surplus value and women's employment. For it is recognized that the full entry of housewives into social production requires the replacement of formerly unpaid household services, a substitution which can only be achieved through the purchase of additional wage goods and services.

The point is put more strongly by Gardiner, Himmelweit and Mackintosh. Necessary labour (equivalent to the value of the means of subsistence) is not equivalent to the total labour performed in the reproduction and maintenance of labour-power. Wages alone (equivalent to necessary labour) have never been adequate to the standard of living of the working class and domestic labour contributes directly to this by making up the deficiency. Thus domestic labour also contributes *indirectly* to surplus value, for it in a sense subsidizes wages. Aside from the material gains to male workers, 'domestic labour permits capital to provide a wage lower in terms of use values than the total subsistence level of the working class. In this sense its existence benefits the production of surplus value and indeed makes that production possible.'[13] Although other forms of maintenance (in particular the state) must also be taken into account, it is still the case that the subsistence level is primarily achieved by varying the relative contribution of commodities purchased with wages and domestic labour, and the flexibility of the latter and its nature as personal service is especially important. This does not mean we can calculate the contribution of domestic labour to reproduction; domestic labour and wage labour are not analogous. But that we cannot equate domestic 'labour time' and socially necessary labour time, and that we cannot talk about its creation of value, is not to say that domestic labour is irrelevant to the reproduction of labour power conceptualized as a cost. Domestic labour is not surplus labour transferred into profits. Nor does it *create* surplus value, but it *benefits* the production of surplus value by *allowing for* necessary labour to be lower than actual subsistence.[14] Domestic labour is indeed an 'external condition of existence' of capitalist production. There may be difficulties in specifying empirically the precise connection between domestic labour as such and capital accumulation, but this hardly denies a relationship which, albeit indirect, is substantial and material nonetheless.

Conditions of Women's Proletarianization

It is easy enough to show that the rate of surplus value increases very considerably from employing all men and women as individuals with responsibility only for themselves and substitutes, even allowing for a rise in the value of labour-power (the cost of reproducing the whole 'family') due to the loss of women's domestic labour. The comparison, following Marx, is typically between a family dependent on a male breadwinner and one where both adults are fully employed, spreading the cost of reproduction between them, and with therefore a reduced value to male labour-power. This contrast of extremes completely ignores the current arrangement whereby most working class family support is achieved in the long run through two wage workers earning different incomes.[15]

Beechey has argued that where married women are dependent for part of their total costs of reproducing their own labour-power and that of children they have a correspondingly lower value to their labour-power compared with men. As well as being partially dependent on sources other than their own wage they are not heavily dependent on the state for income maintenance insofar as it does not recognize married women as individuals.[16] Now a situation where married women are partially dependent on their husbands can also produce a rise in surplus value overall at least equivalent to, and possibly even greater than where women and men are self-sufficient. This will be the case even if married women are employed full time and the cost of family reproduction (value of 'family' labour-power) rises following the need to substitute wage goods for domestic labour.[17]

As long as there is demand for cheap female labour-power domestic labour is unlikely to disappear. The dependence of women on men may not as such require its performance if wages, even differential wages, are sufficient to substitute, although in practice unpaid services (and not just sexual) are likely to be exchanged in return for economic support (marriage), even if child care is socialized. Of course women's cheaper labour-power might also be related to their concentration in less skilled jobs requiring less training etc. But, as Philipps and Taylor have pointed out, it is highly questionable that 'women's work' is objectively less skilled than men's or that it has been more deskilled. As they suggest the subordination of women in the labour market which results in ghettoized female labour is premised much more on existing power relations between men and women which are structured through female subordination in the family.[18] Of this women's responsibility for domestic labour is a major component. It legitimates the weaker claim of women on scarce resources (particularly in periods of recession) and it accounts for their availability for part-time employment.

There is also the fact of the difference between wages and the value of labour-power. While fully proletarianizing all women reduces the value of individual male workers' labour-power (assuming no support of a dependent wife), it is far less likely that male wages will fall to this level without resistance. In the long run the value of labour-power as a whole may fall with cheapened wage goods but another aspect of socialization is that 'work which as housework is not paid for as such ... becomes wage work, commanding payment in accordance with what is generally expected in the labour market.'[19] True, an 'acceptable' rate does not have to be the same as that for men but only providing there are other means of ensuring the subordination of female wage labour and weakening the claims of trade-union bargaining on behalf of women workers.

Higher wages and a tendency to equalize the wages of women and men may well be a cost that capital can sustain given the ability or need to expand production and the internal market (consumption). Wage rises occasioned by the rise in the value of labour-power can be offset by cheapening the means of sub-sistence and may in any case be provided in exchange for rises in productivity, for instance shiftwork.

But in the long run wages must rise less than productivity. For as Mandel puts it, 'What may seem quite realistic for the individual capitalist – namely to regard all proletarians other than his own workers as potential customers with a purchasing power that could grow without limit – is void of meaning for the capitalist class as a whole.'[20] And in addition rises in produc-tivity are also required to finance the growth in unproductive investment that accompanies the expansion of commodity pro-duction. This concerns not only state provision of child care necessary to women's wage labour on a large scale but the un-productive sector in capitalism as a whole. It is argued by Mandel that the limits to this, and the compulsion to limit wages, can be offset by transforming services into commodities (and consumer credit etc.) and to the degree that married women's earnings help close the gap between family consump-tion needs and individual male wages. This has much to be said for it but there are limits too to these 'countervailing' tendencies, limits which in the long run are also to a large ex-tent limits of eroding domestic labour and women's cheaper labour-power.

Some domestic labour tends initially to be replaced by com-mercial services which do not become productive merely be-cause they are organized on capitalist lines and purchased with wages. The extent of service replacement depends in part on the precise definition of unproductive labour, but, more impor-tant, laundries, 'diaper services' and the like can clearly be com-moditized, as witness the current promotion of the single domestic machine that washes and tumble dries in one single action.

Of course the major exception to productive replacement of personal services is child care. The full proletarianization of women requires equal wage labour unencumbered by responsi-bility for children as much as husband's meals, in order to be free for shiftwork or indeed even an '8-hour' day.[21] Conveni-ence foods and ready-made meals may be far less important than adequate provision of pre-school nurseries and after-school care. Of course capital may well be willing to bear the cost, or part of it, in certain circumstances (and not only war-time), and there is no inherent reason why child care should be provided by the state rather than by employers. If child care is provided by private agencies it can clearly be profitable for them individually but it remains a service and thus part of the unproductive sector. The limits on state provisions are subject to the same limits as apply to social spending generally, in particular its relationship to profitability.[22]

The limits for capital as a whole of unproductive expenditure is obviously not just a question of unproductive substitutes for domestic labour since, apart from child care, these are in the long run insubstantial. It is rather of the degree to which women as well as men can be absorbed into productive employment. But in any case the valorization of productive capital and the realization of value become an increasing problem in advanced capitalism of which the growth in commercial and service capital is symptomatic.[23] It is no coincidence that women are drawn disproportionately into unproductive employment. Ultimately such growth areas can only expand at the cost of productive capital or wages. Since a drain on productive capital reduces the average rate of profit, there will be, from capital's point of view, a more or less constantly present necessity to increase the rate of exploitation, in particular of productive workers, which of course applies no less in the long run when services are converted into commodities. It is worth spelling out the implications of this for the significance of domestic labour to capital accumulation.

Aside from lowering the value of labour-power, which while increasing surplus labour time also 'benefits' labour (other things being equal) raising the rate of exploitation can be achieved, *inter alia*, by drawing on cheaper labour-power, by lowering wages directly, reducing employment or reducing wages below the value of labour-power. Raising prices can also raise the rate of profit at a given rate of exploitation. The effects on the family of these measures and the ways in which women's labour can compensate depend on the degree and nature of proletarianization. As with calculating how much surplus value is extracted from ending 'domestic slavery', it is erroneous to assume, either from the point of view of capital or the working class, that it is a question of either domestic labour or women's wage labour.

Lower wages and unemployment obviously lower workers standards of living, as do rising prices which, even if originating in Department I (production of means of production) will be passed on to consumer goods unless offset by rises in produc-

tivity. Clearly as long as married women are not fully proletarianized their further employment can constitute a solution
although this will also critically depend on trade unions' response to the erosion of male jobs or earnings. If it is cheaper
female power that is drawn upon then this in itself will stem
from and perpetuate women's economic dependence. But even
supposing equalized wages mean that women can truly substitute for the loss of husbands' earnings some intensification
of domestic labour is also necessary to maintain the standard of
living given the reduced time available for housework. (New
labour-saving devices are likely to be purchased given a constant income or rise in wages.) The material basis of the family
will therefore be retained unless there is a rise in state income
maintenance or a fall in the value of labour-power. And a rise
in state income maintenance would have to be financed out of
profits or wages.

While a reduction in domestic labour initially raises the value
of labour-power as more wage goods are necessary, a reduction
in the value of labour-power through cheapened commodities
clearly does not increase the necessity for domestic labour. On
the one hand a lower wage packet may purchase an equivalent
amount of cheapened goods and services. On the other, at a
given level of income, domestic labour can decrease in as much
as the same wage buys more goods and services. It is only in
this latter case that we could expect the erosion of domestic
labour, or at least its reduction to a minimum sufficient to
permit the full subsumption of women's labour by capital.

How far though can the means of subsistence be cheapened?
This requires either reduced prices of raw materials, heightened
use of technology or cheaper labour-power. If women no
longer constitute such a reserve (as the 'proletarianization' argument assumes) then productivity can only rise with other
sources, notably migrants, or through technology which ultimately creates valorization difficulties for individual capitals
and capital as a whole. As regards services this is also limited
in respect of technical constraints and quality, child care being
a case in point,[24] in which cheap labour is far more effective.
More generally, once women are fully proletarianized, raising
the rate of exploitation through lowering wages or employment
or wages inadequate for family or self-sufficiency inevitably reproduces the material necessity for domestic labour if the
standard of living is to be maintained, and without doubt the

183

disposability of married women's wage labour is premised on their having 'a sphere of their very own' to which they can return, namely the family.

It is clear from the above that there is no even relationship between wages and domestic labour. Domestic labour may 'permit a wage lower in terms of use values than the total subsistence level of the working class.' But even aside from state maintenance there are too many other factors to be considered to allow for some crude association between money wages, employment levels and the performance of domestic labour, particularly since the relations of marriage and parenthood influence the amount, nature and flexibility of domestic labour. It is this complexity which partly accounts, along with non-economic forces, for the difficulties of trying to explain specific historical connections between the family and production in terms of the significance of privatized reproduction.[25]

Undoubtedly women's wage labour is needed in particular periods in both productive and unproductive sectors, and an extension of socialized child care and of working class purchasing power may be necessary to the expanded reproduction of capital, along with some erosion of sexual divisions. But levels of female employment (as well as socialized housework and child care) are affected by what Mandel refers to – but only in passing – as 'oscillations in the business cycle'. Since cyclical variations in capitalist accumulation are the rule rather than the exception it would seem prematurely optimistic to regard the material basis of the family as eroded.[26] Given the benefits of cheap, disposable female labour power and the cyclical effects of production on the necessity for domestic labour to workers' standards of living, there is far from being an absolute sense in which the full proletarianization of women, the socialization of reproduction and the disappearance of the family are economically ordained.[27]

NOTES AND REFERENCES

1 K. Marx, *Capital* vol. 1, London: Allen and Unwin, 1946, p. 585.
2 The blurring of the distinction between labour-power as use and exchange value is the fundamental error in M. Dalla Costa and S. James, *The Power of Women and the Subversion of the Community*, Bristol; Falling Wall Press, 1972, where it is claimed that the home is a 'social factory', a centre of 'social production'.
3 Arguments that domestic labour creates value are put forward by, for instance, W. Seccombe, 'The housewife and her labour under capitalism', *New Left Review*, 83, Jan.-Feb. 1974 and 'Domestic labour – reply to critics', *New Left Review*, 94, Nov.-Dec. 1975; J. Harrison, 'The political economy of housework', *Bulletin of the Conference of Socialist Economists*, vol. IV, no. 1, 1974. On the implications of these positions see note 5 below. The discussion that follows here is drawn chiefly from three critiques: J. Gardiner, 'Women's domestic labour', *New Left Review*, 89, Jan.-Feb. 1975; PEWG, 'Women's domestic labour', *On the Political Economy of Women*, CSE Pamphlet no. 2, London: Stage One, 1976; P. Smith, 'Domestic labour and Marx's theory of value' in A. M. Wolpe and A. Kuhn, *Feminism and Materialism*, London: Routledge & Kegan Paul, 1978.
4 On the different situation in petty commodity production see Gardiner, op. cit., p. 49, and Smith, op. cit., pp. 204–9.
5 Whether wives received a measure of their domestic labour time or not capital would neither gain nor lose: value-creating domestic labour would be unique in capitalism in providing no surplus, in being, in principle, fully 'paid for' (Gardiner, op. cit., p. 50). In fact, as in Harrison's formulation (op. cit., p. 43), capital could only benefit from any *value* created by domestic labour if wages were always below the value of labour-power (means of subsistence plus domestic labour). But if no measure can be made of the value created by domestic labour, the concept 'value of labour-power' becomes merely notional and incapable of substantiation. Seccombe (1974, op. cit., pp. 12–13) has

suggested the labour origins of the wage are further obscured by the backstage, unseen contribution of domestic labour to the value of labour-power. But this would be an 'ideological' rather than economic function of domestic labour.

6 Surveys by *Woman's Own*, National Opinion Poll and the National Consumer Council found that between twenty and twenty-eight per cent of husbands had not increased housekeeping allowances in the previous year and that the lower the income the more likely the wife to go short; the *Guardian* 17 Sept. 1975 and 12 Jan. 1978.

7 M. Coulson, B. Magaš and H. Wainwright, ' "The housewife and her labour under capitalism" – a critique', *New Left Review*, 89, Jan.–Feb. 1975, p. 67. They emphasize the contradictions in women's position from the combination of domestic and wage labour.

8 Strictly domestic labour is neither productive nor, unproductive because it is not abstract social labour. But the economic significance of domestic labour is missed by those who suggest that domestic work is not really labour at all. See, for example, M. Cousins, 'Material arguments and feminism', *m/f* no. 2, 1978, p. 68.

9 E. Mandel, *Late Capitalism*, London: New Left Books, 1975, p. 391. See also the argument in H. Braverman, *Labor and Monopoly Capital*, New York: Monthly Review Press, 1974, especially chap. 13; and I. Breugel 'What keeps the family going?', *International Socialism*, Series 2, no. 1, July 1978.

10 Gardiner, op. cit., pp. 55 and 57.

11 Mandel, op. cit., pp. 388 and 393.

12 There are a number of other approaches to that discussed here and in note 5 above. Coulson *et al.* (op. cit., pp. 68–9) note also the relationship of domestic labour to privatized consumption and unequal distribution. Others see absolute limits to the abolition of domestic labour in capitalism, e.g. O. Adamson, C. Brown, J. Harrison and J. Price, 'Women's oppression under capitalism', *Revolutionary Communist*, no. 5, 1976. They note that the replenishment of labourpower can only end with the end of its consumption by capital. But on that replenishment *in* capitalism they do not see that the socialization of *reproduction* might well be in capital's interest just because 'no surplus value can be produced by domestic work.' See also a different argument in

S. Himmelweit and S. Mohun, 'Domestic labour and capital', *Cambridge Journal of Economics*, 1, 1977.

13 J. Gardiner, S. Himmelweit and M. Mackintosh, 'Women's domestic labour', *Bulletin of the Conference of Socialist Economists*, vol. IV, no. 2, 1975, p. 9. See also Gardiner, 1975, op. cit., pp. 53–4.

14 Gardiner's formulation (1975, op. cit.) speaks of domestic labour 'keeping down' necessary labour. The meaning is in fact quite clear but failure to appreciate it has led certain critics to suggest that she confuses the effects of domestic labour on subsistence with the determination of necessary labour itself. Of course Smith (op. cit., p. 216, note 4) is correct to note that necessary labour is a function of the value of labour-power, but this in no way prevents both being concretely dependent or contingent on the structure of the family. 'The value of labour power is ... *premised* both on the role of women in the wage economy [women's wage labour both raises it and spreads it over the whole family] and on a particular level and organization of domestic labour,' PEWG, op. cit., pp. 11 and 5 (my emphasis). This revised version of the 1975 CSE article (see note 13) does not make explicit the implications of the above for capital accumulation.

15 Currently half of *all* married women are officially counted as in the labour force but the proportions are notably higher in the age group from twenty to fifty-nine: *Social Trends*, HMSO, 1979, Table 5.3, p. 84. On part-time employment and rates among women with children see below.

16 V. Beechey, 'Some notes on female wage labour in capitalist production', *Capital and Class*, no. 3, Autumn 1977.

17 With women employed part time, rates of surplus value would still be a great deal higher than in the case of the family dependent on one breadwinner, even without the possibility of extracting greater productivity and surplus value from part-time labour.

18 A. Phillips and B. Taylor, 'Sex and class in the capitalist labour process', paper given at the Nuffield Deskilling Conference, Windsor, Dec. 1978.

19 Gardiner, op. cit., p. 54.

20 Mandel, op. cit., p. 398.

21 In fact, more significant in contemporary capitalism is the high rate of part-time, irregular, semi- and unskilled work among women with young children. Almost two-thirds are

employed part-time; only one in seven works a standard
seven- or eight-hour day, one in fourteen works evenings,
early mornings or at night. Semi- and unskilled jobs are the
lot of half or more with a child under ten. Recent FES data
indicates employment among four in ten women where the
eldest child is under five, and among two-thirds with their
eldest at primary school, which figures should not surprise
us given the existence of 'self-employment'. Most women
without responsibility for young children escape low-grade
manual work but even in their absence a non-standard work
pattern is rather more typical than a regular day. See P.
Moss, 'The current situation' in N. Fonda and P. Moss,
Mothers in Employment, Brunel University Management
Programme and Thomas Coram Research Unit, 1976, pp.
6–14.

22 Gardiner, op. cit., p. 56. State services (especially all-day
care) rarely compete favourably with other priorities in
periods of restricted expenditure. Neither state nor, in general, private provision expands commensurately with increases in women's employment. Private nursery places have
long been as significant as local authority ones, especially
given restricted eligibility to the latter, but the most important provision of all is childminding. See, for example,
Moss, op. cit.; N. Fonda, 'Current entitlements and provisions' in Moss and Fonda, op. cit.

23 Mandel, op. cit., e.g. pp. 387–8, 400–1; Braverman, op. cit.,
part IV.

24 'Adequate socialized preschool child care requires a minimum of one adult to five children, without taking account
of administrative and ancillary workers. If one compares
this with the average family with its two-and-a-half children
to one woman, one gets a rough estimate of no more than
a fifty per cent saving of labour,' Gardiner, op. cit., p. 54.

25 Some of these connections are explored with special reference to industrial capitalism in my 'Some notes on the
changing relationship of domestic labour to the reproduction of labour-power', mimeographed paper, Department of Sociology, University of Bristol, April 1979. It is
worth noting here though that the ideology of motherhood
is often not autonomous of economic constraints, including
the tendency to the 'partial' proletarianization of women.
See H. Land, 'Women: Supporters or Supported?' in D
Leonard Barker and S. Allen, *Sexual Divisions and Society*,

Process and Change, London; Tavistock, 1976; M. McIntosh, 'The state and the oppression of women' in Wolpe and Kuhn, op. cit.

26 The impact of recession only underwrites the significance of the double shift for married women. It is *part*-time employment that both expands to compensate for pressure on living standards and frequently masks, if not at times corresponds to, a decrease in full-time especially men's employment. On official figures, for instance, most of the years between 1971 and 1976 show substantial increases in women part-timers yet a fall in the numbers of male and full-time women employees: N. Fonda and P. Moss, 'The next five years' in Fonda and Moss, op. cit., and more generally J. Gardiner, 'Women and unemployment', *Red Rag*, no. 10, 1975. On the underestimates of official statistics on both women's employment and unemployment see, for example, H. Land, op. cit.; A. Oakley and R. Oakley, 'Sexism in official statistics' in J. Irvine, I. Miles and J. Evans, *Demystifying Social Statistics*, London; Pluto, 1979.

27 For advice, not always heeded, and support in preparing this article I would particularly like to thank Liz Bird, Miki David, Will Guy, Theo Nichols, Marilyn Porter, Margaret Rowe and Dalbir Singh.

5 Education and Work

Education and the Long Shadow of Work

Samuel Bowles and Herbert Gintis

> Every child born into the world should be looked upon
> by society as so much raw material to be manufactured.
> Its quality is to be tested. It is the business of society, as
> an intelligent economist, to make the best of it.
>
> LESTER FRANK WARD,
> *Education*, c. 1872

It is not obvious why the US educational system should be the
way it is. Since the interpersonal relationships it fosters are so
antithetical to the norms of freedom and equality prevalent in
American society, the school system can hardly be viewed as a
logical extension of our cultural heritage. If neither technological necessity nor the bungling mindlessness of educators
explain the quality of the educational encounter, what does?

Reference to the educational system's legitimation function
does not take us far towards enlightenment. For the formal,
objective, and cognitively oriented aspects of schooling capture
only a fragment of the day-to-day social relationships of the
educational encounter. To approach an answer, we must consider schools in the light of the social relationships of economic
life. In this chapter, we suggest that major aspects of educational organization replicate the relationships of dominance
and subordinancy in the economic sphere. The correspondence
between the social relation of schooling and work accounts for
the ability of the educational system to produce an amenable
and fragmented labour force. The experience of schooling, and
not merely the content of formal learning, is central to this
process.

In our view, it is pointless to ask if the net effect of US education is to promote equality or inequality, repression or liberation. These issues pale into insignificance before the major
fact: the educational system is an integral element in the
reproduction of the prevailing class structure of society. The

educational system certainly has a life of its own, but the experience of work and the nature of the class structure are the bases upon which educational values are formed, social justice assessed, the realm of the possible delineated in people's consciousness, and the social relations of the educational encounter historically transformed.

In short, and to return to a persistent theme of this book [*Schooling in Capitalist America*] the educational system's task of integrating young people into adult work roles constrains the types of personal development which it can foster in ways that are antithetical to the fulfilment of its personal developmental function.

Reproducing Consciousness

> ... children guessed (but only a few
> and down they forgot as up they grew
> autumn winter spring summer)...
>   e e cummings, 1940

Economic life exhibits a complex and relatively stable pattern of power and property relationships. The perpetuation of these social relationships, even over relatively short periods, is by no means automatic. As with a living organism, stability in the economic sphere is the result of explicit mechanisms constituted to maintain and extend the dominant patterns of power and privilege. We call the sum total of these mechanisms and their actions the reproduction process.

Amidst the sundry social relations experienced in daily life, a few stand out as central to our analysis of education. These are precisely the social relationships which are necessary to the security of capitalist profits and the stability of the capitalist division of labour. They include the patterns of dominance and subordinacy in the production process, the distribution of ownership of productive resources, and the degrees of social distance and solidarity among various fragments of the working population – men and women, blacks and whites, and white-and blue-collar workers, to mention some of the most salient.

What are the mechanisms of reproduction of these aspects of the social relations of production in the United States? To an extent, stability is embodied in law and backed by the coercive power of the state. Our jails are filled with individuals who have operated outside the framework of the private-ownership market system. The modern urban police force as well as the National Guard originated, in large part, in response to the fear of social upheaval evoked by militant labour action. Legal sanction, within the framework of the laws of private property, also channels the actions of groups (e.g., unions) into conformity with dominant power relationships. Similarly, force is used to stabilize the division of labour and its rewards within an enterprise: dissenting workers are subject to dismissal and directors failing to conform to 'capitalist rationality' will be replaced.

But to attribute reproduction to force alone borders on the absurd. Under normal conditions, the effectiveness of coercion depends at the very least on the inability or unwillingness of those subjected to it to join together in opposing it. Laws generally considered illegitimate tend to lose their coercive power, and undisguised force too frequently applied tends to be self-defeating. The consolidation and extension of capitalism has engendered struggles of furious intensity. Yet instances of force deployed against a united and active opposition are sporadic and have usually given way to détente in one form or another through a combination of compromise, structural change and ideological accommodation. Thus it is clear that the consciousness of workers – beliefs, values, self-concepts, types of solidarity and fragmentation, as well as modes of personal behaviour and development – are integral to the perpetuation, validation, and smooth operation of economic institutions. The reproduction of the social relations of production depends on the reproduction of consciousness.

Under what conditions will individuals accept the pattern of social relationships that frame their lives? Believing that the long-term development of the existing system holds the prospect of fulfilling their needs, individuals and groups might actively embrace these social relationships. Failing this, and lacking a vision of an alternative that might significantly improve their situation, they might fatalistically accept their condition. Even with such a vision they might passively submit to the framework of economic life and seek individual solutions to social problems if they believe that the possibilities for realizing change are remote. The issue of the reproduction of consciousness enters each of these assessments.

The economic system will be embraced when, first, the perceived needs of individuals are congruent with the types of satisfaction the economic system can objectively provide. While perceived needs may be, in part, biologically determined, for the most part needs arise through the aggregate experiences of individuals in the society. Thus the social relations of production are reproduced in part through a harmony between the needs which the social system generates and the means at its disposal for satisfying these needs.

Second, the view that fundamental social change is not feasible, unoperational, and utopian is normally supported by a complex web of ideological perspectives deeply embedded in the cultural and scientific life of the community and reflected in the consciousness of its members. But fostering the 'consciousness of inevitability' is not the office of the cultural system alone. There must also exist mechanisms that systematically thwart the spontaneous development of social experiences that would contradict these beliefs.

Belief in the futility of organizing for fundamental social change is further facilitated by social distinctions which fragment the conditions of life for subordinate classes. The strategy of 'divide and conquer' has enabled dominant classes to maintain their power since the dawn of civilization. Once again, the splintered consciousness of a subordinate class is not the product of cultural phenomena alone, but must be reproduced through the experiences of daily life.

Consciousness develops through the individual's direct perception of and participation in social life.[1] Indeed, everyday experience itself often acts as an inertial stabilizing force. For instance, when the working population is effectively stratified, individual needs and self-concepts develop in a correspondingly fragmented manner. Youth of different racial, sexual, ethnic, or economic characteristics directly perceive the economic positions and prerogatives of 'their kind of people'. By adjusting their aspiration accordingly, they not only reproduce stratification on the level of personal consciousness, but bring their needs into (at least partial) harmony with the fragmented conditions of economic life. Similarly, individuals tend to channel the development of their personal powers – cognitive, emotional, physical, aesthetic, and spiritual – in directions where they will have an opportunity to exercise them. Thus the alienated character of work, for example, leads people to guide their creative potentials to areas outside of economic activity: consumption, travel, sexuality, and family life. So needs and need-satisfaction again tend to fall into congruence and alienated labour is reproduced on the level of personal consciousness.[2]

But this congruence is continually disrupted. For the satisfaction of needs gives rise to new needs. These new needs derive from the logic of personal development as well as from the evolving structure of material life, and in turn undercut the reproduction of consciousness. For this reason the reproduction of consciousness cannot be the simple unintended by-product of social experience. Rather, social relationships must be consciously organized to facilitate the reproduction of consciousness.

Take, for instance, the organization of the capitalist enterprise ... Power relations and hiring criteria within the enterprise are organized so as to reproduce the workers' self-concepts, the legitimacy of their assignments within the hierarchy, a sense of the technological inevitability of the hierarchical division of labour itself, and the social distance among groups of workers in the organization. Indeed, while token gestures towards workers' self-management may be a successful motivational gimmick, any delegation of real power to workers becomes a threat to profits because it tends to undermine patterns of consciousness compatible with capitalist control. By generating new needs and possibilities, by demonstrating the feasibility of a more thoroughgoing economic democracy, by increasing worker solidarity, an integrated and politically conscious programme of worker involvement in decision-making may undermine the power structure of the enterprise. Management will accede to such changes only under extreme duress of worker rebellion and rapidly disintegrating morale, if at all.

But the reproduction of consciousness cannot be insured by these direct mechanisms alone. The initiation of youth into the economic system is further facilitated by a series of institutions, including the family and the educational system, that are more immediately related to the formation of personality and consciousness. Education works primarily through the institutional relations to which students are subjected. Thus schooling fosters and rewards the development of certain capacities and the expression of certain needs, while thwarting and penalizing others. Through these institutional relationships, the educational system tailors the self-concepts, aspirations, and social class identifications of individuals to the requirements of the social division of labour.

The extent to which the educational system actually accomplishes these objectives varies considerably from one period to the next ... recurrently through US history these reproduction mechanisms have failed, sometimes quite spectacularly. In most periods – and the present is certainly no exception – efforts to use the schools to reproduce and extend capitalist production relations have been countered both by the internal dynamic of the educational system and by popular opposition.

... the two main objectives of dominant classes in educational policy are the production of labour power and the reproduction of those institutions and social relationships which facilitate the translation of labour power into profits. We may now be considerably more concrete about the way that educational institutions are structured to meet these objectives. First, schooling produces many of the technical and cognitive skills required for adequate job performance. Second, the educational system helps legitimate economic inequality ... The objective and meritocratic orientation of US education reduces discontent over both the hierarchical division of labour and the process through which individuals attain position in it. Third, the school produces, rewards, and labels personal characteristics relevant to the staffing of positions in the hierarchy. Fourth, the educational system, through the pattern of status distinctions it fosters, reinforces the stratified consciousness on which the fragmentation of subordinate economic classes is based.

What aspects of the educational system allow it to serve these various functions? We shall suggest in the next section that the educational system's ability to reproduce the consciousness of workers lies in a straightforward correspondence principle: for the past century at least, schooling has contributed to the reproduction of the social relations of production largely through the correspondence between school and class structure.

Upon the slightest reflection, this assertion is hardly surprising. All major institutions in a 'stable' social system will direct personal development in a direction compatible with its reproduction. Of course, this is not, in itself, a critique of capitalism or of US education. In any conceivable society, individuals are forced to develop their capacities in one direction or another. The idea of a social system which merely allows people to develop freely according to their 'inner natures' is quite unthinkable, since human nature only acquires a concrete form through the interaction of the physical world and pre-established social relationships.

Our critique of education and other aspects of human development in the United States fully recognizes the necessity of some form of socialization. The critical question is: What for? In the United States the human development experience is dominated by an undemocratic, irrational, and exploitative economic structure. Young people have no recourse from the requirements of the system but a life of poverty, dependence, and economic insecurity. Our critique, not surprisingly, centres on the structure of jobs. In the US economy work has become a fact of life to which individuals must by and large submit and over which they have no control. Like the weather, work 'happens' to people. A liberated, participatory, democratic, and creative alternative can hardly be imagined, much less experienced. Work under capitalism is an alienated activity.

To reproduce the social relations of production, the educational system must try to teach people to be properly subordinate and render them sufficiently fragmented in consciousness to preclude their getting together to shape their own material existence. The forms of consciousness and behaviour fostered by the educational system must themselves be alienated, in the sense that they conform neither to the dictates of technology in the struggle with nature, nor to the inherent developmental capacities of individuals, but rather to the needs of the capitalist class. It is the prerogatives of capital and the imperatives of profit, not human capacities and technical realities, which render US schooling what it is. This is our charge.

The Correspondence Principle

> In the social production which men carry on they enter into definite relations which are indispensable and independent of their will; ... The sum total of these relations of production constitutes ... the real foundation on which rise legal and political superstructures, and to which correspond definite forms of social consciousness.
>
> KARL MARX, *Contribution to a Critique of Political Economy*, 1857

The educational system helps integrate youth into the economic system, we believe, through a structural correspondence between its social relations and those of production. The structure of social relations in education not only inures the student to the discipline of the work place, but develops the types of personal demeanour, modes of self-presentation, self-image, and social-class identifications which are the crucial ingredients of job adequacy. Specifically, the social relationships of education – the relationships between administrators and teachers, teachers and students, students and students, and students and their work – replicate the hierarchical division of labour. Hierarchical relations are reflected in the vertical authority lines from administrators to teachers to students. Alienated labour is reflected in the student's lack of control over his or her education, the alienation of the student from the curriculum content, and the motivation of school work through a system of grades and other external rewards rather than the student's integration with either the process (learning) or the outcome (knowledge) of the educational 'production process'. Fragmentation in work is reflected in the institutionalized and often destructive competition among students through continual and ostensibly meritocratic ranking and evaluation. By attuning young people to a set of social relationships similar to those of the work place, schooling attempts to gear the development of personal needs to its requirements.

But the correspondence of schooling with the social relations of production goes beyond this aggregate level. Different levels of education feed workers into different levels within the occupational structure and, correspondingly, tend towards an internal organization comparable to levels in the hierarchical division of labour. As we have seen, the lowest levels in the hierarchy of the enterprise emphasize rule-following, middle levels, dependability, and the capacity to operate without direct and continuous supervision while the higher levels stress the internalization of the norms of the enterprise. Similarly, in education, lower levels (junior and senior high school) tend to severely limit and channel the activities of students. Somewhat higher up the educational ladder, teacher and community colleges allow for more independent activity and less overall supervision. At the top, the elite four-year colleges emphasize social relationships conformable with the higher levels in the production hierarchy.[3] Thus schools continually maintain their hold on students. As they 'master' one type of behavioural regulation, they are either allowed to progress to the next or are channelled into the corresponding level in the hierarchy of production. Even within a single school, the social relationships of different tracks tend to conform to different behavioural norms. Thus in high school, vocational and general tracks emphasize rule-following and close supervision, while the college track tends towards a more open atmosphere emphasizing the internalization of norms.

These differences in the social relationships among and within schools, in part, reflect both the social backgrounds of the student body and their likely future economic positions. Thus blacks and other minorities are concentrated in schools whose repressive, arbitrary, generally chaotic internal order, coercive authority structures, and minimal possibilities for advancement mirror the characteristics of inferior job situations. Similarly, predominantly working-class schools tend to emphasize behavioural control and rule-following, while schools in well-to-do suburbs employ relatively open systems that favour greater student participation, less direct supervision, more student electives, and, in general, a value system stressing internalized standards of control.

The differential socialization patterns of schools attended by students of different social classes do not arise by accident. Rather, they reflect the fact that the educational objectives and expectations of administrators, teachers and parents (as well as the responsiveness of students to various patterns of teaching and control) differ for students of different social classes. At crucial turning points in the history of US education, changes in the social relations of schooling have been dictated in the interests of a more harmonius reproduction of the class structure. But in the day-to-day operation of the schools, the consciousness of different occupational strata, derived from their current milieu and work experience, is crucial to the maintenance of the correspondences we have described. That working-class parents seem to favour stricter educational methods is a reflection of their own work experiences, which have demonstrated that submission to authority is an essential ingredient in one's ability to get and hold a steady, well-paying job. That professionalism and self-employed parents prefer a more open atmosphere and a greater emphasis on motivational control is similarly a reflection of their position in the social division of labour. When given the opportunity, higher-status parents are far more likely than their lower-status neighbours to choose 'open classrooms' for their children.[4]

Differences in the social relationships of schooling are further reinforced by inequalities in financial resources. The paucity of financial support for the education of children from minority groups and low-income families leaves more resources to be devoted to the children of those with more commanding roles in the economy; it also forces upon the teachers and school administrators in the working-class schools a type of social relationship that fairly closely mirrors that of the factory.

NOTES AND REFERENCES

1 Herbert Gintis, 'Welfare Criteria with Endogenous Preferences: The Economics of Education,' *International Economic Review*, June 1974; Alfred Schutz and Thomas Luckmann, *The Structure of the Life-World*, Evanston, Illinois: Northwestern University Press, 1973; and Peter L. Berger and Thomas Luckmann, *The Social Construction of Reality: A Treatise in the Sociology of Knowledge*, Garden City, L.I., N.Y.; Doubleday and Co., 1966.

2 For an extended treatment of these issues, see Herbert Gintis, 'Alienation and Power' in *The Review of Radical Political Economics*, vol. 4, no. 5, Fall 1972.

3 Jeanne Binstock, 'Survival in the American College Industry,' unpublished Ph.D. dissertation, Brandeis University, 1970.

4 Burton Rosenthal, 'Educational Investments in Human Capital: The Significance of Stratification in the Labor Market,' unpublished honors thesis, Harvard University, 1972; and Edgar Z. Friedenberg, *Coming of Age in America*, New York; Random House, 1965.

Working-Class Kids and Working-Class Jobs

Paul Willis

The main emphasis so far has been upon the apparently creative and self-made forms of opposition and cultural style in the school. It is now time to contextualize the counter-school culture. Its points of contact with the wider working class culture are not accidental, nor its style quite independent, nor its cultural skills unique or special. Though the achievements of counter-school culture are specific, they must be set against the larger pattern of working class culture in order for us to understand their true nature and significance. This section is based on fieldwork carried out in the factories where 'the lads' get jobs after leaving school and on interviews with their parents at home.

In particular, counter-school culture has many profound similarities with the culture its members are mostly destined for – shopfloor culture. Though one must always take account of regional and occupational variations, the central thing about the working class culture of the shopfloor is that, despite harsh conditions and external direction, people do look for meaning and impose frameworks. They exercise their abilities and seek enjoyment in activity, even where most controlled by others. Paradoxically, they thread through the dead experience of work a living culture which is far from a simple reflex of defeat. This is the same fundamental taking hold of an alienating situation that one finds in counter-school culture and its attempt to weave a tapestry of interest and diversion through the dry institutional text. These cultures are not simply layers of padding between human beings and unpleasantness. They are appropriations in their own right, exercises of skill, motions, activities applied towards particular ends.

The credentials for entry into shopfloor culture proper, as into the counter-school culture, are far from being merely one of the defeated. They are credentials of skill, dexterity and confidence and, above all, a kind of presence which adds to, more than it subtracts from, a living social force. A force which is *on the move*, not supported, structured and organized by a formal named institution, to which one may apply by written application.

The masculinity and toughness of counter-school culture reflects one of the central locating themes of shopfloor culture – a form of masculine chauvinism. The pin-ups with their enormous soft breasts plastered over hard, oily machinery are examples of a direct sexism but the shopfloor is suffused with masculinity in more generalized and symbolic ways too. Here is a foundryman, Joey's father, talking at home about his work. In an inarticulate way, but perhaps all the more convincingly for that, he attests to that elemental, in our culture essentially masculine, self-esteem of doing a hard job well – and being known for it:

> I work in a foundry ... you know, drop forging ... do you know anything about it ... no ... well you have the factory down in Bethnal St with the noise ... you can hear it in the street ... I work there on the big hammer ... it's a six tonner. I've worked there twenty-four years now. It's bloody noisy, but I've got used to it now ... and it's hot ... I don't get bored ... there's always new lines coming and you have to work out the best way of doing it ... You have to keep going ... and it's heavy work, the managers couldn't do it, there's not many strong enough to keep lifting the metal ... I earn eighty, ninety pounds a week, and that's not bad, is it? ... It ain't easy like ... you can definitely say that I earn every penny of it ... you have to keep it up you know. And the managing director, I'd say 'hello' to him you know, and the progress manager ... they'll come around and I'll go ... 'Alright' [thumbs up] ... and they know you, you know ... a group standing there watching you ... working ... I like that ... there's something there ... watching you like ... working ... like that ... you have to keep going to get enough out.

The distinctive complex of chauvinism, toughness and machismo on the shopfloor is not anachronistic, neither is it bound to die away as the pattern of industrial work changes. Rough, unpleasant, demanding jobs which such attitudes seem most to be associated with still exist in considerable numbers. A whole range of jobs from building work to furnace work to deep-sea fishing still involve a primitive confrontation with exacting physical tasks. The basic attitudes and values most associated with such jobs are anyway still widely current in the general working class culture, and particularly in the culture of the shopfloor. The ubiquity and strength of such attitudes is vastly out of proportion to the number of people actually involved in heavy work. Even in so-called light industries, or in highly mechanized factories where the awkwardness of the physical task has long since been reduced, the metaphoric figures of strength, masculinity and reputation still move beneath the more varied and visible forms of workplace culture. Despite the increasing numbers of women employed, the most fundamental ethos of the factory is still profoundly masculine.

Another main theme of shopfloor culture – at least as I observed and recorded it in the manufacturing industries of the Midlands – is the massive attempt to gain informal control of the work process. Limitation of output or 'systematic soldiering' and 'gold bricking' have been observed from the particular perspective of management from Taylor onwards, but there is evidence now of a much more concerted – though still informal – attempt to gain control. It sometimes happens now that the men themselves to all intents and purposes actually control at least manning and the speed of production. Again this is effectively mirrored for us by working class kids' attempts, with the aid of the resources of their culture, to take control of classes, substitute their own unofficial timetables, and control their own routines and life spaces. Of course the limit to this similarity is that where 'the lads' can escape entirely, 'work' is done in the factory – at least to the extent of the production of the cost of subsistence of the worker – and a certain level of activity is seen as necessary and justified. Here is the father of one of 'the lads', a factory hand on a track producing car engines, talking at home:

> Actually the foreman, the gaffer, don't run the place, the men run the place. See, I mean you get one of the chaps says, 'Alright, you'm on so and so today'. You can't argue with him. The gaffer don't give you the job, they swop each other about, tek it in turns. Ah, but I mean the job's done. If the gaffer had gi'd you the job you would ... They tried to do it one morning, gi'd a chap a job you know, but he'd been on it, you know, I think he'd been on all week, and they just downed tools (...) There's four hard jobs on the track and there's dozens that's ... you know, a child of five could do

it, quite honestly, but everybody has their turn. That's organized by the men.

Shopfloor culture also rests on the same fundamental organizational unit as counter-school culture. The informal group locates and makes possible all its other elements. It is the zone where strategies for wresting control of symbolic and real space from official authority are generated and disseminated. It is the massive presence of this informal organization which most decisively marks off shopfloor culture from middle-class cultures of work.

Amongst workers it is also the basis for extensive bartering, arranging 'foreigners' and 'fiddling'. These are expanded forms of the same thing which take place in school amongst 'the lads'.

The informal group on the shopfloor also shows the same attitude to conformists and informers as do 'the lads'. 'Winning' things is as widespread on the shopfloor as theft is amongst the lads, and is similarly endorsed by implicit informal criteria. Ostracism is the punishment for not maintaining the integrity of the world in which this is possible against the persistent intrusions of the formal. Here is the father of another of 'the lads' on factory life :

A foreman is like, you know what I mean, they're trying to get on, they're trying to get up. They'd cut everybody's throat to get there. You get people like this in the factory. Course these people cop it in the neck off the workers, they do all the tricks under the sun. You know what I mean, they don't like to see anyone crawlin' (. . .) Course instead of taking one pair of glases [from the stores] Jim had two, you see, and a couple of masks and about six pairs o' gloves. Course this Martin was watching and actually two days after we found out that he'd told the foreman see. Had 'im, Jim, in the office about it, the foreman did, and, (. . .) well I mean, his life hasn't been worth living has it? Eh, nobody speaks to him, they won't give him a light, nobody'll give him a light for his fag or nothin' . . . Well, he won't do it again, he won't do it again. I mean he puts his kettle on, on the stove of a morning, so they knock it off, don't they, you know, tek all his water out, put sand in, all this kind of thing (. . .) if he cum to the gaffer, 'Somebody's knocked me water over', or, er, 'They put sand in me cup' and all this business, 'Who is it then?' 'I don't know who it is'. He'll never find out who it is.

The distinctive form of language and highly developed intimidatory humour of the shopfloor is also very reminiscent of counter-school culture. Many verbal exchanges on the shopfloor are not serious or about work activities. They are jokes, or 'pisstakes', or 'kiddings' or 'windups'. There is a real skill in being able to use this language with fluency: to identify the points on which you are being 'kidded' and to have appropriate responses ready in order to avoid further baiting.

This badinage is necessarily difficult to record on tape or re-present, but the highly distinctive ambience it gives to shopfloor exchanges is widely recognized by those involved, and to some extent re-created in their accounts of it. This is another foundry worker, father one of the Hammertown 'lads', talking at home about the atmosphere on his shopfloor:

> Oh, there's all sorts, millions of them [jokes]. 'Want to hear what he said about you', and he never said a thing, you know. Course you know the language, at the work like. 'What you been saying about me?' 'I said nothing.' 'Oh you're a bloody liar', and all this.

Associated with this concrete and expressive verbal humour is a well-developed physical humour: essentially the practical joke. These jokes are vigorous, sharp, sometimes cruel, and often hinged around prime tenets of the culture such as disruption of production or subversion of the boss's authority and status. Here is the man who works in a car engine factory:

> They play jokes on you, blokes knocking the clamps off the boxes, they put paste on the bottom of his hammer you know, soft little thing, puts his hammer down, picks it up, gets a handful of paste, you know, all this. So he comes up and gets a syringe and throws it in the big bucket of paste, and it's about that deep, and it goes right to the bottom, you have to put your hand in and get it out ... This is a filthy trick, but they do it (...) They asked, the gaffers asked X to make the tea. Well it's fifteen years he's been there and they say 'go and make the tea'. He goes up the toilet, he wets in the tea pot, then makes the tea. I mean, you know, this is the truth this is you know. He says, you know, 'I'll piss in it if I mek it, if they've asked me to mek it' (...) so he goes up, wees in the pot, then he puts the tea bag, then he puts the hot water in (...) Y was bad the next morning, one of the

gaffers, 'My stomach isn't half upset this morning'. He told them after and they called him for everything, 'You ain't makin' our tea no more.' He says, 'I know I ain't not now'.

It is also interesting that, as in the counter-school culture, many of the jokes circle around the concept of authority itself and around its informal complement, 'grassing'. The same man:

He [Johnny] says, 'Get a couple of pieces of bread pudding Tony [a new worker] we'll have them with our tea this afternoon' see. The woman gi'd him some in a bag, he says, 'Now put them in your pocket, you won't have to pay for them when you go past, you know, the till' (...) Tony put 'em in his pocket didn't he and walked past with his dinner (...) When we come back out the canteen Johnny was telling everybody that he'd [i.e. Tony] pinched two pieces of bread pudding (...) he told Fred, one of the foremen see, 'cos Fred knows, I mean ... Johnny says, 'I've got to tell you Fred', he says, 'Tony pinched two pieces of bread pudding', I mean serious, the way they look you know (...) he called Johnny for everything, young Tony did: Fred said, 'I want to see you in my office in twenty minutes', straight-faced you know, serious. Oh I mean Johnny, he nearly cried (...) We said, 'It's serious like, you're in trouble, you'll get the sack', you know and all this (...) they never laugh. He says, 'What do you think's gonna happen?' Well what can happen, you'll probably get your cards' (...) 'Oh what am I gonna do, bleeding Smith up there, he's really done me, I'll do him'. I says, 'Blimey, Tony', I says, 'It ain't right, if other people can't get away with it, why should you 'a' to get away with it'. 'Ooh'. Anyway Fred knocked the window, and he says, 'Tell Tony I want him'. He says, 'You've got the sack now Tony', you know. 'Hope I haven't', he says, 'I dunno what I'm gonna do' (...) After they cum out, laughing, I said, 'What did he say to you Tony'. He says, 'He asked me if I pinched two pieces of bread pudding', so I couldn't deny it, I said I had. He says, 'All I want to know is why you didn't bring me two pieces an' all'.

The rejection of school work by 'the lads' and the omnipresent feeling that they know better is also paralleled by a massive feeling on the shopfloor, and in the working class generally, that practice is more important than theory. As a big

205

handwritten sign, borrowed from the back of a matchbox and put up by one of the workers, announces on one shopfloor: 'An ounce of keenness is worth a whole library of certificates'. The shopfloor abounds with apocryphal stories about the idiocy of purely theoretical knowledge. Practical ability always comes first and is a *condition* of other kinds of knowledge. Whereas in middle-class cultures knowledge and qualifications are seen as a way of shifting upwards the whole mode of practical alternatives open to an individual, in working class eyes theory is riveted to particular productive practices. If it cannot earn its keep there, it is to be rejected. This is Spanksy's father talking at home. The fable form underlines the centrality and routinization of this cultural view of 'theory'.

> In Toll End Road there's a garage, and I used to work part-time there and ... there's an elderly fellow there, been a mechanic all his life, and he must have been seventy years of age then. He was an old Hammertown professional, been a professional boxer once, an elderly chap and he was a practical man, he was practical, right? ... and he told me this (...) I was talking to him, was talking about something like this, he says (...) 'This chap was all theory and he sends away for books about everything', and he says, 'Do you know', he says, 'he sent away for a book once and it came in a wooden box, and it's still in that box 'cos he can't open it'. Now that ain't true, is it? But the point is true. That in't true, that didn't happen, but his point is right. He can't get at that box 'cos he don't know how to open the box! Now what's the good of that?

This can be seen as a clear and usually unremarked class function of knowledge. The working-class view would be the rational one were it not located in class society, i.e. that theory is only useful insofar as it really does help to do things, to accomplish practical tasks and change nature. Theory is asked to be in a close dialectic with the material world. For the middle class, more aware of its position in a class society, however, theory is seen partly in its social guise of qualifications as the power to move up the social scale. In this sense theory is well worth having even if it is never applied to nature. It serves its purpose as the *means* to decide precisely which bit of nature one wants to apply it to, or even to choose not to apply it at all. Paradoxically, the working class distrust and rejection of

206

theory comes partly from a kind of recognition, even in the moment that it oppresses, of the hollowness of theory in its social guise.

Even the non-conformists in the high status grammar school in the most exclusive part of the larger conurbation recognize the *social* essence of theory as it is articulated with practice in our society. For them, qualification is choice and mobility in a class society. It is not simply the ability to do the job better. It is this central realization, in fact, which characteristically limits their anti-social feeling:

> Larry:
> ... What I want to do, I want to get me 'A' levels [he had only just finished his 'O' levels and decided to carry on to 'A' level] and then go touring the world, then OK, live it fairly rough for a few years, just dossing around, then I'll carry on, but at least then I've got the choice of whether I want to carry on, whether I want to go back and get a decent job. If you've got qualifications, then you can choose what you want to do: if you want to drop out, or whether you want to carry on being part of the system. But if you haven't got, you know ... if I didn't have the qualifications, I don't know what I'd do, this is all according if I get them, but if I do get them, at least I'll know I'll have a choice of whether I want to get a steady job and you know pension scheme, car, two kids and wife and house mortgage and everything like, or whether I just want to roam the world.

It is, of course, the larger class dimension which gives the working-class counter-school culture its special edge and resonance in terms of style, its particular force of opposition and its importance as an experiential preparation for entry into working-class jobs. Although all forms of institution are likely to breed their own informal accretions, and although all schools of whatever class always create oppositional cultures, it is the crucial conjunction of institutional opposition with a working class context and mode which gives the special character and significance to 'the lads' ' culture. Institutional opposition has a different meaning according to its class location and expression. The non-conformists in the high status grammar school, although sharing similar attitudes to school, know that they are different from the Hammertown lads. They cannot through institutional means alone transcend their class location. Ulti-

207

mately, they have not only a different attitude to qualifications but also an inevitable sense of different social position.

> Larry:
> A lot of kids that you've been talking to [in Hammertown], they'd regard us as poufs, 'cos we go to a grammar school. Not only 'cos we go to a grammar school, but because we're from here in the first place which is regarded as a snob area.

Some of the non-conformist group in the grammar school are, in fact, from working class families. Despite even their origins and anti-school attitude, the lack of a dominant working-glass ethos within their school culture profoundly separates their experience from 'the lads'. It can also lead to artificial attempts to demonstrate solidarity on the street and with street contacts. That the working-class cultural forms of school opposition are creative, specific, borne and reproduced by particular individuals and groups from afresh and in particular contexts – though always within a class mode – is shown by the cultural awkwardness and separation of such lads. The lack of the collective school-based and generated form of the class culture, even despite a working-class background and an inclination to oppositional values, considerably weakens their working-class identity:

> John:
> Kids (...) have casually bracketed me as that [a snob] (...) I live near a school called The Links, and there's a lot of kids there, 'Oh he goes to grammar school. Oh'. Well, my attitude's been, I never want to be called anything like that, I think it's really horrible, so for a start, I've never tried to improve my language. I have these basic things of doing things daft, doing things daft. It's mainly just to make sure that everybody knows that I'm not a typical Percival Jones (...), he's got a really posh accent, 'Old chap', Lady Byron Lane type [indicating a middle class accent] of person, you know, not one of us kind, proud of the school and all that (...) I've said to kids who've really been getting on my nerves, you know, 'I know I'm better than you', you know, but these things when I muck about, that's trying to make sure that everybody knows I'm not.

It could be suggested that what non-conformists in middle-class schools – no matter what their individual origins – are struggling for is some kind of conversion of their institutional opposition into a more resonant working class form. Insofar as they succeed ... so does their future 'suffer'. Insofar as they fail, or insofar as, for instance, conformist working-class boys in a working-class school are insulated from working-class culture, and become free from its processes, so they are likely to 'succeed'.

PART IV

Management and its Relation to Capital and Labour

Introduction

'When we come to the managers,' writes the economic historian Sidney Pollard in his *The Genesis of Modern Management*, '... the figures are missing or unhelpful.'[1] Hobsbawm, too, notes the absence of good figures for the decline in owner-management or the rise of technicians and managers.[2] There are various reasons for the relative paucity of such historical information. But rather more startling has been the lack of attention that many Marxists have paid to politico-theoretical questions to do with management, at least until recently.

Of course, at an ideological level, various sections of the left have often seen it as important to counter the thesis that a so-called 'managerial revolution' has occurred. Typically, the managerialist argument runs that this or that society is no longer capitalist, or, if capitalist, beneficent, or if not capitalist or beneficent, beyond change.[3] In one form or another it has been common to many revisionist initiatives and justifications for reformism. Because of this, with every new generation it has had to be rebutted anew. But in Britain and America in the 1950s and 1960s the 'radical' counter-attack was not pitched at a particularly high theoretical level.[4] Not in hindsight anyway. For at the turn of the 1970s a particular collision took place between British and French Marxism, in the persons of Miliband and Poulantzas.[5] In this, Poulantzas made differences in the mode of analysis of the separation of ownership and control to serve the wider purpose of advancing the cause of an Althusserian-inspired, and highly theoretical, structuralism.

There was, it appeared, a political, indeed tactical, as well as a theoretical edge to what Poulantzas had to say. The gist of this was that Miliband,[6] in his attempt to counter the orthodoxies of bourgeois political science, had allowed himself to fight on the enemy's ground, and with his weapons. Poulantzas held managerialism to be a 'false problem' and considered issues to do with the motives of managers (or capitalists for that matter) to be beside the point. He claimed that Miliband had allowed himself to be unduly influenced by 'the problematic of the subject', that is, one couched in terms of men, their values and inter-personal relations, rather than one couched in terms of 'objective structures' which made men the 'bearers' of deeper social relations. It was thus by a concern to demonstrate that the motivation of conduct of managers was not as the managerialists argued it was, that Miliband had, in the very act of seeking to refute bourgeois ideology, placed himself on its terrain. 'To characterize the class position of managers', Poulantzas argued, 'one need not refer to the motivations of their conduct, but only to their place in production and their relationship to the ownership of the means of production.'

Now just how far Miliband was trapped by the very bourgeois problematic in which the thesis he attacked was inserted, and whether in any case there are good arguments for seeking to discredit or destroy a competing problematic and its facts *before* (even as a *pre-condition to*) theorizing in a different way – these are not matters that can be gone into here.[7] But what can be said is that to the extent Poulantzas' critique, and the much more broadly based theoretical movement from which it stemmed, encouraged Marxists in Britain and America to go back to basics, this has led, among other things, to a deepening of the understanding of the separation of ownership and control beyond that which was current in the 1950s and 1960s. As can be seen from the piece by Michel de Vroey, in the modern Marxist conception the rise of the joint stock company and the separation of ownership and control are once more firmly situated within the contradictory historical process of socialization that the drive towards accumulation generates in the capitalist mode. The evidence assembled by earlier radical-Marxist investigators was not inconsistent with such an understanding, but it rarely amounted to the same thing. For whilst they used such evidence to fight against those who argued that capitalism was dead, it was only rarely that they themselves talked the language of history and of contradiction and adequately conveyed its meaning.[8]

Begin with the idea that science and technology are ideologically neutral; add to this a rather mechanistic interpretation of the thesis that the forces of production, as they develop, stand in ever greater contradiction with capitalist social relations; stir into this the notion that all available manual, technical, professional and intellectual skills – and management as we know it – are to be retained on the road to socialism; then serve up this medley of ideas with an analysis of classes according to which the working class includes pretty well everybody ... Do all this, and as Andre Gorz has said, you are likely to end up with a working class politics 'feared only by the monopolists – and by the proletariat.'[9] But you are also likely, once having thought about the possible existence of such a constellation of ideas, to begin to think about politico-theoretical questions to do with management. The fact is that any adequate theorization of the class location of managers must consider the neutrality or otherwise of the work of co-ordination that they perform and their technical expertise. And it is implicit in the loose set of ideas sketched out already that *productivism* constitutes one important axis around which a unity of theory and practice can form – a theory and practice which is of course sharply crystallized in scientific management, to which we come in Part V (see pages 269–75).

Very shortly some consideration will be given to a non-productivist theorization of the place of managers in the technical division of labour and class relations. One of the readings below also provides a sketch of some of the mechanisms that one writer, Carchedi, sees to be at work in the 'proletarianization' of employees.[10] For the moment, however, it is necessary to specify some of the different relations that are all too easily blurred over by the use of the general occupational category 'manager'.

A useful way of doing this is to distinguish, one, control over investment and resource allocation; two, control over that part of the means of production that is constituted by labour-power; and three, control over the other part of the means of production, physical means of production. The first of these central relations involves a relation of economic ownership as in de Vroey's statement on the separation of ownership and control, the stress is of course on real control, on a substantive social process, not on juridical categories of legal ownership). The second and third control relations – those over labour-power and physical means of production – involve two aspects of a relation of possession.

Now those managers who control investment and resource allocation stand in a dominant place in relations of real economic ownership and are part of the bourgeoisie. On this all Marxists agree. But what of other managers? What of those – the vast majority – who lack a dominant place in relations of economic ownership and yet are engaged in the performance of relations of possession? If we follow Wright,[11] these may be said to occupy a 'contradictory class location' – 'contradictory', that is, between the capitalist class, which is marked by a dominant place in all three processes of class relations, and the proletariat, which is marked by an exclusion from control, again over all three. Wright's larger argument is that it is the contradictory location of class at the economic level which affects the extent to which political and ideological relations act as a determinant of class position. But in fact, although Wright provides a thorough critique of Poulantzas' *Classes in Contemporary Capitalism*,[12] which he charges with inconsistency in the priority that is accorded to the economic, the political and the ideological, he is, in the end, himself inconsistent. And despite some very real limitations to Poulantzas' analysis (his concept of productive labour, for example) there is still something to be learnt from his work in the present context. This is not simply because (as Wright complains), Poulantzas regards managers as part of the bourgeoisie, even when they are excluded from major investment and resource allocation decisions and are only bearers of relations of possession. Rather, it is because of the reasoning that lies behind this.[13]

Central to this reasoning is the assertion that: 'the separation and dispossession of the workers from their means of production, the characteristic of capitalist exploitation, means that *there is no division or co-ordination of tasks that simply corresponds to purely "technical" requirements of "production", and exists as such.*' (My italics.) Poulantzas is quite explicit that foremen and supervisors, for instance, do not have a double class membership (working class and capitalist); implicitly, he denies that they are marked by a contradictory class location either. As Poulantzas sees it, the work of supervision is *simultaneously* the performance of a co-ordinative function and a process by which the capitalist consumes labour-power. Accordingly 'the reason why these agents do not belong to the working class, is ... the dominance of the political relations that they maintain over the aspect of productive labour in the division of labour. Their principal function is that of extracting surplus-value from the workers ... They exercise powers that derive from the place of capital, capital that has seized hold of the 'control function' of the labour process.'[14]

In some ways a similar refusal to isolate the technical from the social is to the fore in the work of Marglin; it is a refusal to abstract the technical division of labour from the social, from class relations; and, in particular, a refusal to abstract the origin of the capitalist workplace from these same class relations. His theme is that 'the key to the success of the factory, as well as its inspiration, was the substitution of capitalists for workers' control of the production process; discipline and supervision could and did reduce costs *without* being technologically superior.' Marglin's historical work echoes with the spirit of the Marx who saw the factory code as 'merely the capitalist caricature of the social regulation of the labour process which becomes necessary in co-operation on a large scale.' (See pages 237–54.)

To argue that the way in which capitalist factories were organized was not (and is not) simply a function of their technical superiority is to unsettle both the defenders of the capitalist faith, who are quite sure that hierarchy is inescapable, and to buttress the resolve of those Marxists who eschew productivism. To be numbered among the latter are probably quite a few of those whose hackles rise at Engels' 'On Authority,' with its deathly line: 'Wanting to abolish authority in large-scale industry is tantamount to wanting to abolish industry itself.'[15] Is it?

NOTES AND REFERENCES

1 Sidney Pollard, *The Genesis of Modern Management*, London, Edward Arnold, 1965, p. 135.
2 E. J. Hobsbawm, *Labouring Men*, p. 309n.
3 For a recent attempt to situate the thesis within the broader

theme of arguments about the 'new middle classes', in terms
of which he claims, with justification, that 'an entire history
of political sociology could be written,' see George Ross,
'Marxism and the new middle classes', *Theory and Society*,
5, 2, March 1978, p. 163. One way to grasp the strength of
certain continuities between early revisionist and modern
reformist thought is to compare Eduard Bernstein, *Evolutionary Socialism*, New York, Schocken Books, 1961 (first
published 1899), and C. A. R. Crosland, *The Future of
Socialism*, London, Jonathan Cape, 1956. For a comparison of various sorts of managerialism – Berle, Burnham,
Dahrendorf, etc., see my *Ownership, Control and Ideology*,
London, Allen and Unwin, 1969, part I.

4 For British examples, see, from the Communist Party, Sam
Aaronovitch, *The Ruling Class*, London, Lawrence and
Wishart, 1961; from the 'New Left', Michael Barratt Brown,
'The Insiders', *Universities and Left Review*, No. 3, 1958
and, 'The Controllers', *Universities and Left Review*, No. 5,
1959. (These were replied to by C. A. R. Crosland in *The
Conservative Enemy*, London, Jonathan Cape, 1962.) For
American examples, see H. M. Gerth and C. Wright Mills,
'A Marx for the Managers', in R. K. Merton, *et al.* (eds)
Reader in Bureaucracy, New York Free Press, 1952; and
D. Villarejo, 'Stock Ownership and the Control of Cor-
porations', *New University Thought*, Chicago, Autumn
1961 and Winter 1962.

5 See John Urry and John Wakeford (eds), *Power in Britain*
London, Heinemann, 1973, chaps. 24 and 25.

6 The occasion for Poulantzas' attack had been the publi
cation of Ralph Miliband's, *The State in Capitalist Society*
London, Weidenfeld and Nicolson, 1969. His review, firs
published in *New Left Review* 58, 1969, followed up a mor
general critique in 'Marxist Political Theory in Grea
Britain,' *New Left Review*, 43.

7 Part of the problem is of course that Poulantzas makes :
seemingly total separation between ideological and theoreti
cal work. Another is that, despite the clatter of his attack
he is careful to say that Miliband has been (only) 'undul'
influenced' by a bourgeois problematic. He has a goo
point, but it is easy to exaggerate the differences. Conside
this: 'What matters are the constraints imposed upon thos
involved by the imperative and objectively determined re
quirements of capitalist activity' (from Miliband's lates

consideration of the separation of ownership and control, in *Marxism and Politics*, Oxford, Oxford University Press, 1977, p. 27).

8 For the most extensive review of writing in this area, see M. Zeitlin, 'Corporate Ownership and Control: the Large Corporation and the Capitalist Class', *American Journal of Sociology*, 79, 5, 1974. For an interesting Russian view of America, see S. Menshikov, *Millionaires and Managers*, Moscow, Progress Publishers, 1969.

9 Andre Gorz, 'Technology, Technicians and Class Struggle' in Gorz (ed.) *The Division of Labour*, pp. 159–60.

10 For a critique of Carchedi's theoretical analysis, see Anthony Cutler *et al.*, *Marx's Capital and Capitalism Today*, London, Routledge and Kegan Paul, 1977, vol. 1, pp. 301–3; and on management, p. 303–12. For a descriptive analysis of the forces acting on managers and foremen in one company, see *Living with Capitalism*, chaps 3, 4 and 5.

11 Erik Olin Wright, 'Contradictory Class Locations', *New Left Review*, 98, July 1976.

12 Nicos Poulantzas, *Classes in Contemporary Capitalism*, London, New Left Books, 1975.

13 For an attempt at a fuller exposition of Poulantzas, see Theo Nichols, 'Social Class: Official, Sociological and Marxist', in J. Evans, J. Irvine, I. Miles (eds), *Demystifying Social Statistics*, London, Pluto, 1979. As to whether Wright's complaint against Poulantzas is justified, see *Classes in Contemporary Capitalism*, p. 229.

14 For the above quotations from Poulantzas (which have a direct bearing on what some of his critics call his 'politicization' of relations of production), see ibid., pp. 226–9.

15 Cited by Marglin in 'What Do Bosses Do?', *Review of Radical Political Economics*, 6, 2, Summer 1974, p. 33. Engels was, of course, amongst other things, an employer.

6 Managers and Class Relations

A Marxist View of Ownership and Control

Michel de Vroey

INTRODUCTION

The idea of a separation of ownership and control in large corporations is widely accepted among economists. Its paternity is usually attributed to Berle and Means whose classical work, *The Modern Corporation and Private Property* [5] appeared in 1932. As Nichols states, this book was

> the first attempt to provide detailed empirical data about stock ownership in order to substantiate the claims that shareholders were becoming less influential in the conduct of corporation affairs and that the 'control' function of ownership is being superseded by that of management. [44, p. 14]

The importance of the idea of a divorce of control from ownership can be properly understood only if placed in a larger context which takes into consideration the alleged consequences of the phenomenon. Indeed, according to the managerial writers,[1] this divorce has radically modified the working of the capitalist system and has thereby constituted one of the major changes in the economic institutions of the twentieth century.

The separation of ownership and control is also often used by bourgeois economists as an attack against Marxism, by which they hope to refute what is often presented as its core, i.e. the assertion of a contradiction in capitalism between the private property of the means of production and the socialization of productive forces. To quote Nichols again, 'most managerialists have assumed that property is the cause of conflict

218

and that it therefore follows that the interests of (non-propertied) managers are not in conflict with those of employees' [44, p. 46]. Insofar as ownership has simply become a 'legal fiction', to borrow the expression of the well-known sociologist Daniel Bell [4, p. 21], the bases of conflicts of interests in capitalist society would thus be suppressed. This ideological utilization of the thesis of a separation of ownership and control is well demonstrated by Sweezy in his criticism of Gailbraith's book, *Economics and the Public Purpose*:

> In that case, control over the key sector of the economy has slipped out of the grip of the owning or capitalist class into the relatively weak hands of a new technocratic stratum. And this same stratum is also supposed to have gained control over the state. According to this view, the task of the reformer has been vastly simplified and eased compared to what it used to be. No more need for class struggle or related unpleasantness. Just enlighten the public, emancipate the state, and downgrade the technostructure to its proper subordinate role. [55, p. 5]

The aim of this article is to expound what Marxist theory has said on the subject of the separation of ownership and control.[2] More specifically, it will argue that, paradoxically enough, the idea of this separation has been originally put forward by Marx himself who could thus be considered as its true founder. Consequently, Berle and Means' originality simply consisted in presenting the first systematic empirical description of the phenomenon.[3] Of course, if Marx perceived the incipient occurrence of this separation, the place that he attributed to it and its assigned impact upon the general evolution of capitalism were quite different from those which are currently attributed to it as a consequence of the Berle and Means managerialist interpretation. In a first section, I will expose what I understand to be the Marxist interpretation of the separation of ownership and control. A second section will deal with the differences in approach between the managerialist and the Marxist views. . . .

I. THE MARXIST VIEW

Marx's treatment of the separation of ownership and control is to be found in Book III of *Capital*, especially in chapter 23 ('Interest and Profit of Enterprise') and in chapter 27 ('The Role of Credit in Capitalist Production'). Therein he distinguishes two functions or roles played by capitalists: firstly, the contribution of funds, which is the role performed by the 'money-capitalist' and, secondly, their utilization in the process of production by the 'industrial capitalist':

In Marx's words,

> the employer of capital, even when working with his own capital, splits into two personalities – the owner of capital and the employer of capital; with reference to the categories of profit which it yields, his capital also splits into capital-*property*, capital *outside* the production process, and yielding interest of itself, and capital *in* the production process, which yield a profit of enterprise through its function. [38, book III, part 5, chap. 23, p. 375]

If the industrial or functioning capitalist is also the owner of the funds put into operation, he pockets the whole surplus-value produced. On the contrary, if he is not the owner of these funds but rather a borrower, surplus-value will be divided into interest paid to the owner/lender of the money capital and into profit of enterprise. From the point of view of the individual capitalist, these two categories of revenue are seen as antithetical. However, from the point of view of capital as a whole (which is the only correct viewpoint in the analysis of the production of surplus-value), 'both are merely parts of the surplus-value and this division (into interest and profit of enterprise) alters nothing in the nature, origin and way of existence of surplus-value.' [38, book III, part 5, chap. 23, p. 380]

Even if these two roles are actually performed by the same person – Marx underlines – they still must be analytically distinguished in order to grasp the dual function performed by capital.

We must proceed from the assumption that the money capitalist and industrial capitalist really confront one another not just as legally different persons, but as persons playing entirely different roles in the production process, or as persons in whose hands the same capital really performs a two-fold and wholly different movement. The one only merely loans it, the other employs it productively. [38, book III, part 5, chap. 23, p. 372]

However for Marx the historical trend is that these functions, which at the rise of capitalism were often performed by the same person, tend to become separated with the development of the capitalist mode of production. In Marx's terms:

Stock companies in general – developed with the credit system – have an increasing tendency to separate this work of management as a function from the ownership of capital, be it self-owned or borrowed [...]. The mere manager who has no title whatever to the capital, whether through borrowing it or otherwise, performs all the real functions pertaining to the functioning capitalist as such, only the functionary remains and the capitalist disappears as superfluous from the production process. [38, book III, part 5, chap. 23, pp. 387–8]

When the two functions are completely separated, profit assumes the pure form of interest. Thus,

even if the dividend which they (the owners of capital) receive includes the interest and the profit of enterprise, i.e., the total profit (for the salary of the manager is, or should be, simply the wage of a specific type of skilled labour, whose price is regulated in the labour-market like that of any other labour), this total profit is henceforth received only in the form of interest, i.e., as mere compensation for owning capital that now is entirely divorced from the function in the actual process of reproduction, just as this function in the person of the manager is divorced from the ownership of capital. Profit thus appears [...] as a mere appropriation of the surplus-labour of others, arising from the conversion of means of production into capital. [38, book III, part 5, chap. 27, pp. 436–7]

This functional differentiation is thus linked with the emergence of joint-stock companies as a new form of ownership. But this emergence itself must be understood as a manifestation and a stage of the process of socialization of capitalist production. It permitted the passage from individual capitalist ownership to socialized capitalist ownership.

As the French Marxist Delilez writes:

> since the triumphant period of capitalism, the corporation was the means to overcome (of course, only partially) the contradictions between the socialization of production (and concomitantly the necessarily growing amount of capital needed) and the individual detention of funds. The individual capital could no longer 'contain' the ever-increasing social character of production. [16, p. 95]

In Marx's words:

> the capital which in itself rests on a social mode of production and presupposes a social concentration of means of production and labour-power, is here directly endowed with the form of social capital (capital of directly associated individuals) as distinct from private capital, and its undertakings assume the form of social undertakings as distinct from private undertakings. It is the abolition of capital as private property within the framework of capitalist production itself. [38, book III, part 5, chap. 27, p. 436]

Thus Marx himself anticipated the occurrence of a functional differentiation between ownership and management. The socialization process however, accelerated by the formation of joint-stock companies, brought about other aspects which were not pointed out directly by Marx, but by later Marxists, especially R. Hilferding, the author of *Das Finanz Kapital*, which appeared in 1910. [33] Hilferding chiefly emphasized another consequence of the emergence of stock-companies, namely the dispersion of stock. But his interpretation of the latter phenomenon was quite different from that which was later developed by managerialists, according to which the dispersion of stock would ultimately lead to a dispersion of power. Indeed Hilferding's contention is that the corporate system has brought about an actual concentration of power, paralleling the dispersion of shareownership. In his view, the corporate system allows an increase of the power sphere of big capitalists who now control larger economic units with a reduced proportion of legal ownership.

> With the extension of the shares system, the capitalist ownership is increasingly transformed into a restricted ownership, giving nominal rights to the capitalist without allowing possibility to exert any real influence on the production process [...]. The ownership of a great number of capitalists is constantly being restricted and their unlimited disposition of the productive process is suppressed. But, on the other hand, the circle of masters of production becomes more restricted. Capitalists form a society in the governing of which most of them have no voice. The effective disposition of the means of production is in the hands of people who have only partially contributed to it. [33, p. 190]

The emergence of the joint-stock companies has thus generated two lines of phenomena, firstly a functional differentiation between ownership and management and secondly, a dispersion of shareownership among the public, going alongside with a concentration of power into the hands of big stockholders. Now these two aspects can be considered in a more analytical way by pointing out some conceptual distinctions which lie at their roots. Although they are quite simple, they permit the avoidance of confusions in which managerialism has fallen. They are described by the French Marxist economist Bettelheim in his book *Calcul économique et forme de propriété.*[6] According to him, three levels should be distinguished: possession, ownership as a relation of production or economic ownership[7] and, finally, legal ownership. The first concept designates the ability to put the means of production to work. It thus pertains to the management of capitalist factories.[8] The second, 'ownership as a relation of production consists of the power to assign the objects on which it bears (especially the means of production) to specific uses and to dispose of the products obtained through these means of production.' [8, p. 58]

Ownership as a relation of production must be distinguished from legal ownership, although they are linked. Indeed the power of assignment and disposition rests on the control of the voting system, to which legal ownership entitles participation. It thus depends upon the holding of an amount of legal ownership large enough to avoid a defeat at stockholders' meetings.

But of course, legal ownership does not automatically imply this power of assignment and disposition.

The two lines of evolution, flowing from the process of socialization of production and described above, can now be restated in terms of Bettelheim's distinctions. It then appears that *the concept of separation of ownership and control contains a twofold dimension*. In a first aspect, it refers to *the separation of ownership and management*, the functional differentiation pointed out by Marx himself. To translate this in Bettelheim's terminology, it is a separation between the agents holding actual 'possession' and those holding 'ownership as a relation of production' (or 'economic ownership'). As stressed by Marx, this functional differentiation itself flows from the distinction between capital as property and functioning capital. In a second aspect, particularly pointed out by Hilferding, the idea of a separation of ownership and control refers to a different reality, namely the dispersion of stock and the consequent split between small and big owners. In Bettelheim's terminology, this second aspect points to a *disassociation between legal ownership and ownership as a relation of production*. Here the Marxist interpretation is that there is a dispersion of legal ownership but not of economic ownership.

It should be noticed that the two aspects do not necessarily occur in parallel. For example, one may conceive of a corporation whose main stockholder is a family owning 10 per cent of the total stock, with the remaining stock widely dispersed among small holders. If this family is active in management, the case exhibits a high degree of stock dispersion but no separation of ownership and management. And, of course, the opposite situation is also very conceivable. This would be the case where there is very little dispersion of stock but at the same time no participation of the chief owners in management. It is therefore very important to distinguish these two aspects, as will appear below.

II. THE DIFFERENCES IN APPROACH BETWEEN MARXISM AND MANAGERIALISM

Having thus far described the Marxist view about ownership and control, the next task is to point out the differences between this view and its managerialist counterpart. Three points will be especially stressed: the impact of a separation of ownership and control, the methodology used in the two approaches and their interpretation of empirical studies. They will be examined in turn.

A. Differences Concerning the Impact of a Separation of Ownership and Control

The Marxist view on this is very clear. A separation of ownership and control, in the twofold meaning of the concept explained above, in no way alters the fundamental dynamics of the capitalist mode of production. Marx's view was rather that it renders exploitation more evident since it helps to avoid a confusion between profits and the owner's salary as a manager.

> With the development of co-operation on the part of the labourers, and of stock enterprises on the part of the bourgeoisie, even the last pretext for the confusion of profit of enterprise and wages of management was removed, and profit appeared also in practice as it undeniably appeared in theory, as mere surplus-value, a value for which no equivalent was paid, as realised unpaid labour. [38, book III, part 5, chap. 23]

The lack of impact can be demonstrated for each of both aspects of the separation of ownership and control. Concerning the first one, i.e. the separation of ownership and management, the Marxist assertion is that it indicates only a change in the forms in which the system is operating. In other words, it only refers to the question of whether the bourgeoisie itself does the job of making capital function or whether this is done through a delegation of power. If this is the case, then we may speak of a separation of ownership and management, understood as a functional differentiation and nothing more. As Sweezy said, one should not confuse

> making decisions within a given frame and deciding what goals are imposed by this frame on those operating within it [...]. The ultimate purpose of enterprise is determined not by any individual or group but by the very nature of the business system, or, as Marxists would say, the nature of capital as self-expanding value. [55, p. 4]

Concerning the second aspect of the separation of ownership

C.L.—H

and control, i.e. the dissociation between legal ownership and ownership as a relation of production, the Marxist interpretation is as follows: the dispersion of stock among a large number of small owners is accepted as a matter of fact, and explained as a means to mobilize the ever-increasing amount of capital needed for accumulation. But rather than seeing the dispersion of stock as an obstacle to concentrated control, Marxism interprets it in exactly the opposite way: as a means for reinforcing the actual control of big stockholders, who thus succeed in commanding an amount of funds out of proportion to their actual ownership. Paradoxically, dispersion of stock thus favours the centralization of capital. As stated by Gilbert,

> the greater the number of shareholders and the smaller the size of the average shareholding, that is the greater the degree of dispersion and fragmentation of share ownership, the smaller is the proportion of the entire voting stock which is in practice needed to exercise effective control. [26, p. 17]

In other words, Marxists assert the lasting existence of the bourgeoisie as a social class. It collectively holds shares of corporate ownership sufficiently concentrated to permit it to monopolize the power of assignment and disposition of the means of production and to use this power for its specific class interests, i.e. to produce and realize surplus-value.

Factual grounds for this affirmation can be found, at least in a first approximation, in studies of the distribution of wealth. In the USA, according to Smith and Franklin [53], 1 per cent of the households owned 51 per cent of corporate stock in 1969. In the UK, according to Glyn and Sutcliffe [27, p. 53], 0·4 per cent of the adult population held 68 per cent of total value of shares on the average during 1964–69. In France, in 1970, 0·8 per cent of the households declared 24 per cent of the incomes derived from stockholdings [51, p. 42] In Belgium, in 1964, 49 per cent of the corporate wealth was owned by 0·5 per cent of the taxpayers. [22] Despite their crudeness, these figures provide a first indication about the contours of the bourgeoisie as a social class and about the division of capitalist societies into classes, since, in the Marxist view, economic ownership of the means of production is the fundamental basis for this division.[9]

Thus Marxism asserts that the separation of ownership

and control does not alter the inner nature of capitalism. Rather, this should be looked for within the sphere of production itself, with its double transformation process: that of the labour-force into a commodity and that of the means of production into capital. As Yaffe states, capitalism is primarily capital production, this being 'the production of surplus-value as additional exchange-value.' [59, p. 7] As long as this process subsists, as well as the class relationships in which it is embodied, the capitalist mode of production continues to exist. However morphological changes, like the separation of ownership and management and the dissociation between legal ownership and economic ownership, should not therefore be considered as mere accidents. On the contrary. Let us repeat that they are themselves the consequences of capitalist accumulation and that they evolve precisely in such a way as to make possible the further development of the capitalist mode of production. They express the ever-increasing socialization of capital or, in other words, its depersonalization.

> The progressive *depersonalization* of property brought about by the development of the great modern 'limited liability' company, implied the emergence as a *subject* of the *object* of property itself, i.e. the complete emancipation of property from man himself, with the result that the firm seemed to acquire an independent life of its own as though it were nobody's property [Coletti, (13), p. 98]

The managerialist view of course takes quite another stand, since its main contention is precisely that the separation of ownership and control has led to a qualitative change in the capitalist system. Thus, according to this view (which, with Burnham's 'Managerial Revolution' and Berle and Means' *The Modern Corporation and Private Property* emerged more than half a century after Marx's writings on the subject), the government of corporations by bureaucrats is more than a functional differentiation – it marks the end of the capitalist system. However this conclusion is arrived at through defective reasoning. Indeed managerialist writers tend to define capitalism in terms of one basic feature, namely the prevalent form of ownership. Capitalism is then associated with a private ownership system. For example, Dahrendorf argues that the term 'capitalist' is only applicable when the legal owner of the factory is at the same time the practical manager and the supreme commander of his workers. [14, p. 40] This rather narrow definition (which hardly corresponds with the Marxist view, although managerialists would often pretend the opposite) makes the reasoning tautological. Indeed if an economic system is defined only by its type of ownership, then a change in the latter leads *ex definitio* to a change of the system.

B. Methodological Differences

If the two views oppose each other on the impact of the evolution of capitalist ownership structure, this is because they radically differ in the way in which they approach the study of capitalism. The categories which they use, and the levels of abstraction in which they evolve, are quite different. In the eyes of Marxism, managerialism is just a specimen of bourgeois science, since the fundamental criticism, which it deserves, is that it 'remains in the estranged outward appearance of economic relations'. This will be demonstrated in respect to two specific points.

The first one concerns the unit of analysis at the basis of managerialist studies. They consider only what happens to individual firms. From the Marxist point of view, this is quite clearly a mistaken approach for grasping capitalist reality in its essence. Rather, the analysis of the capitalist mode of production must start from social aggregates. As said by Yaffe, commenting on Marx's *Grundrisse*,

> In order to develop the concept of capital it was first of all necessary to abstract from many capitals or the action of capitals on one another through competition. The latter would be analyzed after the consideration of what they (many capitals) have in common, as *capital* [...]. The analysis of 'capital in general' is still the starting point of any analysis of contemporary capitalism. [53, pp. 9, 10]

Thus, in its highest level of abstraction, Marxism proceeds on the assumption that there is but one unity of capital, called by Marx 'capital in general' or 'the capital of the whole society'. The consideration of separated units of capital, in competition one with each other, comes only at a second level of abstraction as a specification of the first. The question of the creation and realization of surplus-value must be considered at the first level, disentangled from that of the division of surplus-value into its components and of the appropriation of the surplus-value among individual units of capital. Hence, while the individual firm may apparently be the *unit of decision* in the capitalist economy, in Marxist methodology it cannot be used as *the unit of analysis*.[10]

A second criticism, linked to the preceding one and even more striking, is that the managerialist analysis is always pursued in terms of people's motivations. The conduct of corporations seems then to depend mainly upon the goals of their heads. Indeed it is because one assumes that the manager's objectives differ from those of the owners that a change of the goals of the system is inferred from the shift in persons. Even though the plausibility of this difference in orientation is empirically subject to heavy doubt,[11] more fundamentally it is the crucial role attributed to motivations in the analysis which is liable to criticism. In opposition to the managerialist approach, the Marxist analysis does not focus on individual actors. Rather, it considers them as personifications or supports of social relationships. As Marx wrote in his Preface to the first German edition of *Capital*, 'individuals are dealt with only insofar as they are the personifications of economic categories, embodiments of particular class-relations and class-interests.' [38, p. 10] While managerialists just ask the question 'who (which individual) rules the corporations?', Marxists' main question is: 'For which class interests are the corporations ruled?' Here, one questions the logic of the actions, and this logic goes beyond motivations, being inherent to the mode of production and the place of the individuals within it. (cf. Godelier [28] and Poulantzas [48])

C. Differences in Interpretations of Empirical Reality

One could imagine that, despite the above depicted differences, the two views could still be in agreement on the occurrence of the phenomenon. However this is not the case, as will be demonstrated.

In the first place it should be noticed that only a small number of empirical studies have been made with the aim of measuring the separation of ownership and control.[12] Although some original work on the subject has been done by Marxist writers (Perlo [47] and Menshikov [40]), the most-known and almost exclusively quoted studies were made either with a purely descriptive purpose or within a managerialist framework.[13] Their investigation consisted in examining, corporation by corporation, the proportion of total stock held by the main owner or nucleus of main owners. As soon as this proportion was less than a certain percentage (generally 10 per cent) the conclusion was that the corporation was under management control; thus an overall conclusion was that in 1963, 88·5 per cent of the 200 largest non-financial US corporations were under management control. (Larner [34])

No detailed criticism of these studies will be provided here[14] in order to concentrate the analysis on the fundamental weaknesses which nearly all of them share. Their first defect is their lack of distinction between the two aspects composing the phenomenon of separation of ownership and control. As pointed out earlier, the same notion covers two quite different realities, a separation of ownership and management, on the one hand, and a dissociation between legal property and economic property, on the other. Now by a sort of intellectual myopia, managerialists have always overlooked this, and speak indifferently of a separation of ownership and control or of a managerial revolution (see, for example, Larner's often-quoted articles [34]). What we face here is more than a confusion of vocabulary. It is a theoretical weakness which leads to unfortunate consequences in empirical testing. Indeed, managerialist writers limit themselves to the empirical examination of one aspect of the phenomenon while pretending however to verify the entire phenomenon. In fact, these studies investigate only the degree of dissociation between legal ownership and economic ownership.[15] Furthermore, in a Marxist perspective, these studies are also defective even in regard to the measurement of this dissociation. Indeed what they really examine is whether there still exists an individual private ownership or, in other words, whether the take-over from individual capitalist ownership towards socialized capitalist ownership has extensively occurred. Of course, they find a drastic diminution of the first type of ownership. This is, however, not very original and was already alleged by Marx one century ago, as said above. Thus, the managerialist studies are only able to confirm the most evident part of Marx's affirmations, about the evolution of the forms of ownership, namely that individual private property is progressively becoming an exception. There is a deep discrepancy between what they actually measure and the conclusions which they pretend to derive from this measurement, and hence the assertion, often made, that these studies have verified a separation of ownership and control or a managerial revolution, is completely illegitimate.

Only a few Marxists, like Perlo [47] and Menshikov [40], or radical authors, like Villarejo [58], have made empirical research based upon the assumption of a coalition among big owners and aiming at assessing the existence of a concentrated collective economic ownership. And indeed, when the problem is framed in this way, the investigations lead to conclusions which confirm the Marxist view of concentration of ownership.

What comes out of the examination of the managerialist empirical studies is that they actually focus on only a small aspect of the whole problem with which they pretend to deal. Therefore they can in no way be considered as a refutation of the Marxist view. The conclusion of our investigation is thus paradoxical. At the intellectual level and when the Marxist view is properly understood, managerialism fails entirely in its attack against Marxism. It is illegitimate to affirm that the separation of ownership and control has changed the nature of capitalism and has rendered the Marxist analytical framework obsolete. However, at the ideological level, the confrontation has resulted in another outcome, since the managerialist interpretation has nevertheless pervaded most parts of the American culture. Despite its radical origin and its consistency with the Marxist paradigm, the use of the concept of separation of ownership and control has been almost entirely left over to managerialists and has thus been deformed into an anti-Marxist ideological instrument.

NOTES

1 I call managerialists all those writers who base their analysis of the corporate system upon the premise that there has been a shift in power in large corporations from owners to managers. Hence, people as different in other regards as Berle and Means, Crossland, Mason, Kaysen, Dahrendorf, Galbraith, Marris, Williamson, etc., can be labelled as managerialists.

2 It is *not* the aim of this article to present a detailed analysis of the managerialist theory itself.

3 Other writers who have presented the idea of separation of ownership and control prior to Berle and Means, are Veb-

len, Tawney, and Marshall. Cf. Child ([11], p. 37).

4 This was also the view held by a Revisionist Marxist like Bernstein. Cf. Colletti's study 'Bernstein and the Marxism of the Second International' [13].

5 More recently, a similar view is put forward by Mandel: 'the corporation is a veiled form of expropriation of small investors, not to the profit of an anonymous might but to the profit of the big capitalists, who thus succeed in commanding an enormous amount of funds going far beyond their own ownership' ([37], vol. 2, p. 100).

6 They have also been taken over by Poulantzas in his book *Political Power and Social Classes* [49]. See also his article 'The Problem of the Capitalist State' reprinted in [48].

7 Henceforth both terms will be used indistinctively.

8 For further developments on the notion of possession in its articulation with the process of production, cf. Poulantzas ([50], pp. 132–40).

9 For further elaboration of the delineation of the ruling class, cf. Mills [42], Domhoff [20], [21] and D. Nichols [43]. For more theoretical considerations see Poulantzas [48] and [50].

10 Unfortunately, this Marxist principle, that the analysis of the capitalist mode of production would be made in terms of social aggregates, has sometimes been lost sight of even by people who claim to be Marxists, as witnessed in the recent debate about finance capital.

11 Cf. Miliband [41] and Nichols [44].

12 I am speaking here only of studies focusing on the *measurement* of the separation, and not of those examining the behavioural effects of a separation. For a general consideration of the latter, see de Alessi [15].

13 The studies focusing on the American situation are the following ones: Berle and Means [5], TNEC [57], Villajero [58], Larner [34], Chevalier [9], [10], Sheehan [52], Burch [8]. They are individually reviewed in De Vroey [18]. Other valuable information can be found in studies whose main object was different from the separation of ownership and control. The 'Patman Report' [56] should especially be mentioned in this regard.

14 Cf. de Vroey, [18], Beed [3] and Zeitlin [60].

15 The other aspect of the evolution of the ownership structure, i.e. the separation of ownership and management, has rarely been examined in a global and systematic manner.

A Marxist View of Ownership and Control

Two exceptions are Gordon's work [30] and de Vroey's [17] and [19]. A certain number of studies exist which investigate decision-making within corporations, but they are of little help in getting a general picture of the distribution of functions between big owners and managers. Some of these studies, as Bower's 'Managing the Resource Allocation Process' [7], constitute a systematic and in-depth study at a micro-level, but are confined to individual cases. Others deal more with leadership style as Heller's 'Managerial Decision-Making' [31]. Finally, some provide information about the working of Boards of Directors but without distinguishing clearly the ownership status of Directors and without sufficiently describing the sample on which they are based, as Mace's 'Directors: Myth and Reality' [36].

REFERENCES

[1] Atkinson, A. B. 1973. *Wealth, Income and Inequality*, London, Penguin Modern Economic Reading.
[2] Baran, P. and Sweezy, P. M. 1966. *Monopoly Capital*, New York, Monthly Review Press.
[3] Beed, C. S. 1966. 'The Separation of Ownership from Control', *Journal of Economic Studies*, pp. 29–46. Reprinted in Michael Gilbert (ed.), *The Modern Business Enterprise*, London, Penguin Books, 1972.
[4] Bell, D. 1971. 'The Corporation and Society in the 1970's', *The Public Interest*, 24, Summer.
[5] Berle, A. A. and Means, G. 1967. *The Modern Corporation and Private Property*, New York, Macmillan (revised edition).
[6] Bettelheim, C. 1970. *Calcul économique et formes de propriété*, Paris, Maspero.
[7] Bower, J. 1972. *Managerial Revolution Reassessed*, Lexington, Mass., Heath.
[8] Burch, P. H. Jr. 1969, *A Post-1960 Appraisal of the Extent of Managerial versus Family Control of Most of America's Large Corporations*, unpublished.
[9] Chevalier, J. M. 1969. 'The Problem of Control in Large American Corporations', *Antitrust Bulletin*, Spring.
[10] Chevalier, J. M. 1970. *La structure financière de l'industrie américaine et le problème du contrôle dans les*

grandes sociétés américaines, Paris, Cujas.

[11] Child, J. 1969. *The Business Enterprise in Modern Industrial Society*, London, Collier-Macmillan.

[12] Child, J. 1969. *British Management Thought – A Critical Analysis*, London, Allen and Unwin.

[13] Colletti, L. 1972. *From Rousseau to Lenin, Studies in Ideology and Society*, London, New Left Books.

[14] Dahrendorf, R. 1959. *Class and Class Conflict in Modern Society*, London, Routledge and Kegan Paul.

[15] de Alessi, L. 1973. 'Private Property and Dispersion of Ownership in Large Corporations', *Journal of Finance*, vol. 28, no. 4, September.

[16] Delilez, P. J. 1970. *Les monopoles. Essai sur le capital financier et l'accumulation monopolistique*, Paris, Editions Sociales.

[17] de Vroey, M. 1973. *Propriété et pouvoir dans les grandes entreprises*, Bruxelles, CRISP.

[18] de Vroey, M. 'The Separation of Ownership and Control in Large Corporations: a Critical Review', *Antitrust, Law and Economic Review* (forthcoming).

[19] de Vroey, M. 'The Owner's Interventions in Decision-Making in Large Corporations. A New Approach', *European Economic Review* (forthcoming).

[20] Domhoff, G. W. 1967. *Who Rules America?*, New Jersey, Prentice Hall.

[21] Domhoff, G. W. 1971. *The Higher Circles*, New York.

[22] Duvivier, P. 1972. 'La répartition de la fortune mobilière en Belgique', *Courrier Hebdomadaire du CRISP*, Bruxelles, no. 561, May.

[23] Fitch, R. and Oppenheimer, M. 1970. 'Who Rules the Corporations?', *Socialist Revolution*, vol. I, no. 4, pp. 73–108; no. 5, pp. 61–114; no. 6, pp. 33–94.

[24] Fitch, R. 1971. 'Reply to James O'Connor', *Socialist Revolution*, vol. II, no. 7, Jan.–Feb.

[25] Fitch, R. 1972. 'Sweezy and Corporate Fetishism', *Socialist Revolution*, vol. II, no. 12, Nov.–Dec. pp. 93–127.

[26] Gilbert, M. (ed.). 1972. *The Modern Business Enterprise*, London, Penguin.

[27] Glyn, A. and Sutcliffe, B. 1972. *British Capitalism, Workers and the Profit Squeeze*, London, Penguin Books.

[28] Godelier, M. 1973. *Rationality and Irrationality in Economics*, London, New Left Books.

[29] Gogel, R., Koenig, T., Sonquist, J. 1974. *Who Rules the*

Corporations? Paper delivered at the Pacific Sociological Association, Annual Meeting, March.

[30] Gordon, R. A. 1961. *Business Leadership in the Large Corporation*, Berkeley, University of California Press (second edition with a new preface).

[31] Heller, F. A. 1971. *Managerial Decision-Making*, London, Tavistock.

[32] Herman, E. 1973. 'Do Bankers Control Corporations?', *Monthly Review*, June.

[33] Hilferding, R. 1970. *Le capital financier*, Paris, Editions de Minuit.

[34] Larner, R. J. 1966. 'Ownership and Control in the 200 Largest Nonfinancial Corporations 1929 and 1963', *American Economic Review*, September, pp. 777–87.

[35] Lenin, V. I. 1933. *Imperialism*. New York, International Publishers.

[36] Mace, M. L. 1971. *Directors: Myth and Reality*, Boston, Harvard Graduate School of Business Administration.

[37] Mandel, E. 1962. *Traité d'économie marxiste*, Paris, Collection 10/18, 4 vol.

[38] Marx, K. 1967. *Capital*, New York, International Publishers, 3 vol.

[39] Meek, R. L. 1967. 'Karl Marx's Economic Method' in *Economics and Ideology and Other Essays*, London, Chapman and Hall.

[40] Menshikov, S. 1969. *Millionaires and Managers*, Moscow.

[41] Miliband, R. 1969. *The State in Capitalist Society*, New York, Basic Books.

[42] Mills, C. W. 1956. *The Power Elite*, New York, Oxford University Press.

[43] Nichols, D. Autumn 1972. 'Ruling Class as a Scientific Concept'. *Review of Radical Political Economics*, vol. IV. no. 5.

[44] Nichols, T. 1969. *Ownership, Control and Ideology*, London, Allen and Unwin.

[45] O'Connor, J. January-February 1971. 'Question: Who Rules the Corporations? Answer: The Ruling Class', *Socialist Revolution*, no. 7, vol. II, pp. 117–48.

[46] Palmer, J. 1972. 'The Separation of Ownership from Control in Large U.S. Industrial Corporations', *Quarterly Review of Economics and Business*, vol. 12, no. 3.

[47] Perlo, V. 1957. *The Empire of High Finance*, New York, International Publishers.

[48] Poulantzas, N. 1972. 'The Problem of the Capitalist State', in Blackburn, R., ed., *Ideology in Social Sciences, Readings in Critical Social Theory*, New York, Vintage Books, 1973; London, Fontana.

[49] Poulantzas, N. 1973. *Political Power and Social Classes*, London, New Left Books.

[50] Poulantzas, N. 1974. *Les classes sociales dans le capitalisme aujourd'hui, Paris, Seuil.*

[51] République Française, Ministère del l'Economie et des Finances, Sept. 1973. *Statistiques et Etudes Financières*, no. 297.

[52] Sheehan, R. 15 June 1967. 'Proprietors in the World of Big Business' *Fortune Magazine*, pp. 179–83.

[53] Smith, J. D. and Franklin, S. D. 1974. 'The Concentration of Personal Wealth, 1922–1969', *American Economic Review*, May, pp. 162–67.

[54] Sweezy, P. M. 1971. 'The Resurgence of Financial Control: Fact or Fancy?' *Monthly Review*, November, included in Sweezy, P. M., 1972, *Modern Capitalism and Other Essays*, New York, Monthly Review Press.

[55] Sweezy, P. M. 1973. 'Galbraith's Utopia', *New York Review of Books*, vol. XX, no. 18, November, pp. 3–6.

[56] US Congress, House, Committee on Banking and Currency. 1968. *Commercial Banks and Their Trust Activities. Emergent Influence on the American Economy*, Staff Report for the Subcommittee on Domestic Finance, 90th Congr., 2nd session.

[57] US Temporary National Economic Committee. 1940. *The Distribution of Ownership in the 200 Largest Nonfinancial Corporations*, Monograph no. 29, Washington D.C.

[58] Villarejo, D. 1961. 'Stock Ownership and the Control of Corporations', *New University Thought*, Part I, Autumn, pp. 33–77; Part II: Winter 1962, pp. 47–65.

[59] Yaffe, D. 1972. 'The Marxian Theory of Crisis, Capital and the State', *Bulletin of the Conference of Socialist Economists*, Winter, pp. 5–58.

[60] Zeitlin, M. 1974. 'Corporate Ownership and Control: The Large Corporation and the Capitalist Class', *The American Journal of Sociology*, vol. 79, no. 5, March.

The Origins and Functions of Hierarchy in Capitalist Production

Stephen Marglin

The minute specialization that was the hallmark of the putting-out system only wiped out one of two aspects of workers' control of production: control over the product. Control of the work process, when and how much the worker would exert himself, remained with the worker – until the coming of the factory.

Economic historians customarily ascribe the growth of the factory to the technological superiority of large-scale machinery, which required concentration of productive effort around newly harnessed sources of energy – water and steam. The first factories, according to T. S. Ashton, arose in the beginning of the eighteenth century when '*for technical reasons*, small groups of men were brought together into workshops and little water-driven mills.'[1] But the beginnings of the modern factory system are usually associated with Richard Arkwright, whose spinning mills displaced the domestic manufacture of cotton yarn. Arkwright's water frame, it is said, dictated the factory organization of spinning: 'Unlike the jenny, the frame required, for its working, power greater than that of human muscles, and hence from the beginning the process was carried on in mills or factories.'[2] Other authorities agree. Thus Paul Mantoux: '... the use of machines distinguishes the factory from (the putting-out system), and gives its special character to the new system as against all preceding ones ...'[3] And, more recently, David Landes has written

> The Industrial Revolution ... required machines which not only replaced hand labour but compelled the concentration of production in factories – in other words machines whose appetite for energy was too large for domestic sources of power and whose mechanical superiority was sufficient to break down the resistance of the older forms of hand production.[4]

These authorities, it should be said, recognize the other advantages the factory afforded, particularly a system of discipline and supervision that was impossible under the putting-out system. 'It was', as Ashton says, 'the need for supervision of work that led Peter Stubbs to gather the scattered filemakers into his works at Warrington.'[5] Mantoux also notes the 'obvious advantages from the point of view of organization and supervision'[6] of bringing together many workers into a single workshop. According to Landes the need for discipline and supervision turned 'the thoughts of employers ... to workshops where the men would be brought together to labour under watchful overseers.'[7] And elsewhere Landes is even more explicit. 'The essence of the factory', he writes in an introduction to a volume of essays on the development of capitalism, 'is discipline – the opportunity it affords for the direction of and co-ordination of labour.'[8]

Nevertheless, the advantages of discipline and supervision remain, in the conventional view, secondary considerations in accounting for the success of the factory system, if not for the motivation behind it. In the same breath as Mantoux notes the organizational advantages of the factory, he concludes that 'the factory system ... was the necessary outcome of the use of machinery.'[9] Similarly, while identifying discipline as the essence of the factory, Landes attributes its success to technological factors: 'the triumph of concentrated over dispersed manufacture was indeed made possible by the economic advantages of power-driven equipment. The factory had to beat cottage industry in the marketplace, and it was not an easy victory.'[10]

The model underlying this reasoning is easy to identify: the factory survived, therefore it must have been a less costly method of production than alternatives. And in the competitive market economy, only least-cost methods are technologically efficient, provided efficiency is defined in an economy-wide sense. Hence the factory must have been technologically superior to alternatives.

However, the very mention of supervision and discipline as motivations for the factory ought to put one on guard against a too-easy identification of cost-minimization with technological efficiency. In the competitive model, there is no scope for supervision and discipline except for that imposed by the market mechanism.[11] Any recognition of the importance of supervision and discipline as motivating forces behind the establishment of factories is tantamount to admission of important violations of the assumptions of perfect competition, and it follows that cost minimization cannot be identified with technological efficiency. Thus, technological superiority becomes neither necessary nor sufficient for the rise and success of the factory.

It will be argued presently that the agglomeration of workers into factories was a natural outgrowth of the putting-out system (a result, if you will, of its internal contradictions) whose success had little or nothing to do with the technological superiority of large-scale machinery. The key to the success of the factory, as well as its inspiration, was the substitution of capitalists' for workers' control of the production process; discipline and supervision could and did reduce costs *without* being technologically superior.

That the triumph of the factory, as well as the motivation behind it, lay in discipline and supervision, was clear to at least one contemporary observer. The leading nineteenth-century apologist for the factory system, Andrew Ure, quite explicitly attributed Arkwright's success to his administrative prowess:

The main difficulty (faced by Arkwright) did not, to my apprehension, lie so much in the invention of a proper self-acting mechanism for drawing out and twisting cotton into a continuous thread, as in ... training human beings to renounce their desultory habits of work, and to identify themselves with the unvarying regularity of the complex automaton. *To devise and administer a successful code of factory discipline, suited to the necessities of factory diligence, was the Herculean enterprise, the noble achievement of Arkwright.* Even at the present day, when the system is perfectly organized, and its labour lightened to the utmost, it is found nearly impossible to convert persons past the age of puberty, whether drawn from rural or from handicraft occupations, into useful factory hands. After struggling for a while to conquer their listless or restive habits, they either renounce the employment spontaneously, or are dismissed by the overlookers on account of inattention.

If the factory Briareus could have been created by mechanical genius alone, it should have come into being thirty years sooner; for upwards of ninety years have now elapsed since John Wyatt, of Birmingham, not only invented the series of fluted rollers, (the spinning fingers usually ascribed

239

to Arkwright), but obtained a patent for the invention, and erected 'a spinning engine without hands' in his native town ... Wyatt was a man of good education, in a respectable walk of life, much esteemed by his superiors, and therefore favourably placed, in a mechanical point of view, for maturing his admirable scheme. But he was of a gentle and passive spirit, little qualified to cope with the hardships of a new manufacturing enterprise. *It required, in fact, a man of a Napoleon nerve and ambition, to subdue the refractory tempers of work-people accustomed to irregular paroxysms of diligence* ... Such was Arkwright.[12] [Emphasis added.]

Wyatt's efforts, and his ultimate failure, are shrouded in mystery. Indeed, it is impossible to sort out his contribution from the contribution of his collaborator, Lewis Paul. No model of the Wyatt-Paul machine survives, but Mantoux supports Ure's judgement that Wyatt and Paul anticipated Arkwright in all technical essentials. Arkwright's machine, according to Mantoux, 'differs from that of Wyatt only in its details. These trifling differences cannot explain Arkwright's triumphal success.'[13]

Contemporary evidence suggests that the problems of organizing the workforce played a substantial part in the failure of the Wyatt-Paul enterprises. The correspondence between the principals and their officers suggests a continuing preoccupation with discipline. Edward Cave, a financial backer as well as a licensee, set up shop with hand-powered equipment in anticipation of finding a suitable water mill. Early on he wrote to Paul: 'I have not half my people come to work today, and I have no great fascination in the prospect I have to put myself in the power of such people.'[14] Discipline did not improve once the Cave factory became mechanized. When Wyatt visited the new spinning mill at Northampton in 1743 he found that 'only four frames were regularly at work, since there were seldom hands enough for five.'[15] The search for new methods of discipline continued. A month later, Cave's lieutenant wrote Wyatt:

I think they [the workers] have done as much in four days this week as they did in a week when you were here ... There were not hands enough to work all five engines but four is worked complete which did about 100 skeins a day one with another, nay some did 130. One reason for this extra advance is Mr Harrison [the mill manager] bought 4 handkerchers one for each machine value about ½p. each and hung them over the engine as prizes for the girls that do most ...[16]

These crude attempts to 'subdue the refractory tempers of work-people' by judicious use of the carrot apparently came to nought. One of the few indisputable facts about the Wyatt-Paul attempts is that they failed. And between Wyatt and Arkwright no one managed to bring Wyatt's invention to a successful conclusion, a remarkable failure indeed if the defects of machine spinning were primarily technological in nature.

There is additional evidence for the assertion that factory spinning did not depend for its success on a superior machine technology. Factory spinning took hold in the woollen industry as well as in cotton, and its success in the wool trade could only have been for organizational reasons. The technology of wool-spinning for many years after the factory made its appearance was the same in factory as in cottage; in both the 'spinning jenny' was the basic machine well into the nineteenth century.[17] The Hammonds suggest that factory spinning dominated by the beginning of the century:

By 1803 the transformation was practically complete. The clothiers had one by one introduced the system of 'spinning houses' on their own premises, and the weavers were filled with apprehension lest they too should be forced to work under their employer's roof.[18]

At some places water power may have been used for working the jennies,[19] but this does not appear to have been the general case. Benjamin Gott, called by Mantoux the 'first of the great Yorkshire spinners'[20] never used power in his spinning (or weaving) rooms during his quarter-century career as factory master and nevertheless appears to have made a satisfactory profit.[21] Certainly Gott never abandoned spinning and weaving to domestic workshops, although these handpowered activities could have been carried on separately from the operations to which Gott applied steam-power scribbling and fulling. Indeed, the customary practice when Gott began his factory in 1793 was for scribbling and fulling to be a trade distinct from spinning and weaving.[22]

In weaving the case is even clearer than in spinning. Gott's handloom weaving sheds were not unique. Long before the powerloom became practicable, handloom weavers were brought together into workshops to weave by the same techniques that were employed in cottage industry. Clearly, the handloom shops would not have persisted if it had not been profitable for the entrepreneur, and just as clearly the source of profits could not have been in a superior technology. There is no evidence that the handloom in the capitalist's factory was any different from the one in the weaver's house.

I have found no comprehensive quantitative estimates of the relative importance of handloom factories, and it would probably require a major research effort to make even a reasoned guess.[23] A recent study of the history of cotton handloom weaving concludes that 'although [the handloom weaving shed] was never anything like the predominant form of organization in cotton weaving, it was not negligible, nor was it confined ... to fancy goods only.'[24] The author of this study continues:

> According to the historian of Rossendale, in the period 1815–1830, when 'the trade of cotton weaving on the handloom was at its briskest, there were at the lowest computation thirty weaving shops, apart from the looms in dwelling houses, in the forest of Rossendale.' The distinguishing feature of the sheds was that they employed a number of weavers on handlooms outside their own homes and families; they were substantially larger than the small shops of four or six (looms) run by a master weaver and apprentices in some of the more specialized lines at Bolton or Paisley. Isolated cases have been found with as many as 150 or 200 handlooms, quite a few with between 50 and 100, and a considerable number with 20 or more. Such sheds were to be found in town and country throughout the weaving area.
>
> ... For both employers and workers, the handloom shed represented a transitional stage in the organization of cotton weaving between the true domestic system and the power driven factory. It does not necessarily follow, however, that the handloom shed was a comparatively late development in cotton, or that it was a conscious imitation of the powerloom factory. With the coming of the dandyloom (an improved handloom) in the late 1820s, there was a probable increase in the number of such sheds, but there is some evidence from notices in the local newspapers for their existence in the 1780s and 1790s.[25]

*

Even as late as 1838, the weaver's animosity might, as in the case of Thomas Exell of Gloucestershire, be directed against the handloom shop and its owner, not against the powerloom. 'Exell was, according to Wadsworth and Mann, "lamenting ... the concentration of handlooms and jennies in the clothier's shop" when he wrote "They have driven us away from our houses and gardens to work as prisoners in their factories and their seminaries of vice." '[26]

The early years of the nineteenth century saw the concentration of outworkers into workshops in other trades too. Supervision appears to have provided not only the motivation for 'Peter Stubbs to gather the scattered filemakers into his works at Warrington,' but a sufficient economic rationale for maintaining a factory-like organization in place of the putting-out system. Ashton's careful study of the Stubbs enterprise[27] does not suggest any technological argument for bringing the filemakers together, at least none he considers to be compelling. Nor does Ashton suggest that the new method of organizing work was ever abandoned. On the contrary: some of the original workshops were still standing in his own day.[28]

None of this is to deny the importance of the technological changes that have taken place since the eighteenth century. But these changes were not independent causes of the factory. On the contrary, the particular forms that technological change took were shaped and determined by factory organization. It is not accidental that technological change atrophied within the putting-out system after Hargreaves's jenny but flourished within the factory. On the demand side, the capitalist provided the market for inventions and improvements, and his interest lay – for reasons of supervision and discipline – with the factory. The supply side was only slightly more complex. In principle, an inventor might obtain a patent and license the use of his inventions to putter-outers or, indeed, to independent producers. In practice, as long as production took place in scattered cottages, it was difficult if not impossible to detect and punish piracy of patent rights. It was much easier to enforce patent rights with production concentrated into factories, and this naturally channelled inventive activity into the more remunerative market. And of course many improvements were by their very nature non-patentable, and their benefits were under capitalist economic organization capturable only by entrepreneurs.

This argument may be thought to imply a *dynamic* technological superiority for the factory system, for it may fairly be interpreted as suggesting that the factory provided a more congenial climate for technological change. A more congenial climate for innovation does not, however, imply technological superiority, dynamic or static. For the factory's superiority in this domain rested in turn on a particular set of institutional arrangements, in particular the arrangements for rewarding inventors by legal monopolies vested in patents. An invention, like knowledge generally, is a 'public good': the use of an idea by one person does not reduce the stock of knowledge in the way that consumption of a loaf of bread reduces the stock of wheat. It is well understood that public goods cannot be efficiently distributed through the market mechanism; so patents cannot be defended on efficiency grounds.

Indeed, the usual defence of patents is in terms of the incentives afforded for invention. But the argument is hardly compelling. There is no *a priori* reason why society might not reward inventors in other ways. In the eighteenth century, for example, Thomas Lombe was voted £14,000 in lieu of a renewal of his patent for silk-throwing machinery, a small amount in proportion to the £120,000 he earned during the fourteen-year term of his patent, but a tidy sum nevertheless, presumably enough to coax out the secrets of all but the most diffident genius.[29] To be sure, as it was practised in Great Britain at least, the public reward of inventors was a fitful and unreliable arrangement, but this does not mean that a way could not have been found to make the system workable had the will existed. Had the patent system not played into the hands of the more powerful capitalist, by favouring those with sufficient resources to pay for licences (and incidentally contributing to the polarization of the producing classes into bosses and workers), the patent system need not have become the dominant institutional mode for rewarding inventors.

There remains one loose end in this account of the rise of the factory: why did the market mechanism, which has been supposed by its defenders from Adam Smith onwards to harness the self-interest of the producer to the public interest, fail to provide adequate supervision and discipline under the putting-out system? Discipline and supervision, it must be understood, were inadequate only from the point of view of the capitalist, not from the point of view of the worker. And though it is true that in a sufficiently abstract model of perfect competition, profits are an index of the well-being of society as a whole as well as capitalists' well-being, this identity of interests does not characterize any real capitalist economy, no more the 'competitive' capitalism of Adam Smith's day than the monopoly capitalism of our own. In the perfectly competitive model, there are no capitalists and no workers, there are only households that dispose of different bundles of resources, all of which – labour included – are traded on markets in which no one possesses any economic power. For this reason, labourers can equally well be thought to hire capital as capitalists labour, and the firm plays no significant role in the analysis. By contrast, the hallmark of the putting-out system was a specialization so minute that it denied to the worker the relatively wide (competitive!) market that existed for products, replacing the product market with a narrow market for a sub-product that, in a limited geographical area, a few putter-outers could dominate.[30] The perversion of the competitive principle, which lies at the heart of the capitalist division of labour, made discipline and supervision a class issue rather than an issue of technological efficiency; a lack of discipline and supervision could be disastrous for profits without being inefficient.

The indiscipline of the labouring classes, or more bluntly, their laziness, was widely noted by eighteenth-century observers.

> It is a fact well known [wrote a mid-century commentator] ... that scarcity, to a certain degree, promoted industry, and that the manufacturer (worker) who can subsist on three days work will be idle and drunken the remainder of the week ... The poor in the manufacturing counties will never work any more time in general than is necessary just to live and support their weekly debauches ... We can fairly aver that a reduction of wages in the woollen manufacture would be a national blessing and advantage, and no real injury to the poor. By this means we might keep our trade, uphold our rents, and reform the people into the bargain.[31]

Indiscipline, in other words, meant that as wages rose, workers chose to work less. In more neutral language, laziness was simply a preference for leisure! Far from being an 'unreasonable inversion of the laws of sensible economic behaviour,'[32] a backward bending labour-supply curve is a most natural phenomenon as long as the individual worker controls the supply of labour.

At least no devotee of the conventional indifference-curve

approach to leisure-goods choices would dare argue that there is anything at all peculiar about a backward bending labour-supply curve.[33] Central to indifference-curve analysis of consumption choices is the separation of substitution and income effects. A rising wage makes leisure relatively more expensive to the worker, to be sure. But against this negative 'substitution' effect must be considered the 'income' effect; besides changing the terms of trade between leisure and goods, a rising wage is like a windfall that makes the worker able to afford more leisure. As long as leisure is a 'normal' good (one for which the income effect is positive), substitution and income effects work in opposite directions. And the outcome is unpredictable; certainly no neo-classical economist worth his salt would argue that the substitution effect must be stronger than the income effect.[34]

In a competitive market, however, the shape of the labour-supply curve in the aggregate is of little moment. By definition, any individual capitalist can hire as many workers as he likes at the going wage. And the wage he pays is reflected in the market price of his product. He earns the competitive rate of profit, whether the going wage is low or high. But for the oligopsonistic putter-outers, the fact that higher wages led workers to choose more leisure was not only perverse, it was disastrous. In 1769, Arthur Young noted 'the sentiment universal' among the cotton manufacturers of Manchester 'that their best friend is high provisions.'[35]

Thus the very success of pre-factory capitalism contained within it the seeds of its own transformation. As Britain's internal commerce and its export trade expanded, wages rose and workers insisted in taking out a portion of their gains in the form of greater leisure. However sensible this response may have been from their own point of view, it was no way for an enterprising capitalist to get ahead. Nor did the capitalist meekly accept the workings of the invisible hand.

His first recourse was to the law. In the eighteenth century, Parliament twice enacted laws requiring domestic woollen workers to complete and return work within specified periods of time. In 1749 the period was fixed at twenty-one days, and in 1777 the period was reduced to eight days.[36] But more direct action proved necessary. The capitalist's salvation lay in taking immediate control of the proportions of work and leisure. Capitalists' interests required that the worker's choice become one of whether or not to work at all – the only choice he wa to have within the factory system.

To a great extent, supervision and discipline meant the same thing in the factory. Under the watchful eye of the foreman, the worker was no longer free to pace himself according to his own standards. But supervision was important for another reason : under the putting-out system materials inevitably came under the control of the workman during the process of manufacture. This created a variety of ways for the workman to augment his earnings; in the woollen trade a worker might exchange poor wool for good, or conceal imperfections in spinning, or wet the wool to make it seem heavier.[87] Above all, there was the possibility of outright embezzlement. It seems likely that these possibilities multiplied as trade developed and grew, for disposing of illegally-gotten goods would appear to have been easier as the channels of trade multiplied and expanded. In any event, capitalists increasingly utilized the legislative, police, and judicial powers of the state to prevent workers from eroding their profits during the course of the eighteenth century.[38] Indeed, even the traditional maxim of English justice – that a man was innocent until proven guilty – counted for little where such a clear and present danger to profits was concerned. A Parliamentary Act of 1777 allowed search of a workman's home on mere suspicion of embezzlement. If suspicious goods were found on his premises, it was up to the worker to prove his innocence. Otherwise he was assumed to be guilty – even if no proof were forthcoming.[39]

The worker's 'dishonesty', like his 'laziness', could not be cured by recourse to the law, however diligently Parliament might try to serve the interests of the capitalist class. The local magistrates might not be sufficiently in tune with the needs of the master manufacturers,[40] particularly one would imagine, if they were members of the landed gentry. In any event, enforcement of the law must have been cumbersome at best, especially where manufacturing was dispersed over a relatively wide geographical area. It is no wonder that, as Landes says, 'the thoughts of employers turned to workshops where the men would be brought together to labour under watchful overseers.' As late as 1824, a correspondent of the *Blackburn Mail* specifically urged the factory system as a means of combating embezzlement :

It is high time ... that we should have a change either to powerlooms or to (hand) loom shops and factories, when at least one sixth part of the production of cotton goods is affected by [embezzlement].[41]

It is important to emphasize that the discipline and supervision afforded by the factory had nothing to do with efficiency, at least as this term is used by economists. Disciplining the work force meant a larger output in return for a greater input of labour, not more output for the same input.[42] Supervising – insofar as it meant something different from disciplining – the work force simply reduced the real wage; an end to embezzlement and like deceits changed the division of the pie in favour of capitalists. In the competitive model, innovation to improve the position of one individual or group at the expense of another may not be feasible. But the history of employer-worker relations under the putting-out system belies the competitive model. Embezzlement and other forms of deceit were exercises in 'countervailing power', and pitifully weak ones at that.[43] The factory effectively put an end both to 'dishonesty and laziness'.

The factory system, then, was not technologically superior to the putting-out system, at least not until technological change was channelled exclusively into this mould. But was it in any event efficient? Was it not better than available alternatives not only for the capitalist, but for the factory worker as well, however severe the consequences (mere 'pecuniary diseconomies' in technical language) for those who persisted in cottage industry? After all, nobody was legally compelled to work in a factory. The worker, no less than the capitalist, 'revealed' by the very act of entering the factory a 'preference' for factory organization, or at least for the combination of factory organization and factory pay[44] – or so neo-classical logic goes.

How applicable is this logic in fact? First of all, it is a strange logic of choice that places its entire emphasis on the absence of legal compulsion. Judging from the sources from which factory labour was originally drawn, the workers had relatively little effective choice. According to Mantoux:

In the early days factory labour consisted of the most ill-assorted elements: country people driven from their villages by the growth of large estates (that is, by the enclosure movement), disbanded soldiers, paupers, the scum of every class and of every occupation.[45]

The question is not so much whether or not factory employment was better for workers than starving – let us grant that it was – but whether or not it was better than alternative forces of productive organization that would have allowed the worker a measure of control of product and process, even at the cost of a lower level of output and earnings.[46] But to grow and develop in nineteenth-century Britain (or in twentieth-century America) such alternatives would have had to have been profitable for the organizer of production. Since worker control of product and process ultimately leaves no place for the capitalist, it is hardly surprising that the development of capitalism, while extending the sway of the market in labour as well as goods, and extending the range of occupations, did not create a long list of employment opportunities in which workers displaced from the traditional occupations of their parents could control product and process.

Where alternatives to factory employment were available, there is evidence that workers flocked to them. Cottage weaving was one of the few, perhaps the only important, ready alternative to factory work for those lacking special skills. And despite the abysmally low level to which wages fell, a force of domestic cotton weavers numbering some 250,000 survived well into the nineteenth century. The maintenance of the weavers' numbers is, in the light of attrition caused by death and emigration, convincing evidence of persistent new entry into the field.[47] However, the bias of technological change towards improvements consistent with factory organization sooner or later took its toll of alternatives, weaving included.[48] The putting-out system, with its pitiful vestiges of worker control, virtually disappeared in Great Britain by mid-century. And weaving was about the last important holdout of cottage industry. Where this alternative was not available, the worker's freedom to refuse factory employment was the freedom to starve.

NOTES AND REFERENCES

1 T. S. Ashton, *The Industrial Revolution 1760–1830*, Oxford University Press, London, 1948, p. 33 (emphasis added).
2 ibid., p. 72.

3 P. Mantoux, *The Industrial Revolution in the Eighteenth Century*, Harper and Row, New York, 1962, p. 39. (First English edition published in 1928).

4 D. S. Landes, *The Unbound Prometheus*, Cambridge University Press, Cambridge, 1969, p. 81.

5 *The Industrial Revolution*, op. cit., p. 109. See also Ashton, *An Eighteenth Century Industrialist*, Manchester University Press, Manchester, 1939, p. 26.

6 *The Industrial Revolution in the Eighteenth Century*, op. cit., p. 246.

7 Landes, op. cit., p. 60.

8 D. S. Landes (ed.) *The Rise of Capitalism*, Macmillan, New York, 1966, p. 14.

9 Mantoux, op. cit., p. 246.

10 ibid., p. 14, C. F. Herbert Heaton, *The Yorkshire Woollen and Worsted Industries*, Oxford University Press, Oxford, 1920: 'the major part of the economic advantage of the factory springs from the use of machinery capable of performing work quickly, and the use of power which can make the machinery go at high speed.' p. 352.

11 Ronald Coase appears to be unique in recognizing that the very existence of capitalist enterprise is incompatible with the reliance of perfect competition on the market mechanism for co-ordinating economic activity. Coase, however, sees the capitalist firm as the means not for subordinating workers but for saving the costs of the market transactions:

> ... a firm will tend to expand until the costs of organizing an extra transaction within the firm become equal to the costs on the open market or the costs of organizing in another firm.

See 'The Nature of the Firm,' *Economica*, vol. IV, 1937, pp. 386–405, reprinted in Stigler and Boulding (eds), *Readings in Price Theory*, Irwin, Chicago, Illinois, 1952, pp. 331–51. The quotation is from p. 341 of Boulding and Stigler.

12 A. Ure, *The Philosophy of Manufacturers*, Charles Knight, London, 1835, pp. 15–16. Military analogies abound in contemporary observations of the early factory. Boswell described Mathew Boulton, Watt's partner in the manufacture of steam engines, as 'an iron captain in the midst of his

troops' after a visit to the works in 1776. (Quoted in Mantoux, op. cit., p. 376.)

13 Mantoux, op. cit., p. 223. Wadsworth and Mann differ. See Alfred P. Wadsworth and Julia DeLacy Mann, *The Cotton Trade and Industrial Lancashire*, Manchester University Press, Manchester, 1931, pp. 482–3.

14 Quoted in Julia DeLacy Mann, 'The Transition to Machine-Spinning' in Wadsworth and Mann, op. cit., p. 433.

15 ibid., p. 436.

16 ibid., p. 437.

17 'Up to the close of the period (1820), and probably until after 1830, when Crompton's mule had been made "self-acting", it made no headway in the woollen industry.' W. B. Crump, *The Leeds Woollen Industry 1780–1820*, Thoresby Society, Leeds, 1931, p. 25.

18 J. L. Hammond and Barbara Hammond, op. cit., p. 146.

19 ibid., p. 148.

20 Mantoux, op. cit., p. 264.

21 Crump, op. cit., esp. pp. 24–5, 34.

22 ibid., p. 24.

23 Albert P. Usher, *An Introduction to the Industrial History of England*, Houghton Mifflin, Boston, 1920, reports some statistics for 1840, but does not give his source: 'In the Coventry ribbon district, there were 545 handlooms in factories, 1264 handlooms employed by capitalists outside the factories, and 121 looms in the hands of independent masters. At Norwich 656 handlooms were in factories out of a total of 3398 for the district as a whole.' p. 353.

24 D. Bythell, *The Handloom Weavers*, Cambridge University Press, Cambridge, 1969, p. 33.

25 ibid., pp. 33–4.

26 Wadsworth and Mann, op. cit., p. 393.

27 *An Eighteenth Century Industrialist*.

28 ibid., p. 26.

29 Mantoux, op. cit., pp. 195–6. In the case of Lombe and his brother, genius, apart from organizing talent, consisted in pirating an Italian invention.

30 On the power of bosses over workers see, among others, Landes, op. cit., p. 56; E. P. Thompson, *The Making of the English Working Class*, Random House, New York, 1963, chap 9, especially the quotations on pp. 280, 297. Adam Smith was quite explicit: 'Masters are always and every-

where in a sort of tacit, but constant and uniform combination, not to raise the wages of labour above their actual
rate. To violate this combination is everywhere a most
unpopular action, and a sort of reproach to a master among
his neighbours and equals. We seldom, indeed hear of this
combination, because it is the usual, and one may say, the
natural state of things which nobody hears of.' *The Wealth
of Nations*, op. cit, Book 1, chap. 8, pp. 66–7.

31 J. Smith, *Memoirs of Wool* (1747); quoted in E. P. Thompson, op. cit., p. 277.

32 The characterization is Landes's, *Unbound Prometheus*,
p. 59.

33 Contrary to Landes's implication, 'a fairly rigid conception
of what [is] felt to be a decent standard of living' [ibid., p.
59] is not required for a backward bending supply curve of
a good or service that (like time) affords utility to the seller.

34 It may be slightly ironic that an important necessary condition for the indifference-curve model to be applicable to
one of the most fundamental problems of economic choice
is inconsistent with capitalism. For the indifference-curve
model to be applicable to goods-leisure choices, control of
the hours of work must rest with the worker. But this is
inconsistent with capitalist control of the work process and
hence with capitalism itself.

35 A. Young, *Northern Tour*; quoted in Wadsworth and
Mann, op. cit., p. 389.

36 Heaton, op. cit., p. 422. These laws had historic precedents.
Unwin reports a municipal order dating from 1570 in Bury
St Edmunds requiring spinsters to work up six pounds of
wool per week. Employers were to give notice to the con-
stable in the event any one failed to obey the order (op. cit.,
p. 94).

37 Heaton, ibid., p. 418.

38 See Heaton, ibid., pp. 418–37 for an account of the woollen
industry, Wadsworth and Mann, op. cit., pp. 395–400 for
the cotton industry.

39 Heaton, op. cit., p. 422.

40 Heaton, ibid., p. 428.

41 Quoted in Bythell, op. cit., p. 72.

42 In technical terms, the shift from workers' control of goods-
leisure choices to capitalists' control meant a shift *along*
a given production function not a shift in the function
itself.

43 Any comment on the alleged immorality of these defences is probably superfluous. This was after all an era in which unions were illegal 'combinations', proscribed under common law of conspiracy (and later, by statute).

44 Factory wages for handloom weaving were higher than wages earned for the same work performed in the worker's cottage – presumably the reward both for longer hours and for submitting to the factory supervision and discipline. See Bythell, op. cit., p. 134.

45 Mantoux, op. cit., p. 375.

46 'Better' is used here in a broader sense than it is conventionally used by economists when comparing different bundles of commodities even when they bother to count leisure as one of the goods. Integrity – personal and cultural – can hardly be represented on an indifference curve. For a discussion of the effects of economic change on cultural integrity; see Karl Polanyi, 'Class Interest and Social Change' originally published in *The Great Transformation*, Rinehart, New York, 1944; reprinted in *Primitive, Archaic and Modern Economies*, George Dalton (ed.), Doubleday, Garden City, New York, 1968, pp. 38–58.

47 On the size of the labour force in domestic cotton weaving, see Landes, op. cit., pp. 86–7; Bythell, op. cit., pp. 54–7. On wages, see Bythell, ibid., chap. 6 and appendices; Sydney J. Chapman, *Lancashire Cotton Industry*, Manchester University Press, Manchester, England, 1904, pp. 43–4.

48 The amazing thing is that the cottage weavers held out as long as they did, testimony as Landes says, 'to the obstinacy and tenacity of men who were unwilling to trade their independence for the better-paid discipline of the versity Press, Manchester, 1904, pp. 43–4.

The reluctance of cottage weavers to submit to factory discipline was widely commented upon by contemporaries. As late as 1836, a noted critic of the factory, John Fielden, wrote 'they will neither go into [the factories] nor suffer their children to go.' Quoted in Bythell, op. cit., p. 252. Another critic testified to a Select Committee of Parliament that a cottage weaver would not seek factory employment because 'he would be subject to a discipline that a handloom weaver can never submit to.' Select Committee on Handloom Weavers' Petitions, 1834; quoted in E. P. Thompson, op. cit., p. 307.

Whether the cottage weavers' inadaptability to the factory

was a matter of taste or of the lack of psychological attitudes essential to factory discipline is a question of present as well as historical significance. (Ure, for what his opinion is worth, clearly sides with the view that the cottager *could* not adapt as opposed to the view that he *would* not.) For the argument that the role of schools is precisely to inculcate attitudes conducive to labour discipline see Herbert Gintis, 'Education, Technology, and the Characteristics of Worker Productivity', *American Economic Review*, May, 1971.

The Proletarianization of the Employees

Guglielmo Carchedi

We can subdivide the process of devaluation of the employee's labour-power, the dequalification of their functions and positions, into three phases which roughly correspond to the advent of the industrial revolution (i.e. the stage of individual capitalism dominated by real subordination of labour to capital), the advent of monopoly capitalism until the Second World War, and the stage of monopoly capitalism following the Second World War up to the present. In the first phase the function of capital is still basically carried out by the individual entrepreneur. The employee is a sort of extension of the entrepreneur. For example, he substitutes for the entrepreneur when the latter has to be absent. In this respect he performs the function of capital which is not yet a global function of capital because the work of control and overseeing has not yet been delegated to a hierarchically organized structure but is still the task of the entrepreneur (and of the few who help him). Usually, he also performs the function of the collective worker (if, for example, he takes care of bookkeeping) because he then takes part in the labour process as a whole. The fact that the employee is here a sort of extension of the entrepreneur[1] is the basis for the explanation of a whole series of phenomena. First of all, as there are only few entrepreneurs compared to the total industrial population, so there are also few employees: the ratio of the employees to the total industrial population is very small. Secondly, the relation between entrepreneur and employee is personal and direct, with no in-between links. Thirdly, his place in the capitalist production process (partial performance of the function of capital) ensures him a position of privilege and thus a salary much higher than the workers' wages. Finally, this place in the capitalist production process requires a legal and economic education which means, given the elitist character of the school system, that usually his social origin is either petty bourgeois or bourgeois. For all these reasons the employee, during this phase, belongs politically and ideologically to the petty bourgeoisie.

During the second phase, the number of employees increases. As we know, the joint-stock company leads to the appearance of that complex organization, both bureaucratic and hierarchical, within which the function of capital is carried out globally. The transformation of the function of capital into the global function of capital implies that many of those who perform the global function of capital also perform the function of the collective worker. That is to say, the position of the employee moves further and further away from that of the entrepreneur and thus the personal relation between the two is broken. The increased complexity of the production process and the performance of the function of capital by a complex structure of agents, the steadily increasing articulation of the technical division of labour, are all causes of the increase in the number of employees. Although he is no longer an extension of the entrepreneur and his labour-power has been devalued, he is still far from being proletarianized. He still performs both the function of the collective worker and the global function of capital, even though the former tends to become increasingly important. His position of relative privilege expresses itself in a whole series of characteristics proper to his position : he does not work in unhealthy environments; he has a certain degree of autonomy in performing his functions (even though the first forms of specialization, leading to a reduction of that autonomy, already start appearing); he has a degree of freedom to determine when he should be at the office (because his presence is not strictly checked by the entrepreneur or managers); he still requires a broad culture for the performance of his function (a fact which makes his replacement difficult); he has a higher salary and has the possibility, individually speaking, of making a career. That is, he can, at the end of a long career, reach the highest levels of the enterprise's hierarchy or at least the lower reaches of those levels. It is during this phase that the ideology of career-making is born; an ideology which becomes the centre of the employee's life, and which ties him strictly to the enterprise's interests. Not only is his level of salary much higher than the worker's level of wages but he also receives much better treatment as far as the non-monetary elements of his income are concerned, such as the length of holidays, the quality of health care, etc. For these reasons, the employee has a privileged position which explains his identifying his interests with those of the dominant classes. During this period the stratum of the employee is, politically speaking, very conservative and, ideologically speaking (while no longer completely integrated with the entrepreneurial class) still has the entrepreneur as his reference group, to the extent of attempting to imitate the life style and the consumption pattern of the entrepreneur. Ingredients of the employee's ideology are individualism, career-making, defence of his higher socio-economic status (already threatened, however, by the creeping devaluation of his labour-power), defence of the enterprise as the guarantor of his higher status and, therefore, defence of the concept of private ownership of the means of production. These remarks should be enough to explain why during this period the employees never sided with the working class; neither in industrial disputes nor on general political questions. Of course, during this phase we witness not only the tendency to dequalify the employee's functions and positions, but also the creation of new functions (just think of the managers of big corporations) which ensure for some the possibility of climbing the organizational structure. We notice here, for the first time, a phenomenon which we will observe again and again: the constant tendency to devalue the labour-power of many and to create higher positions for a few.

During the third phase the number of employees increases not only absolutely, as during the second phase, but also relatively to the total industrial population. At the same time there is an acceleration of the process of dequalification of the employee's functions; of devaluation of his labour-power, i.e. of the knowledge and training necessary to carry out functions which become more and more fragmented, more and more specialized, more and more repetitive in nature. Not only the size but also the composition of the employee stratum changes: the female part becomes increasingly important (typists, lower-level secretaries, card-punchers, etc.) and the average age drops due to the technological changes introduced by monopoly capitalism and the new division of labour.[2] The separation between the entrepreneur and the employee reaches now its highest degree. While on the one side positions of privilege are constantly and increasingly eroded with the decline of the global function of capital, on the other side it is important for the entrepreneurial class to retain the ideological support of the employee. Thus, the employee finds himself in an increasingly contradictory situation: his condition approaches more and more the proletarian one, while he is asked to stick to an

C.L.—I

ideology and political practice which is based on a lost position of privilege.

The process of devaluation of the employee's labour-power and thus the progressive disappearance, in his position, of the global function of capital, has deep-going effects, which tend to bridge the gap originally existing between the worker (as member of the proletariat) and the employee (as member of the petty bourgeoisie). First of all, from the economic point of view, the progressive disappearance of the global function of capital and the tendential reduction of the employees' labour-power to simple labour-power (due to the technical dequalification of positions, itself a consequence of automation) imply not only the progressive disappearance, in the income of the employee, of the revenue part (i.e. of the part connected with his position of privilege) but also a reduction in the wage part due to the dequalification of his functions.[3] Therefore, for many strata of the employees, the difference between the employee's salary and the worker's wage tends to be bridged and it is nowadays not unusual for a skilled worker to earn more than the lowest strata of the employees.[4] The fact is that for these layers, i.e. for those strata which have been proletarianized, the distinction between 'worker' and 'employee' is no longer relevant, at least as far as the economic aspect is concerned, when identifying their place in the social structure. The only difference between a girl punching cards and a worker on the conveyor-belt, is that the former works on a 'paper conveyor-belt'. Any sociological distinction, of the type that the former performs manual labour while the latter performs intellectual labour, is simply absurd.[5] Both meet the requirements needed to be classified within the working class, i.e. neither owns the means of production, both perform the function of the collective worker, are economically oppressed (or exploited) and are paid a wage the extent of which is determined by the value of their labour-power. It is therefore perfectly logical that a skilled 'worker' earns more than an unskilled 'employee' (logical, that is, from the viewpoint of capital). Secondly, this loss of his position of privilege is reflected in a variety of phenomena, all symbolizing the fact that the employees, or at least a large section of them, become, from the subject of the work of control and surveillance, its object. For example, his private room has been substituted by a large area where he works with tens of his colleagues. The private desk is increasingly substituted by a counter, a symbol of the loss of individuality, of his approaching the stage of the 'paper conveyor-belt'. Now he does not take care of the whole dossier but only of a few specialized aspects of it. For example, one employee computes the basic wages and then passes on the dossier to another employee who computes the piecework points, etc. Even those elements of the job which give it the personal touch, such as personal answers to letters, are eliminated by the introduction of standard forms. Thirdly, the employee's changed status is also reflected in the variables so dear to the sociologist: alienation (the employee, who used to be able to place his activity in the wider context of the production process, whose work gave him a global view of this process, is now, with the proletarian, just a small cog in a complex machine: the purpose of his activity escapes him completely), status (his status drops with the dequalification of his functions even though there might be lags), etc. In this connection, it should be mentioned that terms such as 'white collar' only serve to confuse the issue because they are not scientific but ideological in nature. White collar jobs, in terms of production relations, encompass both sections of the new middle class and sections of the working class, including both the technician who also carries out work of supervision and management and the typist.[6] Since the process of rationalization and mechanization traditionally applied to the 'blue collar' jobs has been applied, especially after the Second World War, to 'white collar' as well, devaluation through dequalification plays an important part in the devaluation of these agents' labour-power. Sometimes specific sectors of the 'white collar' (e.g. clerical) workers have their labour power devalued to such an extent that their average income falls below the average income of the 'blue collar' production workers. In the USA, in 1969, the former's income was $105·00 per week while the latter's weekly income was $130·00 (Braverman 1974, p. 34). However, it can happen that, because of the traditional lag between school system and production requirements – as well as a host of other reasons – the dequalified positions are filled by agents with the same or even higher educational qualifications. These higher qualifications not only do not command higher wages (which are determined by the value required) but represent spilled social labour (i.e. labour which went into the production of the unused skills of those agents). Hence the discontent to be found not only among 'blue collar' but also among 'white collar' workers and the application of job enrich-

259

ment schemes to 'white collar' workers even more than to 'blue collar' workers. Let us quote H. Braverman:

> Traditionally, lower-level white collar jobs in both government and industry were held by high school graduates. Today, an increasing number of these jobs go to those who have attended college. But the demand for higher academic credentials has not increased the prestige, status, pay, or difficulty of the job. For example, the average weekly pay for clerical workers in 1969 was \$105·00 per week, while blue-collar production workers were taking home an average of \$130·00 per week. It is not surprising, then, that the Survey of Working Conditions found much of the greatest work dissatisfaction in the country among young, well-educated workers who were in low-paying, dull, routine, and fractioned clerical positions (1974: 34). It is interesting to note that although the discussion of job enrichment, job enlargement, and the like began in connection with factory work, most actual applications have taken place in offices (1974: 36).

Fourthly, and contrary to the trends depicted so far, the official ideology tries to foster the employee's loyalty to the enterprise by attempting to create or perpetuate the image of the employee as the hard worker who never strikes. The process of proletarianization that the employee perceives or feels, rather than understands, is the objective basis for his fear for social change; a fear that creates a common view with the members of the old middle class and which is of course amplified by the mass media. But the contrast between the reality of the social process unfolding itself and the ideological view which denies it (just think of the atmosphere of harmony and co-operation propagated by the enterprises' internal bulletins and papers) is too big and this ideology is doomed to loosen its hold even more. Years of this accelerated process have led to a situation in which the traditional hostility of the employees towards the workers is being replaced, at least in the lowest strata already proletarianized, by a new consciousness of a community of interests between workers and employees. It is not by chance that, starting from the May 1968 events in France and the 'hot' autumn of 1969 in Italy, the workers and employees have often formed a united front in industrial disputes. The ultimate cause must be sought in the process of devaluation of labour-power in many employee strata and finally in their proletarianization. This is not to suggest, of course, that proletarianization necessarily brings about proletarian class consciousness. This was recently the case in Italy because of a host of political and ideological factors, both international (the influence of the Vietnam War, of the Chinese Cultural Revolution, of the May 1968 events in France and the crisis in the bourgeois ideology brought about by these events) and internal (the combativeness of the working class which becomes a point of reference for the employees, the direct and indirect influence of the student movement, the so-called 'crisis of representation' of the traditional left-wing parties, therefore the rise of strata of the working class not politically and ideologically hegemonized by these parties, etc.) (*I Comitati Unitaru di Base*, 1973.)

What has been said so far could lead one to think that technical innovations, the change in the technical and social content of positions, etc., only lead unilinearly to a devaluation (even though in various degrees) of the employees' labour-power. In effect, if this is true for a great part of the employees, there is also a small part for whom positions of privilege connected with an increase in the global function of capital within their functions, are created.[7] In other words, the process of devaluation of labour-power splits the stratum of the employees into two parts, the largest of which is pushed towards the bottom of the organizational chart where the work of control and surveillance is greatly reduced and tends to disappear, while a minority is pushed closer to higher management positions. At least two important consequences are detectable. First of all, the middle management section – those who decide through experience – becomes increasingly thinner because increasingly substituted by the computer. Secondly, and this is a direct consequence of the first point, the employee gets closer to the worker also with respect to the ever-decreasing vertical mobility, since the intermediate steps tend to disappear.

NOTES AND REFERENCES

1 See also Braverman, *Labor and Monopoly Capital*, pp. 259–260, 293–5.
2 See *I Comitati Unitari di Base*, Quaderni di Avanguardia

Operaia, no. 6, Sapere Edizioni, Milan, 1973, pp. 36–7.

3 The reader will recall that the income of those agents performing both functions is made up both of a wage component and of a revenue component.

4 These are, usually, employees who have been already proletarianized.

5 See also Braverman, *Labor and Monopoly Capital*, pp. 293–358.

6 'The industrial managers range from the production engineer and designer at the top to the foreman immediately above the workmen at the bottom.' C. W. Mills, *White Collar*, Oxford University Press, 1961, p. 82. White collar people are, for Mills, a residual category: 'Their position is more definable in terms of their relative differences from other strata than in any absolute terms.' See ibid., p. 75.

7 'In its early stages, a new division of labour may specialize men in such a way as to increase their levels of skill; but later, especially when whole operations are split and mechanized, such division develops certain faculties at the expense of others and narrows all of them. And as it comes more fully under mechanization and centralized management, it levels men off again as automatons. Then there are a few specialists and a mass of automatons.' Mills, op. cit., p. 227. See also p. 245.

PART V

The Labour Process and Class Struggle

Introduction

As we saw in the Introduction to Part I, an important distinction in Marx's own analysis of the labour process under capitalism was that made between the production of absolute and relative surplus value. In outline, surplus value emerges because workers produce a greater value than is necessary to maintain and reproduce them. There are two general ways in which the rate of surplus value can be increased. In one, the length of the working day is extended to produce *absolute* surplus value. In the other, which is clearly evidenced in the large-scale industry characteristic of the real subsumption of labour under capital, *relative* surplus value is produced in a circumstance where the length of the working day is *given* and specific capitals are subject to a constant revolution of their means of production.

Now increases in the rate of relative surplus value occur through the *intensification of labour* and through increasing its *productiveness*. In Marx's own words: 'Once the capitalist mode of production has become the established and universal mode of production the difference between absolute and relative surplus value makes itself felt whenever there is a question of raising the rate of surplus value. Assuming that labour-power is paid for at its value, we are confronted with this alternative: on the one hand, if the productivity of labour and its normal degree of intensity is given, the rate of surplus value can be raised only by prolonging the working day in absolute terms; on the other hand, if the length of the working day is given, the rate of surplus value can be raised only by a change in the relative magnitudes of the components of the working day, i.e. necessary labour and surplus labour, and if wages are not to fall below the value of labour-power, this change presupposes a change in either the productivity or intensity of the labour.'[1]

Through the *intensification of labour*, workers are driven to work harder and faster. More of the potential that is labour-power is squeezed out into actual production. 'Works' time' or 'company time' – the time that makes the employer money – comes further to drive out what is left of 'own time' or 'free time' in each moment of the working day. The practices that can be employed to achieve this are legion. The speed of machines is increased; the same worker is given a greater quantity of machinery to operate, so that, say, one worker does what was formerly the work of two; tea breaks are cut; and so on. In the classic historical case, to which we will come shortly, employers sought to ensure that workers really did expend more labour-power by the piecework method of payment. Through increases in the *productiveness of labour* more power is put at the workers' elbow via increased mechanization and organizational change. In practice, of course, intensification and increased productiveness can occur simultaneously, and often do. Both can also be said to increase *productivity*, in the sense of the same number of workers producing more, or fewer of them producing the same amount, hence the awkward term 'productiveness' above. (Insofar as intensification and increased productiveness are applied to the production of goods for working class consumption, they can also have effects on the value of labour-power generally, and so, indirectly, bring about a reduction in the relative time devoted to necessary – as opposed to surplus labour).

In general terms it can be said that the pursuit of relative surplus value through mechanization[2] forms the basis for the 'completion' of the development of the real subsumption of the labour process and the labourer to capital – as capitalist control is *objectified* in machinery; as technical calculation and organization by capital displaces craft expertise; and as the development of the reserve army of labour exerts its discipline on workers. But, as a recent commentator has noted,[3] this 'completion' is not uniform or entirely coherent. The surplus-value producing process retains its contradictions. Capitalism still develops unevenly both in relation to other modes of production and in its 'internal' relations; and the objectification of capitalist control in machinery, and the augmentation of the reserve army of labour press *variously* on *different* sectors, and in different phases of the cycle of accumulation.[4] Because of all this, it is always necessary to take into account the specific historical context in which such dynamics of the production of surplus value are actually worked out. A set of propositions pitched at a high level of abstraction, even though a good and necessary beginning, cannot by itself get us very far.

From the abstract towards the concrete then – payment systems, scientific management, 'participation' and other mechanisms for the control of labour under capital.

The first readings in Part V mainly concern *payment systems*, especially piecework.

Piecework has a long history. In the fourteenth century it was officially recognized by labour statutes in France and England. With the early period of large-scale industry in England at the end of the eighteenth century, it served as a lever for the lengthening of the working day and the reduction of wages. But after this contribution to the production of absolute surplus value, it became, following the Factory Acts, a device whereby employers sought to intensify labour and to increase the rate of relative surplus value – became in fact, as noted earlier, the distinctive method of payment by which industrial capitalists sought to ensure that workers really did expend more labour-power in a given working day. In 1851 the factory inspector Leonard Horner observed piecework to be 'daily on the increase'; in 1854 J. R. McCullock attributed the superiority of British industry to piecework;[5] in 1858 the factory inspectorate reported that four-fifths of those employed in factories were paid by the piece.[6] No wonder, then, that in 1867, Marx should call it 'the form of wage most appropriate to the capitalist mode of production'.[7]

Piecework[8] is intended to make it in the immediate interest of workers to strain their labour-power as intensely as possible – 'interest' here being considered in absolute cash terms of course, since such increases in effort expended may have quite different implications for their safety,[9] for their solidarity, and for their security of employment. From the standpoint of capital, additional advantages of piecework lie in those particular schemes which are regressive (each increment of production being paid at a lower rate than the preceding one) and, generally, in the fact that it can represent a saving on the cost of supervision. Marx himself remarked on the 'superintendence

265

of labour becom[ing] to a great extent superfluous' with this form of wage.[10]

Sometimes piecework has been used precisely because management cannot provide adequate supervision on a job – thus Hobsbawm's examples of deep pits being sunk on time-wages for the first few hundred feet and on piecework thereafter.[11] Sometimes it has also been used in conjunction with subcontract and piece-mastering to bring about the alienation in which, to quote Marx, 'the exploitation of the worker by capital takes place through the medium of the exploitation of one worker by another.'[12]

Yet piecework, like any other payment system, can have its disadvantages for capital. Thus Leslie Blakeman, an ex-labour relations officer at Ford's, has gone on record as saying that though 'a day-rate plant probably requires 25 per cent more supervision than one on payment by results ... this is a small price to pay for freedom from disputes and control over costs and methods'.[13] The truth is, of course, that workers are apt to try to take advantage; indeed, the industrial sociology literature on 'restriction of output' is for the most part a documentation of how workers regulate and minimize the effort that they expend, *despite* the apparent advantages to employers of piecework schemes.

As Brown has put it: 'a payment system does not exist in a vacuum'.[14] Amongst other things this means that we can expect payment systems to *change* according to their effectiveness and the balance of power. Experienced, organized workforces are likely to awaken their managment's interest in new methods; methods which, in the words of one expert,[15] are designed to ' "freshen up" the works atmosphere' (a most inept phrase for techniques more than likely to increase sweat and toil). It also means that if, for example, we find what appears to be a 'nineteenth century' payment system – 'the lump', in the modern British construction industry – then we have no business to write this off as an 'anachronism', or to characterize the industry's employers as 'backward'. We have to investigate the specifics of the industry, and to see how these relate to its particular context of class struggle (as Terry Austrin does below).

Payment By Result (PBR) systems are difficult to classify, but in Britain in 1961 about one third of all workers in all industries (and 42 per cent of those in manufacturing) were subject to them, compared to a quarter in 1938.[16] During the 1960s, however, aided by a long stretch of full employment, organized labour in Britain grew in strength, there was 'wage drift' (or what Cliff calls 'wage-*drive*'[17]) and there came about what has been called a 'crisis' in wage payment methods.[18] One indication of this was the interest which managements began to take in measured day work systems (MDW). As a management consultant[19] has nicely put it, MDW 'guarantees to workers the same amount of money all the year round – provided that they maintain a certain level of output.' Yet notwithstanding the trimmings – talk of becoming salaried like management etc. – this form of payment system was not uniformly welcomed by the British labour movement.

The brute fact noted already, that piecework is a mechanism which managements may bring into play in a relationship of exploitation – and that according to an old craftsman's adage 'piecework is the ruination of any job' – does not preclude workers wringing certain advantages from it. And it some circumstances, aggressive piecework bargaining has enabled them to jack-up rates of pay and to establish a measure of control over production. In 1967 Hugh Scanlon, then President of the AUEW, summed up the complexity of the situation confronting many trade unionists in the 1960s: 'I've attributed most of the ills of the engineering industry to an iniquitous piece-work system,' he said. 'Yet ... we fight ... to retain it, and correctly so. Because with piecework you have the man on the shop floor determining how much effort he will give for a given amount of money.'[20]

The adoption of, and advantages of, particular payment systems must always be set in particular contexts, account also being taken of particular sectors and even particular capitals and their special circumstances. For instance, under state incomes policy, workers on piece-rate have sometimes been allowed to get ahead of others in the same industry or locality who work on a different payment system. Now, from the standpoint of 'capital' – conceived in a blanket sense – incomes policy is clearly a 'good thing', but to *particular* capitals it can prove otherwise, and in the mid-1970s some managements have had cause to regret that the *absence* of piecework – which it sometimes took a hard battle to abolish – has left their workers relatively deprived of opportunities to 'drift' round inflexibilities of internal organization and to avoid problems with differentials. To take a case in point. In 1977, in the city of Coventry, toolmakers' wages *varied* by up to £34 a week, with the highest-paying firms being those on piecework. As Leyland management might testify, being plagued as it has been by its (MDW paid) toolmakers' demands for the removal of glaring anomalies, this is not necessarily an ideal situation for companies who pay by MDW.[21]

Clearly the state can seek to limit the room for manoeuvre of particular capitals, for the good of capital in general (as is indeed the case with incomes policy). When it accomplishes this, it does something which 'capital' cannot achieve, because of the anarchy of the separation of capitals. But just because of this anarchy, there are also occasions when the state actually tries to influence the development of specific techniques of exploitation. In fact, Martyn Nightingale argues in his piece on British productivity deals that their changing nature during the 1960s can be understood in terms of the working out in a particular context of just these sort of tensions between the interests of individual capitals and those of capital in general as articulated by the state.

Turning now to consider MDW at a little greater length: this might look most appropriate as a system of payment when consistent output is required; when the rate of output is largely machine- or process-paced; when operations are closely interlinked; when low materials wastage is important; and when high or consistent quality is wanted and management wants to control production flow. Such a view is indeed quite widespread.[22] But, as with any other payment system, decisions about the introduction, or discontinuance of MDW cannot be abstracted from the historically specific struggle between capital and labour. As Terry Austrin argues below, the precise form of wage payment can be as much an object of struggle as the amount of the wage itself.[23] It is instructive to look at the British coal industry in the light of these remarks.[24]

When the National Coal Board was formed in 1947 the industry was dominated by localized piecework bargaining. But after the mechanization of the mines (and the number of power loading machines grew rapidly from 280 to 1052 between 1954 and 1957) standard shift payments were introduced via the 1966 National Power Loading Agreement. At this time the NCB wanted to move away from piecework for several reasons: because it was thought that mechanization made piecework increasingly inappropriate (productivity now depending less on the intensification of physical effort than on increased productiveness through the utilization of machines – a move away from payment by results also followed containerization on the docks); because piecework had been a source of many stoppages and disputes; because standardized wages allowed greater flexibility of men from face to face; because it was easier to control wages; and because long-established practices might thereby be considerably changed.

Yet, in 1974, only eight years after the NPLA had been introduced – *and* following the only two national miners' strikes for nearly half a century, in 1972 and 1974 – the NCB was again talking of 'productivity'; with a suggestion for a partial return to a payment system based on direct financial incentives.[25] The day-wage structure had had the disadvantage, to the NCB, that ca' canny and various forms of work regulation could be practised without necessarily affecting earnings. The drive was on to further intensify labour and to use the new machinery to the full. In 1976 a joint management-union study visit to the pieceworking mines of Poland rubbed the message home: 'The Poles, who are almost as highly mechanized as we are, have shown that bonus systems can produce extra output and extra wages' (it also claimed that since 1966 in the NCB 'more efficient and powerful machines have been introduced but they are not always used to their full capacity').

By 1978, following prolonged and bitter dispute within the union, productivity deals were *in*, and being negotiated *locally*. In this way miners from the more easily worked pits were encouraged to intensify their labour. At the same time, disunity was fostered about a £135 wage claim for underground workers.

The strength of the miners in the 1970s had stemmed in part from the *national* unity they derived from the 1966 agreement. The extent to which, as a union, they will be weakened by these changes remains to be seen. But certainly the move away from, and back to, incentive payments was not the result of a merely technical decision but one which involved *inter alia* the state incomes policy (of a Labour government), the consequences of the energy crisis, the competitiveness of British coal, the traditions and interests of different coalfields, and considerable struggle between left and right factions in the miners' union, the NUM.

Finally, if we now look across to the world of management science, it should come as no surprise that payment systems do not always work as their adherents would wish, nor sometimes quite as they would have us believe. For instance, it now seems that F. W. Taylor's wretched 'Schmidt' and his gang of rate

269

busters (who were, incidentally, initially subject to physical intimidation by other workers to prevent them volunteering to load pig-iron by the piece) did not succeed in getting other workers to follow in their steps simply by virtue of the higher earnings that they received, as Taylor himself reported. Something else happened as well. A change was instituted whereby men who were injured, or tired from excessive work, were no longer forced to lose time (as they had been at first) but were given 'easier' work until they could return to loading pig-iron. It wasn't some scientifically ordained management technique, but improved conditions, that reduced 'the prejudice against piecework'. Even in the hands of F. W. Taylor, it might be said, piecework was an *incomplete* management practice.[26]

Scientific Management. As a model of social organization, the factory has impressed its image upon an increasing number of aspects of contemporary society (including the educational system, as Bowles and Gintis argue on pages 190–9 above). But perhaps its most notable conquest has been the *office*. Without doubt, one of the most powerfully effective parts of Braverman's *Labour and Monopoly Capital* is his description of what has happened to clerical work this century.

Braverman argues that there is little similarity between the modern office worker, usually female, and the privileged stratum of clerks (usually male) who characterized the pre-monopoly phase of the nineteenth century. He argues that within the productive corporations the growth of production brought an advance in the division of labour, administrative complexity, and an increase in clerical work. Hand in hand with this there developed commercial concerns involved with the sale and purchase of commodities, rather than with their production; also, financial institutions, banks and credit agencies. Increases took place in the work of record-keeping and accountancy, both internally to given capitals and – in a system of private property ownership – to regulate the mounting transfers of ownership rights and obligations between them. (To these developments have to be added the economic support and regulative functions of the state, and the emergence of a 'welfare state' – more so in some countries than others of course – which have also led to an increase in clerical employment.) This new clerical work became, as Braverman put it, a labour process in its own right; one that became subject to 'office management'. For, as is detailed in the extract, the methods of scientific management – initially developed in the factory – came to be further applied to the office itself.

Braverman's work has the great distinction, compared to the bulk of sociological literature, that it is not only written with clarity and force but that it actually argues a thesis: that monopoly capitalism generates a generic impulse towards *deskilling*. From F. W. Taylor's own forthright formulations Braverman was able to demonstrate most adequately what the purpose of scientific management was. His book also abounds with illustrative material by which he strongly supported his case that capital could benefit from deskilling. This was both because it permitted labour-power to be bought at a lower cost and because what he termed 'the separation of conception and execution' and subsequent to this a management monopolization of 'conception' (of relevant knowledge, planning functions etc.) made for *control* over every step of the labour process and its mode of 'execution'. However, Braverman conveyed the impression that deskilling was a necessary feature of monopoly capitalism; and that control really had been effectively secured in this manner. Yet as we have had cause to note before (Part I, pages 358–69) and as Schwarz and Elgar suggest below, amongst Marxists the linkages claimed between monopoly capitalism and the labour process have often owed more to assertion than investigation, and upon inspection are not always very convincing.

Braverman's work has been criticized on several counts. For instance, it has been questioned how far, as a former craftsman himself, his focus on deskilling betokened a sentimental attachment to what has always been a small part of the working class. Related to this, his failure to explore the politics and ideology of craftsmen has been said to beg the question of what, historically, has given way to what. Indeed, it has often been mentioned that the analysis of Marx from which Braverman's general thesis derives was one in which the process of deskilling had been located in the decline of handicraft, that is, in a situation prior to the full development of the capitalist mode of production.

Questions have arisen, too, about the level at which Braverman conducted his analysis. For his primary emphasis on the *job* and the 'degradation' of the work involved in it tended to get in the way of a recognition of the various other mechanisms that can be brought to bear on the valorization process and the relationships – consciously designed or not – which can structure it. Consider the internationalization of the labour process, for example. Or the replication of jobs, skilled or not, so as to weaken labour's bargaining power (a possibility which becomes more clearly evident with multi-national corporations). Or attempts to smash trade unions. Or to incorporate them. Or, at the level of the state, intervention in the form of incomes and employment policies etc. These can fall well outside the parameters of a predominantly capital *v.* labour point of production analysis, as did, for instance, the recent politico-economic orchestrations of a British Chancellor of the Exchequer (Healey) through whose April 1976 budget trade union leaders were quite explicitly promised tax reductions if they held down wage increases as the government's six-pound limit expired and threatened with tougher monetary policies (i.e. with higher unemployment, more competition for jobs and consequent lowering of wages) if they did not. All of these are possibilities.

An important lesson to be drawn from the work of Braverman is, therefore, that since there can be considerable variation in the sets of conditions under which actual labour processes take place, all analyses which are couched in terms of any one level, single factor, development or generic tendency, are to be very carefully scrutinized. But it has to be said loud and clear, too, that his direct linkage of one albeit rather abstractly conceived capitalist impulsion, to control labour-power, to just one particular management practice, deskilling, did, at the very least, actually forge a link between *capitalism* and *work*. If you like, Braverman re-united capitalism and the labour process.

The long-term consequence of Braverman's *Labour and Monopoly Capital* may prove to be some actual historical work to compensate for his own isolation of theory from class struggles and to provide the historical specificity that his theoretically inclined critics and commentators have (rightly) found lacking.[27] If so, the rather unilinear development of capitalist control that he implied, the lack of attention he paid to worker organization and consciousness, his apparent insensitivity to some possible contradictory effects of deskilling (for flexibility and, within limits, an active involvement in production can also be of interest to capitals[28]), all these could in time come to be regarded as a small price to pay for putting back the *capital* into *capitalism* at the level of the labour process.

However, scientific management is not confined to the capitalist West. And this, in a roundabout way – through posing its relation to socialism – brings us to a sensitive and complex area within Marxism, not least as it finds its expression in the writings of Gramsci and Lenin.

'Where a horse shits', wrote Gramsci, 'a hundred sparrows feed'.[29] He was bitterly hostile to a large part of the population of cities like Naples – the type of city which was 'not itself productive, nor ... directed towards satisfying the needs and demands of the productive classes'. This hatred of parasitism and of feudal remnants formed the backcloth to the *productivism* from which he approached 'Americanism', which, as he saw it in the Italian context was to represent a highpoint of capitalist development. Yet, as can be seen from the *Prison Notebooks*, this stress on the positive aspects of the development of the productive forces – which as was noted in Part IV forms one important strand in Marxism (see page 213) – runs awkwardly into ideas of a humanist kind.

'Taylorism', Gramsci tells us in his note on 'Taylorism and the Mechanisation of the Worker', 'supposedly produces a gap between manual labour and the "human content" of work. On this subject', he continues – and it is worth listening to him at some length – 'some useful observations can be made on the basis of past history and specifically of those professions thought of as amongst the most intellectual, that is to say the professions connected with the reproduction of texts for publication ... If one thinks about it, it is clear that in these trades the process of adaptation to mechanisation is more difficult than elsewhere. Why? Because it is so hard to reach the height of professional qualification when this requires of the worker that he should "forget" or not think about the intellectual content of the text he is reproducing ... The medieval copyist who was interested in the text changed the spelling, the morphology and the syntax of the text he was copying ... he was a bad scribe because in reality he was "remaking" the text ... in the Middle Ages ... there was too much time in which to reflect, and consequently "mechanisation" was more difficult. The compositor has to be much quicker; he has to keep his hands and eyes constantly in movement, and this makes his mechanisation easier. But if one really thinks about it, the effort that these workers have to make in order to isolate from the often fascinating intellectual content of a text (and the more fascinating it is the less work is done and the less well) its written symbolisation, this perhaps is the greatest effort that can be re-

273

quired in any trade. However, it is done, and it is not the spiritual death of man. Once the process of adaptation has been completed, what really happens is that the brain of the worker, far from being mummified, reaches a state of complete freedom. The only thing that is completely mechanised is the physical gesture; the memory of the trade, reduced to simple gestures repeated at an intense rhythm, "nestles" in the muscular and nervous centres and leaves the brain free and unencumbered for other occupations ... The same thing happens and will go on happening in industry with the basic gestures of the trade. One walks automatically, and at the same time thinks about whatever one chooses. American industrialists have understood all too well this dialectic inherent in the new industrial methods. They have understood that "trained gorilla" is just a phrase, that "unfortunately" the worker remains a man and even that during his work he thinks more, or at least has greater opportunities for thinking, once he has overcome the crisis of adaptation without being eliminated: and not only does the worker think, but the fact that he gets no immediate satisfaction from his work and realises that they are trying to reduce him to a trained gorilla, can lead him into a train of thought that is far from conformist.'[30]

Gramsci's idea above about how a 'dialectic inherent in the new industrial methods' confronts American industrialists is an interesting one. But his whole essay on 'Americanism and Fordism' – in which he earlier states that American industrialists like Ford 'are not concerned with the "humanity" or the "spirituality" of the worker, which are immediately smashed'; that though the Taylorist phase is more brutal than its predecessors it 'represent[s] simply the most recent phase of a long process which began with industrialism itself'; that it will be superseded by a 'psycho-physical nexus' of a new superior type; that there is 'a forced selection ... ineluctably tak[ing] place; a part of the old working class ... be[ing] pitilessly eliminated'[31] – all this is threaded with a certain ambiguity about how the process of deskilling (as it would now be called) is regarded by Gramsci. Is it to be regarded as the tearing off of petty bourgeois artisanal remnants? At least one commentator has argued that his productivism, and the welcome he gave to 'scientific managment' in the name of productivity, was a 'great mistake'.[32]

Of course, any real depth of understanding of Gramsci's (rather sketchy) notes on scientific management requires that they be related to the context in which they were written, including the problem of fascism. In the case of Lenin it is to be welcomed that his views on scientific management have recently been more firmly located in this way; in particular, in relation to the changing circumstances of pre- and post-revolutionary Russia.

Thus it has been shown[33] that his discussions of Taylorism in 1913/14 point both to its role in increasing the exploitation of the worker *and* to the rationality it introduces into the organization of labour, which he contrasts to the anarchy of capitalist production as a whole.

In his preparatory notes for his work on imperialism, Lenin's assessment of Taylorism concentrates mainly on its effect in reinforcing the labour aristocracy through wage increases and the use of a part of the work force in supervisory functions. At the same time he comments euthusiastically on its effects in standardizing and generalizing the operation of manual labour, which appears to prepare the way for a society in which everyone would take part in this.

On the eve of the October revolution Lenin returns to a discussion of Taylorism, this time with reference to the conditions necessary for the working class to wield state power. It is seen that Taylorism, by increasing the productivity of labour, will under socialism liberate the time and energies of the masses which 'will enable everybody without exception to perform "state functions" and this will lead to a complete withering of every form of state in general'. In the spring of 1918 Lenin pursues this point and suggests that Taylorism could be collectively controlled by the worker: 'the Taylor system, properly controlled and intelligently applied by the working people themselves, will serve as a reliable means of further greatly reducing the obligatory working day for the entire working population, will serve as an effective means of dealing, in a fairly short space of time, with a task that could roughly be expressed as follows: six hours of physical work daily for every adult citizen and four hours of work in running the state.'

But for all this, as Kelemen has noted,[34] the consequences of Taylorism in bureaucratizing the labour process and widening the separation between mental and manual labour did not enter within Lenin's theoretical horizon.

'Participation' and all that. In the literature of the studies in-

dustrial and organizational, scientific management has typically been counterposed to other 'approaches to industrial behaviour' (especially 'human relations'). We are told: 'Taylor's worker is a monstrosity', 'a greedy machine indifferent to its own pain and loneliness'; and that it was against such 'sociological barrenness', 'the psychological emptiness of this mechanistic conception' and the 'crudity of its economism' that other approaches developed – better, more sophisticated *social* ones.[35] The limitations of formulations of this sort have been heavily underscored elsewhere.[36] But as far as Marxists are concerned, it is arguable that those of them who operate at the level of management-worker relations also face problems. And perhaps two above all others.

First, the surplus-value producing process cannot be reduced to the labour practices of managements and the immediate issue of the control of labour-power. Even the issue of the control of labour-power requires explorations outside of production, and into practices and ideologies that are not directly initiated or reproduced by capital. (Although this is no excuse to *neglect* this level, as until recently has been the case with a lot of academic Marxism in which it is all too readily forgotten that, *for workers*, bosses are part of the problem of capitalism.) Second, there is the danger of collapsing management's potentially wide-ranging repertoire of practices at this level into essentially two – Taylorist ones, and non-Taylorist ones. Friedman, who contrasts two 'strategies' – 'direct control' (basically Taylorism) and 'responsible autonomy' (basically non-Taylorism) – comes close to this position. But at the very least he makes it clear that *each* of these alternatives is subject to what he calls 'the continuation of management control in the absolute or identifying sense'.[37] Because of this, he does not see 'participation' to endanger the capitalist enterprise, or system.

In this sense, Friedman's view might be taken to represent one common element in a loosely identifiable Marxist orthodoxy about 'participation'. Another element is the view that if the sphere of workers' participation *does* extend beyond narrow limits 'one can be sure that the capitalist class will attempt to regain full control of the labour process.'[38] But of course the main stress tends to be on the improbability of any authority being ceded in the first place. In Britain, the context and the fate of the *Bullock Report*[39] clearly suggest that such a view has a lot going for it. For instance, it was spelt out in the Conclusion to the Report that there was no more to fear for 'the country's stability and prosperity' from an extension of industrial democracy 'than there had been from the extension of the franchise, despite the threat that this, too, had been considered to be at the time' (para. 10). Yet the employers' representatives (including Sir Jack Callard, formerly chairman of Britain's reputedly most 'progressive' corporation, ICI[40]) were adamant. They signed a Minority Report. 'There is no evidence whatsoever that the changes will be beneficial,' they said (which was probably no more than the truth, from the standpoint of capital, or labour), but, they added, 'the risks are enormous' (para. 78).

In short, then, even though the *Bullock Report* was almost certainly right that the employers had nothing to fear from worker directors, the balance of class forces in 1977 was such that they felt strong enough to reject it —to take no risks with labour at all. Just such an outcome might well be anticipated from a reading of Ramsay's historical review. For there is solid foundation for his argument against the view that capitalism is naturally 'progressive'.

What is interesting about the following analysis by Bosquet is that he does see 'participation' – or more exactly 'job enrichment' – to endanger capitalist authority. 'Job enrichment', he tells us, 'spells the end of authority and despotic power for bosses great and small.' And, in parody of the bosses, but apparently in agreement with them too : 'The more you give [workers] the more they want. Give them a bit of power and they want it all.'[41]

It is a virtue of Bosquet's analysis to emphasize that there are circumstances in which capital may seek to *engage* workers' labour-power more fully. In this he shares an assumption which has been quite widespread amongst management spokesmen and advisers, and which, in Britain, informed the *Bullock Report* : that 'the problem ... is not a lack of native capacity in its working population so much as a failure to draw out their energies and skill to anything like their full potential' (Conclusion, para. 2). There is no doubt that such an approach as Bosquet's, when historically situated – for what is to be heard of 'participation' today? – goes beyond the ideological critique of liberal-radical sociology, according to which, as per C. Wright Mills, 'Human Relations' is castigated as a 'con' or 'manipulation'.[42] Less certain, however, is the idea that from questioning 'meaning' workers will come to question the 'purpose' of capitalist production, so that management's initiatives

277

will 'boomerang' against capital. Capital's representatives are not blind to such possibilities, as the mention of 'risk' in the *Bullock* Minority Report should remind us. Indeed, as another writer has sensibly noted, whether or not a 'participation' programme gets 'out of control' will depend on several factors: the nature and extent of the programme introduced, the technology and work organization, the character of the union, the political consciousness of the workers.[43] And as has been noted elsewhere, the way some managements have actually gone about introducing for instance job enrichment strongly suggests that they do not need to read sociology books to learn about 'unintended consequence'.[44]

To some extent jobs can be and have been 'enriched'. More or less safe mechanisms exist within capitalism to enable this. Thus, the example has been given of how the American Telephone and Telegraph Co. modified the processing of telephone bills. The process was initially organized in a way analagous to that of an industrial production-line, with nine different operations – to put envelopes in special containers; to put invoice cards and cheques through a vibrator to separate them; to compare the sum on the cheques and that on the invoice cards etc., etc. But a group of twenty workers, performing extremely fragmented tasks, set and divided up by a supervisor, was cut to fourteen workers, each of whom now performed a 'recomposed' operation – with each worker being made 'responsible', to *specified* customers. In this way, as Pignon and Querzola put it: 'Any mistake detected by a customer is immediately attributed to the employee responsible'[45] – and external control imposed through the market partly dispenses with control hitherto imposed by a supervisor.

However, just as the above example underlines how important it is to keep in proportion the extent of those changes which have been made, so it is equally important not to exaggerate how widespread they have been. Whatever happened at Volvo, for example – and though there is still no adequate research on this, Volvo has seen to it that there has been massive publicity – cannot be generalized to Sweden as a whole.[46] Even Bosquet's seemingly straightforward report of what happened at ICI Gloucester can benefit from closer study.[47] And it is always as well to remember both *who* it is that is subject to 'enrichment' and *how* they experience this. As to the question *'who?'*, for the most part it could prove misleading to think of militant, well-organized or male, manual

workers. Even according to that veritable plum fairy of 'enrichment', the American consultant psycho-sociologist Frederick
Herzberg, this has not been the case.[48] As to *how* workers themselves actually *experience* 'job enrichment', for myself it's difficult to forget the words of a worker at 'ChemCo': 'You move
from one boring, dirty, monotonous, job to another boring,
dirty, monotonous job,' he said. 'And somehow you're supposed to come out of it all "enriched". But I never feel "enriched" – I just feel knackered.'[49]

The structure of this book has meant that, beginning with Marx
on the labour process, and going on to questions of forced and
free labour, it has proceeded through a consideration of some
aspects of the reproduction of the labour force (migrant labour;
the family, domestic and wage labour; education) to issues
concerning management and its place in class relations, and
has only now arrived at this Part, which comes closest to those
issues usually associated with 'the point of production'. But
today 'the *point*' that is 'the point of production' is by no means
clear. One reason for this has been implied already: the extent
to which the functions of finance and so on have spawned
labour processes of their own. However, there is another reason,
namely, that production itself now constitutes more of a network than a point.

Three cardinal facts of capitalist production are: the concentration and centralization of the means of production; the
creation of a world market; and, of especial concern to us
here, the organizations of labour itself into social labour,
through co-operation, division of labour and the uniting of
labour with the natural sciences.[50] Now at a certain level of
abstraction the vast webs of complexity and interdependence
that reflect these three cardinal facts can be seen to have the
makings of an inter-connected, world-wide working class. But
classes do require *making*, and this same network/web/struc-
ture, call it what you will, when it is viewed by workers – so to
speak from the underside up – though it is undoubtedly a potential strength, can look to constitute a heavy burden: it can
appear a source of division rather than unity; something too
complex, too much a mystery, too big, too powerful to budge.
And the roots of the sort of Marcusian[51] pessimism, to which
such an observation as this lends itself, do not stop here. For
insofar as the drive for the production of relative surplus-value
increases the objectification of capitalist control – flows, speeds,

tolerances becoming 'programmed' into the technology for instance – it can also more easily come to appear that the enemy is not a class one at all. Instead, the problem and the cause all the more readily can appear to resolve themselves into the inevitability and insurmountability of 'technical progress'; in short, science itself becomes the enemy, rather than science and technology as developed and applied in a particular mode of production. Or then again the problem can appear to be 'red-tape' – bureaucracy. The objectification of capitalist control in bureaucratic hierarchies and procedures can be just as mystifying as the objectification of this control into mechanical, chemical, and particularly now, computerized systems. A specific example of this is provided by what can happen with, say, a job grading system.[52] But consider also, in the context of ideas about the entrapment and enmeshing of British workers, the probable post-*Donovan Report* (1968) increase in the attempted incorporation of local trade union representatives like conveners,[53] and, at national level, the holding down of wages by governments that work extensively through union leaderships. In both these cases, it can certainly appear to workers that 'their' union stands over and against them and that they lack weapons sharp enough to cut through the web of procedures, understandings, contracts, compacts, concordats.

Over-much can be made of all this though. In reality, everything is not as tightly planned and as smoothly incorporated as the above might imply. Co-operation, division of labour and the uniting of labour with the natural sciences has not spelt the suffocation – or the total 'subsumption', to use Marx's word – of the working class. So, three comments on the broader political parameters.

One. An apparatus of total repression would be extremely costly. Even when slaves have been made into industrial workers, they have resisted[54] – as did the *chibaro* workers we introduced in Part II. As their employers saw it, desertion, theft, sabotage and a system of passive resistance meant that 'to obtain a good day's work' was 'an impossibility'. In fact these black miners were able (in an employer's words) 'to defeat the objects of a master who desires value for his money', despite compound 'police', spies, censorship, the *sjambok* and much else besides.[55] And as Hilary Partridge shows in her work, which deals with a quite different time and place, despite FIAT's definite attempts to repress certain types of working class union and political activity in Turin in the 1950s, workers there were alas still able to 'draw the line' and did so, quite literally, in defending themselves against speed-up (see pages 416–32).[56] 'The Rabbit Years' she describes were moreover a mixture of hard *and* soft touches, which brings us to the second point.

Two. 'Take care for me that the ... worker following his heavy labour and his long day is able to recuperate. Take care that these men can for once learn to forget the day's burdens'. Thus Hitler to Ley, leader of the Labour Front in Germany in 1935.[57] In that year seven oceanic steamships were kept constantly occupied by Strength Through Joy with tours to Norway, Lisbon, Madeira, the Azores and elsewhere. In fact between 1936 and 1938 holiday trips were taken by six million people annually ...[58] In Nazi Germany, then, holidays for workers; and, to anticipate, at FIAT, mass sackings for the workers *and* a football club; in the south, in Donald Roy's lexicon of anti-trade unionism, 'Fear Stuff', *and* 'Sweet Stuff' *and* 'Evil Stuff'; and at 'ChemCo', a specious smoothness of operation, lubricated by management psycho-sociology, held in place by the objectification of control in technology and bureaucratic procedure,[59] but no guarantee that the iron hand will not be revealed from beneath the velvet glove.

The second point, then, is that as with automation and technical innovation, so with the development of socio-political forms of control. There is no inevitable, unilinear progression: in the first case to the fully-automated 'play society', in the second to the 'soft' form of incorporation of the working class. Perhaps, however, two other items are worth a mention here as well. The first is that whereas the 1971 Industrial Relations Act should remind us that the coercive system of the strong state is a possibility in Britain, the years that followed should also remind us that strong-arm measures, and indeed the *threat* of coercive measures, can pave the way for a softer approach. After all, one reason that the 1974–9 Labour government could enter into such relatively 'good' relations with the trade union leaderships was the talk from 'responsible' sources about a seemingly assured and mechanical relation between high levels of inflation and fascism. (Of course, there is no such automatic link: fascism, like socialism, takes making; even if it is an extreme part of the repertoire of capitalist systems). The second additional note concerns the fact that whether employers and the state incline towards the 'soft' way of the office and the committee or the 'hard' way, ultimately of the prison or worse – and these are not necessarily clear-cut alternatives – depends on many things; including most obviously the trade unions, where they exist; and the strength and estimation of strength and the expectations of those who support and lead them. To deny this is to deny that there is a class struggle fleshed of living men and women with a specific history. But to accept it is to render highly problematic all statements about the future balance of coercion and incorporation that are not based upon the most detailed historical knowledge. There are no easy short-cuts to the understanding of 'what will happen next'. Progressivist predictions (of the ilk 'more participation *must* come') are not to be trusted.

Three. The possibilities of change are best understood by beginning from a recognition of the contradictions that actually beset the capitalist systems – like that between the *organization* of production in the given workshop/factory/firm and the *anarchy* of production in society generally. For as is argued in the last reading, whereas some planning is possible, and is increasingly practised at the level of the company, it is not possible at the level of society; not, that is, in a system that is dominated by the separation and anarchy of capitals. The situation is not, therefore, as the earlier remarks might imply, that capitalism is akin to some gigantic self-lubricating, sealed mechanical bearing, flawed only by the odd speck of dust. Right from the beginning it has to be grasped that the system is irrational, that it doesn't work well – or well enough for many metropolitan capitals. Moreover, planning, real planning, requires control, including control over wage costs. And this, to end on a sober note, could result, according to some not very far-fetched scenarios, in a growing limitation of the right to strike and of the freedoms of association, assembly, demonstration and publication – '*if*', that is, as Mandel rightly stresses, 'capital were to triumph'. Today, an awful lot hangs on that '*if*'.

NOTES AND REFERENCES

1 *Capital*, vol. 1, p. 646.
2 For Marx there was a further consequence of mechanization as a method of increasing relative surplus value that

stemmed from the labour theory of value. Very briefly, only living labour creates value. On certain assumptions, then, insofar as, for example, increased mechanization signifies an increase in the *organic composition of capital* (the ratio of 'dead' to 'living' labour), the growth of constant capital in relation to variable capital will necessarily lead to a fall in the rate of profit and thus spell the demise of the entire system. To eschew this line of argument is not of course in any way to deny that *actual* rates of profit are a most important seismograph of the major forces acting on specific capitals and capitalist systems. For Marx's statement on 'The Law of the Tendency of the Rate of Profit to Fall', see *Capital*, vol. 3, part 3, chaps. XII–XV. For a readable critique see 'The Falling Profit Rate and the Collapse of Capitalism' in G. Hodgson, *Trotsky and Fatalistic Marxism*, Nottingham, Spokesman Books, 1975, pp. 65–88.

3 Tony Elger, 'Valorization and "Deskilling": A Critique of Braverman', *Capital and Class*, No. 7, Spring 1979.

4 Consider the case of microprocessors, for example. The much vaunted 'chip revolution' – heralded in Britain by former Prime Minister Callaghan as presaging 'the most rapid industrial change in history' – can, of course, be regarded as but one further instance of capital's drive to increase the production of relative surplus value. But it would be a strange kind of Marxism that could say only this, and to say more requires painstaking empirical work.

Certainly Marxists, because of the way the theoretical ground upon which they stand is contoured, should be able to 'see' certain openings, possibilities, likely twists and turns. Thus, if it is hazarded that, because of the chip, unemployment in Britain alone may swell to 7 million, they will (should) know that this will not be *evenly* distributed; also that what unemployment actually *does* result will not come about through some inexorable technological *logos*, outside of the struggle of classes, politics and economics; and indeed that the technical changes which microprocessors facilitate and which *could* lead to a direct substitution of labour, are only likely to take place when it is cheaper to 'employ' them than human labour-power. They will remember, *in fact*, that the production of microprocessors themselves has involved not only the highly valued labour-power of the scientists of West Coast America's 'Silicon Valley' but also the far less celebrated labour-power

– the cheap labour in fact – of workers in Hong Kong, Taiwan and South Korea.

These Marxists of ours will also be sensitive to the possible implications of the new technology for the better control of quality of raw materials, energy, stocks – *and* human labour-power. Given the use of the grand term 'objectification' in the text, this is worth a comment here, for there now exist monitoring devices for surveillance and control at work (and outside of course, which is what the media tends to stress, 'privacy' etc.) that make the time clock look antediluvian: e.g. monitored check-outs in supermarkets, tachographs in driving cabs, detectors to track speeds and timings on the buses, and other computerized facilities for management information and control, even computerized keys to record time spent out of the work area in factories and offices. Thus a French insurance company is reported to have fitted glass partitions on all landings and glass doors to all exits and entrances (providing no handles to the doors) and to have installed a small gadget, to be operated by personal plastic cards which recorded workers' movements off the job for coffee, the toilet, etc. Unauthorized absences of five minutes or over were deducted from employees' work units under the flexi-time system that was in operation.

From where they stand, these Marxists of ours should be well placed to 'see' such developments and to question some much-vaunted possibilities. But no one sees anything unless they look. (For Callaghan, see *Financial Times*, 7 December 1978; for the 7 million unemployed, see Colin Hines, *The 'Chips' Are Down: The Future Impact of Microprocessors and Computers on Employment in Britain*, London, Earth Resources Research Limited, April 1978; on the French insurance company see 'Computers and Capital', *Capital and Class*, no. 2, Summer 1977.)

5 Horner and McCullock are both quoted in E. J. Hobsbawm's now classic essay, 'Custom, Wages and Work-load in Nineteenth-Century Industry' in his *Labouring Men: Studies in the History of Labour*, London, Weidenfeld and Nicolson, 1964, chap. 17, p. 357. Both are further cited in Geoff Brown, *Sabotage: A Study in Industrial Conflict*, Nottingham, Spokesman Books, 1977, p. 83.

6 Cited in *Capital*, vol. 1, p. 699.

7 ibid., p. 698.

8 For information on the varieties of payment by results generally see 'Payments by Results', *Ministry of Labor Gazette*, vol. 69, 9, September 1961: R. B. McKersie, 'Changing Wage Payment Systems', *Royal Commission on Trade Unions and Employers' Associations*, Research Papers 11, London, HMSO, 1968; National Board for Prices and Incomes, *Payment by Results Systems* (Supplement), London, HMSO, 1968.

9 As Haraszti indicates in the extract below. Although from Hungary this is included in these readings on the capitalist labour process because it constitutes such powerful testimony to the nature and effects of this form of payment system, about which no one has written better. For a review of the relationship between piecework and industrial accidents see John Wrench, *The Piecework Effect: Payment by Results and Industrial Safety*, Sociology Group Occasional Paper 3, University of Aston, Birmingham, May 1978. For some cases, see Theo Nichols and Peter Armstrong, *Safety or Profit: Industrial Accidents and the Conventional Wisdom*, Bristol, Falling Wall Press, 1973; and Theo Nichols, 'The Sociology of Accidents and the Social Production of Industrial Injury' in G. Esland, G. Salaman and Mary-Anne Speakman, *People and Work*, Edinburgh, Holmes McDougall and the Open University, 1975.

10 *Capital*, vol. 1, p. 695.

11 'Custom, Wages and Work-Load', p. 353.

12 *Capital*, vol. 1, p. 695.

13 Reported in *Financial Times*, 19 November 1968.

14 *Sabotage*, p. 364.

15 McKersie, 'Changing Wage Payment Systems', p. 31.

16 Department of Employment and Productivity, *British Labour Statistics: Historical Abstract, 1886–1968*, London, HMSO, 1977, Table 80. For more recent information on PBR as related to region, size of firm, industry and skill level, see Department of Employment, *British Labour Statistics Yearbook 1975*, London, HMSO, 1977.

17 Tony Cliff, *The Employers' Offensive: Productivity Deals and How to Fight Them*, London, Pluto, 1970, p. 40.

18 McKersie, 'Changing Wage Payment Systems', p. 31.

19 Anne Shaw, 'Measured Daywork: One Step Towards a Salaried Work Force', *Manager*, 32, 1, 1962.

20 Cited in Brown, *Sabotage*, p. 314 from an interview with Scanlon in *New Left Review* 46, Nov.–Dec. 1967.

21 'Measured Daywork or PBR?', *Labour Research*, July 1977, pp. 159–60.

22 Such conditions are cited by both trade union and management sources. Cf. Anne Shaw, 'Measured Daywork' and *Labour Research*, July 1977.

23 For a brief description of the results of such struggles in the US steel industry – following a shift from the sliding scale of wages for skilled workers and the contract system in the case of their helpers, to, first, flat rates, then piece rates, see Katherine Stone, 'The Origins of Job Structures in the Steel Industry', *Review of Radical Political Economics*, 6, 2, Summer 1974.

24 For a most useful account, heavily relied on here, see Brown, *Sabotage*, chap. 15. His chap. 16, 'The Car Industry and Measured Day Work' is also useful in this connection.

25 Interestingly, Leyland car bosses were soon thinking of a move in the same direction, seeking to introduce plant productivity bonuses, which would pay extra according to improvements in collective productivity and thereby engender a more receptive attitude to changes in working arrangements. According to a *Sunday Times* report (12 November, 1978) they did not see the problem 'as a lack of individual effort (which piecework aims to maintain) but as collective attitudes'.

26 Taylor's often-rehearsed account of the 'scientific selection' of Schmidt (see for instance Braverman, *Labour and Monopoly Capitalism*, pp. 103–6) could have been 'incomplete' too. More precisely – to quote two rather upset management scientists who also reported the business about 'easier' work above – it was 'completely fictional'. See C. D. Wrege and A. G. Perroni, 'Taylor's Pig-Tale: A Historical Analysis of Taylor's Pig-Iron Experiments', *Academy of Management Journal*, 17, 1, March, 1974. Taylorism was not of course simply about piecework; see Littler who stresses its relation to the decline of sub-contract and the rise of management hierarchy proper, Craig R. Littler, 'Understanding Taylor', *British Journal of Sociology*, 29, 2, June 1978.

27 For the most exhaustive statement see Tony Elger, 'Valorization and "Deskilling": A Critique of Braverman'. (Note the similarity between what, at the end of the 1970s, is now said about Braverman and the labour process and what is now often said about work on the family and capitalism,

which had had a similar gestation period, cf. Elger, ibid., and Middleton, cited at page 112.)

28 The underplaying of such contradictory possibilities is all the more striking in view of the fact that Braverman's entire analysis is founded on his observations, following Marx, about 'labour-*power*', 'human *capacity*', '*potential*', and on the sort of remarks made about '*variable* capital' etc., in the Introduction to Part I of the present book. See *Labour and Monopoly Capital*, chap. 1, pp. 45–58.

29 'Americanism and Fordism', *Selections from the Prison Notebooks of Antonio Gramsci*, ed. and trans. Quintin Hoare and Geoffrey Nowell Smith, New York, International Publishers, 1971, p. 283.

30 ibid., pp. 308–10. 'Trained gorilla' is a reference to F. W. Taylor's claim that pig-iron handling 'is so crude and elementary in its nature that the writer firmly believes that it would be possible to train an intelligent gorilla so as to become a more efficient pig-iron handler than any man could be,' *The Principles of Scientific Management*, 1911, p. 40. Some of the ideas presented by Gramsci in this passage will no doubt remind some readers of Baldamus' concept of 'traction'; see *Efficiency and Effort*, pp. 59–65.

31 ibid., pp. 302–3.

32 Martin Clark, *Antonio Gramsci and the Revolution that Failed*, New Haven and London, Yale University Press, 1977, p. 9.

33 See Robert Linhart, *Lenine, Les Paysans, Taylor*, Paris, Editions du Seuil, 1976.

34 In his review of Linhart's *Lenine* in the CSE publication *Head and Hand*, no. 1, 1978 which is the source of the above commentary. For further comments on Lenin and Taylorism, see K. Bailes, 'Alexei Gastev and the Soviet Controversy over Taylorism, 1918–24', *Soviet Studies*, 29, 3, 1977, pp. 373–94; R. Bendix, *Work and Authority in Industry*, London, Chapman and Hall, 1956, pp. 206–7; and Charles S. Maier, 'Between Taylorism and Technocracy: European Ideologies and the Vision of Industrial Productivity in the 1920s', *Journal of Contemporary History*, 5, 1970, pp. 50–1.

35 See, for example, Michael Rose, *Industrial Behaviour: Theoretical Development since Taylor*, p. 62.

36 Above all by Braverman, *Labor and Monopoly Capital*, pp. 86–7.

37 Friedman, *Industry and Labour*, p. 83.
38 E. O. Wright, 'Class Boundaries in Advanced Capitalist Societies', *New Left Review*, 98, July–August 1976, p. 29n.
39 *Report of the Committee of Inquiry on Industrial Democracy*, London, HMSO, Cmnd 6706, January 1977.
40 For some comments on 'participation' at 'ChemCo', see Theo Nichols and Huw Beynon, *Living with Capitalism: Class Relations and the Modern Factory*, London, Routledge and Kegan Paul, 1977. (This according to the ICI Shop Stewards' newspaper *ChemCo News* (No. 1, March 1978) describes a situation 'all too familiar to ICI workers'.)
41 A view shared by another Marxist writer on this subject, see Andrew Zimbalist, 'The Limits of Work Humanization', *Review of Radical Political Economics*, 7, 2, Summer 1975, p. 56. A slightly different translation of Bosquet's article appears as 'The Prison Factory', *New Left Review*, 73, May 1972.
42 This is not to deny that it *is* 'manipulation'. For further comments, see Theo Nichols, 'The "Socialism" of Management: Some Comments on the New "Human Relations"', *Sociological Review*, 23, 2, May 1975; also 'Management, Ideology and Practice' in *Politics of Work and Occupation 2*, Open University 1976.
43 Zimbalist, 'The Limits of Work Humanization', p. 56.
44 See, for example, 'The "Socialism" of Management', pp. 261–4.
45 Dominique Pignon and Jean Querzola, 'Dictatorship and Democracy in Production' in Andre Gorz (ed.) *The Division of Labour: The Labour Process and Class Struggle in Modern Capitalism*, Hassocks, nr Brighton, The Harvester Press, 1976, pp. 76–7.
46 Goran Palm's *The Flight From Work* (Cambridge, Cambridge University Press, 1977) is a useful corrective here, as well as containing some good things on the complexities of industrial workers' experience, not least on piecework.
47 See 'The "Socialism" of Management', p. 265n.
48 See the '17 populations' that he cites in 'verification of the theory' (the theory being his so-called 'motivation-hygiene theory') in F. Herzberg, *Work and the Nature of Man*, London, Staples Press, 1968, chap. 7, table IV. (Of course, the most virgin of workforces can turn nasty, once it becomes aware that it has been 'experimented' upon, as Daniel

Bell once gleefully pointed out, with reference to the classic industrial social psychological work done at the Harwood Manufacturing Co. See his *The End of Ideology*, New York, Collier Books, 1961, p. 423n.)

49 *Living with Capitalism*, p. 16.

50 For Marx's original statement see *Capital*, vol. 3, p. 266.

51 Herbert Marcuse, *One Dimensional Man; Studies in the Ideology of Advanced Industrial Society*, London, Routledge and Kegan Paul, 1964.

52 For a close-up analysis of such a scheme in one company see Peter Armstrong in *Workers Divided*, London, Fontana 1976, Part Two.

53 Richard Hyman notes that it can no longer be suggested, as *Donovan* argued, that 'it is the exception, rather than the rule, for a chief shop steward to have a room at his disposal as an office' (p. 107) and that a new layer of full-time conveners and senior stewards has quadrupled during the past decade, see 'British Trade Unionism in the 1970s: The Bureaucratization of the Rank and File'. C.S.E. Conference Paper 1978, now published as 'The Politics of Workplace Trade Unionism', *Capital and Class*, 8, Summer 1979; see also, W. Brown and M. Terry, 'The Future of Collective Bargaining', *New Society*, 23 March 1978.

54 Robert S. Starobin, *Industrial Slavery in the Old South*, chap. 3, 'Patterns of Resistance and Repression'.

55 *Chibaro*, p. 242.

56 For a brief treatment of later developments at FIAT see *Working Class Autonomy and the Crisis: Italian Marxist Texts of the Theory and Practice of a Class Movement: 1964–79*, Red Notes/CSE Books, London, 1979, esp. 'The Struggle at FIAT', pp. 167–95.

57 Cited in Robert A. Brady, *The Spirit and Structure of German Fascism*, London, Gollancz (Left Book Club), 1937, p. 145.

58 ibid., p. 146; C. W. Guillebaud, *The Social Policy of Nazi Germany*, Cambridge, CUP, 1941, pp. 38–9.

59 For a systematic listing of the many matters which shop stewards did not have any right to determine, see *Workers Divided*, Part I.

7 Payment Systems and Productivity

Piecework and 'Looting'

Miklos Haraszti

How do you earn money? Learning to calculate this is harder than mastering the job itself. Even so, some calculations are just as important for earning a living as the most strenuous labour. They give me money in exchange for my work, but after that I have to go through all the sums they have done to arrive at my pay. Otherwise I could easily fool myself. Neither the gleaming heap of finished jobs, nor my leaden fatigue, dry mouth and trembling stomach tells me anything about whether or not my work has been successful. I must learn to measure myself against the standards of the factory. I have to add up the value of months, days and hours on the basis of what minutes are worth, and I can hardly afford to be generous. They have already calculated each minute into so much for so much. The method is simple. They have converted my minutes into jobs done, and my output into piece-rates.

'Work-sheet' – that's what is printed on the form which comes with each batch. There is one sheet for each run. Once the inspector has checked them off, I get the carbon copies. The workers simply call the sheets 'money'. My instructor explains it to me immediately : 'The first thing to do when you get a job is to check the "money", and, if the people from the office haven't sent one down, you demand it straightaway.' Then, brushing aside the jumble of mysterious letters and figures with a sweep of his hand, he says, 'None of that need bother you. Here, these are your holy words.' And, with that, he taps a box at the corner of the sheet. 'That's the piece-rate. That's the only thing we look at. Take it as being in fillérs for a single piece; turn it into forints for a hundred. Just forget about the rest,' he says, rubbing the point home.

There must have been a time when he was interested in all the headings on the 'money' – for instance piece-time and 'work category'. But, like the others, he knows from experience that it is an illusion to think that the piece-rate depends on factors such as the time allowed for each item. 'Just ask them yourself. They'll go on at you until your head swims. Everything's fine on paper; there's no point in opening your mouth about it. But, if that lot up there want to slash the piece-rate – otherwise called "readjusting the norms" – they have only to give the order, and down it comes by such and such per cent. They just sit there with the rate-fixers, add, multiply, divide and rub out, and, at the end of all this, the piece-rate has dropped. But on paper it all looks fine; you can study it for as long as you like. It figures. Look, I'm telling you: just watch the piece-rate. That's all . . .'

I do study my 'money' and try to anticipate the results. When I have accumulated a good bundle of work-sheets, I take them home with me. At work, I don't have time to check the piece-rate, simply because I'm on one. And the race against the clock follows me right into my home. I have to rest for hours on end doing nothing, otherwise even the most simple multiplication becomes such a strain that my hands tremble.

It doesn't take long to realize that my calculations bear out my neighbour. The boxes headed 'Preparation Time' and 'Preparation Payment' are blank. And so the period allowed for a job (and the corresponding pay for it) does not take into account the preparation and setting of the machine, although this must take up my time even if the setter helps. My machine remains idle while it is prepared, as the rate-fixer knows full well. Just as I must know that if I want to do 'paid' work then – as my neighbour pointed out – I must also do things for which I will never be paid, even nominally. This kind of unpaid work is not just a miller's privilege. It is the right of every worker on piece-rates.

But perhaps this lost time is taken into account when the overall time for the job is calculated? After all, what is this 'piece-time'? How is it assessed? Why do the others obstinately ignore it even when, according to the work-sheet, wages are directly dependent upon it? 'Money', on its own, does not answer these questions. And so, for days on end, I put them to my machines, to try and work it all out.

I take the piece-time, as given on the work-sheet, quite literally: I follow the blueprint meticulously, and I run the machine at the prescribed speed. The technical instructions determine both the quality and the safety of the work. I only have to fix

291

the speed, the rate of feed, and the cutting depth, then I'm ready to start off a run of fifty pieces. As soon as the inspector has accepted my first piece, I look at the workshop clock. Then, everything ceases to exist except the passing seconds. The machine turns at its set speed; only my own movements can gain me time.

After the fiftieth piece, I look at the clock once more, I pull out the work-sheet, and I begin to calculate. The sheet says: time per piece, 3·3 minutes; payment per piece, 4·1 fillérs. I completed the run of fifty in three and a quarter hours; instead of the 3·3 minutes which I am supposed to be able to meet, I have taken about 4 minutes a piece, and that does not include the time needed to set up the run. I have made 20 forints and 81 fillérs, and the better half of my working day has gone.

The result is more or less the same in all my trials: out of ten operations, two, at the very most, come close to the official time. (This is not because of lack of experience: some months later I will repeat these tests again, always sticking to the instructions, and the results will be hardly any better.)

My neighbour smiles again: 'What are you trying to prove with these alchemical calculations? You'll never earn more like that. While you did your sums, I made at least 10 forints. And I knew the result before you started: you're broke.'

The calculations I make at home show even more conclusive results. I establish that it is impossible for me to reach the norm given on the work-sheet. Even if I could – even if my output was one hundred per cent – I could hardly earn any extra. This is important. Because up to now I'd thought that it in some way depended on me.

From all this it turns out that the piece-rate is an hourly rate in disguise, or more precisely, a straightforward rate per minute: only those minutes during which the machine is running are paid for. None of the workers I spoke with realized that they were working for a dolled-up time rate; the deception is shrewdly masked behind the piece-rate system ...

More and more, piece-rates appear to me in the guise of a man who typifies the managerial spirit; a man who, up to this point, seemed to me, like the bosses themselves, to be severe but just, and who judged me according to the standards of a machine. Just: because he allowed me to pull myself up to the level of the machine; if I showed myself capable of a productivity comparable to the machine, then I received payment for each of my movements, just as the machine itself received electric current. Severe: because he punished me for being only a man; he did not pay me for the time when I was not a machine, during which I prevented the machine from giving birth to a piece. But my calculations around this one hundred per cent performance reveal a further characteristic of piece-rates. They are insatiable. They fix a norm, but take good care that I am forced to surpass it by making sure that even one hundred per cent performance is not enough to live on.

Anyway, the norms are not unreasonable only because pauses have to be taken during work, they are impossible to fulfil in any case if one keeps to the technical instructions that determine the quality of the job, and a certain level of safety. Another line of reasoning confirms my first alchemical calculations. The rate-fixers cannot but set a production time which demands a superhuman effort, since the whole point of the norms is to hold wages down to a level fixed in advance. If, for example, the sum of 61 forints has been fixed as the wage for a day's work at one hundred per cent performance, the rate-fixers are obliged to set the time per piece so that a minute of work does not yield more than the level fixed for the category; that is, the wage for a full minute's work. Even if the workers don't think like this, the rate-fixers are doing so all the time. Their point of departure is the pay itself – the 'incentive' of a danger to one's living standards – and not their experience of the true time taken to make a piece. Their stop-watches give a result which has been determined in advance, and this is the reason why the allocated times per piece, with very few exceptions, are unrealizable.

Piece-rate workers make neither analysis nor alchemical calculations: they learn from experience. Quite simply, they *know* that the time per piece is purely formal, that it is the payment per piece which counts, and nothing else. They only concern themselves with one sum: how high is the piece-rate for the job in hand? And how many must I produce to earn a day's wage? A sociologist would write: 'In the system of the people's economy, founded upon incentives, the norm plays the role of an indispensable fiction.' The man next to me says, 'The norm is a rip-off.'

I no longer think about the time-norm and other mysterious headings any differently from the others. My colleagues would think a worker had gone off his head if he came home on pay-day saying 'I am not bringing back a lot of money, but I kept to all the technical instructions, and fulfilled the norm.' The norm anyway can't be realized. There is only one way out of this vicious circle: every young worker knows it even before he stands at his machine for the first time, and so does the rate-fixer, from the day when he gets his first commission.

LOOTING

Safety Regulations for Milling Machines

1. Throughout working hours, work-clothes must always be worn and firmly fastened. Women must wear a head-scarf, men with long hair must wear a cap.
2. The wearing of rings, watches, bracelets, and chains during work is forbidden.
3. Before beginning work, check that machines are in good working order and that the safety devices operate. If there are any malfunctions it is forbidden to start work.
4. Jobs must only be carried out as laid down by the prescribed technical instructions. (The specified cutting speed, feed and depth must all be observed.)
5. Make sure that both the job and the tools are properly fixed and fastened.
6. It is forbidden to regulate tools, adjust a job, take measurements on or clean a machine which is running.
7. Whenever wharf is generated, protective goggles or a plastic face-guard must be worn.
8. In the event of any malfunctioning, the machine must be switched off immediately and the foreman notified of the fault.
9. Wharf may be removed only with the appropriate tools. It is forbidden to clean the machines with compressed air.
10. Machine hands must not carry out any repairs, whether electrical or mechanical, on their machines.
11. See that tools and gears are stored safely and are kept clean and tidy.
12. All accidents must be reported to the foreman immediately.

The Management

A copy of these rules is stuck to the side of every milling machine. When I started work in the factory, I was asked whether I had read them. I was then put through a sort of test. I had to recite all the points, one after another. I was asked questions about them in a relaxed, casual sort of way. The safety officer and I then signed the foreman's paper, which has since been attached to my personal file. If anything should happen because I'd not complied with these rules, the foreman would only have to get out my signature and everything would become clear: *I knew the rules, but I failed to apply them.*

In the galvanizing section of a factory where I used to work previously, and which was even bigger than this one, we spent the whole day plunging heavy pieces of metal into tubs of cyanide, chrome, hydrochloric acid, caustic soda, and other lethal poisons. We were paid, exactly as we are here, according to output. The safety test, no more searching than here, lasted five minutes. It did not make much sense anyway: apart from a feeble ventilation system, which made unendurable noises and draughts – we always unplugged it after a few seconds – there was nothing to protect our health. In spite of the rules, we handled chemical substances without using either goggles or the safety devices intended to stop the bottles from turning over. Who had the time to go and look for them? Our rubber gloves would always rip open just in the middle of an electrolysis and, to prevent this treacherous anointment from eating our skin, we used to wash our hands in hydrochloric acid after work. One man used to say that we were each entitled to half a litre of milk a day, to help avoid toxication. But he wasn't sure about that.

Before the test, they showed us a short documentary. 'The actors are great artists; it's really most instructive,' the safety officer told us, to whip up our enthusiasm.

And indeed, one after the other, the favourites of Budapest cabaret appeared on the screen. Ervin Kibédi played the part of the arrogant, disorganized, work-shirking malcontent, riddled with faults and quite unconcerned about the safety regulations. In his typical upper-class Jewish accent, he told what were supposed to be workers' jokes, rather in the way that he parodies car-owners' complaints in publicity films. László Keleti was the furious foreman, solely preoccupied with productivity. At first, he completely ignored the safety regulations, but later on – this was a bizarre touch – he fell on his face, hurting himself so that he had to go about squinting. In the end, he was converted. He put forward an angel-faced young worker as an example for everyone. This youth had charming manners, measured gestures, and demonstrated for all the world to see that even from the point of view of productivity it was best to obey the safety regulations. Our young hero argued with the foreman, 'Think how many hours of work are lost each month through accidents!' He was so sure of himself, our good youthful worker, that he made an ally of the manager himself, whom the film carefully avoided embellishing with any comic touches. In the beginning, and also at the end, the manager trusted the foreman. But the day when he discovered that things were going badly, he joined forces with angel-face to put everything right. It was even made to appear that the manager knew the individual workers better than the foreman – even though he was over-burdened with work. He was carrying out research towards an important breakthrough, and this sort of incident disrupted his studies – but only for a few hours, we hoped.

The film went down very well with the apprentices. At each accident, presented as a joke and without any sign of real blood, they muttered all sorts of comments and remarks. They anticipated every *faux pas*, and laughed in advance. 'What a load of bullshit,' they said when it was over.

The fate of the twelve points in our factory was much the same as that of all 'twelve points' generally.* The first two are possibly exceptions, as no time is lost by observing them. If it wasn't for the fact that they are laid down as rules and regulations even the young workers might well apply them, for they are just a matter of common sense. However, every section has its undisciplined, long-haired rebels.

But all the other points are our enemies, and a burden to the bosses, whose bragging about work safety increases in proportion to their distance from the machines.

The fourth point is the most important. Under the piece-rate system, and any other form of payment by results, its breach is both inevitable and tolerated. A piece-rate worker does not earn money just by working, but rather because he works without observing the regulations.

My work-mates have long since given up the idea of their labour producing useful goods of high quality. They find it quite natural to be bound by special rules governing elementary matters of common sense, and equally natural to resist these rules, even when the price they pay is their own health.

But who batters his own head against a wall unless someone

---

* Both the revolution of 1848–9 in Hungary and the uprising in 1956 began with a declaration of 'twelve points'.

else is forcing him to do so? What immense force is capable of killing in the worker – who creates everything – the instinct for good work? You can, like the newspapers, believe that there is a point to a worker's life. But why should one be shocked by the indifference with which even workers who make a good living turn the page without hesitation when a newspaper article purports to give his life some other meaning than this simple desire to live well? 'You have to alleviate the *cancer*, but not cut it out.' Even the most well-intentioned say some such thing when they talk about the improvement of workers' pay or the relations which surround their work – they say nothing about the pitiless inhuman absurdity of paid labour itself.

When we work on a machine – whose output is basic to the calculation of our pay – and when we run it faster than the prescribed rate, then, officially, that is not called self-destruction (an inconceivable self-destruction which calls into question our whole universe) but 'cheating the norm'.

A strange kind of cheating which does so much harm to the cheater! If a fraud is perpetrated, then someone has to be defrauded. In this case possibly the employers, since increased production does not result, as they might wish, solely from the extreme tension of our nerves and muscles, but also from speeding up the machines.

If we received a satisfactory wage for one hundred per cent performance then, all right, it would be cheating pure and simple. Because we would produce no more than the one hundred per cent, but would do so with less effort, and the quality would be worse. But this isn't it. What would spur us on constantly to increase output if one hundred per cent performance was really feasible, and its corresponding pay satisfactory?

And so, when the jobs come out of the machine quicker than the norms lay down, it could well be called a sort of cheating, but for us, this only means – and that's what they intend – that we finish more jobs than are officially reckoned to represent an output of one hundred per cent. It's not a matter of working less. Exactly the opposite in fact: we work more to produce more in order to earn an acceptable wage, and this is possible only by cheating.

One might well ask: who is being done? Certainly not the bosses who in the final count can only be satisfied, because we produce more. The machines perhaps? They can take the pace. It is the norm which is swindled, only the norm and the piece-rate system itself. And suddenly, this norm begins to

297

take on a concrete existence: it assumes the appearance of a boss, any boss, whom one then imagines one is cheating.

The workers call cheating the norm 'looting'. Millions of piece-rate workers use this word quite naturally, without the least trace of guilt. No doubt the god of piece-rate workers receives millions of prayers every day, which beg him to provide their daily loot. This meaning of the word is not to be found in any dictionary. Entries under 'cheating the norm' do not describe what the workers actually do, but mention bribery, fiddling the accounts, and so on, things which are unknown in the factories.

But management knows all about looting. After all, it is not just the workers who practise it, and live off it, but the bosses as well. If they fix my pay for a hundred per cent performance at around 8 forints an hour, then, quite literally, they force me to loot. Just how could their production plan be implemented if this compulsion was not built into it in the first place?

There is no need for them to go through all those calculations which I made to work out my wage per minute. All they have to do is to set the time for a job low enough, so that it compels me to loot.

Every boss banks on his piece-rate workers looting. If he sometimes reprimands them about this, it's invariably in a cautious, low-keyed, impersonal way, often with humour. This usually happens only when looting too obviously affects the quality of work, perhaps when there are many more defective pieces than are allowed for in the calculated reject rate.

No boss would ever openly encourage us to loot. 'You can take money home by the sackful,' says the head foreman. 'It's entirely up to you.' Of course, he doesn't add that the hourly wage is a farce and the prescribed speeds can't be taken seriously.

M gave me my first lesson in looting. He said he couldn't stand to see the way my machine crawled along. 'You're not giving them any sleepless nights. If you don't work out how to make your money yourself, they won't slip the missing hundred forint bills into your pocket. Well now, what do you do when the setter has finished?'

I was going to tell him that I knew all about my machine, but he stopped me with a wave of his hand. 'This is what you do: you set it all over again. And if you begin without the setter, then forget about the technical instructions. He sticks to the blueprint. That's what he's paid for. But you've got a head of your own, haven't you? Well then, step up the cutting speed and feed the job through faster. Just make sure you don't blow yourself up. If you want to make a living here you can't let things run along smoothly.'

It's not easy. As soon as I start, the accelerated pace brings on an extreme state of nerves. My eyes are transfixed by the hail of sparks; my whole body strains towards the lever; sometimes I can't bear the tension any longer and pull too soon. The machine trembles and shrieks. The excessive stress on the material induces ominous knockings and vibrations. Their crescendo induces in me cramps and waves of guilt and fear. My torpid concentration collapses.

I concentrate on one machine. The other, timed for a different run, comes to the end of its operation; the milling disc hits against harder material and breaks, making an infernal din. The broken milling teeth shoot past my head like bullets. I stop both machines. My inner trembling gets the better of my hands. When this happens to experienced workers, they set about sweeping up shavings to master their impulse to run away. The unmistakable sound and the sudden quiet that follows makes the others look up from their own noisy machines. Their looks don't condemn and their remarks help me through a difficult moment. Slowly and unobtrusively, my neighbour strolls over and examines the shattered head. 'There are plenty of these in the stores,' he says. 'It's a disposable tool.' (At every production meeting, the foreman tables the same motion: 'The level of consumption of disposable tool parts is too high throughout the section.') . . .

'Nerves' brought about by the necessity of looting cannot be calmed by anything except loot itself. We have to stake all our inventiveness, knowledge, imagination, initiative and courage on getting it. And when this comes off, it brings a certain feeling of triumph. This is why workers on piece-rates often feel that they have beaten the system, as if they'd got the better of someone. But looting does not make the work any easier; it intensifies the physical and mental effort demanded. The time won is used to make even more pieces. If we stopped, carried away by the sheer joy of success, we should lose all the advantages we had gained. Despite this we talk among ourselves about our looting with an air of conspiracy, as if it was a decisive blow in the unending, daily battles.

M is decidedly proud of his reputation. Even the turners

speak with respect about his looting, although they have a traditional contempt for the millers' dirty trade. He really does get up to some fantastic tricks. One of his favourites is to lay the huge, heaviest pieces on the milling table, without fastening them down, and to lean against them with the whole weight of his body while the table moves to and fro, and the cutters screech. Just to watch him sends cold shivers down your spine. A grain of impurity in the material, or a fault in the casting, and the insane speed of the head will rip the piece from between his hands. But if he doesn't do it that way, he will lose the two minutes to be gained from every ten.

L, who is coming up to retirement, has been given the chance of doing exactly the same work every day. He mills the gaps in between the teeth on cog wheels. Each piece has to be worked on three sides. This is how he grabs his loot: when he has finished on one of the three sides he uses one hand to loosen the clamps (which are anyway fewer than the number laid down in the regulations) as the table comes back at full speed and the spindle continues to rev. When the table gets back to its initial position, he can immediately pivot the piece around without stopping the milling head, so that he can then let the machine carry on with its cycle while he tightens the clamp on to the new position. Is it safe to work with so few clamps? Does he have time to check that they are fastened tightly enough or that the piece isn't going to smash into the revolving head? He never asks questions like this. If he worked to the rules, in one fell swoop his job would be metamorphosed into 'bad' work, and he would have lost his 'living'.

Around Christmas time, we were made tragically aware of the way L worked. In the adjacent section there was an accident involving another miller who put L's pieces through their next operation. This worker also took advantage of the chance to pivot the pieces around. The milling head tore off the fingers from his right hand. The stretcher on which they carried him out passed right in front of old L's machine.

The foreman sent for the millers and gave us a little talk in his office. 'On the occasion of this most regrettable incident, I would like to take the opportunity of emphasizing to you that in our section we can boast about the fact that we have had very few accidents indeed. It is in all our interests' – this was his favourite phrase – 'to keep things this way. This scramble at the end of the year isn't very pleasant for anyone, but it involves all of us, because the final outcome will affect us all.

It would therefore be a good thing if we kept our safety record to its present level, and finished the year without an accident. We must learn from what has just happened. You are grown men, I know, but you shouldn't be ashamed to learn. Has anyone got any questions? Now, please sign the minutes of this *ad hoc* meeting.' On the sheet of paper, you could read that the foreman had drawn our attention to the importance of keeping to the technical regulations, and the workers had registered their agreement. We went back to the section, and everyone continued exactly as before: including old L.

The 'Lump' in the UK Construction Industry

Terry Austrin

The nationally negotiated closed shop form of trade union agreement does not operate in the construction industry. Trade unions have been unable to enforce it. The effect is that in that sector of the construction industry dominated by the private firm – in 1973 there were 73,420 such firms[1] – the firms and their casually employed labour forces pay little attention to the centralized bargaining machinery that exists. They also operate with a variety of forms of wage contract. These can be legal or illegal, union sanctioned or non-union.

The construction industry is both casual and labour intensive. Workers are employed for particular construction projects which have a limited duration, hence the negotiation and renegotiation of wage contracts is a continuous process begun anew at each new project. But the fact that there is no fixed form of contract – itself an indication of trade union weakness – means that the use of different contract forms can fluctuate according to the problems posed for capital and labour in particular regional labour markets. From the trade union point of view this has two direct implications. Firstly, trade union strength is determined by the degree to which local branches of the national building union can control local labour markets. Secondly, the object of trade union struggle in the industry has always been the particular wage contract *form* as much as the *amount* of wages. Further, the industry has been characterized by a very uneven development of trade union struggle. Violent, bitterly fought strikes over wages and wage contracts, lasting up to and longer than a year, can co-exist in the same industry with non-unionism of a most passive kind.[2] In the post-war period these struggles took the form of shop steward struggles over the incorporation of bonus into the union wage contract and struggles against the non-union 'lump'.

The struggle against the lump, fought against individual building firms, reached its height in the period 1970–73. It was a struggle within one industry, between a unionized and non-unionized workforce, in which up until 1970 the building unions had been the losers. In fact, in the face of the growing use of building workers on lump wage contracts, traditional craft building unionism had atrophied and collapsed. In 1965 the bricklayers' union, the Amalgamated Union of Building Trade Workers (AUBTW), had reported that it was 'financially bleeding to death as a union'. In June 1971 an age-old hope of building workers was realized by the amalgamation of the AUBTW with the carpenters' union, the Amalgamated Society of Woodworkers (ASW), to form a new union with the declared aim of one union for the construction industry. UCATT – as the new union was called – was a forced embrace of national union leaderships brought on by bankruptcy. It was a desperate attempt to keep independent building unionism alive, not fought for by construction workers but rather negotiated by their leaderships. The alternative they had faced was clear. Either merger with one of the two big general unions – and both had made it clear that they were prepared to expand their membership in the construction industry – or continued decline.[3]

This crisis and reconstruction of trade unionism was a direct product of construction workers ignoring their trade unions and opting to negotiate their own wage contracts and conditions on the lump rather than relying on, or fighting for, union regulated work. The figures on the growth of this form of working are very revealing. Between 1965 and 1973 the numbers of building workers classified as operating some form of labour-only contracts grew from an estimated 160–200,000 to 400,000. Paradoxically, the impetus for this substantial reorganization of labour on non-union contracts was provided by acute shortages of skilled and unskilled labour. In 1973 – a boom year for construction – the National Economic Development Office produced a report that calculated that in the south and east of England there were ten vacancies for every bricklayer and that across the country the average was five to one. There were also three jobs for every carpenter and three for every plasterer.[4]

The increased freedom to negotiate, and mobility between firms, that this market afforded construction workers forced firms to pay wages well above the standard union rate. But under the labour-only sub-contracting form that was offered – and which many workers chose – it did not provide for the growth and further establishment of national trade unionism. It was a situation in which construction workers didn't feel the immediate need for shop stewards or trade unionism because every worker was in a position to do his own bargaining. Trade unionism was thus drained of its membership in a situation normally understood as ideal for union growth.[5]

However rather than assign the lump to the existence of a particularly backward capitalist sector of industry we will seek here to clarify how it differs from a union negotiated form of contract; the conditions in which workers took up the lump contract; and the conditions under which construction firms could successfully block trade unionism by using that contract.

The Lump

Generally the lump was characterized by a main contractor who contracted out work, the sub-contractor who contracted for a piece of that work and the worker who was hired out, on a labour-only basis, to the main contractor by the sub-contractor. Accordingly, the worker, in cases where he did not directly negotiate his own individual contract, was placed into a position of dual dependence; upon the sub-contractor for his wage and the main contractor for the supply of work. In addition the contract was negotiated outside of union control: it generally broke all forms of union agreements on hours, wages, safety and training and further could involve the illegal appropriation of tax.

A government report on the construction industry defined it in the following way:

Under the labour-only sub-contract the main contractor himself provides the materials and most of the equipment required for some part of his task, and pays the sub-contractor for carrying out the work. That the sub-contract is for 'labour only' distinguishes it from the predominant form of sub-contract known as 'supply and fix', in which the sub-contractor himself provides the materials and equipment as well as the labour needed to perform a specified part of the whole task under the main contract. Generally the labour-only sub-contractor provides only hand tools, but sometimes he is required to provide some other forms of equipment – in bricklaying for instance he may be required to provide his own scaffolding. The payment fixed in the sub-contract may take the form of a lump sum for the completion of a specified task in joinery, for instance so many £'s for the 'first fixing' of a given house; or a piece-rate, so much for instance, per 1000 bricks laid; or even an hourly rate, but this is quite unlike the familiar basic hourly rate, in that it is the sole and comprehensive source of the payment due to the sub-contractor.[6]

Such a contract could, according to the state of the labour market, give the individual worker both very 'high' earnings and a freedom to determine his own pace of work. A bricklayer lists the advantages and disadvantages to him:

> For the past seven years I have been a labour-only sub-contractor (a subby). To become a subby has certain disadvantages. In the first place I must become self-employed. To be self-employed means I lose the right to unemployment pay, workmen's compensation and the opportunity of a secure job with a building firm and promotion prospects. I am also responsible for stamping my own cards and those of anyone I employ. This is seldom, as I prefer to work on my own. The benefits that accrue are that I pay less income tax than I would on PAYE and in the short run I can earn more money than working as an employee.[7]

But the lump could also lead to wage cutting and to the complete undermining of national trade union conditions outlined in the national working agreement. This was the main union argument against it. For the unions it contained the potential for being a 'scabs' charter. It was a practice that could destroy everything that trade unionism had ever fought for; most importantly the guaranteed weekly wage.

The arrangement of the lump contract varied from the examples listed above to sub-contractors who operated as small firms to the gang system with all the members of the gang operating as self-employed workers. Further variations on these forms were the gang system under a leader, or labour master, who may himself have worked part of the time, but who also took the sub-contract himself, paid the other members of the gang terms agreed with them and bore an employer's responsibility towards them. A gang leader of this sort may have controlled simply one small gang or taken on several gangs at once. In all of these situations the employers' liabilities, the stamping of insurance cards and the deduction of tax could be, and were, avoided.

An increasingly important method of sub-contract that grew

in the late 1960s was the use made of labour agencies. Workers employed in this way worked for an hourly rate paid by the agency that sent them out on contract to the employers. The employers' payment was to the agency who then paid the sub-contracted men a certain proportion of that payment. This particular form flourished through the establishment of the national labour agencies, Manpower, Labour Force and SOS. It is important to note that their legal status gave a legitimation to the lump that was generally denied in the other forms which tended to be tied to tax and insurance evasion.

As a variation on a piecework system of working the lump form of contract was not new to the building industry.[8] The justification for the contract in the nineteenth century was that it was suited to the industry's needs, that it was a natural method of working conforming in some way with an assumed psychology of building workers. This justification was repeated in the second half of the twentieth century. In the words of a government report (1968) the lump offered the 'opportunity for an enterprising worker to gain independence.'[9] The same report went on:

> The men feel that they are working for themselves ... Their whole attitude to work is energised by the thought that they are working for no man's profit but their own.[10]

This rationale always forgot to add that the construction unions always opposed the practice.

A dominant feature of this form of contract – as noted by the bricklayer above – was that it placed the lump worker in the tax category of the self-employed. This categorization legitimated the conception of freedom that is generally associated with piecework and allowed the lump worker the tax privileges normally associated with the self-employed class. This tax category did not however alter the social position of the lump worker, rather it operated as a legal category with no distinct social content. The lump worker was not directly employed in the legal form of a direct contract between himself and the employer, but the different legal form (sub-contract) in no way altered the economic relationship between them. He produced for the employer; he neither owned nor controlled his own capital but remained as a seller of labour-only. The fact that the wage incentive in the case of the lump could be further enhanced by the self-employed category, and by the opportunity to evade tax given in that category, was not an indication of a new type of system but rather an expression of the level to which tax payments had risen in the period after 1945.[11]

The lump, then, was not a career ladder out of the working class. The lump worker remained very different from the owner of a small building firm and rather than removing himself from the social world of the ordinary construction worker he actually reinforced its *casual* nature. Significantly this situation was not misunderstood by the National Federation of Self Employed. Lump workers did not find acceptance in an organization catering for the traditional petty bourgeois. In fact lump workers formed no organization, for to have done so would have necessarily pointed towards trade unionism.[12] Under their form of contract the general relation between capital and labour had not been transformed. They earned their money because they broke the rules.[13]

Trade Unionism

Trade unions in the construction industry opposed the lump because it broke and undermined their control of training apprentices and wages. Historically the struggle over these two issues was in fact crucial to the development of the craft union forms in the industry. They stood against the lump because, firstly, it undermined their ability to regulate uniform *time* wages and, secondly, because piecework (or the lump) was traditionally the employers' method of breaking trade union control of the labour process. The lump was understood to be an attempt to lower the standards of training in the industry. In this sense it was a practice that aimed at lowering wages. The craft form of control, then, was rooted in the attempt to control and regulate apprenticeship training in order to maintain both craft standards and wages.

The success of the British building unions in achieving this form of control was however partial because they failed to develop any autonomous methods of regulating the labour market. In the casual conditions of the construction labour market the tie of the worker to his union was his skill, but this tie was never unilaterally enforced through such practices as union control over hiring and firing. In the post-war conditions of labour shortage, combined with the break-up of craft skills that characterized the development of the industry, this structural weakness of the construction unions was clearly brought into the open. The boom period of labour shortage strengthened bargaining at the point of production, thereby displacing traditional craft arguments concerning wage cutting, but it also displaced trade unionism itself. In this curtailment of trade union strength there was however no contradiction in employers maintaining combination against trade unionism whilst individually buying labour-power by raising wages on lump contracts. For the object was not to drive down wages but to raise wages to attract labour – but significantly, only to raise them temporarily.

That these wage rises were not expressed in, or a consequence of, trade union strength was important. In the short run it could be argued that lump contracts could place a wide degree of control of work in the hands of the worker; in practice however it meant that wages and working conditions were negotiated for individually and hence were never *established* or *consolidated* through collective practice or custom.[14] Thus in a period of profitable production and labour shortage, high wages were passed on through the lump contract but work rules controlling production, whilst generated, were not stabilized. And perhaps more importantly for the employers, those rules that had been in existence were openly discarded in the struggle for production in the shortest possible time. In a period in which skilled construction workers were being progressively deskilled this atomization of the work force through lump contracts was crucial.

For these reasons the practice of the lump was not understood by the unions to be a legitimate form of piecework or bonus system. The employers used the lump to organize and control casual labour in a situation of extreme labour shortage. The lump was perfect for this because the negotiation of the complete contract at the point of production lacked any form of collective regulation or any conception of training skilled workers. Bonus schemes were different. Their introduction into the industry (1947), although a product of the long-term desire of employers' to organize craftsmen's work into a number of clearly defined repetitive tasks with a view to raising productivity, was accepted by the unions because they believed they could regulate them without detriment to craft training or themselves. Bonus, then, was negotiated for on top of collectively agreed union conditions; the lump however was always a one-off contract with no continuity of organization.

The lump worker was treated as an individual, responsible

for his work but as a craftsman totally indifferent to it – and thus not subject to the collective control of the workforce or trade union. If the contract was taken in group form then the size of the unit of responsibility was enlarged, but the principle of division within the workforce was maintained. Whereas wages under trade union control were known and generalized throughout the workforce, wages under the competitive conditions of labour-only sub-contract remained a private affair. This of course meant that men could work alongside one another ignorant of the amount of money being paid. In many cases a site foreman or site agent would not have known how much certain workers were being paid since the lump contracts were negotiated indirectly.

Official government reports have been very clear about the basic mechanism at work here

> Where firms found themselves short of labour, and raised their bid to attract it, they would add less to their costs if they paid more to a marginal group under the guise of a sub-contract, than if they paid them normally, when they could hardly refuse to extend the higher pay to all other workers.[15]

Obviously to have established trade union control in such conditions it would have been necessary to overthrow the lump contract.

The point to be stressed is that the system of wage payment is as much an object of struggle as is the amount of the wage itself. Further, that though trade unionism is an expression of wage labour, it is not at all the case that all forms of wage labour are compatible with trade unionism. Piecework can be compatible but the significance of the lump contract in the boom years of construction in the 1960s and early 1970s was that trade union control was precluded. A whole generation of construction workers were thus habituated to work through the lump. In the words of a Liverpool shop steward 'they were born and bred on the lump, they never knew trade unionism or what it was for.'

The historical examples of the use of the contract conform to this pattern. It has always been lumps of casual labour power that the employer bought. The intended effect has always been to reinforce the atomization of individual workers and small groups and thus impede any effective trade union regulation of the industry. The overcoming of a casual labour market as a condition of work is of course the fundamental problem of construction trade unionism.

The State and the Employers

In the literature dealing with the nineteenth century the lump contract is normally described as operating in those industries lacking a developed management structure. The advantage of the contract in that situation was that it supplied a 'self-acting stimulus which dispensed with the necessity of incessant supervision.'[16] To that condition of nineteenth-century production must be added that it also dispensed with trade unionism for well developed management structures in the twentieth century. In both historical periods it functioned as a wage form that secured the appropriate organization of labour according to the problems posed by the prevailing conditions of the social reproduction of capital.

In the 1960s and early 1970s the major problem of capital was an acute shortage of skilled and unskilled labour. A government report of 1966 clearly presented the employers' case for lump working under these conditions. It argued that the lump was a consequence of labour shortages and that attempts to eliminate or control the system should not be taken since such attempts could give rise to more serious difficulties for the industry.[17] This position of 1966 was adopted by the Tory government that followed Wilson's Labour government in 1970 and was reaffirmed under the re-elected Labour government of 1974. It was further enhanced by government reports that praised the productivity and character of labour working on lump contracts:

> The Labour-only group will have attracted the type that is most ready to work harder and longer in order to earn more, that is, the type that will in any case be more responsive to incentives. This explains why the high gearing of the lump sum incentive, with earnings wholly dependent on output and with no basic hourly rate or fall-back for hours lost through bad weather, should be acceptable under labour-only as it is not in direct employment.[18]

Clearly the lump contract was understood to be a valuable spur to production in conditions of labour supply which might otherwise have undermined labour productivity.

Governments, then, were prepared to support the employers' use of the lump contract. This was so even when high lump payments were used to circumvent the incomes policy requirements of both Labour and Tory administrations. As James Prior, a Tory Minister put it in an interview with the employers' national journal:

> The major problem with the building industry is that it goes from slump to boom and back to slump again. When you are in a boom period there is no chance of getting an income policy as far as the building industry is concerned, and when you are in a slump you do not need one.[19]

In this form of governmental logic the construction industry is understood to be a special case, not because of low wages or trade union strength, but rather because the lump contract allowed the direct regulation of wages by market forces without any form of trade union intervention.

The State also however reserved the right – as it does with all forms of wage contracts – to regulate the different forms in which the lump contract was operated. In the case of the lump this meant legislation to deal with the tax evasion that accompanied the practice. On these grounds the State received support from the unions but no active encouragement from the employers. The first piece of legislation that dealt specifically with the lump was the Tory government's 1971 Finance Act. The details of the clauses (special sections 29–31, schedule 5) made it necessary for a sub-contractor to be in possession of a tax exemption certificate which was obtainable from the Inspector of Taxes. If the sub-contractor did not hold the certificate then the employer was required to deduct 30 per cent as tax payment from all wage payments made.

The result was that 400,000 people took out the tax exemption certificates and an elaborate black market trading of the certificates developed in which both workers and employers engaged. The Labour government's 1975 budget attempted to tighten up on this by recalling all the certificates and issuing new ones. Their success was limited, but more to the point was the fact that by 1975 the lump was no longer a preferred method of working. The onset of recession conditions in the industry in 1974 had eliminated the need for the contract.

Cases did come to light in later years. In 1976 one concerned Mr Ronald Carr, a company director, who made lump workers the directors, shareholders and secretaries of 'off the peg' companies, the men receiving their wages in full from Carr's agency, Labour Force Limited, without the 30 per cent deduction required by the Finance Act.[20] Another involved the building firm of J. Murphy & Sons and led to three of its directors being fined more than £78,000 for a gigantic swindle to avoid paying tax.[21] In this case the London Region of the National Federation of Building Trade Employers considered expelling the firm but was urged by the national organization not to do so. No condemnation was made of the firm by the employers' organization.

These cases were however rare, for the majority of prosecutions involved workers and by this time the lump had receded with the slump in construction. In 1973 the number of unemployed construction workers was listed as 90,000. By February 1978 the recorded figure had reached a total of 221,817. The Department of the Environment estimated that between 1973 and 1976 287,000 jobs were lost in construction.[22] The position of the worker in construction was therefore reversed from the 'boom' conditions up to 1973. The consequence was unemployment and the beginnings of a large export of skilled and unskilled construction workers to the construction sites of West Germany and the Middle East. The trade union struggle against the lump contract turned into a defence of trade unionism in conditions of chronic unemployment.

Conclusion

Considered in the ordinary way, the problem of the lump revolved around what was 'fair and just'. The contract could have legal status and was therefore just, what was unjust was the action of individuals – workers and employers – who resorted to tax evasion. For the unions the contract was both unfair in that it violated national working rules and unjust in that it took illegal forms. Essentially their argument was that the union contract was somehow fair. This was an argument that cut no ice with lump workers. When union struggles on the lump were successful, as in Birmingham between 1970–72, the success of the union drive was based upon equalling and going beyond lump payments by forcing through local employer-union agreements and organizing sites through high bonus payments.

The employers justified the contract the way they did all forms of piecework – by claiming that it directly rewarded effort with wages. That the direct consequence was the decline and declared irrelevance of national centralized bargaining and training did not concern them. They were however concerned to maintain a low national trade union rate and indeed in the three-month national strike of 1972 showed a very high degree of unity on resistance to a trade union demand of £30 for thirty-five hours. At the same time construction workers, both unionized and lump, could earn up to and over £100 a week on contracts negotiated at the point of production. It was quite clear, then, that the employers were concerned at all costs to avoid strengthening trade unionism in a period of labour shortage. Thus whilst there was no love lost between employers in the competition for labour employed on lump contracts, they formed – and in this they were assisted by the State – a block against the unions on the subject of eliminating the contract and raising wages through the union.

The reproduction of this system of lump wage labour was however only guaranteed insofar as wages were rising and workers could negotiate 'high' wages without trade union backing. These 'high' wages offset the tendency for construction workers to combine and were tied ideologically to the idea of individual achievement and effort in the production process. In reality, they excluded the unions from the direct regulation of wages and wages expressed the conditions operating in local labour markets.

This was the condition of suitability to the employers. The lump contract enabled them to retain the casual nature of their industry in employment conditions which tended to undermine it. It was a temporary contract for temporary employment. It was designed to facilitate the movement of labour so that it was available where and when it was needed and did not constitute a liability when it was not needed.

That liability can be understood to have been the threat of a trade-union-organized construction industry in conditions of full employment.

The Labour Process and Class Struggle

NOTES AND REFERENCES

1 The construction industry is broadly composed of a public and private sector. The private sector is by far the larger. It employs approximately 85 per cent of all construction workers. The public sector is mainly composed of direct labour workforces employed by local authorities. These workforces are mainly employed on maintenance work and local authority housebuilding and unlike the private sector are highly unionized.

2 The most vivid expression of this were the events of the 1972 national building strike. For details of this see my *Industrial Relations in the Construction Industry*, Ph.D. thesis, University of Bristol, 1978.

3 In fact the TGWU also operated with the policy of one union for the construction industry. Hence the creation of UCATT produced a situation in which in one industry two unions fought each other on the same policy.

4 See *Sunday Times*, 5 August 1973.

5 This is a generalization which can't be held to be true for the whole of the country. The north of England is generally recognized to be better unionized than the south and the cities of Liverpool and Glasgow have always been noted for their trade union strength.

6 E. H. Phelps Brown, *Report of the Committee of Inquiry under Professor E. H. Phelps Brown into certain matters concerning Labour in Building and Civil Engineering*, London, HMSO Cmnd. 3714, 1968.

7 Max Gagg, 'The Subby Bricklayer' in R. Fraser *Work*, Vol. 2, Pelican, 1969, p. 113.

8 The ASW rule banning piecework/lump work dates from 1892. This rule was relaxed in the case of piecework (bonus) in 1941 due to agreements made during the war and finally given up in 1947.

9 E. H. Phelps Brown, op. cit., 1968, p. 15. This subjectivist interpretation of the lump/piecework was of course nothing new.

10 There has always been a controversy over the subject of piecework. Marx argued that the worker could gain a sense of freedom under piecework systems. This in part

314

stems from the fact that the contract dispenses with direct supervision. For a brilliant attack on the system of piece-rates, see M. Harastzi, *A Worker in a Worker's State*, Penguin, 1977.

11 This refers to both taxes on workers' wages and taxes on capital. Particularly important in this respect was the Selective Employment Tax which taxed firms according to the number of employees. This tax, in part aimed at the construction industry, increased the tendency for firms to employ labour on the lump.

12 In 1977 tunnellers in the construction industry, who up until then had been employed on lump contracts, began organizing for higher 'lump' rates of pay. When these were not granted the tunnellers first applied to join the TGWU and then attempted to set up their own union. See 'Militant Mole digs his heels in for £1000', *Sunday Times*, 16 August 1976.

13 In principle it does not seem impossible that unions could actually have organized lump contracts. Unionized workers could have operated such contracts by demanding union conditions, including a minimum guaranteed wage and then have the right to negotiate wages in a lump contract form over and above the union rate. This would of course negate the use the employers made of the lump but it does indicate that the lump wasn't in any absolute sense anti-trade union.

14 See D. Lamb, *The Lump: An Heretical Analysis*, Solidarity Pamphlet, 1974, for a positive evaluation of the lump.

15 Phelps Brown, op. cit., 1968, p. 122.

16 A. J. Taylor, 'The Sub-Contract System in the British Coal Industry' in *Studies in the Industrial Revolution*, L. S. Pressnell (ed.), London, London University 1964, p. 216.

17 Report on 'Labour-Only-Sub-Contracting', *Ministry of Labour Gazette*, May 1966, p. 220.

18 Phelps Brown, op. cit., 1968, p. 128.

19 *National Builder* May 1976, p. 140.

20 *Guardian*, 25 May 1976.

21 See *The Times*, 25 March 1976.

22 For these statistics see *Building with Direct Labour* published by Housing Workshop of the Conference of Socialist Economists, 1978.

UK Productivity Dealing in the 1960s

Martyn Nightingale

Introduction

For nearly a decade in the 1960s, workers were subject to a wave of productivity bargaining. As critics pointed out at the time, many deals were only thinly disguised attempts to increase company profitability at the expense of shop-floor workers. Yet for Allan Flanders, a leading British industrial relations specialist, they were to be applauded as a means by which managers could somehow increase their control and share it at the same time.[1]

On the basis of the UK experience, however, it would be misleading to reduce the process of productivity bargaining as a whole to the status of a crude 'employers' offensive', perpetrated against 'creeping worker control'. Nor should it be seen as a process which contains some inexorable logic that will eventually lead workers to reject the whole framework of capitalist social relations.[2] Such claims are too abstract and risk obscuring the true significance of a complex development: a development which was characterized above all by *unevenness*, since, for various reasons, its attractiveness was limited to particular companies and industries and varied over time. Even the response of workers to the productivity experience was not uniform; the degree of acceptance or resistance varied considerably according to both general economic and political circumstances and technological conditions within particular companies and industries. To appreciate better the complex significance of productivity bargaining in the 1960s, it is useful to focus on three inter-related but analytically separable facets of productivity bargaining – the economic, the ideological and the political.

(a) *Economic*

Marxist critics, like Tony Cliff, had been quite correct to link the advent of productivity bargaining in the early 1960s with the general crisis of profitability facing British capital. It was accurate, too, to stress that the inception of productivity bar-

316

gaining indicated an intention on the part of managers and employers, later to be supported by the state, to take the initiative by reasserting their prerogatives and controls at the point of production. But the novel aspects of the productivity bargaining process lay in the *methods* by which managements chose to increase relative surplus value in order to restore profitability.

Most deals took the form of a comprehensive 'package' involving a wide variety of changes in work practices and payment systems. Often, previously non-negotiable work practices (craft-demarcations etc.) were brought into the wage-work bargaining arena and thus within the orbit of managerial control. This was done on a continuing basis as part of the productivity bargaining *process*. To put it simply, this represented a move away from traditional incentive payment schemes, of which piece-rate systems were the most widespread, towards more wide-ranging and subtle techniques of controlling the relationship between earnings and output. There had been much debate throughout the 1950s and 1960s about the inadequacy of these 'traditional' methods. Evidence suggested that piece-rate systems gave workers the ability to push up their earnings and maximize their 'unproductive time'. They had consequently 'boomeranged' against capital. The Donovan Report published in 1968 added fuel to the fire. It suggested that this process had a 'political' dimension. The growth of plant-bargaining had encouraged the development of an informal shop-steward system which had seriously undermined the ability of management and the State to control labour productivity at the point of production. From this point of view, both wage-drift and the growth of the shop-steward system were symptomatic of 'loose' managerial control. Productivity bargaining offered a possible solution. By the introduction of the 'package' including job flexibilities (deskilling), measured daywork, grading systems and the like, it was hoped that control could be 'tightened'. In essence, new forms of control were to be established: the discipline of the piece was to give way to the discipline of supervision, in order to effect a planned restructuring of social organization at the point of production.

(b) *Ideology*

The concept of productivity bargaining was the product of a 'new philosophy' – a particular stream of managerial ideology, whose origins were to be found in pluralism, which has distinct historical and intellectual roots. Of course, particular agreements contained elements of other more traditional managerial ideologies and in some respects pluralism itself was based upon some very 'traditional' theoretical assumptions. But the basic tenets of pluralism were certainly widely accepted by the industrial relations prophets of productivity bargaining and there was a commitment to this 'new philosophy' on the part of many managers. In the face of the economic crisis there was indeed a recognition, by capital, the State, and to a large extent the trade unions, that a new pluralistic style of management had become appropriate.[3] Managers often prided themselves that by extending the nature and scope of the wage-work bargain they were 'facing up to reality'. The shift away from 'unitary' notions (of management by fiat) towards 'participation', 'joint regulation' and the like also suited most trade union negotiators. For they, too, were suffering a certain 'looseness' of control in terms of their members. Collective bargaining had proved inadequate on both sides of the table.

Despite the increased centralization of collective bargaining machinery, the ability of trade union officials to police agreements had been continually undermined by aggressive shopfloor bargaining. In this context, as Donovan pointed out, productivity bargaining provided a means through which the trade unions' institutional structure could be rationalized in such a way as to provide 'strong leadership'. 'Formalization' was the key word. At local levels the new apparatus of productivity bargaining, works committees, productivity councils, etc., could provide a suitable framework for *all* wage-work bargaining, thus preventing the situation, most common under piecework, where individuals and groups could determine the 'rate for the job', without recourse to local or national officials. For employers and trade union officials alike, national level 'framework' agreements offered the advantage of removing the question of rates of pay from the shop floor altogether. As other commentators have noted in this context, productivity bargaining represented 'the quintessence of corporate rationality'.[4]

(c) *Political*

Finally, and in some respects most significantly, productivity bargaining marked a crucial stage in terms of the intervention of the state apparatus within the sphere of capital–labour relations. The state has played an increasing part in the restructuring of these relations since the war and increased labour productivity has been a central objective of state policies. What is so well illustrated by the case of productivity bargaining, is the positive nature of state intervention and the degree of 'autonomy' which it exercises *vis-à-vis* individual units of capital. There is, for example, some evidence to suggest that many agreements were essentially 'pseudo-deals'. But the Labour government took strong measures to avert this, and, in so doing, encouraged agreements which were in the interests of capital *as a whole*.

However, just as productivity bargaining illustrated this positive aspect of State intervention it also highlighted the limits which constrain it. Despite the sophistication of the new approach, the end of the 1960s marked a return to confrontation and more coercive attitudes to industrial relations. Paradoxically, what was from management's point of view the very strength of productivity bargaining – its comprehensiveness – was simultaneously its weakness. It affected many facets of shop-floor relations and met with correspondingly widespread opposition. This opposition was stimulated by the kinds of changes introduced through productivity agreements, such as increased supervision and higher work rates. Trade union officials were less and less able to control this resistance, and by the late 1960s there was growing evidence of a widening gulf between officials and their members. While, therefore, the increasing incorporation of the trade union bureaucracies offered possibilities for the 'management of discontent' it also posed a severe threat – the loss of the very basis of trade union power – rank and file support. As already stated though, the development of productivity bargaining in the UK was itself an uneven process. To consider further its development two stages have to be distinguished, the periods 1960–66 and 1966–70.

PRODUCTIVITY BARGAINING: PHASE I 1960–66

In 1960, 2461 workers at an Esso oil refinery at Fawley led the way and the fruits of their experience soon became widely known through the publication in 1964 of Allan Flanders's pioneering study, *The Fawley Productivity Agreements*. By

319

December 1966 about half a million other workers were affected by productivity deals, and by the end of 1969 the Department of Employment and Productivity register recorded some 3000 agreements covering nearly 6 million workers or about 25 per cent of all those employed.[5] Productivity bargaining essentially involved the restructuring of workplace organization, and the development of procedures by which this could be achieved on a long-term basis. Previous attempts to secure increases in productivity, through incentive schemes like piecework, or simply by the more efficient use of existing resources of manpower, had mainly taken place on an *ad hoc* basis. Productivity bargaining systematically located such attempts within the broad context of the wage-work bargain. Workers' representatives and managements negotiated on a 'package deal' basis, which involved increased remuneration, or other benefits, in return for the introduction of new methods of work or organization aimed at increasing the productivity of labour.

During the early years, the *content* of particular productivity agreements varied widely, notably between different industries and the pattern was complicated as new elements emerged throughout the 1960s. But the most common changes in work methods included reductions in, or elimination of, overtime working; reduced levels of manning; increases in 'flexibility' between craft and non-craft workers; 'interchangeability' amongst all workers; and the introduction of work study techniques associated with the rationalization of pay structures. The latter were most often achieved through 'grading' systems or 'measured day work'. Significant changes, all of these, since they involved the displacement of control through economic incentives by control through the supervised application of closely defined rules and standards.

Agreements were implemented in different forms, usually being 'comprehensive' (e.g. plant-based), 'partial' (e.g. agreements of limited scope) or of a 'framework' (i.e. company- or industry-wide) type. The Fawley lead had been a 'comprehensive' one. Individual aspects of it had been introduced previously in other organizations, but never before in the form of a site-wide package which significantly extended the scope of collective bargaining. The agreement, signed in 1960, was certainly ambitious, and in its negotiation managers constantly stressed the need to secure the 'consent and cooperation' of workers. In this the Fawley managers were fortunate. They were unfettered either by commitment to company- or industry-wide negotiation procedures, or by the prior existence of payment-by-results incentive schemes, which had never been particularly appropriate to the technology of such industries. But the economic problems faced by Esso were typical of those confronting British industry as a whole. The originality of Fawley lay in management's forthright acceptance of its own need to regain control over all facets of workshop organization. Implicit was the belief, voiced by Flanders at the time, that productivity bargaining was the only effective means of achieving this: 'The most telling argument in favour of productivity is the lack of a practical alternative. It is the only method that promises to be effective in present circumstances.'[6] One of the key lessons Flanders drew from the Fawley experience was that neither coercion nor manipulation would do. A fundamentally new approach was needed if the barriers to increased profitability were to be breached. In particular, management *control* over pay and work had to be strengthened.

The declining profitability of oil refining in the United States had encouraged Standard Oil to look closely at all aspects of manpower utilization, and the British managers at Fawley, being particularly aware of unfavourable comparisons with the parent company, saw the 'underemployment' of manpower, caused primarily by the prevalence of 'systematic overtime', as the major factor constraining returns on capital. The cost of labour bore no relation to its contribution to output. This had been of concern to British industry and the government for some time prior to the 1960s. When William Allen, the US management consultant at Fawley, suggested that Britain was a 'half-time country' by comparison with the US he was only restating the findings of many previous investigations.[7] Though such an estimate risked over-generalization, there was evidence of a growing 'productivity gap', of between a half and one third in respect of the labour productivity of British and US industries, even allowing for the latter's greater capital-intensity. Furthermore, the average annual increase in output per head in Britain, about 2½ per cent between 1957–64, compared unfavourably with most other European industrial countries, as did overall rates of growth.

In the 1960s managers became increasingly aware that this under-utilization of manpower was endemic to the framework of British industrial relations. 'Excessive' manning levels, restrictive practices and lack of flexibilities between different groups of workers, were all held to threaten profitability in

C.L.—L

an era of growing international competition. Productivity bargaining, it was increasingly felt, offered a new solution to these long-standing problems. At Fawley, as at many other companies where incentive schemes had not been applicable, 'systematic' as opposed to 'occasional' overtime had been encouraged both as a source of supplementing basic rates of pay, and as a means of coping with labour shortages. Weak management, Flanders argued, had thus allowed overtime to become 'institutionalized'. This situation was by no means peculiar to Fawley and most early productivity agreements attempted to reduce or eliminate overtime working. Loss of earnings suffered by workers was usually compensated for by increased basic rates. The reduction in actual hours worked was offset by the introduction of more 'exacting' work methods to increase the total volume of work done in normal working hours – or, in other works, by increased work rates.

At Fawley it had been overtime payments that had contributed to wage-drift, that is the gap between basic rates, negotiated at industry or plant level, and actual take-home pay. Elsewhere 'drift' had been encouraged by other factors; piece-rate working in 48 per cent of cases, and other payment by results schemes and bonus systems. In terms of British industry as a whole this drift was estimated to be between about 2 and 4 per cent during the early 1960s. Whichever form wage-drift took, it represented a failure by management to control labour costs and more directly, the social force which determined these costs, namely the bargaining strength of workers on the shop floor. It was the recognition of this, and of the implications for profitability, that led the managers at Fawley and elsewhere to consider the relevance of productivity bargaining. For the real significance of productivity bargaining in this period lay in the attempt to increase profits by restructuring the relationship between earnings and productivity. Workers had developed informal practices to push up their earnings. By means of a 'jointly-regulated' collective bargaining process, management hoped to re-establish its initiative where it was weakest – on the shop floor. In this way it hoped to secure the introduction of important new working methods.

Between the time of Fawley and the state-imposed 'standstill' on wage increases at the end of our first period in June 1966, about 73 productivity agreements were instituted. Aside from the oil companies, other industries, especially capital intensive ones, and notably chemicals, had also been quick to see the potential of productivity bargaining. The type of technology usually associated with capital intensive industries is that of 'continuous process' characterized by a high rate of both technical change and capital investment. The achievement of the most efficient use of capital and labour, through increased flexibility – in both methods and hours of work – and the avoidance of restrictive practices likely to delay the introduction of new techniques, was therefore particularly prized in such areas. And during this early period these deals were concerned with flexibilities between craft and non-craft workers, the rearrangement of working hours by reductions in overtime and increased shift working, as well, of course, as reduced levels of manning. Most agreements favoured the 'Fawley approach', being comprehensive and usually plant-based. One important innovation made by ICI (1965), and then followed by the Electricity Supply Industry (1974/75) and the Mobil Oil Company, Croyton (1965), involved improvements in the 'status' of manual workers as part of the 'package'. This reflected concern for the 'cultural' aspects of productivity bargaining – the contribution it could make to improved industrial relations. Indeed it was characteristic of many agreements in this period, that the notions of 'joint-regulation', 'involvement' and 'participation' were seen as constituting an integral aspect of productivity bargaining. If control was to be regained a whole new approach had to be adopted – a 'new philosophy'. This had been the major lesson of Fawley, and was recognized as such by the prophets of productivity bargaining. It was a lesson, however, that was somewhat forgotten in the second half of the 1960s.

The managers at Fawley had believed in their experiment. The conversion of outsiders to the ideals of productivity bargaining, however, was a slow and uneven process. The TUC and CBI had both been cautious. The leaders of the latter had initially felt that plant bargaining might undermine both the possibility of a centralized incomes policy and the effectiveness of industry level negotiated agreements. More specifically they argued that productivity bargaining could accentuate existing tendencies towards 'leapfrogging'. The TUC had been more optimistic, seeing productivity bargaining as an opportunity to achieve better pay and conditions for trade unionists, 'rationalization' of the structures of collective bargaining and a more 'progressive' system of industrial relations. They were less convinced of the inflationary consequences, but were well aware that plant bargaining could undermine the central authority of both the TUC and their member unions. Consequently, they shared the view expressed by the CBI that productivity bargaining should supplement and not replace the existing national system of collective bargaining. Such cautious optimism was evident in Vic Feather's remark to the TUC in 1966 that the issue of increasing productivity bargaining was 'not one of principle but of time'.

It is more difficult to summarize the attitudes to productivity bargaining of particular unions during these formative years. Not least because negotiations were mostly localized, concentrated on a variety of issues and took place in industries with widely differing technologies. The officers of some unions, however, were noted for their broadly co-operative approach, particularly the TGWU and the GMWU who were involved in a number of the early agreements in the more technologically advanced sectors. The response of other unions, particularly craft ones who were being asked to accept the most radical changes in those early years, was far less enthusiastic. The AUEW, for example, was notably hostile to ICI's deal, known as 'MUPS', and prevented its implementation on some of the trial sites, while DATA, a white collar union, rejected the idea of productivity bargaining on principle. Essentially, however, the approach of most trade unions to productivity bargaining was, as ever, one of pragmatism, with later experience under the Labour government's prices and incomes policy certainly causing many trade union leaders and officers to temper their initial enthusiasm.

For its part, the Labour government had monitored the experiments at Fawley and elsewhere with growing interest. Any possible solution to the continuing post-war problem of inflation was to be welcomed. Since the mid-1950s governments had become increasingly aware that traditional macro-economic policies, aimed at so-called 'demand management', were inadequate in themselves. The Council on Productivity, Prices and Incomes set up in 1957 had recognized this and later institutional developments suggested a growing commitment on the part of successive governments to the need for increased 'planning' in general and for a centrally controlled prices and incomes policy in particular. The establishment of the National Board for Prices and Incomes in March 1965 was the culmination of this trend. And in its very first report, while pointing out certain difficulties associated with productivity bargaining, the members suggested that the innovation could provide the foundation on which to build an effective prices and incomes policy.

The establishment of the Donovan Commission in 1965 to investigate industrial relations in Britain implied that the government was aware of a *political* dimension to the problem of inflation and that the success of its prices and incomes policy depended upon achieving centralized control over wages, on a long-term basis. Productivity bargaining offered formalization, integration and harmony, in place of informality, fragmentation and disorder. But it was by no means seen as a universal panacea, and this kind of government intervention to control wages was to some extent at odds with the 'new philosophy' associated with productivity bargaining – the commitment to 'cultural' changes aimed at eliciting a better spirit of co-operation among workers.

PRODUCTIVITY BARGAINING : PHASE II 1966–70

By 1966, the economic situation had deteriorated.[8] Inflation persisted at the then steadily high rate of 3 per cent and international competition was becoming more acute, resulting in growing balance of payments deficits and the continual threat of devaluation. Centralized bargaining had failed to contain wage-drift. The productivity of British industry still lagged far behind that of its major competitors, the average increase in labour productivity between 1963 and 1966 being 2·6 per cent, compared with France's 5·3 per cent, Germany's 4·7 per cent, Italy's 5·7 per cent and Japan's 8 per cent. In July 1966 the voluntary policy was replaced by a statutory standstill on wage increases, to be followed by a period of 'severe restraint', involving a 'zero norm' which applied until early 1968. During this period 'productivity' was the key criterion for exceptional treatment, and increasingly rigid guidelines were introduced to this end.

By August 1969 the NBPI extended its criteria significantly to incorporate what it termed 'efficiency agreements'. This emphasis on 'efficiency' revealed the Labour government's determination to consolidate and extend the implementation of the quantitative techniques associated with productivity bargaining and not the practices of 'joint regulation' and 'participation' which had been popular in early productivity bargaining. This was in order to cover a wider range of workers and industries. They intended to spread the advantages of earlier agreements, both in terms of increased 'managerial control' and increased work rates, throughout the whole country.

This desire to 'reform pay structures' and 'control costs' had been directly influenced by continued wage-drift resulting to a large extent from PBR systems. Earlier productivity agreements in industries characterized by complex technologies had not regarded such economic reforms alone as sufficient. The reorganization of work practices had been seen to require concomitant ideological changes on the part of managers and workers. But between the period of severe restraint, January 1967 and December 1969, there was a burgeoning in the number of productivity agreements, the major increase occurring in 1968. The DEP register recorded over 4000 cases covering a vast number of workers and these were no longer most prevalent in capital intensive industries. More and more unskilled workers were being affected, as were 'white-collar' workers as the broader 'efficiency' criteria were applied. 'Framework' – or industry-wide agreements – became increasingly popular and affected more workers than any other type of bargain. And, compared with the previous period 1960–66, the content of these agreements changed. While the overall aim remained the same, namely to increase profitability through increased work rates, the emphasis of a far greater proportion was on *direct* changes in the intensity of labour. To do this, agreements introduced measured day work, speed-up, demanning and eliminated 'wasteful' practices and restrictions on output. (See Table 1)

Economic objectives became more central and ideology less so. The ever increasing advocacy of work study and other tools of scientific management was symptomatic of this. Evidently the Labour government was concerned to achieve speedy, short-term, and above all, quantifiable controls over both production and internal wage structures, rather than the more long-term and intangible 'cultural' benefits associated with so-called 'genuine' productivity agreements. The prolonged period of negotiation which had been typical where agreements had introduced changes in the patterns of work of skilled craftsmen were no longer regarded as particularly efficacious.

TABLE 1

Content of Productivity Agreements 1963–69

ACHIEVEMENT FEATURE	NUMBER OF TIMES RECORDED	NUMBER OF TIMES RECORDED AS PERCENTAGE OF TOTAL OBSERVATIONS	RANKING 1967–69	RANKING 1963–66
1. Quantity of Work	2499	30	1	4
2. Nature of Work	1409	17	4	1
3. Working Hours	945	11	5	2
4. Manning	1472	18	3	3
5. Change of Methods	1496	18	2	5
6. Organization of Work	322	4	6	6
7. Responsibility	104	1	7	7
Total	8247	99	—	—

Source: R. B. McKersie and L. C. Hunter, *Pay, Productivity and Collective Bargaining*, London, Macmillan, 1973, p. 76.

Thus an important element of classical productivity bargaining, that it should be a continuous process to secure ideological acceptance of change in order to qualitatively restructure the balance of power at plant level, was replaced by a narrow concentration on the achievement of measurable improvements in 'effort' in return for short-term wage increases. The direct effect of the incomes policy, therefore, was to channel productivity agreements into the realm of pure 'monetary bargains'. Not surprisingly, in the context of wage restraint, the impetus for such 'bargains' came increasingly not from managements mindful of long-term strategy but from workers and their representatives – and the state, intent on finding a quick solution to the intensifying economic crisis.

The inclusion of 'penalty clauses' and 'managerial prerogative clauses' in later agreements suggested a tendency on the part of managers to accept this reversal to 'management by fiat' rather than through 'joint regulation'. Indeed, the key concepts of involvement and participation seemed to have little relevance to the new situation where emphasis lay on 'quantification' and 'effort'. As Barrat-Brown has ruefully remarked,

'Management science did not grow up with industrial democracy in mind.'

Faced with this rapid spread in the number of productivity agreements, the TUC and CBI could no longer remain aloof. Due to government policy productivity bargaining was no longer a 'secondary' or 'supplementary' aspect of collective bargaining. Individual employers and unions were committing themselves to such agreements without reference to their central institutions. It was to avoid the undermining of national control, therefore, that the CBI, accepting the NBPI's guidelines, as well as the importance of plant level bargaining generally, argued in 1968 for the increasing application of 'framework' agreements. They hoped to incorporate plant level bargaining and thus strengthen the authority of national collective bargaining.

The TUC were equally eager to stress the importance of industry-wide bargaining. Whereas the CBI preferred to limit the independence of plant and company levels of bargaining, the TUC felt that such agreements, by introducing new issues, would provide the impetus for extending the scope of legitimate collective bargaining at all levels. Encouraged by the TUC some unions, like the EETU/PTU, emerged as staunch supporters of productivity bargaining during the period of severe restraint and often, under the direction of the national leaderships, took the initiative. Trade unions with ostensibly more 'democratic' organizational structures retained a more pragmatic and less positive attitude, preferring to decentralize the negotiation of these agreements. Both the T & G and the AUEW supported rank and file demands for 'mutuality' and 'opening of the books' as a means of countervailing increased managerial control. Some white-collar unions shared this hard-nosed approach, while a number of craft unions were particularly hostile, fearing the progressive dilution through productivity bargaining of their skills and status.

In practice, however, all the important unions were forced to involve themselves in productivity bargaining in order simply to protect the living standards of their members. And union co-operation declined in the late 1960s, essentially because the process became so clearly associated with the Labour government's discredited incomes policy. Growing discontent from an ever-widening range of workers, some newly affected by productivity bargaining as well as from those whose experience spanned the decade, put pressure on union leaders to resort to other criteria for national and local wage negotiations. This pressure increased as inflation continued to erode living standards.

The nature of productivity bargaining, then, had been changed substantially as a result of intervention by the state. 'Efficiency' criteria, work study, rationalization of pay structures and the like had reduced the bargain to a monetary *quid pro quo*. This was reflected by a hardening of attitudes on both sides. As McKersie and Hunter have aptly noted:

> The use of productivity bargaining as a means of gaining acceptance for systems of work measurement, job evaluation, and measured daywork, was the superficial reflection of a much deeper issue – the extent to which workers and trade unions were prepared to cede control in matters of work rate and pay to management. With growing experience of productivity bargaining involving these sort of control systems, unions became increasingly concerned over their long-term implications, and resistance to productivity proposals based on such systems emerged as an important obstacle to the continuation of productivity bargaining in a number of sectors.[9]

The development of productivity bargaining was uneven, and some later agreements did contain aspects which had been integral to those of the 'classic' phase, but the battle for men's minds, for a new co-operative and jointly regulated system of plant bargaining, no longer took pride of place. Their decline in popularity was closely related to the general failure of the Labour government's economic policies in the late 1960s and to the growing disillusionment felt by many workers with the practical implications of productivity bargaining, both political and economic.

Conclusion
By 1972 it was clear that unemployment rather than productivity bargaining was to be at the centre of the state's economic strategy. Not that the latter had been altogether unsuccessful. On the contrary it did enable some companies to boost profitability. There were many cases, as the NBPI reported, both before and after state intervention where managements felt

that productivity agreements had secured important economic benefits. But the late 1960s saw an increasing number of wage claims based upon general demands for 'parity' and 'equity', with scant attention being paid to productivity criteria. The prophets of Fawley had reason to be dismayed as critics from both the left and right vied for the opportunity to hammer the last nail into the productivity coffin. The rather feeble attempts of the NBPI to justify its very existence fell on deaf ears. And in the changing political context of the late 1960s this was not surprising. From its inception, productivity bargaining had taken on a *political* dimension. It had sought to enhance managerial control over the relationship between earnings and productivity. Implicitly this tackled the 'problem of wage-drift' not just quantitatively but qualitatively, by redefining the balance of power between management and workers, capital and labour. State intervention had the effect of making the degree to which workers and trade unions were prepared to concede control over work rates and rates of pay, through the productivity bargain *explicit* and this led to growing concern about the long-term implications. Even where managers attempted to introduce the more democratic institutional innovations associated with the earlier 'classic' agreements, like joint regulation and participation, they were often met by an increasing reluctance to accept the 'new philosophy' with its inherent assumption of management's 'right to manage' which was central to productivity bargaining. Consequently, some agreements were followed by long and bitter strikes often involving workers in industries not previously noted for militancy; by, for example, post office workers, electrical supply workers and other public sector employees. These strikes were not always overtly concerned with the issue or managerial prerogatives, but there is certainly some evidence to suggest that the effect of many productivity agreements had been to increase workers' awareness of control issues at all levels.[10]

Meanwhile, trade union leaders were in an ambivalent position. The growing number of strikes and disputes related to productivity agreements, many of which were unofficial, suggested that if they were to maintain control over their members they would have to adopt a more radical position. Consequently, in order to counter what many of their members saw as attempts to strengthen managerial authority, some unions put forward demands which, in effect, amounted to increased *worker* control, such as 'opening of the books', 'mutuality' and 'participation'. They did this both in the context of 'productivity' negotiations and as general policy.

Allan Flanders had always stressed that the Fawley agreements did not 'inaugurate an era of sweetness and light, expressed in trouble-free relations.' On the contrary, he had said, 'the immediate effect was to make relations more liable to the confrontation of opposed interest.' He had hoped that the new framework of productivity bargaining would be able to institutionalize such conflicts. From a different perspective socialist critics of productivity bargaining like Cliff and Topham had shared this expectation. They had feared that, by introducing greater formality into the shop-floor situation, productivity bargaining would undermine workers' day-to-day control over their jobs and their ability to bargain over line speeds, the rate for the job, conditions of work, and so on. They expected, too, that union officials and shop stewards, in particular, would become increasingly bureaucratized and remote from their members and that this would have the serious effect of weakening shop-floor organization.

But 'formalization' did not always have such effects. In some cases workers proved able to use the newly formulated rules *against* management. Alternatively, some developed 'informal' controls in ways unanticipated by managements. Nor were shop stewards invariably drawn into the insidious institutional web. Again the experience at Fawley indicated that, far from 'integrating' the shop stewards, a productivity agreement could have the opposite effect of enhancing their independent bargaining power, sometimes at the expense of union officials. In other cases, shop stewards became involved in a whole new range of disputes which arose from the new kinds of authority claimed by management and their supervisors. Moreover, the 'tightening-up' of supervision which accompanied many agreements tended to force them into a new position of militancy on behalf of their members rather than into a 'policing' role. Nor did the union official necessarily become 'professionalized' and more amenable to 'common objectives' in his dealings with managers. Some union officials deliberately opted out of this role, especially where members felt they were being adequately represented by their stewards.

Clearly, then, the experience of the 1960s suggests that the progress towards enhanced managerial control was always problematic and that there were important limits upon the extent to which capital was able to re-establish control over the labour process.

NOTES AND REFERENCES

1 A. Flanders, *Collective Bargaining: Prescription for Change*, London, Faber and Faber, 1967, p. 32.
2 See M. Bosquet, 'The Prison Factory', *New Left Review*, no. 73, p. 23. Also see A. Topham, 'New Types of Bargaining' in R. Blackburn and A. Cockburn, *The Incompatibles* Harmondsworth, Penguin, 1967; and T. Cliff, *The Employer's Offensive: Productivity Deals and How to Fight Them*, London, Pluto, 1970.
3 For a useful outline of the pluralist approach to industrial relations see A. Fox, *Industrial Sociology and Industrial Relations*, Royal Commission on Trade Unions and Employers Associations, Research Paper, no. 3, London, HMSO, 1966. Also the same author's 'second thoughts', A. Fox, 'Industrial Relations: A Social Critique of Pluralist Ideology' in J. Child, ed., *Man and Organization*, London, Allen and Unwin, 1973, p. 185.
4 T. Nichols and H. Beynon, *Living with Capitalism: Class Relations and the Modern Factory*, London, RKP, 1977, p. 113.
5 Sources of information for this section are cited in detail in Martyn Nightingale, *The Sociology of Productivity Bargaining*, Ph.D. thesis, University of Bristol, 1976, chap. 2, 'The Development of Productivity Bargaining 1960–66', pp. 6–14. See also the extensive bibliography.
6 A. Flanders, *Productivity Bargaining*, p. 245.
7 W. Allen, 'Is Britain a Half-Time Country?', *Sunday Times*, 1 March 1964. Most influential were the findings of the Anglo-US productivity teams set up by Cripps between 1948–52 – which suggested that output per man in the USA was far greater than in Britain, see P. Jenkins, 'The Limits of Exhortation', *New Society*, 22 September 1966, p. 435.
8 Sources for this section are cited in detail in Martyn Night-

ingale, *The Sociology of Productivity Bargaining*, chap. 3, 'The Development of Productivity Bargaining 1966–69', pp. 15–22.

9 R. B. McKersie and L. C. Hunter, *Pay, Productivity and Collective Bargaining*, London, Macmillan, 1973, p. 80.

10 A. Topham, 'Productivity Bargaining', *Trade Union Register*, London, Merlin, 1970, p. 85.

8   Scientific Management

The Transformation of Office Work

Harry Braverman

Office Work as Manual Labour

The management experts of the second and third generation after Taylor erased the distinction between work in factories and work in offices, and analysed work into simple motion components. This reduction of work to *abstract labour*, to finite motions of hands, feet, eyes, etc., along with the absorption of sense impressions by the brain, all of which is measured and analysed without regard to the form of the product or process, naturally has the effect of bringing together as a single field of management study the work in offices and in factories. The modern 'science' of motion study treats office and factory work according to the same rules of analysis, as aspects of the unvarying motions of human 'operators'. A typical handbook by a management engineer thus begins with a section headed 'The Concept of the Universal Process', and in discussing work 'in a shop, warehouse, store, office, or any other area,' first takes pains to establish the *general applicability* of work measurement and production control systems to work of every kind: 'Each situation presents a different surface appearance, and so the work which is performed in each of these diverse areas is ordinarily assumed to be very different. But a very marked similarity of basic purpose exists in all of these areas .... The universality of the process may be seen by analysing that which goes to make up the process. To say that wherever humans labour they are performing the same types of work certainly seems to be a ridiculous statement. This seems to be even more inaccurate when it is remembered that much work is mental in nature, and not physical. But the statement is true.'[1] 'Universal standard data,' the collection of which began with an eye principally towards factory work, are now applied at least as frequently to work in the office.

In addition, standard data have been collected specifically

for office purposes, in the form of studies of particularly common office motions that are offered as interchangeable parts from which office managers may assemble their own complete operations. The Systems and Procedures Association of America, for instance, has assembled in compact form such a manual, entitled *A Guide to Office Clerical Time Standards: A Compilation of Standard Data Used by Large American Companies* (Detroit, 1960). The organizations which contributed their materials to this handbook are the General Electric Company, Stanford University, the General Tire and Rubber Company, Kerr-McGee Oil Industries, Inc., Owens-Illinois, Harris Trust and Savings Bank of Chicago, and the Chicago Chapter of the Systems and Procedures Association.*

The clerical standards maintained by these organizations begin with unit time values for the various elements of motion ... but they go on to agglomerate elemental motions into office tasks, and to offer the office manager the standards by which labour processes may be organized and calibrated. For example :

Open and close	*Minute*
File drawer, open and close, no selection	·04
Folder, open or close flaps	·04
Desk drawer, open side drawer of standard desk	·014
Open centre drawer	·026
Close side	·015
Close centre	·027
Chair activity	
Get up from chair	·033
Sit down in chair	·033

* The tables in the *Guide* are published without direct identification of the source corporation, but the information given makes identification clear in most cases. Thus 'Company A', from whose data most of the examples used here are taken, is identified only as a 'large manufacturer of electrical appliances and allied products', but of the co-operating parties, the only organization that fits this description is General Electric, which contributed the office standards used in its Distribution Transformer Department, manufacturer of heavy power-processing equipment. In what follows, we manage to catch a glimpse of the office standards and analyses under which modern office workers are actually supervised, whether they know it or not, and this is superior to looking at textbook standards.

Turn in swivel chair   ·009
Move in chair to adjoining desk or file (4ft maximum) ·050

Walking time is tabulated for distances from one foot to a thousand feet, but since walking within the office requires many turns, 'Walking (confined)' adds ·01 minute for each turn. The reading of a one- to three-digit number is presumed to take ·005 minutes, and of a seven- to nine-digit number, ·015 minutes. To make comparison checks, going from one paper to another, is rated at ·0026 minutes per character. To read typed copy, per inch: ·008 minutes. And to write, not including 'get' or 'release' of pencil or pen:

Numerals, per number	·01 minute
Print characters, each	·01 minute
Normal longhand, per letter	·015 minute

For some reason, the operation called 'jogging' is a favourite of office management experts, and is charted, analysed, and timed in scores of studies. In this instance, the time for 'jog' ('basic times, paper in hand') is given as follows:

1st jog	·006 minute
2nd or subsequent	·009 minute
Pat following jog	·004 minute
Pat following pat	·007 minute

In this table, the time for jogs from one to ten is given, and we are told to 'add ·01 for each jog over 10.'

The time value for 'Cut with scissors' is given as ·44 minute, with '·30 for each additional snip'. *'A snip', we are told, 'includes opening, moving forward and closing the scissors.' Tabulations are given for unit time values for rubber stamping, including the time for getting the stamp, checking the date setting, and putting it aside, and for stamping a series of sheets and putting *them* aside, with allowance for inking

---

* Why it is that, when one is 'jogging' or rapping a stack of papers to align them, the second jog takes longer than the first is not made clear. Nor is it clear why it should take almost half a minute to make the first snip with a scissors, and almost a third of a minute for each additional snip, unless these are misprints.

the stamp at every fourth impression. Also for the time re-quired to collate, gather, lay aside, handle, punch, staple (or remove staples), rubber band (or remove), move material between stations, count, fold or unfold, open mail container (envelope) and remove contents, insert mail in container. Unit times are given for locating a single item in a drawer file, Kardex file, Linedex file, Speed-o-Matic file, binder or folder, log sheet, planning card, or at a specific position on a form. Times are given to file random items, to start a new file, to do numerical and miscellaneous filing, to enter or write, and at this point, still another chart for jogging.

Typing times are subjected to a stringent analysis. The con-ventional standards for words per minute are charted against minutes per inch; but beyond this, time values are assigned to the steps of handling the paper, inserting it in the typewriter, aligning (for various numbers of sheets and carbons), erasing, making strike-over corrections, and 'handling material after.' We are given such intelligence as the 'fact' that back spacing (per space) requires ·0060 minute on a manual machine and ·0025 on an electric model. Further tables cover the time required for various duplicating processes, by offset, spirit, and mimeograph. A tabulation covering the operation of a key-driven calculator includes time values for clearing the machine and turning over each sheet between calculations (·0120 minute) . . .

In the clerical routine of offices, the use of the brain is never entirely done away with – any more than it is entirely done away with in any form of manual work. The mental processes are rendered repetitious and routine, or they are reduced to so small a factor in the work process that the speed and dexterity with which the manual portion of the operation can be performed dominates the labour process as a whole. More than this cannot be said of any manual labour process, and once it is true of clerical labour, labour in that form is placed on an equal footing with the simpler forms of so-called blue-collar manual labour. For this reason, the tradi-tional distinctions between 'manual' and 'white-collar' labour, which are so thoughtlessly and widely used in the literature on this subject, represent echoes of a past situation which has virtually ceased to have meaning in the modern world of work. And with the rapid progress of mechanization in offices it becomes all the more important to grasp this.

The Mechanization of the Office

Machinery that is used to multiply the useful effects of labour in production may be classified, as we have seen, according to the degree of its control over motion. Insofar as control over motion rests with the operator, the machine falls short of automatic operation; insofar as it is rendered automatic, direct control has been transferred to the machine itself. In office machinery, however, the control over *motion* is generally incidental to the purpose of the machine. Thus the rapidity and precision of the high-speed printer are not required in order to print rapidly – there are other and faster ways to ink characters on to paper – but in order to record a controlled flow of information as it is processed in the computer. It is one part of a machine system designed to control not motion but *information*.

Information exists, in the main, in the form of a record of symbolic characters: the alphabet, numbers, and other conventional symbols. Until recently, the processing of these characters – that is to say, assembling and reassembling them in required forms and combining or analysing them according to the rules of mathematics – was directly dependent upon the human brain. While various mechanical means for recording or combining them were in daily office use, such as the typewriter, the adding or calculating machine, and the book-keeping machine, each of these machines could only carry or process information through a very short part of its total cycle before it again had to involve the human brain to move it into its next position. In this sense, the office process resembled a pipeline that required a great many pumping stations at very close intervals. The difficulty lay in the form in which information was recorded: so long as it took the form of a notation which could be apprehended only by the human senses, humans were required to seize it and move or manipulate it. Thus every key-driven mechanical adding or calculating machine depended on the line-by-line keyboard work of the operator, and its storage and processing facilities were limited to the capacities of a few mechanical registers. While this situation continued, every office machine remained on the primitive level of the hand tool, or power-assisted hand tool.

The change began with the machine for counting punched cards invented by Dr Herman Hollerith in 1885 and used to tabulate the United States census of 1890. The importance of this invention lay not in any technical advance, but entirely in the concept it embodied. In recording bits of data, each on its own card, by means of a system that gave to each column and rank of the card a specific meaning, the punched-card system made available a means of 'reading' and 'interpreting' simple data without direct human participation. Now, through one means or another of sensing the holes, machines could sort and classify, combine and tabulate the bits of data on the cards. The significance of the method lay in the recasting of the form of the information so that it could be picked up by a machine.

This revolutionary conception passed through a series of purely technical improvements in the years that followed, first electromechanical, in which electrical impulses were made to control mechanical registers, and then electronic, in which information is handled and stored by means of the electrical impulses themselves and the mechanical elements virtually disappear. The effect upon the storage and handling capacities of computing systems has been enormous. In contrast to the punched card, which in its standard form stores eighty characters on a surface slightly larger than two playing cards, the common type of magnetic disc pack, which consists of eleven fourteen-inch discs mounted a half-inch apart, will hold up to 29 million characters. And these can be transferred at the rate of 156,000 characters per second to or from the computer processing unit, within which they may be manipulated in operations that are measured in millionths or even billionths of a second each. Thus once the information is recorded, bit by bit, by means of key-driven machines, it may be summoned, brought together from diverse sources, arranged, combined mathematically, etc., in very short periods of time, and the results displayed on a screen, or more commonly recorded by the high-speed printer which is itself a typewriter that puts to shame the combined efforts of scores of typists.

The computer system working on these principles is the chief, though not the only, instrument of mechanization of the office. Its first applications were for large-scale routine and repetitive operations which to some extent were already performed mechanically: payrolls, billing, accounts payable and accounts receivable, mortgage accounting, inventory control, actuarial and dividend calculations, etc. But it was soon applied in new tasks, such as for elaborate sales reports, production-cost accounting, market research information, sales commissions, and so forth, all the way up to general accounting, at which point the corporation's books of record are put into computerized form.

This automatic system for data-processing resembles automatic systems of production machinery in that it reunifies the labour process, eliminating the many steps that had previously been assigned to detail workers. But, as in manufacturing, the office computer does not become, in the capitalist mode of production, the giant step that it could be towards the dismantling and scaling down of the technical division of labour. Instead, capitalism goes against the grain of the technological trend and stubbornly reproduces the outmoded division of labour in a new and more pernicious form. The development of computer work has been so recent and so swift that here we can see reproduced in compressed form the evolution of labour processes in accord with this tendency.

For a short time in the 1940s and early 1950s, the data-processing occupations displayed the characteristics of a craft. This was during the period when tabulating equipment based on the punched card dominated the industry. Installations were small and the tabulating craftsman worked on all machines: the sorter, collator, tabulator, calculator, etc.* These machines were programmed by wiring a panel board for each machine, and this operation was learned as the worker gained a general familiarity with all the machines. Thus the equivalent of an apprenticeship was a period of learning the use of all the equipment, and the programming done at that time was simply the highest skill of an all-round trade.

The development of a data-processing craft was abortive, however, since along with the computer a new division of labour was introduced and the destruction of the craft greatly hastened. Each aspect of computer operations was graded to a different level of pay frozen into a hierarchy: systems managers, systems analysts, programmers, computer console operators, key punch operators, tape librarians, stock room attendants, etc. It soon became characteristic that entry into the higher jobs was at the higher level of the hierarchy, rather than through an all-round training. And the concentration of knowledge and control in a very small portion of the

---

* Except for the key punch machine; being a keyboard machine, this was immediately recognized as a job for 'girls'.

hierarchy became the key here, as with automatic machines in the factory, to control over the process.

The upper level of the computer hierarchy is occupied by the systems analyst and the programmer. The systems analyst is the office equivalent of the industrial engineer, and it is his or her job to develop a comprehensive view of the processing of data in the office and to work out a machine system which will satisfy the processing requirements. The programmer converts this system into a set of instructions for the computer. In early computer installations, the programmer was generally a systems analyst as well, and combined the two functions of devising and writing the system. But with the encroachment of the division of labour, these functions were increasingly separated as it became clear that a great deal of the work of programming was routine and could be delegated to cheaper employees. Thus the designation of 'programmer' has by this time become somewhat ambiguous, and can be applied to expert programme analysts who grasp the rationale of the systems they work on, as well as to programme coders who take as their materials the pre-digested instructions for the system or subsystem and simply translate them mechanically into specialized terminology. The training for this latter work occupies no more than a few months, and peak performance is realized within a one- to two-year period. In accordance with the logic of the capitalist division of labour, most programmers have been reduced to this level of work.

Below this level, computer work leaves the arena of specialized or technical skills and enters the realm of working-class occupations. The computer operator runs the computer in accordance with a set of rigid and specific instructions set down for each routine. The training and education required for this job may perhaps best be estimated from the pay scales, which in the case of a Class A operator are on about the level of the craftsman in the factory, and for Class C operators on about the level of the factory operative.

The largest single occupation created by computerization is that of the key punch operator. Since it in many ways typifies the direction being taken by office work, it is worth examining in some detail.

The extraordinary swiftness with which computers process information depends in the first instance upon the careful preparation of a data base for the computer's use. While all other office functions dwindle in the face of the computer, this one tends to grow. First, everything which the computer digests must be translated into uniform codes. Second, the pre-calculated operation of the entire system depends upon the provision of adequate coding to cover every requirement at the time of entering the original data; nothing can be left for later recognition, apprehension, and action by the human brain if it is to be done by the computer in the course of its operations. Third, every preassigned code must be prepared for the computer in accordance with a strict and undeviating form so that it can have the desired effect. And fourth, this must be done in a relatively error-free way, since the computer does not recognize errors (except insofar as they transcend the parameters set in the programme) but acts upon all the information it is given.

This requires the preparation of data according to rigid forms because no matter how ingeniously the matter is approached, the computer cannot interpret any symbols but those that derive their meaning from their form and position. The computer card, punched as desired by a key-driven machine and verified by a repetition on another such machine, is still the most common such form. It is not the only one, however, and a variety of other devices that record data on a magnetic tape, or print out symbols than can be 'read' by an optical scanner, are now in use. Their advantage is not that they 'eliminate key-punching', as some hasty publicists have rushed to announce, but that they simplify the operation still further so that it may be performed on keyboards similar to that of the typewriter, and so divest the coding operation of even the very limited amount of training it now requires. Although the manner of coding may be varied, it cannot be eliminated; and while there are some ways in which the volume of coding may be held in check, in general it tends to grow with the growth of computerization. To describe key punching, therefore, is to describe the sort of work which, in this form or another, is growing rapidly in offices.

The training required for this sort of work has been described in one sociological study as follows:

> Card punching can be a rather monotonous job when it involves large masses of homogeneous data, pre-sorted and prepared in ready-to-copy columnar format. The job can be learned in a matter of a week or two, and satisfactory pro-

duction skills can be attained within some six months. Despite most employers' stated preference a high-school diploma is not essential for satisfactory performance. Some training officials estimated that a ninth-grade reading level and equivalent proficiency in arithmetic provide a good starting base.

For all these reasons, a highly knowledgeable personnel man, in the course of one interview, described key-punch operating as a 'semi-blue-collar' job. He considered the term descriptive not only of the nature of the job, but also of the entry requirements, both formal and informal. In many instances girls who lack formal education or the 'social graces of the office' can be placed in key-punching, whereas they would probably be rejected for other purely white-collar work.[2]

The authors of this study, who like most of their colleagues in the social sciences prefer to look on the bright side, profess themselves 'intrigued' by the view expressed by this personnel manager. They are quick to theorize that key punching can become a handy substitute for unskilled manufacturing jobs which in the past 'served as the first step on the ladder.' But within a page they themselves are forced to characterize key punching as a 'dead-end' occupation: 'Whereas messengers are frequently promoted to file clerks, file clerks to typists, and typists to secretaries, key-punch operators tend to remain key-punch operators.'[3]

The work itself is described by key-punch department managers themselves as 'extremely boring' with 'no intelligence looked for' and a very high turnover rate.[4] Here is a description, reported on the occasion of the changeover from a pre-computer tabulating machine system (which also required punched cards) to a computer system:

One key-puncher reported that before the installation of the computer, her work had been somewhat varied and had occasionally called for the exercise of judgment. This had made it bearable. Every three or four weeks, as the conversion to automation proceeds, several of her associates are transferred from the original group of key-punchers and assigned to the new work, which is more monotonous and repetitious. Since there is no variation in job content, the pace is continuous, steady, and 'pressured'. The most frequent comment among the girls is, 'We are working for the machine now.'

Mrs Duncan described all key-punch girls as 'nervous wrecks'. 'If you happen to speak to an operator while she is working, she will jump a mile. You can't help being tense. The machine makes you that way. Even though the supervisor does not keep an official production count on our work, she certainly knows how much each of us is turning out – by the number of boxes of cards we do.' Mrs Calvin, a former operator for a different company, reported the same kind of tension: 'If you just tap one of them on the shoulder when she is working, she'll fly through the ceiling.'

Both women reported that absenteeism was very high among their group. Mrs Duncan remarked, 'Someone is always saying, "I don't think I'll come in tomorrow. I just can't stand this any longer."' Although the girls do not quit, they stay home frequently and keep supplies of tranquillizers and aspirin at their desks. The key-punchers felt that they were really doing a factory job and that they were 'frozen' to their desk as though it were a spot on the assembly-line.[5]

As in the factory, the machine-pacing of work becomes increasingly available to office management as a weapon of control. The reduction of office information to standardized 'bits' and their processing by computer systems and other office equipment provides management with an automatic accounting of the size of the work load and the amount done by each operator, section, or division:

Precise measurement of clerical output is one of the aspects of the production room approach heightened by if not exclusively new to automated offices. Simplification and routinization of office tasks by automation makes the work much more amenable to objective count and measurement. The American Management Association has published numerous studies reporting the experience of various large firms in developing clerical cost programs by means of time measurement of office operations. These articles refer only indirectly to employee irritation and resistance. In the Standard Oil Company of Ohio, for example, a special name was coined to avoid such terms as 'work measurement', which was considered to be 'irritating to the employees and made it difficult to secure their participation.'

The Seventh Annual Conference on Systems and Procedures in 1958 stressed that the systems profession is devoted to methods improvement or 'working smarter'. Implicit in this was the job of motivating the office worker to greater productivity. Henry Gunders, associate director, Management Advisory Services, Price Waterhouse and Company, Houston, Texas, maintained that in the unmeasured office the rate of clerical output is low. He estimates that such an office is operating on 50 to 60 per cent efficiency, and that with clerical output measured, even unaccompanied by incentives, there would be a 20 to 30 per cent increase in output. It is stated that incentives are most applicable to already mechanized jobs. When an office machine is used, various devices such as stroke counters, automatic sequential numbering, and the like simplify counting. Similarly, pre-numbered documents, processed in sequence, facilitate production counting.

Most of the firms included in this study quantify the operations associated with data-processing. Key-punching, in particular, lends itself to objective count. Government agencies and private business firms reported that this type of work measurement was standard procedure. In some instances, the girls fill out a daily tally form indicating how many inches they have punched, and the verifiers keep count of the errors. An executive of one large insurance company commented that, although it is not generally mentioned, an objective record of productivity is kept, and the operator whose output lags is fired. Many firms rely on the supervisor to keep a visual check which can be objective because she would know the total number of trays of cards processed during any period. One official explained that the careful tally of key-punch output in his firm was made necessary because all service functions must be allocated as to cost, and that check on operators' speed was a secondary consideration. Serial checking on other types of office equipment is the method used by many firms, and is applicable to calculators, check sorters and various machines besides key-punches. 'Industrialization' of clerical work is evident not only in the work count, but also in the use of a moving belt to carry the work from one station to the next. Several companies studied use this method of carrying orders from the point of origin through the various stages of processing to the computer.

The factory atmosphere is unmistakably present. Not only are the office machine operators often required to punch a time clock, but they are not permitted to converse while at work. They are subject to dismissal with as little notice as a week or at most a month. There are few distinguishing marks between the employee in the electronic office and the factory worker in light manufacturing.[6]

As work has been simplified, routinized, and measured, the drive for speed has come to the fore. 'Everything is speed in the work now', said a woman who found herself near a nervous breakdown, and the pace is 'terrific'. And with the economies furnished by the computer system and the forcing of the intensity of labour come lay-offs which selectively increase the tendency towards factory-like work: 'With each reduction in force, the remaining workers are told to increase their output. Automation has reduced the staff in that office by more than one third, and more mechanization is in prospect. The union spokesman said that the categories of jobs which have disappeared are those which require some skill and judgement. Those remaining are the tabulating and key-punch operations, which become even simpler, less varied, and more routinized as work is geared to the computer.' The vice-president of an insurance company, pointing to a room filled with key punch operators, remarked: 'All they lack is a chain', and explained himself by adding that the machines kept the 'girls' at their desks, punching monotonously and without cease.* And the workers themselves are under no illusions about their 'white-collar' jobs: 'This job is no different from a factory job except that I don't get paid as much,' one operator in a large farm-equipment office said.[7]

The educational requirements for this new kind of office work are subject to confusion, some of it deliberate, between

---

* This vice-president gives us a clear illustration of the fetishism which puts the blame for the situation on the 'machines' rather than on the social relations within which they are employed. He knew when he made this remark that it was not the 'machines' but he himself who chained the workers to their desks, for in his next breath he pointed out that a count of production was kept for the workers in that machine room.

the needs of the work itself and other considerations. Thus the authors of a recent study of electronic data-processing in New York write:

> We have already noted the general tendency of employers to specify a high-school diploma as a prerequisite to employment for key-punch operators. It is also true, however, that many successful* operators are hired without the diploma, particularly in a period when the labour market is tight. Our interviews convinced us that a high-school diploma is viewed as something other than a certification of academic or intellectual proficiency.
>
> Some firms, admittedly, relish their ability to state that 'all our employees are high-school graduates,' as an indication of status or prestige. The great majority, however, view the diploma as a certification of responsibility, motivation, and reliability.... 'Sure, we can find out quickly if a girl can really punch cards. But will she come in every Monday? Will she stay after 5 o'clock when we're pushed for overtime? Will she drift to another job after three weeks?' These are the kinds of questions that were repeatedly raised by employers.[8]

Earlier in the computer era, various managements not yet oriented in the field and perhaps somewhat deceived by their own glowing estimates of the mass 'upgrading of the labour force' that would take place, hired the 'wrong kind of labour'. This was particularly true in banking, where the snobbish tradition of 'superior' employees had not yet been overcome by managers. Thus in one study of bank computerization it was decided that personnel managers were 'recruiting girls of too high an intellectual calibre for the new simple machine jobs.'[9] Experience soon showed, in the words of another study of technological change in banking, that 'it would be misleading to assume that a massive upgrading will take place, for a large proportion of jobs created up to this point are relatively low rated. Encoders are a case in point: Encoding "is a low-grade job which is easily and quickly learned, requiring only the ability to operate a 10-key keyboard." At one bank, "Due to the simplicity of operator training for single

---

* This term in itself is quite remarkable, and can only be understood if taken to mean key punch operators who turn out to be successful' hiring strokes for the personnel manager.

pocket proof encoders, the job, as related to our job evaluation scale, has been downgraded three grades and reduced from an average base of $68 to $53 per week."* An EDP clerk is only "a slightly higher grade position than that of encoder. . . ." At the large branch bank referred to above, approximately 70 per cent of the jobs created were low rated, while at the small branch bank they comprised around 50 per cent of the new jobs.'[11] And it is in the nature of the organization of work around the computer system that, like factory work, it does not have the advancement ladder characteristic of the bank and office of several generations ago. This was recognized early in the computer era by the American Management Association, which, in a special report designed to help employers set up data-processing operations, said: 'To be honest – we don't want people to take data-processing jobs as stepping stones to other jobs. We want permanent employees capable of doing good work and satisfied to stay and do it. To promise rapid advancement is to falsify the facts. The only rapid advancement for the bulk of non-supervisory data-processing staff is *out of data-processing!*'[12]

So far as the traditional grades of office labour are concerned, the computerization of office accounting procedures further weakens the position of those skilled in the system as a whole, particularly bookkeepers. The decline of the bookkeeper, which had begun, as we have seen, with the rise of the office manager, was helped along by the rise of the bookkeeping or posting machine, which converted a certain amount of skilled ledger work into a mechanical operation. The decline was continued, especially in banking, by the development of electronic bookkeeping machines, which complete the conversion of bookkeepers into machine operators and at the same time reduce the demand for them sharply. Thus one multibranch bank reported that within eighteen months after installing electronic bookkeeping machines, the bookkeeping staff of 600 had been reduced to 150, and the data-processing staff had grown to 122. This is in line with the experience of most banks, which achieve a reduction in overall labour requirements of 40 to 50 per cent for the same volume of work, and

---

*These pay figures refer to 1963. Elsewhere the job of coder is characterized thus by a data-processing executive: 'The only gal who will stick with this work has to have a husband with two broken legs and five hungry kids. No one else could stand it.'[10]

in the process cut down the bookkeeping people sharply and replace them with machine operators.[13]

Not only bookkeepers, but even the lower grades of management, feel the effects in a similar way. The computer presents management with an enormous temptation to save management time as well as labour time by 'mechanizing' many choices and decisions. It is probably for this reason that Howard C. Carlson, a psychologist employed by General Motors, has said: 'The computer may be to middle management what the assembly line is to the hourly worker.'[14]

The tendency of the labour process exemplified in the various machine jobs is not confined to the workers grouped immediately around the computer. On the contrary, with the exception of a specialized minority whose technical and 'systems' skills are expanded, this tendency increasingly affects all clerical workers. The reasons for this may be separated into two parts.

First, the formal demands of computerization extend far beyond those machine operators who work with the raw materials or finished products of the computer. Since coding operations are performed mechanically according to fixed layouts, the materials prepared by others for the machine rooms must also follow strict rules of form. Thus the clerk who uses nothing but paper and writing instruments, and who apprehends the information in the first instance from original source documents, is governed by the same rules of form. This has led to the possibility of transferring the work of the key punch operator to the other grades of clerk, a change which is now under way and which will undoubtedly accelerate. Under this system, the work of transcribing information into a form that can be used by the computer is spread throughout the office instead of being localized in machine rooms, by means of terminals or other simple keyboard machines that can be operated by any clerk. In this way, machine operation is generalized throughout the office. If, in the first instance, this involves a combination of jobs – that of interpreting being combined with that of keyboard operation – the next step is the simplification and even elimination of the judgemental steps involved in interpretation by tying the new keyboard machine to the computer and utilizing its storage and swift-search capacities. Thus, in a variety of ways, the reduction of data to symbolic form with accurate positional attributes becomes, increasingly, the business of the office as a whole, as a measure to economize on labour costs.

Second, a variety of other machines and systems are applied to other work processes not within the immediate orbit of the computer. For example, file clerks serve elaborate and semi-automatic machine systems which eliminate the need to know the sequence of the alphabet, or even the sequence of numbers; everything is eliminated but the task of placing under the photographic apparatus of the machine, as swiftly as possible, one document after another. Typists, mail sorters, telephone operators, stock clerks, receptionists, payroll and timekeeping clerks, shipping and receiving clerks are subjected to routines, more or less mechanized according to current possibilities, that strip them of their former grasp of even a limited amount of office information, divest them of the need or ability to understand and decide, and make of them so many mechanical eyes, fingers, and voices whose functioning is, insofar as possible, predetermined by both rules and machinery. As an important instance of this, we may note the changes in the work of the bank teller, once an important functionary upon whose honesty, judgement, and personality much of the public operation and relations of the bank used to depend. Attached to mechanical and electronic equipment, these employees have been transformed into checkout clerks at a money supermarket counter, their labour-power purchased at the lowest rates in the mass labour market, their activities prescribed, checked, and controlled in such a way that they have become so many interchangeable parts. And it should be added that the teller's function, limited as it now is, will gradually be replaced by new mechanical-electronic equipment that originated in England and has been spreading in the United States. A cash machine which, activated by a customer card, supplies cash from the customer's account is no more than the first tentative step in this direction. So-called automated tellers are able, on the same principle, to transact any of a number of banking functions, including deposits to or withdrawals from savings or checking accounts, transfers between accounts, and loan repayments.[15] Such equipment requires not so much a revolution in banking technology as the modification of existing equipment so that it may be used directly by the customer, with minimal opportunity for error or fraud. The fact that this is becoming increasingly common in trade and service areas indicates that much automated equipment is so simple to operate that it requires *no training whatsoever*; it also foreshadows the weakening of the demand for labour in fields of employment that have been expanding rapidly.

The trend in what is known as 'secretarial work' assumes great importance in this transformation of clerical labour, for two reasons. First, it is an occupational category of enormous size. Some 2·75 million persons were employed as secretaries in the United States in 1970, according to the census for that year, almost all of them women. This is the largest single category of clerical labour. And second, we are at the beginning of a revolution in this field which will transform the office almost to the same extent as it is now being transformed by the computer. To understand this incipient upheaval, we must review this occupation and its fundamental rationale.

From a functional standpoint, the secretary came into existence as a device to extend the administrative scope of the entrepreneur and proprietor. Later, as the managerial structure grew, the secretary, from this same functional standpoint, came to represent a pure expression of the Babbage principle: it was thought 'wasteful', from the capitalist point of view, to have a manager spend time typing letters, opening mail, sending parcels, making travel arrangements, answering the telephone, etc., when these duties could be performed by labour power hired at anywhere from one-third to one-fiftieth of the remuneration of the manager. But here the operation of the Babbage principle is further stimulated by the fact that the managers are organizing not the distant labour processes of subordinates, but *their own* labour. Since they tend to place an exaggerated value upon their own time, and a minimal value upon the time of others as compared with their own, the Babbage principle goes to work in the offices of managing executives with particular force, all the more so as it is intensified by the prestige attaching to managers with large staffs, the usefulness of a retinue of office servants for the transacting of personal matters, and other career, social, and personal considerations.

Thereafter this system of secretarial assistance spreads to lower ranks as well, as the numbers of managerial and semi-managerial employees increase. Since the Babbage principle operates wherever a mass of work may be subdivided and its 'lower' portions separated out and delegated, it invades all the realms of paper work performed by 'executives', assistants

351

to executives, heads of small departments sometimes consisting of no more than the 'head' and a secretary, professional and even semi-professional employees. The Babbage principle has here transcended its own limits, especially as social and prestige factors come into play and the personal secretary becomes a perquisite of the privileged job as one of its chief privileges. Top managers watched this multiplication of secretaries with nothing more than amusement, until it grew to dimensions which threatened the balance sheet.

For management to tackle this monstrosity in order to reduce the drain on the corporate pocketbook is by no means simple. It is not just a matter of attacking a traditional and entrenched privilege, but one which is enjoyed by the lower reaches of the managerial structure itself, those whose loyalty and interest in the corporation is guaranteed by, among other things, these very trappings and pretences of managerial status. Corporate managements confront the danger, in any such attack, of alienating their own instruments of control over the administrative structure. True, some managements have not allowed such a situation to develop, or have destroyed it at an earlier stage – stenographic pools as a substitute for personal secretaries, for example, are hardly unknown – but many others have shrunk from the task. There is ample evidence, however, that this situation is ending, and that management is now nerving itself for major surgery upon its own lower limbs.

The reasons for this new attitude are various. The most important has already been mentioned: the extent to which this expensive practice has burgeoned, and the immense amounts of payroll it devours, not just through the multiplication of secretaries but through the effect of this arrangement upon the entire functioning of the office. But there are other factors: the completion of the basic work of rationalization in the factory, so far as it can be carried through, freeing management to turn to the office; the maturation of 'systems thinking' among managers to the point where they have reconceptualized the entire problem; the spread of the methods of close calculation throughout smaller firms that might otherwise escape them for a while longer, through the purchase of such firms by conglomerates whose first step is to send in systems engineers (and here the fact that the blame for the changes can be assigned to distant proprietors makes the installation of new systems by corporate management somewhat easier); the perfection of various cheap systems of centralized communications and recording; even the new attitudes of women, who dispute and scorn the body-servant role and make it more difficult to recruit tractable secretaries – all of these are among the factors which both encourage and facilitate the ending of the secretarial explosion.

Office managements have thus entered upon a sweeping campaign to destroy what they call the 'social office', to use a phrase which has recently gained popularity.[16] It is only necessary to follow the periodicals published for top office managers, such as *Administrative Management*, to see that they are attacking on this front not only with a newly systematized armamentarium of ideas and procedures, but with a fresh determination, and that the object of this attack is no longer just the clerk but the comfortable arrangements made by their own lower managers.

There is of course no disposition on the part of office managements to reject the Babbage principle and to have those functionaries who are now assisted by secretaries begin to do their own typing and other chores. This would contradict the basic tenet of management that each task must be performed at the lowest possible rate of pay. Rather, they feel that the time has come to end a system which makes of each functionary a supervisor over the labour of one assistant, because the labour time of secretaries is used wastefully and inefficiently, is subject only to relaxed and friendly supervision by a superior who is more interested in personal convenience than in office efficiency, and because such functionaries often cannot delegate enough work to fully occupy the time of another person.

Secretarial work is analysed into two parts: typing and administrative routine (sometimes reception and telephone answering are separated from the latter as a distinct function). The first is being made the business of what has been named the 'word processing centre'. This centre is a modernized version of the stenographic pool; it does not send stenographers to take dictation from executives, but rather gives each executive a link with the stenographic process through the telephone on his end and recording equipment on the other. These recordings are then 'processed' by typists, and the finished letter, document, brief, contract, script, or any other form requiring typing is brought by messenger for checking and signature. As distinguished from a stenographic pool, which merely held and dispatched labour-power to departments as required, this system visualizes the construction of a separate production department whose business it is to manufacture to order all the correspondence and other documentary work required anywhere throughout the offices of the enterprise. Thus this major portion of the secretarial job now becomes the province of production workers, assisted by electronic equipment. Not unexpectedly, this concept and its application have made the furthest strides in Germany, and an article in *Administrative Management* describes the stress given there to the use of canned texts and automatic typewriters. Word processing is

> a process of having word originators (executives, sales correspondents, lawyers, and the like) select formula clauses from pre-coded, pre-organized clause books. For example, an administrator who would normally dictate the same kind of reply to a letter several times a day, instead selects the appropriate clauses (by code number) from the clause book – or from memory if he's used them often enough. Once selected, clause codes plus individual names, addresses and other variable inserts (such as dates or prices) are either dictated into recorders or jotted down on 'to-be-typed' forms. This source dictation or form is then used by the typist to prepare a final letter. Automatic typewriters repetitively type the 'canned' clauses, and the typist manually keyboards in the new or variable data.... benefits are word originator and typist efficiency, and more work produced from the same number of hours on the job. In addition, less training is required of all the people involved.[17]

This last 'benefit', the reduction of training for 'all', indicates the sensitivity of management to the proliferation of correspondents and other such 'word originators', each of whom is required to know how to formulate a passable paragraph so that it may be understood by the recipient; under the new system, this requirement disappears, leaving only the ability to *select the proper paragraph*.

The other functions of the secretary are taken over by an 'administrative support centre'. The superior who formerly had a secretary is known, in relation to this centre, not as a 'word originator' but as a 'principal', and it is considered that a ratio of four to eight principals to each 'administrative support secretary' will prove adequate. This support centre handles all the non-typing chores formerly required of the secretary, foremost among them being filing, phone answering, and mail handling. 'Filing,' we are told, 'should be performed in the support centre – not in the principal's office.' The clear objective of such arrangements is to prevent the renewal of the previous situation by imperceptible degrees, and to ensure that all secretarial work is performed under centralized production supervision and not under the supervision of the 'principal'. Moreover, 'principals should answer their own phone, but the phone should also ring in the centre so if the principal doesn't pick it up by the third ring the secretary can get it.' Like the 'word processing centre', the 'administrative support centre' is connected to the various offices by phone and messenger service.[18]

Thus, under the new arrangement, the secretarial function is replaced by an integrated system which aims at centralized management, the breakdown of secretarial jobs into detail operations subdivided among production workers, and the reduction of the number of secretarial workers to one half, one quarter, or even smaller fractions of their former number. Among the subsidiary benefits management expects to derive from this arrangement is the reduction and thus cheapening of the skills of administrative employees, and, not the least, the squeezing out of the minutes and hours of labour-power lost in the personal relations and contacts among secretaries and between secretaries and their 'principals' – which is what they mean when they speak of the 'end of the social office'. The force and seriousness of this campaign, which has begun in this form only in the past few years, can be seen not only from its conception as a total system with its own jargon, technology, and specialists, and from the space now being devoted to it in office management periodicals, but also from the launching of new periodicals and organizations devoted entirely to this subject (for instance, *Word Processing Report* and the Word Processing Institute). The total system has been installed in a great variety of corporations, including sophisticated publishing offices in New York, where systems analysts have shown themselves to be sturdy of purpose and impervious to the barbed comments of editors who are being deprived of their secretaries.

We have now described, in its major facets, the conversion of the office routine into a factory-like process in accordance with the precepts of modern management and available technology. The greatest single obstacle to the proper functioning of such an office is the concentration of information and decision-making capacity in the minds of key clerical employees. Just as Frederick Taylor diagnosed the problem of the management of a machine shop as one of removing craft information from the workers, in the same way the office manager views with horror the possibility of dependence upon the historical knowledge of the office past, or of the rapid flow of information in the present, on the part of some of his or her clerical workers. The recording of everything in mechanical form, and the movement of everything in a mechanical way, is thus the ideal of the office manager. But this conversion of the office flow into a high-speed industrial process requires the conversion of the great mass of office workers into more or less helpless attendants of that process. As an inevitable concomitant of this, the ability of the office worker to cope with deviations from the routine, errors, special cases, etc., all of which require information and training, virtually disappears. The number of people who can operate the system, instead of being operated by it, declines precipitously. In this sense, the modern office becomes a machine which at best functions well only within its routine limits, and functions badly when it is called upon to meet special requirements.*

* Managers often wag their heads over the 'poor quality of office help' available on the labour market, although it is their own system of office operations which is creating the office population suited to it. This complaint is, unfortunately, too often echoed by unthinking 'consumers' when they run into trouble with an office, as they often do. Such difficulties will tend to increase in the same way that the quality of factory production tends to decline and the servicing of consumer appliances tends to worsen even as it becomes more expensive, and for the same reasons.

NOTES AND REFERENCES

1 William J. Fuhro, *Work Measurement and Production Control with the F-A-S-T System*, Englewood Cliffs, New Jersey, 1963, pp. 39–40.
2 Boris Yavitz and Thomas M. Stanback, Jr., *Electronic*

Data Processing in New York City, New York and London, 1967, p. 82.

3 ibid., p. 83.

4 Ida Russakoff Hoos, *Automation in the Office*, Washington, 1961, p. 53.

5 ibid., pp. 67–8.

6 ibid., pp. 78–9.

7 ibid., pp. 66–8.

8 Yavitz and Stanback, *Electronic Data Processing*, p. 84.

9 Enid Mumford and Olive Banks, *The Computer and the Clerk*, London, 1967, p. 190.

10 Hoos, *Automation in the Office,* p. 57.

11 Joseph P. Newhouse, 'Technological Change in Banking' in National Commission on Technology, Automation, and Economic Progress, *The Employment Impact of Technological Change*, Appendix Volume II, *Technology and the American Economy*, Washington, D.C., 1966, p. 167.

12 American Management Association, *Establishing an Integrated Data-Processing System*, Special Report no. 11, 1956, p. 113; cited by Hoos, *Automation in the Office*, p. 85.

13 US Department of Labor, Bureau of Labor Statistics, *Technological Trends in Major American Industries*, Bulletin no. 1474, Washington, D.C., 1966, p. 247.

14 *Business Week*, 12 May, 1973, p. 141.

15 'Machines – The New Bank Tellers', *New York Times*, 2 December, 1973.

16 *Administrative Management*, May 1972.

17 ibid., January 1972

18 ibid., May 1972.

Monopoly Capitalism and the Impact of Taylorism: Notes on Lenin, Gramsci, Braverman and Sohn-Rethel

Tony Elger and Bill Schwarz

The basic principles of scientific management have been explained elsewhere: fervently in the proselytizing tracts of Taylor himself, and more soberly and critically by Braverman (1974), and no extensive resumé is needed here. Both of these accounts, in strikingly different ways, focus on the wholesale reorganization of production, the systematic division between the mental and manual functions of the labour process, the intensified pace of work, and the recasting of the wage form (incentive payments and the phenomenon of high wages). The coercive disciplinarian dictate of early paternalist management gives way to a supposedly scientific discourse elaborating the notion of 'objective work measurement', of which management is the sole arbiter: 'It is only through *enforced* standardization of methods, *enforced* adoption of the best implements, and *enforced* co-operation that the faster work can be assured. And the duty of enforcing the adoption of standards and the enforcing of co-operation rests with the *management* alone' (Taylor 1947 p. 83).

These initiatives first acquired importance in the formative period of monopoly capitalism, most obviously in the United States. A key objective was the destruction of skilled, craft control lodged within the productive process, and its replacement by new supervisory and white-collar strata, and this was closely related to the expansion of machine production, the moves towards technical standardization, and underpinned by the emerging organization of mass production (Stone 1973; Landes 1969).

Much of this, however, is implicit in the very logic of capitalist machine production, and point after point in scientific management can be matched by the gradgrindian theories of management developed by Ure (1861) and Babbage (1841) during England's first accelerated push towards mechanized production. This suggests that although the Taylorist move-

358

ment clearly had its origins in the early phases of monopoly capitalism, it did not bring into being a completely new structure to the labour process, one exclusively linked to monopoly capital, as some commentators have supposed, but must be situated historically in the continuous transformation of production set in motion by capital's appropriation of machinery.

We can only address this theme in a preliminary way within the limitations of a short paper by examining some of the major theorists of the relation between scientific management and monopoly capitalism. Of the key issues this literature raises, we want to emphasize:

(i) how the objectives of scientific management can be located within the complex of developments which constitute 'monopoly capitalism': concentration and centralization of capital, and the emergence of cartels and oligopolies; the expansion of the market into an arena of international competition on a world scale with associated imperial rivalry; the increasing centrality of protectionist and imperialist state policies abroad, and of state regulation at home; the development of mass production and consumption, and the recomposition of working class politics around reformism and economic trade unionism; and the incursion of the state into the sphere of the 'private' and domestic, particularly the attempts, both state and non-state, to reorganize the family;

(ii) the need to specify what sort of transformation was involved: how radical was the transformation to monopoly capitalism, and out of what exigencies of capital accumulation did Taylorism arise;

(iii) the significance of particular variants in the development of monopoly capitalism and the specific forms taken by the strategies of 'scientific management' in the context of distinct social formations;

(iv) the contradictions and limitations, and possibilities for class struggle, which beset these strategies.

Many variants of Marxism have explained monopoly capitalism as a particular epoch in the development of the capitalist mode of production, paying particular attention to the international division of labour. This was Lenin's characteristic emphasis in *Imperialism, the Highest Stage of Capitalism*. Although for Lenin the absolutely decisive element in the new phase was the concentration of capital and the growth of monopolization, detailed investigation of the internal recomposition of domestic capitals and the consequent attempts to re-form the working classes is virtually absent. (It is evident from his *Notebooks on Imperialism*, however, that Lenin recognized the significance of Taylorism, and had originally intended to include a section on it as the dynamic for the creation of a new labour aristocracy.)

One effect of this absence is that the socialization of production is viewed as being in itself relatively unproblematic, and only contradictory insofar as it is negated by private appropriation; there is a straight line of determination which immediately links concentration of capital to monopolies; monopolies and cartels to an intensification of contradictions; and these in turn to the terminal situation of capitalism. The significance of the expansion and complexity of the collective labourer is persistently underestimated. Thus there is a failure to grasp the extent to which capital can develop its own forms of socialized labour, articulated by the division of mental from manual labour; there is an unconvincing depiction of a homogeneous working class, duped into reformism by a labour aristocracy which has been bought off by the bourgeoisie; and finally a straightforward identification of significant sectors of the dominant classes as rentier or parasitic, which ignores the tendency in monopoly capitalism for many economic and ideological functions of the collective labourer to be distanced from the actual site of manufacturing production itself. From this basis, Lenin elaborates the other elements of the new period of capitalist development – the fusion of bank and industrial capital into finance capital, the export of capital to the colonies, the creation of international monopolist associations, and the complete territorial division of the world – with the predominant emphasis clearly on the international division of labour, and the contradictions specific to that division.

Writing in the midst of the imperialist slaughter of the 1914–18 war, castigating his political opponents who denied the existence of contradictory social development, it is probably of little surprise that Lenin was so single-minded. To reject his main propositions was either to abandon Marxism or to balance on its extreme right wing. But in hindsight we can perceive more sharply the failure: identification of the immediate piling up of contradictions as the signal of capitalist breakdown, and the period of imperialism as inherently transitional; in many ways, it makes as much sense to see the capitalism of the nineteenth century as 'transitional', and the mode of roduction of this century as a form of developed capitalism.

Next we turn to Harry Braverman, who addresses these issues from the vantage point of the contemporary relations of capital and labour within the United States (marked by the predominance of deskilled mass production and 'business' trade unionism) while giving minimal attention to the international division of labour. He provides a stark account of the relation of Taylorism to monopoly capitalism which admits little scope for variants and contradictions: for him 'scientific management' is *the* characteristic strategy of monopoly capital, developing in a systematic and self-conscious fashion what had earlier only been adopted haltingly and pragmatically.

Braverman emphasizes the location of scientific management within the emergence of monopoly capitalism, but never clarifies his understanding of the connection between them: on the one hand, the relation is contingent – Taylorism merely coincides with' or 'dates from', the onset of monopoly capitalism – on the other, Taylorism assumes a 'functional' role in the new phase of capitalism. The implication is that the process of concentration and centralization of capital simply provided the necessary resources for management to fulfil its inherent logic of detailed control over the labour process. Only once these resources were marshalled was capital able effectively to confront workers' control of the labour process based on craft skills. This vision of the fruition of a generic impulse to destroy craft autonomy both romanticizes and wrenches from historical context the uneven and limited forms of worker initiative characteristic of the competition phase of capitalist development (Elger 1979). It also implies a neo-Marcusian view of virtually contradiction-free capitalist hegemony in monopoly capitalism. Both within the labour process, where craft controls give way to the total regulation of production by capital, and within the sphere of exchange, where domestic production is superseded by commodity production and the manipulation of wage and price movements, capital creates a passive working class. The capacity of monopoly capital to compensate economistic trade unionism from an expanding surplus (note his brief but crucial comments on Fordism and trade unionism: Braverman, 1974, pp. 146–51) sets the seal on this hegemony in a way which renders political and cultural domination automatic and of little independent significance. This emphasis on the profound dominance of capital is qualified only in terms of the persistence of inarticulate working

361

class disgruntlement which might, under the pressure o extreme crisis, reopen the prospects for revolutionary politic (Braverman 1976).

Braverman himself says very little about the dynamics o monopoly capitalism but takes the account of Baran an Sweezy (1968) as his point of departure. For them the con tradictions of the phase of competitive capitalism, which issu in a tendency for the rate of profit to fall, are superseded i the monopoly phase by contradictions focused upon realiza tion/overproduction. This emphasis on contradictions an crises in the sphere of circulation leaves space for Braverman' analysis of production relations in terms of an invariant con tradiction between capitalists' and workers' control of th labour process, rather than in terms of specific problems o accumulation.

Braverman registers in a particularly impressive manner th profound impact of scientific management and technical trans formations upon the composition and politics of the workin class; he identifies as crucial the part played by these strategie in the development of monopoly capitalism; and he suggest very strongly that 'monopoly capitalism' should be seen as developed form of capitalism rather than merely a form o capitalism in crisis. However his account lacks any precis specification of the process of transition to monopoly capital ism, the variant forms that transition might take, and it contradictions and limitations.

Sohn-Rethel (1978) faces these problems more directly, pro viding a contemporary account of scientific management whic has many parallels with Braverman's but which is embedde in a theoretical project with more distant origins in the ex perience of central-European Marxism of the 1920s and 1930 From that experience came Sohn-Rethel's concern with th specific form of the labour process characteristic of monopol capitalism and the possibilties and problems it poses for social ist movements.

In Sohn-Rethel's account Taylorism represents a distinc phase in the development of the capitalist labour process qualitatively intensifying the socialized character of produc tion and bringing its logic into contradiction with capitalis market relations. He emphasizes that the domination of th labour process by capital on the basis of mechanization an the division of mental and manual labour develops *through out* the capitalist period. However Taylorism represents qualitative transformation within this trajectory, which arose out of the specific crisis of accumulation marked by the declining rate of profit during the 'great depression' (1873–96):

> To save the system and to restore profitability two remedies were above all imperative: one, a decisive expansion of the markets and the opening up of new territories, and fields for capital investment, in other words imperialism, and two, a substantial increase in the rate of exploitation of the labour employed in production at home. The first of these remedies recommended itself foremost to the rich creditor nations like Britain and France, while the second was particularly pressant for the USA, then still a debtor country but in full sweep of industrialisation and landed with the world's highest wage level. After 1918 Germany was thrown into the position of a highly industrialised debtor country with little choice but to enhance the exploitation of her national labour force by internal 'rationalisation' in order to work her way back into world competition. The weakened European victor countries from World War I then followed suit in this development as reluctant modernisers, while the USA now came into the position of combining both remedies to become the dominant capitalist world power. (Sohn-Rethel, 1971, p. 61; similarly Sohn-Rethel, 1976, and 1978.)

This account of the differing tempo and context of the adoption of Taylorism is accompanied by an analysis of the manner in which it responds to, and modifies the contradictions of capitalist production. In one aspect the crisis of profitability can be offset simply through 'speed up' facilitated by the 'coercive timing' and mechanical pacing of workers. However, the changes in the organization of production which precipitated the crisis of profitability place further constraints on employers. On the one hand there is pressure towards the expansion of plant to reap scale economies, but on the other such expansion threatens overcapacity, and simple cut-backs in production inflict disproportionate penalties because of increased fixed costs. Thus the capitalist experiences a diminishing capacity to respond to market exigencies and increasing pressure to utilize equipment in the most tightly integrated fashion. Thus Taylorism, and for Sohn-Rethel more especially Fordism, embrace an attempt to impose not only an

363

intensive but a *coherent* economy of time. In so doing they attempt to co-ordinate and control the labour of a multitude of workers as living labour associated with machinery, *prior to* and in tension with regulation/commensuration of labour times through exchange. This Sohn-Rethel conceptualizes as a fundamental contradiction between 'plant economy' and 'market economy': in the former can be seen the potential for social regulation of labour within production emancipated from the domination of machinery, specialized intellectual labour or market relations.

We can take from Sohn-Rethel not only a recognition of the centrality of time-economy in Taylorism (and Fordism) but particularly his bold attempt to specify the differential pattern of adoption of these strategies by different national capitals. Underlying these contributions (and leaving aside the general project of analysing the historical evolution of the segregation of intellectual and manual labour) is his concern to specify more closely the contradictions which beset the capitalist process of production during the transition to monopoly capitalism. The major limitation of his account is the manner in which he characterizes such contradiction in terms of a stark dualism between 'plant' and 'market' economies, designating monopoly capitalism on this basis as transitional. As a recent review suggests 'far from establishing any such "duality" of economic laws, the societization of labour is fundamental to the *consolidation* of capital' (Reinfelder and Slater, 1978, p. 135). Not only does this lead to a dualistic treatment of Taylorism, but it also leaves the relationship between the development of plant economy, contemporary class struggles over intensification of labour, and the emancipation of the collective labourer opaque.

The final account appears slightly more enigmatic: Gramsci's elliptical notes on 'Americanism and Fordism' (1971). Like other commentators, Gramsci recognized the importance of the tendency for the rate of profit to fall, and saw Fordism as the ultimate stage in the attempts to overcome this tendency. But the major impulse behind his analysis was to situate this whole Fordist fanfare in an investigation of social formations, rather than at the more abstract level of the mode of production, concentrating on the actual historical forms of transition from the individualistic capitalism characteristic of the nineteenth century to the various forms of corporate capitalism in gestation by the end of the 1920s. We cannot take up all the themes which occur in these notes: the investigation touches on the economic role of the Italian state, demographic patterns in Europe and North America, the social organization of the family and ideologies of sexuality, the problems of work discipline in capitalist and socialist countries, the cultural formations of Europe and America and so on. But the political logic behind this is clear: just as Lenin elaborated his notions of the American or Prussian routes for capitalist development in order to stake out a political strategy for the Bolsheviks, so Gramsci was examining what forces existed inside the Italian state which favoured the continuation of the fascist route, what forces existed for transforming the State direction of development into less authoritarian forms, and how this might affect the political leverage of the subordinate classes. In this way, the attempts by capital to overcome the tendency of the rate of profit to fall, or to mobilize counteracting tendencies, are seen in terms of their political and cultural conditions, and crucially, of the forms of state power which they require. This is clearly relevant to the question of the possible solutions for capital in this early period in the formation of monopoly capitalism: the dominance of either the imperialist or Taylorist trajectory.

Gramsci was particularly concerned with the internal colonialism of the Italian social formation, with the deep rift which held the south in subordination to the more prosperous, capitalized northern region. Embedded in these notes is the appreciation that the advanced monopoly forms of the north actually perpetuate the underdevelopment of the south, and he knew only too well from his own experience that for a truly popular revolution, the geographical and cultural divide had to be overcome. (Here monopoly capitalism intensifies the division between country and city as surely as it does mental and manual labour.) A common theme in both Gramsci and Lenin was the concept of parasitism, although for each author it carries quite distinct meanings: for Gramsci it referred to the relation of capitalist accumulation to a pre-capitalist formation (which he saw as parasitic), while for Lenin it was the advanced sectors of capital themselves which were parasitic. Thus there is the implication in 'Americanism and Fordism' that the fascist route for the formation of monopoly capitalism tended to reproduce more sharply the division between north and south than would perhaps the American route based on a 'rational' demographic structure.

This recognition of the colonial domination of the south, his own homeland, and the super-exploitation of its peasantry, and his search for more progressive strategies, shaped Gramsci's conception of Taylorism and his assessment of the impact it was beginning to have on the Italian formation. Like Lenin, he was convinced that under capitalist conditions Taylorism imposed unbearable penalties on the workers, which he understood as one of the contradictions at the heart of the new capitalism. But, again like Lenin, he was intrigued with the possibilities for developing under quite different social relations of production what might be rational about Taylorism: the 'unity between technical development and the interests of the ruling class is only a historical phase of industrial development, and must be conceived of as transitory. The nexus can be dissolved' (202). Gramsci did not believe that the contradiction could be overcome by tearing down the factories – first and foremost, in a manner characteristic of all theorists of the Third International, he believed that the revolutionary discipline of the working class was schooled and created in the factory; and secondly, Americanism impressed him as more notable for its development of the complex apparatus of trained and integrated collective labour than for its deskilling and intensification of work, constraints which would be overcome educatively in socialist society by the internalization of a new communist, collectivized work ethic. This approach (shared in its fundamentals by Lenin) persistently renders ambiguous Gramsci's location of Taylorism and its integral relation to the formation of monopoly capitalism, in a way that is never paralleled in his embittered enmity for the whole apparatus of colonial accumulation.

Thus both Lenin and Gramsci, with the conceptual and political resources available, mounted an inadequate critique of Taylorism (Linhart 1975), though the question of what might be 'progressive' about forms of production born in the heart of capitalism cannot simply be dismissed. What Gramsci and Lenin failed adequately to confront was the historically specific and contradictory features embodied in the monopoly capitalist socialization and subsumption of labour, and the forms of class struggle which develop on that terrain. (Gramsci did, however, mention the contradictions inherent in a high-wage strategy based on the precarious monopoly position of innovating firms, and in the continued reliance of employers upon a trained workforce: his account of the progressive features of Americanism should, perhaps, be seen as celebrating a specific, limited development of Fordism still significantly reliant upon workers' skills.) In this respect, current debates have tended to polarize around celebratory notions of either old craft forms (Montgomery, Braverman) or the new homogeneous mass worker (Baldi, Tronti). While appreciating the strategic possibilities presented by the contradictions reproduced in new work processes, we would also emphasize the specific, differentiated forms assumed by socialized labour today.

REFERENCES

Aglietta, M. 1978. 'Phases of U.S. Capitalist Expansion', *New Left Review*, 110.

Babbage, Charles. 1841. *On The Economy of Machinery and Manufactories*, (first published 1832).

Baldi, G. 1972. 'Theses on the Mass Worker and Social Capital', *Radical America*, 6 : 3.

Baran, P. and Sweezy, P. 1968. *Monopoly Capital*, Harmondsworth, Penguin.

Bologna, S. 1976. 'Class Composition and the Theory of the Party', *The Labour Process and Class Strategies*, London, CSE Pamphlet, Stage One.

Braverman, Harry. 1974. 'Labour and Monopoly Capital', *Monthly Review*, London.

—— 1976. 'Two Comments', *Monthly Review* 28 : 3.

Dobb, M. 1964. *Studies in the Development of Capitalism*, London, Routledge and Kegan Paul.

Elger, Tony. 1979. 'Valorization and Deskilling', *Capital and Class*, 7.

Fine, Ben. 1978. 'On the Origins of Capitalist Development, *New Left Review*, p. 109.

Foster, John. 1976. 'British Imperialism and the Labour Aristocracy' in J. Skelley (ed.), *1926 The General Strike*, London, Lawrence and Wishart.

Fridenson, P. 1978. 'The Coming of the Assembly Line' in Krohn, Layton and Weingart (eds), *The Dynamics of Science and Technology*, Dordrecht.

Gramsci, A. 1971. 'Americanism and Fordism' in *Selections From the Prison Notebooks*, London, Lawrence and Wishart.

Hinton, James. 1973. *The First Shop Stewards' Movement*, London, Allen and Unwin.

Hobsbawm, E. J. 1964. 'Customs, Wages and Workload in Nineteenth Century Britain' in *Labouring Men*, London, Weidenfeld and Nicolson.

—— 1968. *Industry and Empire*, Harmondsworth, Penguin.

Lenin, V. 1970. *Imperialism, The Highest Stage of Capitalism*, first published 1916, Moscow, Progress Publishers.

—— 1974. *Notebooks on Imperialism* (Collected Works, vol. 39), London, Lawrence and Wishart.

Linhart, R. 1975. *Lenine, Les Paysans et Taylor*, Paris, Seuil.

Maier, C. 1970. 'Between Taylorism and Technocracy', *Journal of Contemporary History*, 5:2.

Mandel, E. 1975. *Late Capitalism*, London, New Left Books.

Marx, K. 1976. *Capital*, vol. 1, Harmondsworth, Penguin.

Monds, Jean. 1976. 'Workers' Control and the Historians', *New Left Review*, p. 97.

Montgomery, David. 1974. 'Workers' Control of Machine Production', *Labor History*, 17:4.

—— 1976. 'The New Unionism and the Transformation of Workers' Consciousness', *Journal of Social History*, 7:3.

Palmer, Bryan. 1975. 'Class, Conception and Conflict: The Thrust for Efficiency', *Review of Radical Political Economy*, 7:2.

Reinfelder, M. & Slater, P. 1978. 'Intellectual and Manual Labour', *Capital and Class*, 6.

Russell, Jack. 1978. 'The Coming of the Line', *Radical America*, 12:3.

Raphael, Samuel. 1977. 'The Workshop of the World', *History Workshop*.

Sohn-Rethel, Alfred. 1971. 'Mental and Manual Labour in Marxism' in Stuart Hall and Paul Walton (eds), *Situating Marx*, London, Human Context Books.

—— 1976. 'The Dual Economics of Transition' in *The Labour Process and Class Strategies*, London, CSE Pamphlet, Stage One.

—— 1978. *Intellectual and Manual Labour*, London, Macmillan.

Stone, K. 1973. 'The Origins of Job Structure in Steel Industry', *Radical America*, 7:6.

Taylor, F. W. 1947. *The Principles of Scientific Management* (first published 1911), New York, Harper and Row.

Tronti, Mario. 1976. 'Workers and Capital', *The Labour Process and Class Strategies*, London, CSE Pamphlet, Stage One.

Ure, Andrew. 1861. *The Philosophy of Manufacturers* (first published 1835).

9 'Participation'

The Meaning of 'Job Enrichment'

Michel Bosquet

How long, in fact, *can* one go on running a factory by intimidation and repression? What is the value of work carried out by someone with a supervisor breathing down his neck, under threat of punishment or arbitrary harassment? What does this barrack-room atmosphere cost in terms of spoilt parts, discreet sabotage, disabling accidents, breakages, daily disturbances, growing difficulty in replacing the workers who leave? What is to become of an industrial country which has to look as far afield as southern Africa for its manpower because its own citizens, even the unemployed, reject imprisonment in its factories?

Today the CNPF (employers' organization) is having to face all these questions. Since the May 1971 revolt at Le Mans it has felt that its hold on the working class is slipping, that May '68 was no accident and the employers' control mechanisms are disintegrating. Repression only escalates the conflict without solving the problems; if you persist in that direction, before long you can only maintain 'order' in the factories by extending your 'fascism' to the rest of society – if you can do it at all. Most bosses daydream from time to time about introducing fascism (a new *kind* of fascism, naturally) as the lesser of two evils, but the thinking minority is well aware that it would solve nothing: look at the workers' risings in Spain or the insurrections in Cordoba (Argentina). In any case, fascism is bad for business; it's too crude, a last-ditch expedient to be used only when all other means of domination have failed.

This is why last autumn the CNPF began sending factfinding missions all over the world to study possible solutions. Is it possible to reconcile workers to the nature of their work? Are despotic management methods really necessary? Is the fragmentation and hierarchization of tasks *indispensable* in this day and age? Could the jobs performed by assembly-line workers be done away with and replaced by more interesting ones, thus reconciling control by the bosses with the principles of 1789? In its report 'The Problem of Assembly-line Workers' the CNPF study group wrote: 'This problem is both vast and difficult. We believe that it is inescapable.' M. Fontanet, the Minister of Labour, last Tuesday expressed much the same opinion.

The first to take an interest in this problem were almost certainly the American managers of the 1930s. Starting from the viewpoint that man is an infinitely adaptable animal, they concluded that those who did not get used to production-line work were 'unadaptable'; they must, it was felt, suffer from 'psychological problems'. Industrial psychologists were hired to help the workers gently to 'overcome their personal problems'. This opened the era of 'human relations in industry', a gigantic brainwashing enterprise.

After the Second World War, when labour became scarce in the United States, managers started to combine 'human relations' with material incentives in various ways; it had become necessary to give the workers an 'interest' in the level of productivity. They had to be rewarded for agreeing to increase production. The thirst for consumer goods which lasted throughout the 1950s seemed to confirm the managers' basic belief that you can get anything out of a worker provided you pay him for his trouble; that there is nothing a man will not do for money. You can buy his labour-power, his health, his youth, his sanity, his sleep, his very reason.

All good things come to an end. Towards the mid-1960s disquieting rumblings began to be heard in the big factories. A few years ahead of their European colleagues, American workers were beginning to rebel against production-line speeds, the meagreness of rest periods, tyrannical supervisors, the nervous exhaustion resulting from monotonous tasks. In 1963 tens of thousands of Detroit workers stayed out on strike in defiance of their union, which had just signed a package agreement making no provision for rest periods or for the reduction and control of line speeds.

American bosses reacted to this spontaneous rebellion in much the same way as their European counterparts, by replacing those workers with black or brown ones on a larger and larger scale. These workers, seldom represented in the union machinery, isolated and despised by management and skilled white fellow-workers alike, found themselves saddled with jobs nobody else would accept. Production lines manned by blacks travelled 20 or 30 per cent faster than those operated by whites. Black militants ('This isn't automation, it's *negro*mation') formed DRUM, the Detroit Revolutionary Union Movement. The tension became so unbearable that in one 'line incident' a black worker downed tools, walked up to his white foreman, killed him, and left without a word to give himself up to the police.

There was no French 'May' in the US, none of the prolonged rebellions which from September 1968 onward turned Fiat's much-vaunted organization of labour upside down and are still tormenting the Turin firm in the form of arguments over production norms, job-quotas, piecework rates and so on. Absenteeism in the United States has never reached the 15 per cent recorded by large French and Italian firms; it remains between 5 per cent and 10 per cent. Labour turnover attributable to voluntary departures has not yet reached Sweden's 30 per cent per annum, let alone the 100 per cent-plus of certain Fiat plants; at Ford of Detroit annual turnover is 'only' 25 per cent of the total workforce. . . .

According to American statistics (there are no equivalent figures for Europe), in 1966 employees were staying in the same job for an average of 4·2 years. By 1969 this average had dropped to 3·9 years; the latest figure for young people under twenty-four is 0·7 years. In ten years' time the number of young adults (i.e. those under thirty-four) will have increased by 46 per cent, roughly equivalent to 19 million people. Twelve million of them will belong to 'anti-system' age groups and strata; nearly 80 per cent of the country's adolescents will pass through the universities. Without basic changes to the nature of industrial work, it is difficult to see where industry will find its manpower.

The CNPF is facing this question squarely.

It is not unreasonable to predict [wrote the study group quoted above] that in a few years' time there will be jobs for which no labour will be available. It is significant that even immigrant labour only takes certain jobs on a very temporary basis, while there are many functions for which it has always been necessary to import manpower of less and less developed character. . . . Has it occurred to anyone that a more searching economic analysis would undoubtedly show that the cost of employing foreign labour which can be very backward seems infinitely greater if adaptation problems, retouching of sub-standard work and irregular production are taken into account? Even for non-immigrant labour [the report asks] has nobody ever weighed the minutes or seconds gained by a fragmented work process against the cost of retouching, botched work and strikes ... incidents, accidents, absenteeism and labour turnover, not to mention the consequences of a lack of job-satisfaction?

The study group reached some startling conclusions on the 'economic cost' of industrial accidents: 'Losses attributable to accidents, according to company figures, represent an average of 4·5 per cent of labour costs; if, however, the *indirect* cost of accidents, resulting from disturbance of the production process, is taken into account, this figure can be roughly doubled.'

Nothing but good, in fact, can come from 'humanizing' and 'reorganizing' factory work, 'adapting the task to the man' and abolishing the fragmented, repetitive tasks which exhaust the worker with their intense monotony. But is it possible? How is it that the bosses did not think of it sooner? That is the first thing to understand.

The whole history of industrial techniques bears the imprint of the original sin of capitalism: separation of the workers from the means of production. The reason for this separation was not originally a technical one. The first factory bosses were seventeenth-century merchants who monopolized the looms in order to gain possession of the *entire production* of the weavers. The weavers had to be deprived of their machines to prevent them from selling their products on their own account. Once they were obliged to go to work in the boss's own workshop and on his machines, the first proletarians could be subjected little by little to other constraints: they could be required to work to the limit of their strength, something no man will do for long if left to his own devices.

Subsequent technological innovations have always had a dual purpose: to make human labour as productive as possible, and also to force the worker to work to the limit of his capabilities. In the eyes of the classic boss, the need for this constraint goes without saying: the worker is suspected of idleness by definition. How could it be otherwise? Neither the product itself nor the purpose of its manufacture has anything

373

to do with him. The purpose of manufacturing is not to fulfil the workers' needs but to make the largest possible profit, in order to buy more machines which will yield still greater profit. It is possible for the employer pursuing this aim (the accumulation of capital) to rely on the workers' basic will to work; their daily or weekly production must be imposed on them and to this end must be fixed in advance as rigorously as possible.

All that remains is to see how this can be done. The most obvious solution is to link payment to yield, but this is not as simple as one might think; workers doing piecework never go all-out for maximum pay. Beyond a certain level of energy output, they lose interest in money. The tendency is for workers to settle on a cruising rhythm and then to try to get that rhythm to correspond to a reasonable wage. Work study makes no difference: the more they are constrained by shackles imposed from above, the more ingenious workers become in leading the boss up the garden path.

Work study is also extremely difficult to apply to highly skilled workers (e.g. toolmakers, fitters, adjusters) whose jobs demand initiative, intelligence, application and skill – qualities which are resistant to tight control. As long as skilled workers are necessary, the boss will be dependent on their goodwill. Their influence was at its peak in the era of the 'universal machine'. The only way of breaking their power was to simplify the work to such an extent that anyone could do it without the slightest training. From 1920 onward Taylorism provided the means: the work was split up into extremely simple tasks; assembly lines were supplemented by powered conveyor belts and became fully automatic; 'scientific work organization' completed the picture. Fifty years after the beginning of Taylorism, skilled workers have become a marginal 'aristocracy' and work quotas are predetermined with mathematical rigidity.

The rational fragmentation of work has often produced spectacular increases in productivity, but it can be seen today that these increases could have been produced in other ways, and that productivity was not the only objective. A hidden (and successful) aim of these developments was to render the forces constraining the worker to work more anonymous and 'objective'. The work quota is no longer laid down, negotiated and imposed by a human authority which remains open to argument; it is ordered by the machine itself, imposed by the inexorable programmed advance of the assembly line. The compulsion to work now appears as a law of nature reinforced with the wonders of science. Behind the scenes, doubtless, are engineers and technicians, but the worker never meets them face to face any more than he sees the remote boss. All he sees are supervisors and foremen, and it is with these 'boss's lackeys' that he has to deal.

In this way work has been fragmented, simplified and made more and more idiotic mainly to deprive the workers of any vestige of power over the production process, to shield the process from 'human hazards' such as skill and intelligent initiative. Everything, including the workers, has to be mathematically predictable to the nearest thousandth. Prime costs, profits, production plans, the amortizement and investment programmes of a great capitalist enterprise cannot be left at the mercy of 'human hazards'.

But some of the more enlightened big bosses have begun to discover that the organizational passion of technocrats trained and hired to rationalize production down to its last detail can backfire in a way which the technocrats are unable to foresee....

Mishaps of the same kind in the United States have given birth to a new school of psycho-sociology whose leading exponents are (or were) McGregor and Scanlon, Argyris and Herzberg. Stripped of its academic jargon, their reasoning is simple common sense. Workers, they maintain, are concerned primarily with ensuring their subsistence. As long as their primary needs – health, security, food and housing – remain uncertain, it is quite useless to ask psychologists to solve factory problems. And dissatisfaction will persist, however high the wages are, if the working 'environment' is bad and the worker is frustrated in his secondary, affective needs: if he finds a barrack-room atmosphere instead of comradeship.

Before passing to the third point, which is the most important of all, we might do worse than listen to the CNPF beating its breast over the first two. The bosses' report quoted above states that assembly-line workers' wages are 16 per cent lower than in Germany, while engineers' salaries are 11 per cent higher. A qualified engineer is paid four times as much as an assembly line worker, against two and a half times as much in Germany, Britain or the US. The 'environment' of factories is almost universally detestable. Newly employed workers are received by barking supervisors, confronted with their task without preparation or advice, and told to fulfil the norm if they want to keep the job. 'Often, workers *"crack"* after three or four days', suffering 'lasting traumas'. Everything seems designed to convince the workers that factory work is some kind of expiatory punishment. Talking about 'participation' and 'job-interest' in these circumstances is tantamount to asking the oppressed to 'participate' in their own oppression.

This is where we reach the third point. If the pay and environment are good, but the work is moronic, the worker will still try to escape from it in a thousand different ways. Management responds by trying to increase the pressure to work; the results are absenteeism, lowered quality and sabotage. 'Idleness, indifference and irresponsibility', notes Herzberg, 'are healthy responses to absurd work.' It is equally absurd, he adds, to think that work can be made more attractive by varying tasks which are individually fragmented and repetitive: 'The combining of two senseless tasks does not confer any sense on their sum.'

The only correct solution is to reframe, broaden and enrich jobs so as to make them intrinsically interesting. According to this school of psycho-sociology man is an 'active animal' who likes to work provided the work gives him an opportunity for 'self-realization': a flowering of the intellect, an enrichment of knowledge, recognition and appreciation for his ideas and inventions in the context of collective effort and co-operation. In short the fragmentation of work, external pressures and hierarchical quasi-military relations of production should all be abolished.

That's the theory, anyway. It is currently being applied in all or part of two or three hundred enterprises of various sizes: Texas Instruments and IBM-France, Philips (Holland), ICI (Britain), and Lapointe, Donnelly Mirrors and AT&T (the world's biggest private employer) in the US. Here are some of the results.

Environment: create a climate of trust by abolishing the time clock. Abolish obvious class discrimination: the same canteen and the same food for everyone (including the managing director), and as far as possible the same dress. Everyone paid on a monthly basis, and a single salary scale. Abolish timekeepers, checkers, supervisors, slave-drivers and cops. Each worker or work team to be responsible for the quantity and quality of their output, the maintenance and adjustment of their machines and their working methods. Every team or individual to make a complete thing. Managers who do nothing but give orders to disappear; technicians and management are now friendly 'counsellors' who get their hands dirty.

The anticipated result is that workers regain their taste for work and produce more *while expending less energy*; for they are spared the psychological strain of working against their spontaneous inclinations. Does the experience bear out the theory? Here are some examples.

Labour turnover had been particularly high in the claims and invoices departments of American Telegraph and Telephone (AT&T), which has a monopoly of telecommunications in the United States. The work is finicky, involving the sorting, coding, transcribing and verifying of cheques and invoices. 'Attractive' pay and conditions were not successful in keeping employees. The proportion of errors had stood at 13 per cent for ten years, and needed a cumbersome checking system, when in 1966 AT&T called Herzberg to the rescue. He observed that the work of sorting, checking and totalling cheques and invoices was broken down into ten successive operations and run on hierarchial, semi-military lines; when a group of clerks reached the end of a stack of a thousand invoices, the supervisor would send them another thousand. What motivation did these women have to work rapidly and conscientiously? None whatsoever.

Following Herzberg's advice, AT&T decided to make each employee responsible for a different section of town; she would always be dealing with the same clients and would be responsible for their accounts. The work (basically card-punching) did not change, but each operator became free to vary her working speed and, within certain limits, her hours of work. The proportion of errors fell to 3 per cent and a whole superstructure of checkers could be dispensed with. Result: a 27 per cent productivity increase and a saving of $558,000 in one year.

Can the same thing be done for mass-production in the manufacturing industries? The psycho-sociologists claim that it can. Here is the proof. Non-Linear Systems, which makes automatic control systems, had problems with absenteeism, output and reliability. The company could not trust the workers to turn up regularly, and could not rely on the quality of its products. It could try strengthening its quality control, but who would control the controllers? Argyris advised them to approach the problem from the other end: trust the workers, make them responsible for the quality of the product and in return do away with the time clock, fragmentation of tasks and other controls. Each worker would be given the (pre-tested) components of the apparatus and would then assemble them, perform final checks and pack the assembled unit. The firm followed this advice, with the result that the output of its assembly workers doubled in two years, while defects declined by 90 per cent.

At Texas Instruments, which applied the same principles, the time taken to assemble one navigational aid fell from 138 hours to 32 in one year, a productivity increase of 330 per cent.

Philips (Holland) is now beginning to apply 'job-enrichment' to the assembly and adjustment of colour TV sets. Formerly, this job was broken down into a hundred successive operations, each lasting less than a minute, carried out by a hundred workers. The work was monotonous and repetitive in the extreme. Assembly and adjustment are currently being carried out by experimental groups of seven workers who have a stock of components at their disposal, co-ordinate the work themselves, pick their own speed and are free to move about. At this stage output is up by 5 per cent, absenteeism is down by 25 per cent and defects are dropping towards nil.

ICI, which has already introduced 'job enrichment' and 'workers' control' in several factories employing a total of about 5,000 people, has registered a 30 per cent productivity increase in its Gloucester synthetic fibre factory, where former assembly-line workers, freed from the supervision of foremen and specialists, have learned to adjust, maintain and repair machines which are supposed to be very complex.

Given all this, why is it that the great majority of employers (75 per cent in France according to a recent poll) remain stubbornly hostile to the abolition of fragmented, idiotic work? ...

In reality, the bosses' hostility is not motivated by technical or economic factors; it is political. Job-enrichment spells the end of authority and despotic power for bosses great and small. It replaces the order and discipline of the barracks with the voluntary co-operation of workers whose autonomy extends to some real power over their work. It requires that workers 'doing a man's job' be treated as men. The whole hierarchy has to be recast; engineers and management, says the CNPF report, must 'modify their attitudes profoundly'. Social, cultural and hierarchical barriers have to be removed. 'After acquiring some idea of ergonomics, engineers and technicians should spend a year doing workers' tasks in workshops that use their specialized skills. . . .' Finally, the workers themselves have to 'identify problems, discuss possible solutions and then reach collective decisions. Relations will no longer be as between superiors and subordinates. . . .'

Once this road has been taken, in fact, where does it end? Managers and technicians will lose their monopoly of science; the alleged scientific or technical necessities in whose name they give orders will lose their mystery and become open to question, along with the ideology they support. Isn't this the thin end of the self-management wedge? The CNPF report seems to suggest that it is, but without undue alarm; in the democratized and 'enriched' enterprise, management authority will still prevail, provided it changes its style.

But can we be sure? Will workers doing intelligent, creative, responsible jobs feel, as Herzberg wants them to, that work well done carries its own meaning within it? What meaning is there in a job whose products are meaningless? How long can a person remain interested in assembling colour TV sets when the programmes are rubbish, in producing polluting detergents, in weaving textiles that wear out in no time? Is there any meaning in the quest for productivity and output when its purpose is the growth of profits? What is the purpose of profit and growth? Why produce more when we can live better by producing less, provided we live and consume *differently*?

All these questions spring logically from any extension of job enrichment. For this reason the advanced elements of the workers' movement see the struggle to 'recompose splintered work' as being far more than a mobilization issue or a modestly reformist campaign to 'humanize' work. What they call 'workers' control' – the re-appropriation by the workers of some say in the nature and organization of their work - can and should lead workers liberated from brutalization, oppression and boredom to struggle for total emancipation.

This is exactly what the great majority of bosses is afraid of : 'The more you give them, the more they want. Give them a bit of power and they want it all.' True enough. But the CNPF researchers answer this by saying that repression is becoming more and more expensive both politically and economically, that in the final analysis industry has no choice : if it wants to find the manpower it needs without having to face continual rebellions, it must try to make the work interesting and attractive. All these subversive questions raised by job-enrichment are, after all, being asked right now in every possible way by millions of young workers and unemployed in the US and in Europe. For them, work – whatever its nature and whatever the pay – has ceased to be an end in itself.

Do they reject it because they reject its products and its results? The fact is that they do not really agree with Herzberg when he says: 'Leisure today is no more than a frantic effort to forget work. When leisure has a meaning, work will have one too.' The tendency of young people is to approach the problem from the other end: 'Work will have a meaning when its purpose has a meaning. Not before.'

Participation: the Pattern and its Significance

Harvie Ramsay

It has long been conventional among writers on the history of industrial relations in Great Britain to represent the past teleologically. By this I mean that past events are selected as significant and internally represented in a manner which emphasizes their contribution as stepping stones to the present. This is not, of course, a preserve of those authors whose sympathy lies with the current *status quo*. E. P. Thompson was attacking a similar distortion in the work of Perry Anderson and Tom Nairn when he described an effort 'to cut history to fit a model with a vengeance' (1965:340). The consequence for historical understanding (and so for interpretation of the present with which it is evidently so closely tied up) is to elide the massive number of counterforces and potentials which exist at any moment in time, and thereby to drain the account of its substance and colour and of any sense of access. In the history of industrial relations this appears most vividly in those accounts which talk of an 'evolution' or 'growth' of the current system. A good example is offered by Charles (1973), whose text is subtitled 'Studies in the evolution of collective bargaining at national and industry level'. Charles seeks to represent a series of meetings between employers and unions in the period 1911–39, and the setting up of Whitley committees after 1917, as signposts to the future and part of the emergence of the present. He does this despite the evident fact that each of the instances he chooses to focus on was a failure in respect of producing the labour-management co-operation he sees as the essence of the new order. He thereby chooses to dismiss as incidental the intense conflict amidst which these bodies were set up (and to which it will be suggested here they were in the case of Whitleyism defensive reactions, and in the case of the Industrial Council, the National Industrial Conference and the Mond-Turner talks similarly but less concertedly, so more token events).

The general thesis adopted here is that it is more fruitful

to examine past periods of participative innovation as management reactions to a period when their power is felt to be under siege. A major part of such a threat is the undermining of legitimacy of managerial authority. A great deal of emphasis must be placed on how social processes were experienced, i.e. how they appeared to those involved in them; this applies not only to those who challenge management but to those on the other end of the challenge. The key to management action will clearly be their perception of the extent and nature of the threat, and of the justification and likely efficiency, within their understanding of the 'problems', of different responses. Clearly one would expect these perceptions to have some link to what is actually happening (i.e. management is more likely to perceive danger at times when there is widespread discontent amongst labour), but the connection is one which may be mediated and considerably affected by how any events are actually experienced by managers. At any rate, whilst participation is seen partly as a tactic, and certainly (because of the unitary cast of management ideology) as incorporative in intent, the argument here is not simply for the conspiratorial concoction of works councils and the like to 'fool' employees. That is not to say, of course, that there will not be times when such cynicism will after all be justified!

Briggs and After

The earliest period in which participative schemes attracted serious attention from capitalists saw the establishment of some twenty-five profit-sharing arrangements between 1865–1873. That the idea was not new is shown by an examination, for instance, of French history. It was in response to the efforts in this direction by Charles Babbage (significantly a precursor of Taylorism in many respects) that Marx had commented that profit-sharing served only as:

> ... a *special bonus* which can achieve its purpose only as an exception from the rule, and which is in fact, in noteworthy practice, restricted to the buying-up of individual overlookers etc., in the interests of the employer *against* the interests of their class ... or else it is a special way of cheating the workers and of *deducting a part of their wages* in the more precarious form of a profit depending on the state of the business. (Marx 1858:288).

*

In the UK the pioneers were Harry Briggs, Son & Co. Their scheme, explicitly directed at the exclusion of unions from the company, followed a period of progressively worsening labour relations. Early profit pay-outs heralded a period of apparent success in the goals of the plan until a renewal of recession in 1874 saw Briggs acting with other coalmasters to cut wages. To their disgust employees showed little loyalty, and joined a widespread strike against the employers' action. Thus the 'preventative' rather than 'palliative' which the Briggses had advertised in their attempts to publicize their methods had at best temporary impact. The scheme was abandoned at the shareholders' insistence.

It is significant that this and subsequent waves of interest on the part of employers in participation schemes in many respects follow the pattern noted by Allen (1964) for the use of conciliation and arbitration procedures. He too observes a pattern in which apparent concessions were made in those industries and at those times when pressure on employers was greatest, but that despite the frequent embracing of universalistic principles justifying the new arrangements the best efforts were made to avoid formal recognition so that the relationship could be readjusted should 'better' times return. The same analysis can also be applied to employer welfare policies (Hay 1977 [b]).

The analysis of two recent and one rather older study of profit-sharing before the First World War confirms the pattern described above. In Church's words:

> If one examines the subsequent history of profit-sharing down to World War I it is possible to identify a direct relationship between the introduction of profit-sharing or co-partnership schemes with a high level of employment and labour unrest. (1971:10).

A recent study of J. T. & T. Taylor's profit-sharing scheme (Pollard & Turner 1976) illustrates the extension of this policy profile well beyond the period examined by Church. Taylor's scheme was in fact begun during the second peak of profit-sharing inauguration, 1889–92. Where Sedley Taylor had found little interest among capitalists in profit-sharing in preceding years, the conflict of this period brought forth a revival of attention. Subsequent periods of interest in 1908–09 and 1912–14 are associated with similar conditions.

In practice, profit-sharing does not appear to have been very successful in achieving 'enterprise consciousness' (Bristow's term, 1974 : 262), with a failure rate of well over 50 per cent (Bristow, 1974:288). Many cases of the sort of instability shown by the Briggs' scheme are apparent, but on top of these visible failures must be stacked the many schemes which became ritual annual bonuses with little significance to employer or employee, yet surviving for years as a token gesture.

Whitleyism

The profit-sharing schemes reviewed above show plainly the unitary, entrepreneurial/managerial ideology which guided them, and the source of the concern which led to their introduction. The United States saw similar attempts by employers:

> In their ways, employers had been responding sporadically to the demand of their workers with schemes of employee representation.... by instituting schemes of profit-sharing, and by the construction of company towns in which they would exhibit varying degrees of benevolence. By such measures American employers hoped to undermine the appeal of the trade unions, and they reacted vigorously and with hurt indignation when they did not succeed. (Bendix 1956:266).

The coincidence of radical working class movements in many different countries during the twentieth century, commencing with the varieties of industrial unionism and syndicalism in the first two decades, is particularly notable. Then, as now, offers of 'participation' in some form were found in many countries as a consequence, illustrating the extent of interlinkage which has existed for a very long time already between the capitalist nations, and so their crises.

To return, then, to the limited perspective of British experience, but with the parallels elsewhere kept in mind, we find the early years of the twentieth century beset by mounting unrest, the varying causes of which have been severally investigated by authors interested in the generation of the shop stewards' movement from 1915. As the rigours of the First World War precipitated the intensification of conflict between working class movements, widely antagonistic to an 'imperialist war', and their employers, the latter seen as backed by a visibly 'servile State', so middle-class fears grew. The events in Russia did little to calm bourgeois anxiety. At the same time, where the war effort did produce patriotic effort from the shop floor, benefits of co-operative activity were made clear, as were those of dilution for the introduction of more effective technology to speed the labour process. Thus whilst anti-Bolshevik feeling ran high[3] there were also moves afoot to encourage the idea of setting up a joint committee of labour and management representatives in each firm, with a national industrial council in each industry. These moves were first mooted by the Garton Foundation, at the particular instigation of a Quaker, Malcolm Sparkes, and Ernest J. P. Benn (ancestor of Tony Benn). They provoked the establishment of a Government committee under the chairmanship of J. H. Whitley, which in its division between employer and union representatives was in many ways a pre-echo of the Bullock Committee of 1976–7. White (1975) makes clear the contiguity between the tactic of Whitleyism which emerged, to try and ameliorate conflict, and the preparation and utilization of other forms of social control, including coercive repression.

It is significant that Whitleyism is now associated with diluted bargaining industries and other areas of employment with weak union organization. It is even common to find joint consultation grafted on top of these arrangements. This also makes it all too easy to forget the original aspirations and rhetoric which surrounded its emergence, and the initial scope of its coverage. The following quotations from the first interim report of the Whitley Committee are illustrative here:

What is wanted is that the workpeople should have a greater opportunity of participating in the discussion about the adjustment of those parts of industry by which they are most affected. . . .

In conclusion it may be pointed out that the subcommittee has tried to devise, in general terms, a plan which would give opportunities for satisfying the growing demands made by the trade unions for a share in 'industrial control' . . . (quoted in Charles, 1973 : 107, 112).

If this rhetoric is plain, then despite the appending of their signatures to a document which trod with notable skill a rhetorical path into which both employer and union representatives could read their own interpretation, there was also a rejection in part of the conclusions on the part of Smillie *et al.* which is echoed in many caveats today:

> ... a complete identity of interests between capital and labour cannot thus be effected and that such machinery cannot be expected to furnish a settlement for the more serious conflicts of interest involved in the workings of an economic system primarily governed and directed by the motives of private profit. (quoted by Charles, 1973: 101).

What, then, was the result of Whitleyism? At its peak it covered 3½ million workers, in a wide range of employment (Halevy, 1921:130). In an enthusiastic review of experience with works committees existing prior to the implementation of the Whitley recommendations, the Ministry of Labour[4] proclaimed that 'Works Committees have, in the great majority of cases, tended to introduce greater harmony and, through it, greater efficiency' (p. 46). Yet the optimism seems to have been misplaced, for even the full flush of Whitley propaganda, accompanied by the National Industrial Council of 1919, could not make the 'new' system, presented then as now as part of the evolution of industrial relations to a new basis, into a workable one. Behind the grand words, interpretations were inconsistent:

> The workers talk about participation in the management of the business. The employers reply by talking about participation in profits and, in the most favourable cases, concede only the most bastard form of joint control to the workers ... we know very well how illusory this control is, and the appearance of control is intended to create the narrowest possible bond between the interests of the worker and the interests of the employer who hires him. (Halévy, 1919:108).

By 'co-operation', Halévy found unionists talking in terms of the elimination of profits and employers of their grand enhancement. It is not, therefore, surprising to find that Whitleyism was largely ignored or rejected by organized trades who had already attained bargaining rights, and began to disappear fairly quickly in other cases. Some councils exhibited an instability inherent in conflict over the terms of the so-called co-operation, others faded into disuse more quietly. By 1926 only 47 of 78 established schemes remained[5], with many of these almost certainly operating on a ritualistic basis only.

The 1920s had seen a reversal of the power and so the challenge of labour to employers of course, and under this circumstance interest in maintaining the participative pretences declined sharply apart from the impetus in this direction from the widespread failure of the councils in managerial terms. The 1927 Mond-Turner talks, which Charles, Chang (1936) and McDonald & Gospel (1973) all seem to regard as path-breakingly significant, stand out in perspective as confirming the impression of cycle after all, for it was practically ignored by employers (who had prior to the defeat of the unions been so eager) and offered the unions the most sketchy and inoperative of consultations. The treatment of this conference is a good illustration of the way modes of interpretation and evolutionism lay stress on events in such a way as to embarrass any reflexive analytical history.

In the eyes of at least two authors the Whitley committee system's publicity had achieved at least a short-term success for the employers' side:

> The trick had come off, and the system of Whitley councils had done its work. It had allowed capitalism to play state collectivism [material demands] and Guild socialism off against each other and to cancel each other out. (Halévy; 1922 : 152).

> Even before 1920, it was becoming obvious that some employers had only dealt with the idea of shared control as a device to buy time. (Child, 1969a : 48).

To envision so conspiratorial and conscious a strategy is probably somewhat misleading. No doubt there were some employers who did calculate on the value of a delaying device, but there were many others who were at least partly (and rather temporarily) convinced of the need for participation; still others would have always pushed for participation, whether on idealistic or tactical grounds, and their voices would have assumed prominence at a time when this approach was in favour. Such 'pioneers' tend to fade back into being 'eccentrics' when interest fades once more. *Pace* Child this is a far more realistic account of the influence of Quaker ideas.

Similarly, the persistence of Sir Alfred Mond with works councils in ICI during the 1930s, far from undermining the thesis here, conforms well to that maxim which speaks of 'the exception that proves the rule.' Mond's statements never concealed the capitalist nature of his ambitions for these and other methods.[6]

Joint Consultation

The participative panacea was thus displaced by other methods more visibly associated with social control for most of the interwar years. Then the latter years of the 1930s witnessed a revival of the militancy of trade unionism in industries where employment prospects were picking up fastest due to military preparations. Those who rebuilt the severely depleted trade unions were, predictably, extremely hostile to the management establishment that had made to offer so much and then, once the opportunity arose, resorted to all the old tactics once more. Capitalism had, moreover, failed in its project of offering at least the most economically effective and secure system of production and employment. The legitimacy of those who ran industry was thus once again under severe pressure. The Second World War was, however, less straightforward in its impact on this situation than the First had been.

Because of the shared opposition to the Nazi enemy particularly once the Soviet Union had been attacked by Hitler, the labour movement was this time united in its support for the war effort. The result was the appearance of joint production committees, apparently much indebted to initiative from the labour side. The government reacted by giving official approval to these committees and their equivalents in shipbuilding (yard committees) and the mines (pit committees). A committee was set up under the chairmanship of the General Secretary of the TUC, Citrine, to recommend action to set up regional organizations to harness these local efforts (1944 : 110, 14ff). By July 1943 there were 4,169 JPCs covering 2¼ million workers (Clegg & Chester, 1954 : 338), and 4,565 in June 1944 (Flanders, 1968c : 135).

JPCs were forbidden to discuss matters covered by machinery for negotiation Thus they dealt almost exclusively with production and efficiency. As such they came to seem attractive propositions to many managers. It was felt that:

*

... competent managers were given a means of 'putting their plans across' to their workers; that an undoubted enthusiasm on the part of many workers was canalized through the JCPs; and that a number of workers gained some experience of the problems of management.[7]

However, this lack of challenge to management, for them the essence of 'real' participation, encouraged less enthusiasm from employees even under wartime conditions. The left had expected (as, ironically, they hoped again in the 1960s) that access to management decisions would expose the inefficiencies and unscientific nature of management, but then as now the source of ideology ran deeper than mere propaganda. There was a growing reaction to the fact that committees were instead becoming the tool of management control and discipline (see Agar 1944; Calder 1969, 1973). Despite ideal conditions for co-operation, then, Clegg & Chester (1954:339) conclude that there was no more than half-and-half success and failure (what they mean by the terms is unclear) for JPCs. Thus after the war JPCs fell away in numbers, to perhaps 550 in 1948 (Clegg & Chester 1954:339; PEP 1955:181). In fear of the new Labour government introducing a statutory form of participation, some employers preferred not to pursue the matter (Wigham 1973:158).

In the years following the war and the defeat of Churchill in the elections, the Labour government put into operation the public corporation, based not on the diluted workers' control model proposed before the war but on the Morrison scheme. This meant no rights to representation for workers at the executive level; but compulsory establishment of consultative and advisory bodies in the new organizations. Meantime, the threat of an economic crisis like that after the First World War haunted government and many employers, and when the situation worsened in 1947 there emerged a rapidly revived interest in joint consultation in the private sector also. The Ministry of Labour again campaigned for the 'new' arrangements, which again were to be voluntary for each industry and to act in advisory capacity only. They were also to be strictly delimited from areas of acknowledged conflict and so negotiation. By 1949, of 54 chief industries, 26 had agreed to recommend setting up joint committees at factory and workshop levels, 17 had decided to leave it entirely to local management, and 8 had decided existing machinery was adequate. Three had not decided (Flanders 1968c : 135–6; Clegg & Chester 1954: 343).

The spread of joint consultation was rapid and very extensive. Two studies at the very end of the 1940s (NIIP 1952; Brown & Howell-Everson 1950) confirmed that around three-quarters of all companies (and over 90 per cent in engineering) had such councils. (7 per cent had already discontinued, it should be noted). But if the scope of this cycle is so often conveniently forgotten today, so too is the speed of its decline. In a period of growing economic prosperity (and mounting Tory majorities) the rising apparent power of the unions did not constitute a threat to management. Moreover, the consultation system produced rife triviality, offering little to either side of industry now that the common war effort was over. By the early 1960s only one in five firms with over 150 employees reported having consultation committees (Marsh & Coker 1963), and equally interestingly under 30 per cent of these companies reported having such schemes in 1955. Whilst some of these cases can be accounted for by schemes which were retired before 1955, there would have appeared to be a good deal of 'amnesia', whether deliberate or not, on the basis of the earlier known figures. Part of this is probably accounted for at the other end, too, by firms reporting schemes when they were fashionable in the late 1940s which were so token as to be soon forgotten. Some of these which had survived had done so in a ritual form, known only to students of the company rule book.

Participation has, then, attracted management attention on a large scale at particular periods of time, particularly when they have experienced a challenge to their authority from below, this usually coinciding with a crisis in the need for motivation of labour effort. Thus, a cyclical or wave-like pattern emerges. Managements have been the gatekeepers for such arrangements. In consequence, although the schemes may appear as a concession to labour, they take a form which accords with management's conception of how they should operate, i.e. a unitary form. This is intended to integrate labour, and so to restore management authority whilst enlisting worker representatives actively in the causes of productivity and efficiency – the intensified rationalization of the labour process.

However, an historical survey also suggests that such strategies have a severely limited capacity to succeed for management. Participation schemes are more likely to become trivial (where labour is not organized, or where key issues can be transferred to a bargaining channel) or unstable (where conflicts erupt because management vets bargaining). Thus, in the absence of pressure for management to attempt periodic revitalization to cope with a continuing challenge, they will tend to disintegrate or fade away. In some cases, a works council may become a negotiating channel, where management take a pragmatic line. These are the processes behind the broader pattern I have described. They indicate the limits to management's efforts to incorporate labour as well as their persistent intent.[8]

NOTES

1 Church, 1971; Bristow, 1974; Rease, 1913. Similarly telling evidence is also provided by a protagonist of the concept, Sedley Taylor in his 1884.

2 See especially Hinton, 1973; Kendall, 1969; Cole, 1923; Holton, 1976.

3 Cf. White, 1975. The Government received regular reports on the state of revolutionary organization throughout the war and for a good many years thereafter.

4 Ministry of Labour, 1918. This publication confirms strongly the similarity of aspiration, propaganda and method of empirical 'verification' by short, uncritical case studies with current approaches by government and other proponents. See, for instance, the series of case studies in the Department of Employment Gazette during 1977 for comparison. Thus, in 1918 the Introduction by D. J. Shackleton tells us that 'The old trade union machinery has often been overburdened' and that works committees had grown up for communication in these circumstances. In fact, many of the committees examined are early bargaining bodies recognizing the shop stewards' role belying and the unitary, evolutionary aspirations of such propagandists as these.

5 E. Wigham, 'Worker Participation: A New Look At An Old Principle', *The Times.* Flanders (1968:209) gives dif-

ferent though similar figures as does Seymour (1932) in a rather fuller description.

6 Thus Mowat reports Mond's reply to Snowden's 1923 parliamentary speech attacking capitalism, a reply which Mowat describes as 'a panegyric on individual initiative and a condemnation of socialism as a robbing of the rich and a clipping of the wings of enterprise in a bureaucratic, soulless machine' (1955:154).

7 Clegg and Chester, 1954:339. See also, Walpole, 1944; ILO, 1944; and Coates & Topham who find that: 'With a few exceptions, shop stewards and unions alike combined to strengthen orthodox managerial power rather than control it' (1972:48).

8 This account is taken further from productivity bargaining in the 1960s through to Bullock and beyond in Ramsay (1977) and in chap. 8 of my Ph.D. thesis, *Participation For Whom?*

REFERENCES

Agar, T. W. 1944. 'Towards Industrial Democracy' in *Can Planning Be Democratic?* Fabian Essays by Herbert Morrison *et al.*, London, Routledge and Kegan Paul.

Allen, V. L. 1964. 'The Origins of Industrial Conciliation and Arbitration', *International Review of Social History*, 9. Reprinted in Allen, 1971.

—— 1971. *The Sociology of Industrial Relations.* London, Longman.

Bendix, R. 1956. *Work and Authority in Industry: Ideologies of Management in the course of Industrialisation.* New York, John Wiley & Sons. (Page refs to 1963 Harper & Row edition.)

Brannen, P., Batstone, E., Fatchett, D. J., and White, P. 1976. *The Worker Directors: A Sociology of Participation*, London, Hutchinson.

Bristow, E. 1974. 'Profit-sharing, socialism and labour unrest' in K. D. Brown (ed.), *Essays in Anti-Labour History*, London, Macmillan, pp. 262–89.

Brown, W. R. and Howell-Everson, N. A. 1950. *Industrial Democracy at Work: A Factual Survey*, London, Pitman.

Calder, A. 1969. *The People's War: Britain 1939–45.* London, Panther, 1971.

—— 1973. 'Labour and the Second World War' in D. Ruben-stein (ed.), *People for the People*, London, Ithaca Press, pp. 234–40.

Chang, D. 1936. *British Methods of Industrial Peace*, Columbia University Press (reprinted by A. M. S. Press, 1968).

Charles, R. 1973. *The Development of Industrial Relations in Britain 1911–39*, London, Hutchinson.

Child, J. 1969. *British Management Thought*, London, Allen & Unwin.

Church, R. A. 1971. 'Profit-Sharing and Labour Relations in England in the Nineteenth Century'. *Int. Rev. Soc. Hist.* 14. (1), pp. 2–16.

Clarke, R. O., Fatchett, D. J., and Roberts, B. C. 1972. *Workers' Participation in Management in Britain*. London, Heine-mann.

Clegg, H. A. and Chester, T. E. 1954. 'Joint Consultation' in A. Flanders and H. A. Clegg (eds), *The System of Industrial Relations in Great Britain*.

Coates, K. and Topham, T. 1972. *The New Unionism*, London, Peter Owen.

Cole, G. D. H. 1923. *Workshop Organisation*, London, Hut-chinson, 1973.

Flanders, A. 1968. *Trade Unions* (7th edition, revised), London, Hutchinson.

Halévy, E. 1919. 'The Policy of Social Peace in England: The Whitley Councils' in 1967.

—— 1921. 'The Problems of Workers' Control' in 1967.

—— 1922. 'The Present State of the Social Question in England' in 1967.

—— 1967. *The Era of Tyrannies*, London, Allen Lane.

Hay, R. 1977a. 'Government policy towards labour in Britain, 1900–1914: Some further issues', *Scottish Lab. Hist. J.*, 11.

—— 1977b. 'Employers and Social Policy in Britain: The Evolution of Welfare Legislation, 1905–14', *Social History*, 4, pp. 435–55.

—— 1977c. 'Employers' attitudes to social policy and the concept of "social control", 1900–1920' in P. Thane (ed.), *Social History and Social Policy*, London, Croom Helm.

Hinton, J. 1973. *The First Shop Stewards' Movement*, London, Allen & Unwin.

Holton, B. 1976. *British Syndicalism 1900–1914*, London, Pluto Press.

International Labour Office. 1944. *British Joint Production*

    Machinery, Studies and Reports Series A, no. 43, Montreal, ILO.

Kendall, W. 1969. *The Revolutionary Movement in Britain 1900–1921*, London, Weidenfeld & Nicolson.

McDonald, G. W. and Gospel, H. F. 1973. 'The Mond-Turner Talks, 1927–33: A Study in Industrial Co-operation', *Historical Journal*, 11 (4), pp. 807–29.

Marx, K. 1858. *Grundrisse*, Harmondsworth, Penguin, 1973.

Ministry of Labour. 1918. *Works Committees*, London, HMSO.

National Institute of Industrial Psychology. 1952. *Joint Consultation in British Industry*, London, Staples Press.

Plase, E. R. 1973. *Profit-Sharing and Co-partnership: A Fraud and a Failure*, Fabian Tract, no. 170.

Political and Economic Planning. 1955. *British Trade Unionism*, London, PEP.

Pollard, S. and Turner, R. 'Profit Sharing and Aristocracy. The Case of J. T. & J. Taylor of Batley Woollen Manufacturers', *Business History*, vol. XVIII (1), January 1976, pp. 4–43.

Ramsay, H. E. 1977. Cycles of control: A social history of workers' participation in management, *Sociology*, 11 (3), September 1977, pp. 481–506.

Seymour, J. B. 1932. *The Whitley Councils Scheme*, London, P. S. King.

Taylor, S. 1884. *Profit -Sharing Between Capital and Labour*. London, Kegan and Paul, Trench & Co.

Thompson, E. P. 1965. 'The Peculiarities of the English', *The Socialist Register*, pp. 311–62.

Walpole, G. S. 1944. *Management and Men*, London, Cape.

White, S. 1975. 'Ideological Hegemony and Political Control: The Sociology of anti-Bolshevism in Britain 1918–20', *Scottish Labour History Society Journal*, no. 9, June: pp. 3–20.

Wigham, E. 1973. *The Power to Manage*, London, Macmillan.

10 Repression and Incorporation

Fear Stuff, Sweet Stuff and Evil Stuff: Management's Defenses Against Unionization in the South

Donald F. Roy

Is the South now ready to accept labor unions? Among those who note that the growth of the labor movement in our southern states has been slow and halting some ask or answer the question in this form. It seems that they view the South as an assimilating entity of varying inclination or capacity to ingest organizations.

'The South is no longer the same old South', said one prominent AFL-CIO official. 'The day of knee-jerk hostility to trade unions is coming to an end in this area.'[1] The president of an international union echoed, 'Things are changing in the South. More people are sympathetic to the aims and objectives of the American labor movement.'[2] Union leaders feel that 'the South is at last ripe for the enrolling of its millions of unorganized workers into unions.'[3]

With assessment of the situation in terms of its changing structural features, the findings of social scientists lend support to the optimism of partisans of unionization. Pointing to structural indicators, two sociologists have recently shown that the South is 'increasingly becoming indistinguishable from the rest of the United States.'[4] Indicators examined included industrialization, urbanization, occupational redistribution, income and education.

Over twenty years ago an industrial sociologist was saying the same thing, basing his assessment on both attitudes and structural measures. He pointed out that during the previous two decades, 1933 to 1953, there had been a 'reduction in differences between the South and other regions in most of the economic measurements we have come to adopt as mean-

ingful',[5] and that 'recent reports on company attitudes towards
the labor unions indicate that these companies have been
interested not in avoiding labor unions but in avoiding labor
racketeering.'[6] A few years later, in 1959, the Carolinas director
for the Textile Workers Union of America made the forecast:
'In ten years the South will be organized.'[7] If, in the latter
instance, the director's projection was an extrapolation, his
trend line was not based on enrollment in the textile union.
During the previous year the number of Carolinians added to
the TWUA rolls was zero,[8] and during the year of the forecast
the union spent over a million dollars to recruit seven southern
workers.[9]

Labor unions don't spring full blown from the brow of
southern industrialization, nor from the moist eye of sympathy
with objectives. They are generated in human interaction, in
intergroup conflict between employers and union officials. The
two factions, each with its general staff to plan and direct
strategy, compete for the affiliation of employees [10] by offering
inducements, applying restraints, and advancing persuasive
exhortations.[11] In attempts to win or reaffirm worker allegi-
ance, the antagonists utilize available supporting groups,
agencies and circumstances. During an organizing campaign
both sides organize and both sides disorganize. They organize
their own bonds of affiliation and try to disorganize or block
the development of affiliations with the opposition. In a given
campaign this process is carried out over a period of time,
from several months to several years, ordinarily ending in an
election conducted by the National Labor Relations Board
(NLRB). In accordance with the balance of their definitions
of the situation, the voting workers decide whether or not
they want union representation; a majority vote determines
the outcome. In the South, at least, beating down the door,
rather than laying out the welcome mat, would seem to be the
more appropriate imagery for 'readiness to accept labor unions.'
unions.'

Of course, there are structural features that condition the
struggle. They may be winnowed out as relevant context in
accordance with their observed connection with the interaction. For instance, the state of the labor market may affect
the organizers' work if employees are apprehensive about it.
Also, the influence of conditioning features on campaign outcome will vary in accordance with the effectiveness of com-
pensatory actions taken by the handicapped combatants. Un-

favourable conditions may be overcome by ingenuity, special effort and assistance from supporting groups. The two general staffs plan strategic action and plot tactical moves. Thus far in the South management groups, on the whole, have been able to outdo the union forces in mustering effective pressures; inducements, constraints and propaganda. In the enlistment of outside help management, for the most part, has gained the assistance of the more forceful or convincing allies. Approximately 15 per cent of the non-agricultural workers in eight south-eastern states including Alabama, Florida, Georgia, Mississippi, North Carolina, South Carolina, Tennessee and Virginia are unionized. The percentage for North Carolina is eight and for South Carolina ten.[12]

What are the big guns in management's arsenal of defensive weapons that have proven effective in severely limiting labor union organizing in the South? From my field observations, made in Ernie Pyle[13] fashion by accompanying organizers in their campaigns, I present a three-fold classification of management's resistive tactics. Drawing mainly but not entirely on experiences in the textile theatre of conflict, I focus on salient features of a complex and wide-ranging web of defensive operations. In this sorting and highlighting I have come up with two master headings that employ terms used in organizer vernacular, namely, 'fear tactics' and 'sweet stuff'. For the third category I have chosen a label of my own creation, 'evil stuff'. Also, I find that 'stuff' will do as common denominator in the interest of linguistic uniformity. Thus, I refer to the three major union-stoppers as fear stuff, sweet stuff and evil stuff.

Fear Stuff

Fear stuff, as the term suggests, is scary. It has proved so effective, according to all that I have seen, heard and read, that I am moved to wonder why the defenders of Mill Hill bother to try anything else. Fear stuff is old stuff. Its use, in holding the open-shop forts of the southern fiefdom, goes back nearly one hundred years. Application has changed in some details since the 1880s and early expansion of the textile industry, but processes of intimidation have remained essentially the same.[14]

Fright is rich in alternatives. It can be used discriminatingly in selected sectors of the workforce or it can be applied en masse. One organizer listed in off-the-cuff fashion the various kinds of fear that may be stimulated to blunt a union drive:

1. Fear of discharge
2. Fear of closing or moving plant
3. Fear of layoff (threat to operate plant at reduced work week)
4. Fear of loss of loans
5. Fear of loss of company goodwill
6. Fear of loss of favours
7. Fear of not receiving breaks in the future, such as promotions, better jobs (more pleasant kind of work), better shifts
8. Fear of being transferred
9. Fear of being given more work or dirtier jobs
10. Fear of not being given wage increases (especially in the case of hourly-paid skilled workers, who tend to receive individual pay increases)

The first two items in this catalogue of fright have proved, in campaign after campaign, to be blockbusters. Fear of discharge, already endemic in the workforce, may be reinforced to a quaking pitch by timely severance of the pay-roll connections of employees who have become detectibly active in the union cause. Such terminations of employment may be judiciously selective of a few bolder enthusiasts; they may include all known members of the workers' organizing committee; or they may involve a more sweeping roundup to catch in the eviction net anyone who is suspected of strong pro-union sentiments. Under ordinary circumstances the strategic firing of a few leaders, combined with brain-washing sessions for the main body of suspected union sympathizers, will suffice.

'Brainwashing', an epithet extensively employed in union circles, carries a special meaning. It refers to a type of semi-private conversation conducted in the office of an overseer or some other company official. Workers are called to the office, one by one, to chat with several officials, usually two, first about 'this and that and the other thing', then about the union and its prospects. These tête-à-têtes tend to be mixtures of consultation and seance. The worker is consulted in regard to his opinions concerning the values of unionization, and the supervisors provide divinations of a future under the union yoke. Workers have informed me that these desk-side chats can be very disquieting, that, in fact, like the apprehensive schoolboy, just being called to the office is a scary experience in itself.

One terminee, convinced that his sudden embracing of unemployment was due to his union activity, offered a few details in regard to his own trip to the office that suggest the danger that lurks in the brainwashing session. He remarked during the course of an interview:

> They called us all in the office, one a night, for two or three hours. He called in everybody in the plant. Hawkins called me in the office and pumped me. I said, 'If I were for the union I wouldn't tell you.' He said, 'Give me the good points and the bad points about the union.' My dad used to work for Zebulon Weave* during the Second World War. They ran him off like that. He called in sick one day, said he wouldn't be in. And they had his check waiting for him. Hawkins talked about that. I said that if you had a union and worked in a place till you were 50 or 55, they couldn't open the door and say they didn't need you any more. He said, 'Name one case.' I said, 'My old man.' That's when he got it that I was for the union.

The official term used by the NLRB for this kind of brainwashing is 'interrogation'. Like firing for union activity it is banned as against the law. Another commonly used illegal procedure of the fear stuff species is surveillance. It comes in two varieties, house-watching and meeting-watching, and works well in sequence with interrogation. One millhand spoke of a quizzing that followed the detection of an attempted house call by an organizer:

> Owens [personnel manager] ... asked me what a union man's car was doing at my house on Denny Avenue. I wasn't home for lunch, and I even tried to get him to call my husband and see that I wasn't home. He [Owens] said I was home, and the union man was there. He wanted to know what he said. It made them mad. I hadn't even talked to Hogue [the organizer] when Owens called me in. My aunt works in the weave room and lives there. I wasn't there. My car was sitting in there, and Owens saw my car there. That was the first part of December. Owens got mad. He

*Names of plants and persons are fictitious.

said I lied. After that, Millard Creston had me in the office. He's overseer in the cloth room. He just asked me when did I talk with the union man. He looked at me like I was lying. Creston didn't get mad, but he was suspicious. Hogue had a North Carolina license. Owens knows his tags.

An employee of another mill, who had escaped the watchful eye on union callers only to be fired for other suspected delinquencies in union matters, told of management's surveillance practices:

> They drive around town, the second hands, and supervisors, and superintendents, and see if any North Carolina cars are parked at anyone's house. If there are, they might as well look out, because the union headquarters are in Raleigh. [His mistake. Headquarters are in Charlotte.] The union men come and talk to you, but they [company officials] never caught me. They [union men] came here to see me before I was fired, but they didn't catch one here till after I was fired. I know a guy at the mill ... He said the organizers came up to his house two or three times, and he run them off. He said they'd get him fired. He's for the union, but he doesn't want to get fired. Grady [the guy at the mill] thinks that's why we were fired, because the organizers came around to see us.

In most campaign situations workers report a general uneasiness in regard to attending union-conducted 'mass meetings'. In some instances the organizers find it very difficult, if not impossible, to induce other than the most dedicated union enthusiasts to advertise their affiliation by presence at a union-sponsored public gathering. One battery-filler attributed loss of her job to being spotted while entering a building to attend a union meeting held in a city that was a few miles distant from the mill community:

> I went to a union meeting in May, on Saturday morning at 11.30. I paused at the outside door to talk to Hogue. They looked me over then. I asked Hogue who was watching us and he said, 'Oh, I don't know the guy's name. He's from Cartersville [30 miles away]. He's probably shopping.' I said, 'He's sure looking.'
> I went up to the meeting. I never figured the guy knew me.

I stayed at the meeting an hour and a half. I came down with Mildred. The meeting was on Wells Street, at the hall. I went up Wells Street and down York Street. I walked down an alley back of the Sunset Courts. Just as Mildred got outside the doors Owens yelled, 'Hello girls! What are you doing here?'

I said, 'We're just up here.'

Another guy was with him, the guy from Cartersville. That was Saturday morning. I went to work Saturday evening, on second shift, and they started picking on my job. Andy Scoggins, the second hand, said he wanted to look at my job. He said I wasn't filling the batteries right. I wasn't winding the pieces.

I said if it wasn't right I'd take it out and put it back. I didn't see anything wrong. I said 'What's wrong?' He couldn't find anything.

He pointed to another. He said. 'That ain't right.' I said it wasn't my loom. He went on and didn't say any more.

At fifteen to eleven, a week later, Scoggins said, 'I want to see you.' He went to his desk and motioned for me to follow. He took me to his office at the end of the hall and closed the door. He said, 'Mrs Brookes, I want you to look for another job. I want you to go along with us, but I have to be hard-boiled. I have to let you go.'

I said, 'You mean you're firing me?' He said, 'Yes.' I said, 'For what?' He said, 'For this and that. So look for another job.' He said he'd let me work till quitting time, fifteen minutes later.

I said, 'I don't think it's a thing in the world but going to a meeting. When you've been working in a place for ten years you don't blow up and can't do your job.' He said, 'If you can't do your job, we can't keep you.'

I've got my ten-year pin. I got it two weeks before I was fired. They gave me a little speech ... Hobgood, he's supervisor over the weave room on second shift, took me into his little office, complimented me on my loyalty and good work, and said he hoped I'd be there ten more years. That was around the first of May.

In one campaign, which culminated in a close vote, the union attempted to hold two mass meetings. The first one was held in a county court house; in addition to several embarrassed union organizers and visiting speakers one worker attended.

The hazard of exposure was appreciably reduced for the second meeting, held in an abandoned church tucked away in the hollow of a working class residential area. This time the union officials and visiting dignitaries addressed nine mill-hands, two of whom were identified as company stooges, embarrassed, in turn, by their own obvious presence in a small audience.

Sometimes the harsh procedures of firing may be avoided by persuading the pro-union worker to resign. However, resignation doesn't always come easy; long tenure may find the employee rooted in his job and reluctant to quit. The retirement of Lonnie Williams, loom fixer, is a case in point:

I lacked three weeks of working there eighteen years. I was fired last, I think I was fired for union activities. For seventeen and one-half years they praised me, little and big. I thought I was somebody. I got along pretty good until the last six or seven weeks. Then they started riding me.

After I saw what was going on for three or four months, I suspected that it would be happening to me. And I was determined to buck it out and not quit. I'd make them fire me, and not do anything to give them a reason to fire me and leave me a bad record.

Gentry [supervisor] done most of the riding. It was a patrol job. He'd find little ends crossed. He'd appear to try to bother me. He threw a flashlight once, to get my attention, and he'd say 'booooooo' to call me. He told me to go to him when he called me, and he'd show me what he wanted. This went on for about six weeks.

He'd tell me that some ends were crossed. I'd quit whatever I was doing and do what he told me to do. To attract attention he'd hunt up all the quills, have me pick them up off the floor when there were a lot of more important things to do. He'd try to get my attention off my business so I'd make bad cloth. He'd call me to the office and rag me, and say he was going to fire me.

The longer it lasted the rougher it got. They kept tightening down on me. The last hour I thought they had me whipped. Frank [second hand] and Gentry, first one and then the other. So I decided to quit.

When you can't eat or sleep, a man goes crazy. So I

decided for the sake of my family I'd pull away. I tried to do a good job. Finally I wore out and quit. I didn't beg them to let me stay. I made up my mind the day I quit. Three minutes before the whistle I said to the second hand, 'It looks like I can't please you. I'm going to quit.' He just smiled at me.

Of course, organizers take an immediate interest in suspected fired-for-union-activity cases; and, when a case appears to have a reasonable chance for following through on a charge of unfair labor practices, they take depositions and make a report to a regional office of the NLRB. If the Board investigation results in a decision favorable to the discharged worker, the company is ordered to make a job reinstatement with back pay for the work time lost. However, three or four years may pass before restitution is made. The company can and does carry the case to several levels of appeal, through a second level of Board decision and on into a District Court of Appeals. According to an ex-official of the Industrial Union Department of the AFL-CIO, breaking up a union campaign by firing some employees, and thus intimidating the others, pays off. Back pay costs are considerably less than those that would be incurred under collective bargaining. He made a statement to the National House of Representatives:

Some people may ask how a company can afford to fire 250 employees for unionism when the law entitles them to reinstatement with back pay. The answer is simple. About one quarter of the dischargees are too intimidated to even present their cases to the Board; another quarter will find other jobs or drift away. For the 150 whom the Board will finally uphold, back pay will come to about $300,000, whereas a ten-cent-an-hour raise won by the union for all 40,000 workers would cost the company eight to ten million dollars a year.[15]

Back pay costs to the company referred to were actually more than $1·3 million for 289 discharged employees whose claims were upheld by the Labor Board and the courts, including the Supreme Court.[16] Presumably, during the five to seven years that the cases dragged on, the company made its savings. Rarely demonstrated is the threat that 'the mill will close down if the union comes in.' This abandon-ship motif which, if introduced with apt timing, can whip up the endemic, free-floating insecurity of a mill population into visualization of a sort of economic Last Days of Pompeii. Whereas the pruning out of a few millhands who are caught with their union sympathies showing teaches the rank and file that fraternization with labor organizers does not pay, and gives union-oriented strays a chance to recant, closing down the mill would terminate everybody *instanter*. Whereas selective firing would permit company standpatters to remain passively, even scornfully, aloof from disseminators of union propaganda, a threat of boarding up the plant would tend to stimulate universal interest in regard to the outcome of the campaign. Here the vision is powerful. At the same time it vitalizes the pro-company worker and devitalizes the pro-union one with the imagery of grass growing on the weave room floor and wild honeysuckle climbing its walls. If the plant is to close the morning after union victory, then the union becomes not just an organization of weak or doubtful service to the middle-of-the-roaders, but one deadly in contact, like the bubonic plague.

Of course, the portent of gaping ruins where factories once stood is not broadcast by management, at least not by the higher echelons. The forecasts come primarily from members of other groups in the community, such as proprietors of small business, sometimes from hinting plant supervisors. These doomsayers by implication, if not by flat assertion, get across the point that the company won't work with a union. Organizers scoff at these predictions, rebutting them by pointing out that the company is making too much money to close up shop. They are aware, however, that at least one textile establishment closed down immediately after a union victory; and they know that a company with multi-plant holdings could at least reduce production at an unfavored unit.

During one campaign the engaging rumor made the rounds that should the union prove victorious, management intended to shut down the mill and rent its vacated buildings to another local industrial organization for use as a warehouse. In the words of one worker:

> My sister is scared to death. She works on the first shift and lives upstairs at 402 Peach Street. Her name is Nettie Perkins. She's in the Throwing Department. She's signed but scared to death. They told her they'd close the plant if the union

came in. They said they'd rent it to Clayton Metals for a warehouse. Clayton's got its own warehouse. I told her, 'You're not that stupid. The machinery is worth a fortune. Common sense would tell you that.' Lots of them think they'll close the mill down. They told them so.

This miasma of rumor on plant closing that feeds the primal folk-dread of unemployment has some basis in historical fact. For nearly two decades southern organizers have had to work beneath the shadow of one towering example of industrial Götterdämmerung. The sudden and complete dissolution of a textile mill immediately followed a narrow campaign by the union forces. The mill was not only shut down; all machinery was sold at auction, thus minimizing possibilities for restoration under new management. As unfair labor practice the case was fought for thirteen years, twice through the two levels of the NLRB and twice into appeals courts. The Supreme Court examined the case once, passed it back to the NLRB, and refused to look at it the second time around. The union won the final decision involving reinstatement and back pay for the workers involved.[17] But the latter, those who could be found, still await recompense. In the meantime, the leitmotiv of shutdown, faint or loud, pervades textile organizing.

Sweet Stuff

Sweet stuff also takes a variety of forms. It may be dispensed as personal favours, as promises of favours, or as hints of favours to come. It may be put out in a trickle of small, immediate improvements in working conditions or in hazy assurances of eventual substantial reconstruction. It may involve a relaxation of the supervisor's concern over quantity and quality of output, and it may entail an expenditure of time and effort on the part of higher bossmen to bring about a makeshift recrudescence of old-time shirtsleeve paternalism.

Personal favor tactics, reality and dream, may include the seduction of promotion to a supervisory position. In some campaigns a worker active in labor's cause may get elevated to one of the lower command posts, an advancement that lifts him above possible union affiliation and lowers appreciably his zeal for collective bargaining. The gain from use of this tactic is usually more than just removing an opposition leader from the battle. Not only does a leader have followers to carry with him in a shifting of votes, the effect of this defection on the morale of the organizing group may be additionally costly for the union. However, tactful promotion does not always achieve the optimum. In one instance the taming of a black union stalwart brought disappointing results; instead of following him into the camp, his ten millhand relatives regarded his acceptance of promotion as betrayal of the union cause.

Sweet stuff benefactions may be bestowed in much smaller portions. Workers may be induced to switch affiliations by transfer to a more desirable job, by assignment to day shift, or by hiring one's wife. Workers report that there are those who succumb to confidential remarks of overseers on the order of 'You're supervisory material and I'm keeping my eye on you.' Such confidences, as the campaign heats up, appear to be widely distributed.

One rather unusual switch from harsh to sweet treatment was reported by a middle-aged weaver of long tenure who had worked hard for the union in two campaigns and had once been fired for her subversive activities only to be reinstated with over $20,000 back pay by court decision. For months, during her second campaign, she complained of being driven and harassed at her work by supervisors. Then one day she announced that the situation had changed; she was now receiving 'nice' treatment. 'The superintendent even waves to me when he sees me leafleting at the gate and blows me kisses.'

The union's knocking at the door may bring improvements in working conditions. Although they may appear to be of a penny-pinching nature to the more cynical employees, to others minor renovations and refurbishments may be viewed favorably as the beginning of a trend towards bigger and better things. During one campaign, in which the company relied primarily on sweet stuff to sweep to a decisive victory, specification of the tangible benefits received by the workers would make a very short and unimpressive list: the installation of snack-bar machines that dispensed small packets of crackers filled with peanut butter or cheese, small fans for work stations and renovated washrooms. In this instance the promise of bigger and better things to come were made in a series of letters sent out to all employees by the company president. Termed 'love letters' by caustic organizers, they expressed an abiding togetherness entwined with hearty optimism for the future of the enterprise and gave off overtones of 'something good is simmering in the pot for our employees.'

One kind of sweet stuff might be called 'phoney pseudo-paternalism'. Some campaigns feature a sort of revival of paternalism, a rejuvenation more on the order of commemorative extravaganza than a genuine return to Grandpa's way of doing things. Were the show given a longer run than a few spot performances during a campaign, were its leading features institutionalized to become more permanently part of the managerial dramaturgy, then it might be called, simply, 'pseudo-paternalism'. Since phoney pseudo-paternalism can sometimes provide a lethal punch to organizing prospects, the more cumbersome designation could be replaced by something on the order of 'knockout paternalism' or 'union-busting paternalism'.

One tactic of this sort is the 'Dad's back' speech, usually delivered from a prepared manuscript by a leading member of local management to an employee assembly. The speech is invariably well attended, since workers are released from their work to hear it, on company time. It is delivered two days or so before the NLRB election ends the campaign. The gist of the speech is: 'Dad has been busy, unintentionally neglectful; but he is back with you now, to stay, and things will get lots better.' And with Dad back, in a few hundred words, handkerchiefs may make a fluttering appearance to turn the occasion into a flag day, of sorts. Noses blow and union stalwarts in the gathering mutter to themselves. 'There goes your election.'

It is essential that the speech be read in an easy, fluent and earnest manner. The care that law firm experts put into the wording and organization of these speeches may go for naught if the company president stumbles over words, loses his place, or otherwise makes his delivery in a halting or wooden manner. The workers of one large establishment account for their induction into a Teamster local with an ample margin of votes after a nip-and-tuck campaign by the failure of a top company official to read his speech smoothly, thereby disgusting many members of his homecoming audience. 'It was the speech that did it,' agreed a celebrating group of union supporters when the election returns were announced.

Another phoney pseudo-paternalism racket bearing the union number is the picnic, an outdoor event sponsored by local management and given in honour of those who are to exercise their franchise in an impending election. This voting unit constitutes the main consuming unit for the chicken, potato salad and assorted soft drinks. If the campaign drags out, to span several years, there may be two picnics. These festive occasions bring together members of management, workers and their families for renewal of informalities that may have languished since the days when Grandad held his barbecues and pitched horseshoes with his men. At any rate, the younger fellows, those under fifty, may search their memories in vain for recollections of earlier picnics, unless they attended with parental escort in the olden times.

However, the picnic, like the 'Dad's back' speech, may boomerang. Careless catering has in at least one instance resulted in depressed merrymaking and wilted reunion; the outing came a cropper when feathers were discovered in the fried chicken.

A recent innovation in sweet stuff tactics involves the adaptation of a procedure long used in football and other athletic games: substitution. In some campaigns the situation calls for temporary replacement of a hard-nosed top local official with a 'good guy'. The good guy is an executive possessed of personal charm, communication skills and a mandate to cool off human relations in the plant. When the emergency period has passed, say workers and organizers, the good guy disappears and old Hard Rock takes over once again. Reports on the practice of substitution have thus far been limited to multi-plant organizations where resources and numbers of mills are presumably sufficient for keeping good-will ambassadors on the road.

Organizers post early warnings about the deceptive coating of sweet stuff, long before the first titbit is offered. They freely predict that the second hand's features will soften, that the overseer will wave a greeting, that work pressures will lighten. They frankly prophesy that the workers are going to receive pats on the back, hints on their promise as supervisors, invitations to gustatory outings, love letters from top officials and an opportunity to see and hear the company president. However, in spite of such warnings and forecasts sweet stuff wins votes for management.

Evil Stuff
A third variety of management's defensive campaign tactics may be called 'evil stuff'. Like fear stuff, evil stuff accentuates

the negative. Where fear tactics tend to instill dread in regard to what management would do, if sufficiently provoked by treasonous identification with the union, evil stuff aims to propagate a robust detestation of what unions are by nature. By plastering union organizers and their ilk with imputations of wicked intentions, sinister connections, violence and corruption, it is used in an attempt to shatter whatever worker-union bonds have already developed, to bring turncoats back into the fold and to make further apostasy very unattractive.

Evil stuff can elevate the vision of the worker above reality, above the mundane world of bread-and-butter matters played upon by fear stuff, such as the flow of weekly paychecks. In lifting the debate above the denotable, its connections with fact may be as tenuous as the images evoked by Grimm's fairy tales or Verdi's early operas. It shares the campaign's fantasy level with some of the more airy sweet stuff, such as love letters from company presidents. However, in place of the cheery tone, hailing the workers optimistically through a verbal mist, the note is strident and the fog of words carries dark import. The summons is not to pie in the sky; it is to take arms against the forces of evil. With the union exposed as a tool of Antichrist, the call is to the preliminaries of Armageddon and the battle is to take place here below.

If workers can be convinced that labor unions are on easy terms with Mephistopheles, then they are not within joining distance, morally speaking. Not many years ago union organizers were not only pointed out, in southern mill villages, as close associates of Satan, they were looked upon as one of the various forms assumed by that Prince of Darkness as he went about his terrestrial peregrinations. In the sermonizing and ministerial counselling of southern preachers whose windows opened to a view of company offices, organizers wore the horns of the Devil. Although mill workers and union organizers report that employee concern over spiritual losses to be suffered from contact with Satan's manifestations has receded, the devil role of unions is, in a sense, still operative. Organizers are still accused of purveying evil. According to industrial managers their slick talk entices the good and honest but unwary folk from the true path laid out by the company. The switch is to a siding that descends into the hell of strikes, with their violence, hunger, hardship and general destruction of harmonious community and factory life.

The word about the infernal region of strikes and violence reaches workers either through the mail in multi-page letters or by way of captive audience speeches delivered two days before the election. In either case it is a local company official who speaks or signs the letters and one of a few experienced union-fighting attorneys who composes the message. Organizers claim to be able to identify the speech or letter writers by style of composition. The following is an excerpt from a letter sent out by a company official to warn his employees:

> We believe that *any* labor union that can turn good and honest working men and women into vicious, bloodthirsty strikers is an organization that should be avoided by our employees. You can make sure that we *never* have these problems at our Millville plant by voting *NO* on June 30.

A four-page mailing sent to employees as part of an effort to block the union's organizing thrust featured a message from a local minister who had once worked in a cotton mill. He told of what had happened to his fellow workers and their families when the union 'took over' and the inevitable strike made the lights go out in mill and community:

> Today people are out of work ... some have little extra jobs ... they and their children are hungry and unhappy.
> I went to one of the officers of the CIO local. I asked him, 'Why don't you do something to help these people? They've been paying dues for a long time.'
> He told me ... when the mill shut down, the local had $6,000, but the National CIO froze this money ... they wouldn't let the local have one dime. And the National hadn't helped feed the former members, save at first to a favoured few.
> Nearly every mill family owned an auto – now not more than one quarter. They had to give up furnishings and appliances. Many of their children are not in school; they can't buy clothing for them to wear.
> I've never seen a union 'take over in a mill' that a strike didn't follow, sooner or later. And I've never seen a strike that didn't cause hard feelings, a lot of trouble, lots of suffering.
> Let me beg of you good people. Don't take the risk of

letting the CIO come in here. If you do, the time will come when you regret it.

In another campaign, which the union lost by two votes, a minister called upon his millhand parishioners at their homes to induce them to vote NO on union representation.

In this shifting imagery of the evil forces of unionism the propensity to lay waste by strikes is accompanied by a tendency to plunder. While the Bad Man keeps one hand in readiness to push the strike button, he keeps the other in the till. That is, he stuffs his pockets with the union dues, collected from the good and honest and hard-working. Although union officials have at times evoked images of bloated plutocrats and dictatorial bosses in their leaflets, artists on the company side appear to have a decided edge in imaginative resources in the free-hand sketching of bossism and bloat. The union bosses, as depicted in anti-union publications distributed during a campaign, look like much heartier trenchermen. Also, they wear jewellery, smoke king-size cigars and contrast sharply in face and figure with the emaciated workmen clustered around them, who look as if they had been boiling their shoes for nourishment.

For many years, since the 1880s, in fact,[18] a major union repellent lay in the race question. Accusations that labor unions, starting with the Knights of Labor, favored and sponsored race mixing, were bombs difficult to duck. Top union officials, from their redoubts in northern cities, did make statements in favor of civil rights for blacks. The application of imagery that linked union invasion with rapacious intent of dark-skinned savages towards white womanhood had great potency in the South. In one campaign, barely ten years ago, a leaflet distributed anonymously suggested vividly a linkage between unionization and mongrelization. In this instance a sketch showed an ape-like black man in close pursuit of a buxom Caucasian who appeared about to trip over her ripped dress. A second drawing, offered in the same leaflet, showed the pursed lips of a racially mixed pair, black ape and white woman, about to meet in a kiss. A caption under the heart-shaped frame for this romancing read: 'The Kiss of Death – Remember India.'

During the past decade, following development of more advanced stages of the Civil Rights movement and the introduction of more blacks into southern textile mills, the more blatant linking of union leadership with 'nigger-loving' has been checked. The race issue is still operative, however, under the surface in private conversation or, if in the open, in more subtle insinuation. Perhaps not so subtle in intimation was a photographic display that found its way to a company bulletin board during a recent organizing campaign. Adjacent to a blown-up picture of a white youth lying in a pool of blood on a San Francisco sidewalk were newspaper clipping photographs of several black men arrested for the nationally publicized Zebra killings. The response of both black and white members of the workers' organizing committee was 'They're trying to split us up.' Although an ever-increasing proportion of white workers are coming to accept the idea of exerting joint effort with black workers to organize unions, many whites still find repellent the thought of joining a 'nigger union'.

In recent years a correlative epithet applied to union organizers, 'carpet-baggers', has dropped out of use. Organizers are still labelled 'trouble-making outsiders', as far as town and mill communities are concerned, but a Yankee invasion is no longer stressed. This disengagement of the War Between the States from union-management conflict may be largely due to the fact that northerners are now fighting northerners. With the growing development of large chain organization in the textile industry, with control centered in New York offices, top management as well as top union is Yankee.

In their relegation of unions to the Kingdom of the Damned, at least to regions beyond the bounds of prevailing mores, some managerial groups have made use of the imputation that unions play an accessory role in the subversive work of communists. Of late this accusing finger has begun to droop owing, perhaps, to the fact that in the mid-1960s the main hunt for Reds under the bed shifted to student groups and to the possibility that top union leadership USA appears to be more respectable, politically speaking, as the years roll on. However, until the late 1960s, a certain four-page periodical, issues of which millhands found in their mailboxes during, but only during, organizing campaigns, revealed that union bosses and communists were bedfellows. This revelation was perennially intertwined, issue after issue, with discoveries in regard to the corruption, godlessness and advocacy of race mixing grossly flaunted by those same bedfellows. The publication, called

Militant Truth, displayed a representation of the American flag in the upper right-hand corner of page one and drawings of the Bible and the Cross in the upper left-hand corner. That suspicion of communist-linked subversion has not died out in managerial circles was recently discovered by a young organizer, a graduate of the University of North Carolina, who found, to his great astonishment, that some of the supervisors in the mill that he was attempting to organize actually believed that labor unions were communistic. His discovery was especially astounding in light of an additional finding: the supervisors in question were students at UNC during his years of attendance.

For many decades the application of fear stuff, sweet stuff and evil stuff has proven highly successful in repulsing attempts of labor unions to organize southern industrial workers. However, management's last line of defense against the institution of collective bargaining does not lie in preventing victory of the union forces in the organizing campaign. Even if workers vote YES, meaning that the union has won the right to represent them at the bargaining table, it doesn't necessarily follow that a contract will soon be forthcoming. A contract may not be achieved for three, four, or more years, perhaps not at all. By law the parties must bargain in good faith, but good faith is a slippery concept. After a year of periodic meetings without minimally acceptable results, the union representatives may prefer charges of unfair labor practices to the NLRB. They may even conduct short work stoppages based on such charges, with these maneuvers leading to the usual sequence of appeals through NLRB and circuit court levels. The years drag on, first with no contract, then with an unsatisfactory one and a dwindling of worker support for the union. Eventually the company may petition the NLRB for a decertification election; and, if a majority vote against the union, the latter finds itself back at square one.

In one case, watched for nearly twenty years, the union conducted three campaigns, finally winning the third one. Then followed three years of 'bargaining', with two strikes resulting in a poor contract and a long period of running unfair labor practice charges and attendant appeals through the courts. Several years ago a decertification election was held; the union won again. Now, a second decertification election is pending, and this time the union expects to lose.[19] The TWUA won representation in several campaigns in 1971 and 1972, but to date contracts remain out of reach. This tactic is called 'bargaining them to death'.

In the interest of linguistic consistency we might call it 'fatal stuff'.

NOTES AND REFERENCES

1 Bill Arthur, 'Unions Renew Dixie Campaign', *Labor News*, vol. 36, no. 26, Durham, North Carolina, 24 September, 1973, p. 1.

2 ibid.

3 ibid.

4 John C. McKinney and Linda Brookover Bourque, 'The Changing South: National Incorporation of a Region', *American Sociological Review*, vol. 36, June 1971, pp. 399–412.

5 E. William Noland, 'Industry Comes of Age in the South', *Social Forces*, vol. 32, October 1953, p. 28.

6 ibid., p. 31.

7 'Textile Union Had Rough Year', *Charlotte Observer*, Charlotte, North Carolina, 1 February, 1959.

8 ibid.

9 William Pollock and John Chupka, 'Almost Unbelievable: The Story of an Industry, a Union, and a Law', *TWUA Report*, 1961, p. 36.

10 Donald F. Roy, 'The Union Organizing Campaign as a Problem in Social Distance: Three Crucial Dimensions of Affiliation-Disaffiliation', Howard S. Becker, *et al.*, (eds), *Institutions and the Person*, Chicago, Aldine Publishing Company, 1968, pp. 49–66.

11 William A. Gamson, *Power and Discontent*, Homewood, Illinois, The Dorsey Press, 1968, pp. 75–81.

12 Arthur, 'Unions Renew Dixie Campaign', p. 1.

13 See Ernie Pyle, *Here Is Your War*, New York, Pocket Books, Inc., 1944.

14 Melton Alonzo McLaurin, *Paternalism and Protest: Southern Cotton Mill Workers and Organized Labor, 1875–1905*, Westport, Connecticut, Greenwood Publishing Corporation, 1971.

15 Vera Roney, 'Labor Drives to Close the South's Open Shop', *The Reporter*, 18 November 1965, p. 34.
16 *Durham Morning Herald*, Durham, North Carolina, 1 September 1974, p. 11A.
17 'Textile Union Wins 13-Year Fight for Fired Darlington, S.C. Workers', *Labor News*, vol. 28, no. 41, Durham, North Carolina, 24 January 1969, p. 1.
18 McLaurin, *Paternalism and Protest, Southern Cotton Mill Workers and Organized Labor*, pp. 73–4.
19 The decertification did take place.

Italy's FIAT in Turin in the 1950s

Hilary Partridge

The Rabbit Years

> It's important to understand how weak the working class
> was at that time. We used to say amongst ourselves, 'We're
> a load of rabbits.' When you went into the butcher's you
> didn't say, 'Give me half a rabbit.' You said, 'Give me half a
> FIAT worker.'[1]

This article will deal with some of the different forms of control to which capital subjects workers. It is specifically
concerned with the tactics of management at FIAT, Turin in
the 1950s. However, 'hard' and 'soft' tactics are not dependent
on the evil or kind nature of the employer but on expedience
and opportunity. For this reason, before considering how
FIAT management sought to control its Turin workforce it
is necessary to say something more generally about the situation of that time. For in Italy's FIAT in the 1950s, the need to
stay in competition and thus for imperialist expansion was
combined with opportunity provided by the alienation of the
communist vanguard from the mass of workers, which weakened the ability of the labour force to fight against repressive
measures. It was this equation, expedience and opportunity,
that was to be resolved by a period of deep repression in the
factories, linked with a vigorous mechanization drive using
technology largely imported from America to increase the
rate of exploitation and build up capital to finance the beginnings of FIAT's imperialist activities.

FIAT's present massive involvement abroad, extending
through most of Europe and Eastern Europe, South America
and Africa, began in the early 1950s with the inauguration of
SEAT, FIAT's subsidiary in Spain. Argentina, Yugoslavia and
Romania followed in the early 1960s and from 1965 a process
of expansion in Europe was carried out. Since then FIAT has
been responsible for many foreign projects: the building of
the huge plant at Togliattigrad in Russia (1966) and the

416   16

'prestige' hydro-electric projects in Pakistan, Turkey and Peru, to name just a few.

The money to finance this expansionist policy clearly had to come from somewhere. Since the labour force in the Italian car industry was already subject to a high degree of internal discipline, work rhythm, etc., the profits gained in the period of the protectionist policies of the fascist regime and during the arms race were used for recapitalization to increase the rate of exploitation on a relatively unchanged number of workers.

The conditions for a massive increase in investment in the car industry had been maturing for some time. In the period 1937–8 a new Italian prosperity caused largely by the arms race had given the potential for an increased internal car market and the huge Mirafiori plant opened during the war was planned to produce small, popular cars in series to exploit just this market. Production was interrupted because of the war, but in the 1950s the first 'Italian Volkswagens', the Vetturetta Democratica, rolled off the line.

In fact the war proved to be a very brief interruption of FIAT's productive development; by 1948 production in the automobile sector, greatly aided by the communist party's policy of reconstruction before all else, was already back to pre-war levels, and they were able to replace war-damaged plant in the great mechanization drive of the 1950s. This process really took off from 1953, with a very rapid renovation of plant associated with an extensive mechanization of the productive process, and an 'advanced' technology (mostly imported from abroad) adapted to production in series. The following figures demonstrate this tendency:

	CAPITAL (FIXED AND CIRCULATING)	EMPLOYEES	VEHICLES
1947	61,539	58,000	28,490
1948	66,714	52,016	46,795
1949	89,168	56,321	75,000
1955	322,112	74,885	250,299
1960	571,590	92,891	530,665[2]

Thus the increases in investment did not give a correspondingly large increase in employment but went to multiply the rate of exploitation putting up productivity per worker. At FIAT Mirafiori the index of production per worker more than tripled in the eight years between 1948 and 1955.

C.L.—O

$$1948 = 100$$
$$1952 = 206$$
$$1955 = 381[8]$$

Real wages, however increased very little during the 1950s.

The beginning of the 1950s thus marked the dawning of a new era in the history of Italian industrialization; one of an enormous development of the Italian car industry through a restructuring of production; a process of mechanization and rationalization designed to finance the beginnings of FIAT's imperialist expansion.

The new era brought with it a need for a new sort of workforce. It had to be docile enough to give FIAT a free hand with new forms of work organization. A highly organized and militant working class will question and eventually threaten the introduction of labour-saving methods and machinery – hence organization at FIAT had to be broken. Before looking at the tactics FIAT employed to do this, it is first necessary to take account of the role played in this period by the communist party (the PCI, the largest workers' party) and the trade unions.

The PCI had found itself in a strange situation after the war. The workforce, emerging from the period of sabotage and anti-fascist struggle which had been an important part of the Turin Resistance was turbulent with demands for a democratization of work and the purging of fascists from the managerial ranks at FIAT. But ironically it was the PCI which was to do most of the work of controlling and containing the rebellious workforce and restoring order and discipline within the factory. The PCI, underestimating the combined power of the Allies and the Vatican, was trapped in the 'paralysing illusion' that with its participation in the post-war tripartite government it was now at the centre of power. Thus of the PCI's three imperatives: purging, democratization and reconstruction, the latter effectively overrode the former two; the PCI called for industrial reconstruction for a new democratic era before all else.

The following quote from a PCI worker demonstrates some of the confusion resulting from this policy:

When we began to work and make it understood that to be a good communist you had to produce and do your duty, then they called us fascists! We (of the Commissione

Interna) were linked in with the foremen. When the bell rang at 5.15 they'd already been in the cloakroom since 4.00. So I, as a member of the CI had to intervene. They called me fascist because I tried to bring in some discipline because we were working for us now.[4]

Parlanti also talks about the confusion generated by the PCI's ambivalent position:

I remember straight after the war Togliatti came to speak in Piazza Crispi – and then De Gasperi came – and they both argued exactly the same thing; the need to have the economy ... We've got to work hard because Italy's on her knees, we've been bombarded by the Americans ... but don't worry because if we produce, if we work hard, in a year or two we'll all be fine.... So the PCI militants inside the factory set themselves the political task of producing to save the national economy, and the workers were left without a party.[5]

The PCI's obsession with reconstruction was apparently based on the inexplicable belief of the leadership that Italy would come into the Russian sphere of influence after the war and be allowed to retain communist participation in government. But this belief turned out to be very dangerous for the working class. Both the rank and file of the PCI and the labour force were generally weakened, because the PCI acceded to the management policy of mechanization coupled with a new code of discipline. To the new younger workers this strategy of the communist trade unionists was difficult to understand. What was the point of joining or fighting for a union which appeared intent on further tightening factory discipline rather than leading the struggle for their basic needs? The rift was deepened by the different experience of the workforce; the young men with their southern peasant origins and the older men tempered by a long industrial experience and the anti-fascist struggles. In this situation communication between the two groups broke down and FIAT's self-elected task of the destruction of all forms of workers' organization was made that much easier.

Industrial working class organizations in Italy differed from the UK in that it never took the form of trade unions based on trade or category. Unions in Italy were primarily based on locality, linking workers in a local 'camera del lavoro', based on the French idea of 'bourses du travail'. There were a number of reasons for this. Firstly, the sudden and uneven development of Italian capitalism which preceeded the formation of guild-type organizations; secondly, the strong influence of political parties which brought with it a tendency towards a purely 'political' activity, as distinct from negotiation over specific 'trade' issues; and thirdly a permanent abundance of labour which had always meant a pressure for a general representation of labour whether in the factory or not.[6]

As industrialization increased a need was felt for an organizational form to cope with more specific issues. The 'Commissione Interna' (CI), basically a shop-floor grievance committee, developed to fill this role and quickly became a general feature of the factories. The CI was the basis for Gramsci's idea of the factory council system: 'Tomorrow, developed and enriched' they were to become 'the organs of proletarian power which replaces the capitalist in all his useful functions of management and administration.'[7] The CIs were more or less linked into a national trade union federation, the CGIL, although election to the CI did not necessarily entail membership of the union. In 1948 the federation split into the communist-dominated CGIL (with a metalworkers' section from FIOM), the Christian Democratic CISL (with the FIM) and the largely white-collar union UIL (with the UILM).

This, then, is the context in which FIAT carried out its strategy aimed at rendering all forms of workers' organization in the factory innocuous. As part of this strategy they also encouraged the development of a company union, the LLD-SIDA,[8] which with UIL and FIM replaced the FIOM in the CI after the electoral defeat of 1955. In fact after this date the CI lost nearly every function of dissent in the factory – at least for the time being, Gramsci's dream had died.

The management, headed by Valletta, justified itself theoretically by dividing the workers into 'constructors' and 'destructors'. Below I itemize their tactics under several separate headings though many of the practices cited do of course interlink.

The use of the Anti-strike Bonus. In these years of high unemployment and low wages, with families often having only one 'bread-winner' extra money was enormously important. The FIAT management was thus able to use very successfully the 'premio di collaborazione' or collaboration prize. This practice started after a strike of 1952 when FIAT workers participated in a metalworkers' strike of the whole industrial triangle, Milan-Turin-Genoa. Eighty-five per cent of FIAT workers struck. Those who didn't were rewarded with a bonus of 2,000 lire. From the end of 1953 the anti-strike bonus was introduced as normal practice with sums of about 40,000 lire annually given to workers who had not participated in any form of agitation during the year. This bonus was never negotiated with the unions but was given to the workers on the request of the so-called 'democratic unions': the 'yellow' SIDA; the Christian Democratic CISL. This practice continued until 1962, when FIAT broke the unwritten rule of negotiation at a national level between the employers' federation, Confindustria, and the national union federations. FIAT anticipated the national contract and signed a separate agreement which included the incorporation of the anti-strike bonus as part of real wage.

Political Sackings. The 'reprisal' sacking of militants and known union or party sympathizers began in October 1948. The accusations levelled were: having struck; having lead workers' struggles; having distributed union or political publications, even outside the factory gates; having organized meetings; having collected subscriptions to FIOM or the PCI; having struck against the 'legge truffa'.[9] After 1955 the FIAT management only rarely used such explicit anti-union wording in their dismissal of troublesome workers (the reasons became 'loafing' or 'low production').

The 'mass sackings', when troublesome departments or entire factories were 'punished' for a high vote for FIOM in the elections to the CI, began in December 1954:

In	December	1954	630	workers were sacked from				FIAT Aeritalia
,	,	,	320	,	,	,	,	FIAT Grandi Motore
,	,	1955	250	,	,	,	,	FIAT di Modena
,	,	1956	380	,	,	,	,	FIAT Lingotto
,	July	1957	230	,	,	,	,	FIAT Marina di Pisa
,	November	1957	120	,	,	,	,	Officiana Sussidiaria Ricambi[10]

In the last instance *all* OSR workers were sacked and the department was closed: what Roy would call 'fatal stuff'.[11] The sackings and 'internal sackings' (transferals) had the desired effect. At Aeritalia, for example, the FIOM vote in the CI elections dropped from 1340 votes in 1954 to 77 in 1955.[12] Punishment for union sympathy did not, however, stop when the dismissal note arrived on the doormat. Sacked workers were 'blacklisted' and no Turin or Piedmont company would employ them on pain of loss of contracts with the FIAT giant. Sacked FIAT men took the most eclectic work – there were a large number of communist undertakers in this period. Most of the full-time workers at the Camera del lavoro in Turin were ex-FIAT men.

The fear that the sackings inspired was not surprising; few people were prepared to support the union at such a price. The literature on FIAT in this period shows that the workers were afraid to greet or even smile at a known militant, much less talk to one, for fear that they might be seen by a foreman or 'creep'. Workers 'caught' talking to a militant would be called in to the foreman's office for a grilling and warned off sympathy with such men.

Even after the failure of FIOM in the CI elections of 1955, a systematic attempt further to weaken the working class was made. In the remaining years of repression at FIAT, 2000 men were sacked and thousands transferred. As late as 1962, when the workers' resistance began to re-emerge, about 100 workers were sacked in reprisal against the first strike for nine years. A protest strike organized by FIOM for the reinstatement of the sacked men failed dismally.

The Quarantine Departments. As Parlanti put it: 'They'd understood that someone who rebelled at work, even if he wasn't politicized, could sooner or later pass on his ideas, his rebellion, to others, and from rebellion clearly organization could be born, and then from organization politics is born.'[13] FIAT's understanding of this was important in their control of the workforce in these years. Troublesome and individually rebellious workers were moved away from their friends and workmates to noisy or isolated workposts. Worse cases could be sent to the 'reparti confino' or 'quarantine' departments to stop the contagion. If the disease was chronic the worker could then be sacked.

FIAT created many 'reparti confino'. The best known was the 'Officina Sussidiaria Ricambi' nicknamed 'Officina Stella

Rossa' – 'Red Star' – because of the vast number of communists and militants who ended their working days for FIAT there. (Really ended – this was the department which was so heavily left-wing that in 1957 all 120 workers were sacked and the department closed!) There were many other such departments including No. 4 in Aeritalia and No. 24 in Mirafiori. These departments had one common characteristic; they were not really designed for production. Workers carried out more or less unimportant tasks or worked with antiquated machinery, often in deserted hangars taken over for just this purpose.

Racism. Yet another strategy of management in these 'rabbit years' was the encouragement of the division of worker from worker, and one way to do this was through racism. Especially in the late 1950s and early 1960s FIAT ran a sort of advertising campaign in the south to entice workers to Turin with talk of high wages, company houses and many other benefits. The Southerners – the 'Meridionale' – began to arrive en masse, to join earlier immigrants from the south and the Veneto who had been involved in building the great Mirafiori plant.

Forms of racism against the Meridionale, who were largely from a poor peasant background, were and still are fairly common in the north. The lower managerial ranks played on this to create tension and competition between the Piedmontese and southern workers. Parlanti recounts:

The foremen had managed to create hatred between Piedmontese and Southerners. When work was over in the evenings you used to see the Piedmontese talking to their foreman, but there was never a Southerner there. In those days they counted on this hatred to get production figures up. 'Tarrun'[14] the Piedmontese would say – which infuriated the Southerners who'd then push up production to show they were better workers. In those days there was still that terrible concept of North and South, the hatred between us, and very few people realized that the division had been created on purpose by the employers.[15]

In this period there wasn't even one Southern foreman – the Southerners were treated as pure machine fodder with absolutely no chance of promotion. However it was often this most ill-used section of the workforce which sparked off moments of rebellion on the shop floor; but more of that later.

The Hierarchy and Favouring. Racism was not the only tool

used by management to pit worker against worker, hence increasing production and decreasing the chance of organized rebellion. By hinting at better pay or workposts or more overtime in return for 'co-operation' some workers in a team could be persuaded to work harder, creating pressure for a rising production target for the whole team. Usually men who most needed the money and most feared unemployment were picked; men with large families to support. Higher management encouraged such discriminatory policies, giving the foremen a free hand in the sharing out of bonuses and overtime, and sometimes providing a special fund to finance favouring.

A formal hierarchy was also used both to control the workforce by brute force and to tempt it to greater efforts with the chance of promotion. There was a multiple grading of workers into many different levels, from the 'fuori linea' (men who were 'off the line', multi-skilled and able to substitute where needed) up to the 'capo reparto' or departmental foreman. The different grades carried with them different levels of prestige, pay, responsibility and control. This hierarchy also worked magnificently as a 'spy network'; workers who 'told' on militants and union sympathisers were often rewarded with a move up the hierarchy.

In the early post-Liberation years the workers at FIAT and all over the industrial triangle had fought desperately against the reintroduction of wage differentials and incentive schemes. The struggle was lost largely because of the PCI's preoccupation with industrial reconstruction before all else (they made great use of Lenin's writings on Taylorism to back up their arguments). Management thus had a clear road to use a variety of such schemes to encourage even faster work rhythms and create further divisions on the shop floor.

The Purge on Politics. Management went to great lengths in this period to keep political and union material out of the factory, and if possible out of workers' hands completely. In his diary of his days as a member of the CI at RIV (a FIAT subsidiary in Turin), Accornero talks of the struggles over the pinning up of *L'Unita* (the PCI paper):

At 'Grossa torneria' *L'Unita* with an article on yesterday's strike was taken down by Lavagno (the foreman) accompanied by two custodians. In maintenance the paper was taken down by another custodian, who was whistled as he took it away. Another copy was stuck up in the department. After a while the same custodian came back but he couldn't find the paper there in its usual place; he walked round a bit and then gave up. It had been stuck to a pillar this time.[16]

Accornero later recalls how the vigilance of the foremen eventually meant the workers had to resort to writing up information on the walls in chalk.

Parlanti talks of later on in the 1950s, when things had tightened up still further:

> The guard used to come and look in your locker, even, to see what you kept in it, if you had a newspaper, if you maybe had *L'Unita* ... in fact nobody read. It was absolutely forbidden. If a worker brought in a comic, say Mickey Mouse, he was sacked straight off. It wasn't a question of 'Mickey Mouse' but because from 'Mickey Mouse' you could one day go on to bring in maybe a pamphlet or a bulletin, or the paper ... they struck straight away so as not to allow a politicization of the workers.[17]

Election-time Harassment. FIAT's fear tactics made it increasingly difficult to compile the lists of 300-odd names (of candidates, scrutinizers and members of the electoral committee) necessary to present FIOM candidates in election to the CI. The election became an annual confrontation. As repressive and punitive measures hotted up, so fewer workers were willing to 'sign up for the sack' – and those committed few who did, did not usually survive to sign again the following year. Even once the lists had been presented harassment continued: foremen would talk to individual workers promising promotion and favoured treatment to men with the 'right' political attitudes. 'Good' electoral behaviour was rewarded with a bonus for the department and 'bad' behaviour with sackings and transferals. Harassment extended outside the factory gates too. Wives and families of FIAT workers would receive visits or letters from management listing the evils of communism and the union and painting pitiful pictures of the life of the unemployed.

'Soft' Control. The Vallettian management of the 1950s did not, however, only use crude and repressive methods to control and mould the workforce. Whilst they were tightening the screws they were also creating a sort of FIAT hegemony in

Turin, reaching into all corners of the workers' private lives. Propaganda about the privileged position of the FIAT worker was, to a certain extent, true. FIAT wages were considerably higher than those of other companies (a FIAT worker could expect from 85,000 to 90,000 lire as opposed to 45,000 to 60,000 in other factories in the metalworking sector). Side benefits, too, were enormous. FIAT workers' families could (sometimes) live in FIAT houses, their children could be educated in FIAT schools and have their holidays in FIAT 'colonies' in the countryside; sick FIAT workers could be treated under the FIAT 'mutua' scheme (a form of health insurance); whilst healthy FIAT workers could keep themselves fit using FIAT sporting facilities. FIAT even bought its own newspaper (*La Stampa*) and its own football team (Juventus).

The combined effects of all the above methods of control were, not surprisingly, very effective. FIOM lost its majority in 1955:

1954 FIOM ... 32885 votes (63·2%) FIM ... 13175 votes (25·4%)
UILM ... 5889 votes (11·3%)
1955 FIOM ... 18937 votes (25·4%) FIM ... 20910 votes (40·5%)
UILM ... 11628 votes (28·5%)[18]

After this defeat the CI lost virtually all independent character, functioning almost as a body of lower management. The destruction of working class trade unionism at FIAT was utilized in three ways by management: (1), to increase profits by speeding up work rhythms to the physical limit; (2), to introduce new labour-saving technology with a free hand to experiment and to discover how to use it most profitably; (3), to introduce a new sort of labour force of 'virgin' young workers from the south; men who were unskilled and who, at least initially, accepted the killing rhythm for the sake of higher wages and because of their lack of industrial experience.

The first point is self-explanatory. As to the second, in the early 1950s the ignorance and underestimation of the new machinery and work methods by the TU organizations at FIAT much simplified their introduction in the early stages. And as awareness grew the union was simultaneously losing power. FIAT's technique was systematically to select workers (on the basis of lack of militancy and work speed) for a long 'experimental' phase on new equipment, a period of time which was never determined in advance. During this phase the optimum rhythms, production, manning and skill grading would be determined.

Even when these had been worked out FIAT was unwilling to disclose them. If the worker is in the dark about such things he may be more easily 'persuaded' to produce more, by the simple technique of speeding up the line or taking a man off. In fact during the 1950s and 1960s workers could only have access to information about manning and timing through a long and complicated process; initially a demand had to be put through to management from a worker on the job in question, then this demand would be discussed with the foreman. Only after this could the CI be called in to support the worker. For most of the workers this procedure was too intimidating to face on their own, and anyway might single them out for 'special attention'. The workers, to some extent, developed informal and spontaneous weapons to defend themselves against the new technology. Parlanti recalls:

> In fact a comrade, a Southerner, I still remember it, drew a line on the ground with a screwdriver (the floor of the line was of beaten earth, that dark, black, earth). Neither the foreman nor the charge-hand, no-one, understood what that line was. But it was a really strong weapon for the workers ... When the lines go fast, effectively the worker loses his sense of time and he does all the various operations more quickly than normal. You can't even look at your watch, they could even sack you, they thought you were doing it intentionally so you could screw up the timing. The only way you could work out whether you were going faster than normal or not was by comparing the distance you travelled up on the line. And that was what that line on the ground was used for. While he worked, the worker would keep an eye on this line, and when he arrived at it he got off the assembly line ...[19]

Such spontaneous rebellion however was often easily broken. Parlanti concludes the incident: 'But then what happened? After a while they moved everyone around ... and put creeps in our places. They were afraid of the principle of organization which had been created.'

Accornero[20] also demonstrates the failure of workers' organizations to filter and to some extent control the introduction of new technology, even in the days before the total rout of the

427

FIOM (his diary refers to 1953). In this diary he makes frequent reference to a struggle going on in 'Fucinatura', where the men were demanding a bonus, the 'paga di posto' (a pay increment for work in unhealthy or especially tiring posts), as new machinery had worsened conditions in the department, increasing heat and fumes. Accornero first mentions the struggle in February 1953, remarking that the agitation had reduced production from 40,000 to 25,000 piston rings per day. Throughout February there were several brief strikes in Fucinatura, a committee of agitation was formed and a 'chequerboard' strike called – the first shift struck on Monday, the second on Tuesday and so on for a week. (In Italy a full withdrawal of labour was, and still is, impracticable, given the almost total lack of strike pay). In the last months of the struggle FIAT employed the tactic of fines, suspensions and warnings to the men involved. The workers were finally forced to accept management's meagre offer. The struggles had, however, cost FIAT a great deal in terms of lost production; they had won in the end, but in this period FIOM and the CI were still able to cost them time and money.

The introduction of the new machinery was not, though, FIAT's only preoccupation; the workforce also had to be adapted to the technology of the 'new era'. In other words management had to carry out a massive selection and deformation of that section of the working class with which it was involved in order to create the sort of mobile, flexible and unskilled labour force it needed to exploit the new machinery to the maximum. It also needed a primarily youthful workforce, preferably in their first jobs, young men who would accept the monotony of the new 'parcelized' labour process more easily than the older, skilled sections. Here then, we come to the third way mentioned above by which management sought to utilize the destruction of working class unionism.

After the war the FIAT labour force was mostly composed of older skilled men, and the labour process was still largely based on their knowledge, experience and skill. The war and the Resistance had contributed to this imbalance by reducing the supply of young men to replace them. From 1949 the phase of rationalization, begun at Mirafiori, brought the first signs of a reorganization of work and it became necessary to phase out the skilled sector. This process was anyway very welcome to FIAT as the older men also tended to be the more politically conscious in that period – they were a sort of labour aristocracy, involved politically as well as physically in the labour process. Many of them had been involved in the Resistance and earlier anti-fascist struggles and in the post-Liberation 'occupations' when the newly liberated factories were in many cases run on democratic principles through workers' councils.

Valletta's management used the powerful weapon of what Alquati[21] calls 'internal sackings' (transferals and enforced mobility) to move the skilled worker off the line, and also reduce his political effect. An enforced 'voluntary' early retirement, and of course the sack when an excuse could be found, were also used to liberate the factory of skilled workers and create a new labour force suited to the new parcelized labour process.

Management began with the importation of 7,800 workers from auxiliary sectors and the expulsion of 2,000 elderly or un-well workers through voluntary resignation. A huge de-skilling and demoting process followed, beginning with the reclassifica-tion of the majority of workers into the third category, a grade covering unskilled labour. The same package brought in a three-shift system to ensure twenty-four-hour-a-day exploitation. The whole process of de-ranking and the introduction of the shift system was sold to the workforce at the price of the reduction of the working week (to forty-five hours for first and second shift workers and forty-two hours for night shift workers) at wage parity.

The process of 'weeding out' of older skilled men was carried on through the 1950s as the sackings hit hard at the more politicized and militant workers. A survey published by Deaglio[22] is very interesting on this point. This enquiry was carried out in 1959 among sacked FIAT workers and was aimed at finding out who was the 'vanguard' in that period. The 'typical' sacked worker turned out to be a first category (skilled) man who had a long work experience at FIAT and had a history of politicization usually dating back to 1943–5. He was usually a member of the PCI and/or FIOM. In fact 80 per cent of the men in the survey had these characteristics. Out of 79 sacked workers, 79 were FIOM members and 74 were PCI members. Only 16 were taken on to the labour force after the war.

Thus during the 1950s the composition of the labour force at FIAT was changed radically to suit the new technology, and contain militancy. With mechanization and early forms of automation the labour process became 'parcelized'; small elements of the whole product produced monotonously and later, equally monotonously, aggregated into the whole. The skilled and politicized men became obsolete. FIAT needed a labour force which would accept the monotony and which had no experience of organizing to fight for better conditions and pay. The skilled men, the communists and militants, who were ironically the very people who had pushed for discipline and factory order in the early post-war years before the collapse of communist participation in government, were pushed out of the mainstream of the productive process, transferred to isolated work posts, put to sweeping floors, sent to the 'quarantine' departments, forced into early retirement, or simply sacked.

But even the new young workers with little previous work experience to compare with FIAT and no frustrated pride and skill in work, and who had been enticed to Turin by the news of high FIAT wages, housing and privileges, had their breaking point. FIAT had not, in fact, been able to provide in time an adequate superstructure of houses and amenities; and the higher wages didn't go far with the higher prices of the north and the added expenses of laundering and catering that young unmarried immigrants had to face. Gruelling conditions and heavy factory discipline were coupled with the squalid living conditions. Parlanti again:

> But the Southerners, especially, weren't really used to discipline like the Northerners with their school education. They were much more expansive, they talked among themselves, sometimes they didn't give a shit ... they didn't understand anything – but precisely because they didn't understand the rules of FIAT, it was really they who began mass discussions, who began to break discipline.... So I think it was really the Southerners at FIAT with their 'bad manners' ... who started to discuss the problems.[23]

The young Southerners with their 'bad manners' and little education to habituate them to the boredom, routine and discipline of factory life – these were the people who started the movement of strikes and agitations in the industrial triangle in the late 1950s and early 1960s. The workers of FIAT, the most powerful and the largest sector in the industrial triangle, would not, however, join the struggle until 1962; the 'rabbits' of FIAT had to be practically forced out on to the streets by the other

Turinese workers, who had recognized how crucial the FIAT men were to their fight. The chronicles of the journal *Quaderni Rossi*[24] describe how, on 19 June 1962, FIAT workers crossed a deserted, strike-bound Turin on the empty trams to go to work, running a gauntlet of insults, bits of old bread and coins, flung at them by striking workers from other sectors. The FIAT factories were besieged by other workers trying to prod this 'mass of molluscs' into action. But it was not until a general strike on 7 July (called as part of the actions centred around the renewal of contracts for the major sectors) that the car workers, after a 'cease fire' which had lasted nearly nine years, entered the struggle with a vengeance.

After so many years of repression, years in which the instinct to fight back was crippled by the detachment of the union leadership from the 'new' rank and file, the struggle was almost bound to be violent.

On the third day of strikes and picketing, UIL signed a separate and wholly unsatisfactory agreement with management. It was the last straw. Workers' demonstrations in Turin that day turned into riots, and police were called in from outside to put down the revolt with baton charges. Symbolically, it was the UIL HQ in Piazza Statuto that came in for most of the violence. And the riots of Piazza Statuto were the first sign of an energetic mass rejection of the old-style unionism led by a labour aristocracy which had lost contact with the rank and file of young unskilled workers.

The period of 'democratization' and opening up of the organization to the shop floor had, however, only just begun; Piazza Statuto was just the first step in the destruction of the legacy of post-war unionism and the creation of a weapon more suited to the changed battle-ground. Commitment to a new form of organization was growing, but the working class at FIAT and all over Italy remained relatively weak in its confrontations with management right up to the great international cycle of struggles of 1968–9.

NOTES AND REFERENCES

1 This quotation is taken from an interview carried out by the 'Primo Maggio' group with an ex-FIAT worker Luciano Parlanti – 'Da Valletta a Piazza Statuto', *Primo Maggio*, no. 9. I have translated quite a number of passages from this interview to illustrate my argument.

2 Liliano Lanzardo, *Classe Operaia e Partito Communista alla FIAT*, Einaudi, 1971, p. 641.

3 'Nella piu grande fabbrica d'Italia' in *L'Organizzazione del lavoro in Italia*, Maurizio Lichtner (ed.), Riuniti 1975.

4 Canzardo, op. cit., p. 89n.

5 Parlanti, op. cit.

6 See, G. Baglioni, 'Commissione Interna e rappresentanza dei lavoratori' in *Studi di sociologia*, 1–2, January–June, 1970.

7 Antonio Gramsci, 21 June 1919 in *Soviets in Italy*, Institute for Workers Control, Nottingham, 1974.

8 The LLD – Liberi Lavoratori Democratici – or 'Free and Democratic Workers' were a company union formed by a split from the Catholic CISL. After the destruction of the FIOM in the CI, management was often able to impose agreements after consultation with LLD-SIDA and UIL-UILM alone.

9 The last upsurge of industrial agitation for almost a decade occurred in 1953 over the 'legge truffa' or 'swindle laws' (laws intended to bring in electoral arrangements detrimental to the workers' parties).

10 E. Pugno and S. Garavini, *Gli Anni duri alla FIAT*, Einaudi, 1974, p. 72.

11 D. Roy, 'Fear Stuff, Sweet Stuff and Evil Stuff', 1975; see pp. 395–415.

12 E. Pugno and S. Garavini, op cit., p. 72.

13 Parlanti, op. cit.

14 'Tarrun': pejorative term, peasant or 'bumpkin'.

15 Parlanti, op. cit.

16 Aris Accornero, *Gli anni '50 in fabbrica-con un diario di Commissione Interna*, De Donato, 1973, 18 September 1953.

17 Parlanti, op. cit.

18 Pugno and Garavini, op. cit., p. 98.
19 Parlanti, op. cit.
20 Accornero, op. cit.
21 Romano Alquati, *Sulla FIAT e altri scritti*, Feltrinelli, 1975.
22 Enrico Deaglio, *La FIAT com'e*, Feltrinelli, 1975, pp. 66–7.
23 Parlanti, op. cit.
24 *Cronache dei Quaderni Rossi*, no. 1, September 1962.

'ChemCo' – Bureaucratic Control and Psycho-Sociology in England in the Early 1970s

Theo Nichols and Huw Beynon

At Riverside, a technologically advanced chemical complex ... one of the first things that the managers we met ... wanted to talk to us about was trade unionism and the state of unionism on the site. 'There is not a militant on this site,' said one of them knowingly, 'some hotheads but no militants'. He was clear that this was in his interests and in 'the interest of the Company' and that one of the main tasks of management at Riverside was to keep the situation this way. In this, as we shall see, they had a lot going for them.

To begin with the question of 'militants'. If we mean by this workers who have had some experience of dealing with management; who have learned how to stand up to them and how to protect their rights and the rights of other workers; who have learned the need to plan a strategy for dealing with management, the need for meetings, for leaflets, for *organization*; if this is what a militant is, then it is clear that there was no such man at Riverside. If these men had anything in common it was a near-total lack of contact with organized shop-floor trade unionism. They had all worked in a variety of jobs – some 'good', some 'bad' – for a variety of often small employers. They had moved around a lot, sometimes they'd taken out a union card, sometimes not. We talked with only two who had taken any active part in trade unionism before they came to this site – both of these men were shop stewards.

So the workforce at Riverside could not draw upon any traditions of militancy from within its collective past. These men had come from far and wide to an area of England that has been remarkably free from confrontation and industrial strife during this century. They live in different parts of the area, travelling on average some twenty miles to work. Few of them meet a workmate outside work and at work they are split apart too. They work on separate plants; plants that are separated by a half-mile or so, which have different car parks, different changing rooms, different managers. Their existence at work is so separate that none of the workers that we talked to on the acid plants knew *anyone* who worked on the Zap plant. Moreover within each plant the workforce is further fragmented by the Continental shift. Only a quarter of the workers who work on a plant will be there at any one time. Almost all the people we talked to who said that they had 'friends' at Riverside found those friends on their own plant and on their own shift. Taken together the plants and the shift system broke a work-force of almost 200 into a series of very small groups.

One of the men on the Zap plant saw the situation like this:

The big problem is there's no contact between the plants. You don't know what the other hand is doing type of thing. We're becoming a bit friendlier with Zap X since we've been working overtime over there. But there's no *social life* with this plant. There's no social life in work. It's a pretty off-hand plant to work on really.

All this has obvious and very real consequences for the development of 'militancy' at Riverside. A factory militant relies, above all else, upon the collective strength of the workers. This collective strength has been asserted in the past through slogans like 'one out all out'; through the strike and through blacking – the practice whereby workers collectively refuse to do a particular job or piece of work. At Riverside much ran against the development of such a collectivism. Men on one shift who decide to refuse to do particular work find that it is done by men on another shift whom they never see. Such action could of course be coordinated through meetings held off the site at the union office in Provincial but the shift system also makes these very difficult to organize. At any one time half the labour force is either at work or asleep while the other half is preparing to go to work or getting used to being at home.

Now these problems aren't insuperable ones (we know of one site, for example, where for a time two men regularly came to work an hour early and left an hour late so that they could talk with the people on the other shifts and establish particular working practices) but they are significant. They create difficulties for collective organization that aren't encountered in engineering factories that work for one shift a day. And the conjunction between this fragmentation and the experience of the workers who came to Riverside placed ChemCo's management in a very strong position. When it came to changing things, to planning and co-ordination, they were faced with a divided labour force which, by the standards of many British factories – certainly those which hit the headlines – could be considered 'docile' and 'unsophisticated'. Certainly if management had wanted a quiet life they could have had it at Riverside. But that quiet life fits very uneasily into the rationality of monopoly capital. Riverside's management was under pressure throughout the 1960s – but particularly towards the end of that decade – to increase the 'performance of the plants'. And this meant that docility was not enough. In deciding to embark upon the change of attitudes that the NEDC had held to be so necessary for the industry, ChemCo's manager accountants therefore sought to 'motivate' their workforce towards higher productivity. They also rethought their approach to trade unionism. So much so that at Riverside management became directly involved in making the union on site.

The personnel manager at Riverside explained the situation like this:

> They're *still* very equivocal about unionism at Roxborough [ChemCo's oldest northern plant]. Really they don't want the buggers in the place. You see ChemCo has traditionally avoided unions, preferring its own system of consultation through works representatives. Christ, my old dad was a union man in the pits and 'Works Representative' for him was a form of abuse.

But at Roxborough, and elsewhere in the company, they *had* to have 'the buggers' in the place.

> We've had to change. We can't rely on those methods any more and I think this is a better situation morally. Now we have to battle for the minds and wills of the men.

The NWA [productivity deal] and the negotiations which led up to it were central to this battle of wills, and the issue of trade unionism played a central part in all this. It is worth reminding ourselves what was involved in the deal. Partly the deal was about ideology – the negotiations contained strong and clear statements by senior management about the need for new attitudes, the need for commitment, for a 'revolution' in the social relationships within the factory. We have already seen something of the reality of this 'revolution' but it is important to point out that such a message was regularly put across to the workforce at Riverside during the years that we visited the plant. An observer of another British chemical firm during the 1960s noticed similar tendencies.[2]

> In regard to employment at British Chemicals, the firm claims that 'from the outset British Chemicals attached the utmost importance to the well-being of those who worked in it, recognizing that prosperity would be neither deserved nor achieved without the goodwill and co-operation of all of them'. A company booklet speaks of close standing relations with trade unions.... The point is made that British Chemicals has contributed significantly to the growth of the British economy and balance of payments ... a weekly newspaper ... includes news of improvements in welfare and retirement benefits.... There is mention of attempts to 'push responsibility down the line'. Links are made between productivity and personal effectiveness.... [A speech by the Chairman asserts] 'that the needs of the Company and the needs of individuals are interdependent. It is clearly the Company's duty to give opportunities for everyone to make the best of their own abilities and thus get more satisfaction from the work that has to be done. If this can be achieved, then all of us benefit twice – by increased personal satisfaction and by the increased prosperity of the Company – which in turn will enable us to measure up more fully to our other inescapable responsibilities – to customers, to shareholders and to the nation itself.'

At Riverside things were much the same. The site newspaper came out every two weeks and its editorials touched on similar issues. They pointed to the company's profit-sharing scheme as evidence of the fact that 'no one person owns ChemCo.' They argued that the modern corporation serves the interests of *everyone*. That the NWA deal with its stress upon co-operation provided the basis for a new working relationship that would produce more chemicals, more wages, more profit – for everyone. (It was just this argument that ChemCo used in full-page advertisements in the national press when, in 1974, it was threatened with nationalization by its inclusion in the Labour

Party's alleged list of likely companies. A threat which – predictably perhaps – has come to nothing.)

The NWA deal, then, was closely bound up with the continuous production of ideology. But there was much more to the deal than this. Central to the agreement was the establishment of a *national* wage rate. On the introduction of NWA all grades of workers in the company were given a large increase in their basic rate of pay but at the expense of losing all locally agreed bonuses, premium payments and the like. The deal did away with all *local* wage negotiation and replaced it with a centralized, national structure. From then on all 'money talk' was restricted to the conference room in London. In addition to this the agreement established that all jobs in the company would be graded (on a scale from two, the bottom, to seven), each job grade carrying a fixed national pay rate, with a fixed maximum addition for bad working conditions and with a fixed national shift allowance. The stress in this part of the agreement was upon the isolation of local, shop-floor organizations from the collective bargaining process. Such organizations were seen to have a role on the plant-based consultation and productivity committees; but they were, in the company's view, to be the administrative adjuncts of the deal.

For management, then, the presence of trade unionism was seen as a central aspect of the NWA. ChemCo's new approach to unionism was rooted in the 'battle for the minds and wills of the men'. Trade unionism was accepted and the pressure was on to mould it into a functional part of the corporation. NWA marked the quintessence of corporate rationality: within it, ChemCo, having rationalized its own management structures, set about rationalizing the structure of trade unionism as well.

In 1967 very few people who worked at Riverside were members of a union. A branch of the TGWU had been established in 1962 but the branch secretary and the shop stewards from the Zap and Zap X plants were promoted to foremen in 1963, for some time after which there was very little union activity on the site. The branch secretary's job, for example, lay vacant for a while until it was taken on by a man who'd come to ChemCo from the Army.

I came from the Army you see and there you were told to do something and you did it. I went to the chemical industry and I was told that you are expected to join the union. I knew nothing about unions but I thought, 'I've got to have this job and if that's part of the job I'll join.' As it turned out only about 20 per cent were in.

Having joined he decided that 'if I was going to be in something I wanted to have some say in it.' So he attended the branch meeting – and was elected branch secretary.

Men who worked on the plants in the early years remember that 'the union' was badly organized, they remember the stewards who were promoted, they remember trying to join and then giving up.

> I never joined. I was going to join when I first came here like. The shop steward had given me the forms to fill in. I filled them in – I thought I might as well like ... [but] ... he wasn't a very good shop steward and nothing came of it. He couldn't have sent them in. So when he gave me another lot of forms about a year later I told him what he could do with 'em. I said I'm not bothering like. Well, when the firm started stopping it, I joined then.

The 'firm started stopping it' when, as part of the preliminaries to NWA, a 'check-off' arrangement was agreed between the company and the union at national level.

There are arguments in favour of the check-off. It ensures the preservation of the closed shop – at Riverside it brought 100 per cent of the production workers into the union – and it saves shop stewards a lot of routine work while avoiding the problem of members falling into arrears and collectors absconding with the funds. But the check-off also makes it possible for the members to lose an important contact between themselves and the union organization: with the check-off the union dues can become more of a tax than a contribution to an ongoing labour organization. Such considerations have led many well-organized shop steward committees to resist the introduction of such schemes, preferring to retain the traditional method of payment through collectors. At Riverside the check-off was welcomed. The district officer told us that 'management was very keen on the idea and so were we. With the closed shop, you see, we have the ability to discipline our members.'

The closed shop was enforced at Riverside by an agreement between the company and the union. (Management gave an assurance that while they wouldn't absolutely refuse to employ non-trade unionists new recruits would be told very clearly

439

what was expected of them.) Those who were shop stewards at the time welcomed the agreement because it established the union at Riverside and saved them a lot of work. But it also ensured that no widespread, active, recruiting campaign ever took place on site. The union was established without a struggle and this meant that for many of these workers (as for an increasing number in the country generally) their *first* contact with trade unionism came through the personnel officer and a weekly deduction on the pay slip. Alan, a foreman well schooled in union politics, saw this quite clearly:

> After the closed shop was introduced I would say the union collapsed completely.

A strange, but by no means unique, situation.

A union in name only, a paper membership, was not however enough for ChemCo. Given the contrasting difficulties of management by fiat and mass meeting, the very implementation of the NWA rested on the involvement of the union. It was to this end that workers' representatives – shop stewards – who were going to be packed off to productivity and consultative committees, were elected. Foremen were instructed by their plant managers to seek out 'likely material' on the plants and encourage them to stand as shop stewards in the coming elections. In this quest it became clear that while the management ideology of the 1960s differed in important respects from what had gone before the differences were only of degree and not of real substance. The 'management men' amongst the foremen talked often of the 'new role' for shop stewards within the company. They'd stress that foremen and shop stewards have comparable functions – 'they've got their job, and we've got ours and we both have to follow procedure.' One of them told us that:

> A good shop steward is my friend. He's a good man to have on the plant. You see, he knows the procedure; he knows just how far he can go and how far I can go. Oh yes, a good shop steward is my friend. He's an asset.

But in reality – and this is not all that disguised here ('an asset' indeed) – when looking for workers to sponsor for shop steward, they acted on the view of the old-style foremen, for whom 'a shop steward with ChemCo should be a company man.'

It is undeniable that ChemCo management exercised an important – and even determining – influence over the way in which the trade union organization developed at Riverside. Of the six shop stewards who represented the men who worked on the fertilizer plant only two had been in any way active in trade unionism before they came on the site. ... The other four had all been encouraged to stand for the office by their foreman, and two of them soon became the 'deputy foremen' (standing in during the foreman's absence) on their section. Managers tell you that the district officer first made contact with the site on their invitation. They privately boast that many of the shop stewards were their nominees. They justify all this with the language of 'participation'; with talk of the new style and the new modern corporation. But in its practice this ideology is inevitably flawed. When they talk of 'participation' they don't mean 'equal participation'; nor does trade unionism imply equal rights for all. In their view – a view that is firmly established within the structure of corporate capitalism – 'participation' and 'trade unionism' are inevitably subordinate to the need for hierarchy and the need for profit. The need for management to manage.

Many trade unionists would accept this view and a lot of trade union officials act on it regularly in their daily lives. But the fact of the matter is that the establishment of organization amongst workers on the factory floor always poses a *potential* threat to both the authority of the corporate hierarchy and to the accumulation of profit. This potential was well understood by the management at Riverside; as it was by the foreman who insisted that 'the unions shouldn't rule the roost.' For while they are clear that trade unionism now has an important role to play in the future of ChemCo they are also clear that it must be a particular type of trade unionism. 'Real', 'responsible' trade unionism ...

Under the deal the newly elected shop stewards were given facilities to meet every Friday in the admin. block to discuss problems associated with the introduction of NWA. Stewards who were not at work at that time would be paid by the company to attend these meetings. The stewards understood those meetings to be theirs as of right under the agreement. The management accepted this but became very worried when the stewards refused access to the personnel manager. This worried them because they felt that 'they'll not be using those meetings to discuss our deal. Those buggers will be discussing the union in them. It's just not going to be very constructive.' But managers put up with the meetings until NWA was fully operational; until the plant productivity agreements had been ironed out and all the jobs on the site had been graded. Once this was done Sammy Bell argued that, 'the Friday meetings are now simply an unproductive use of time.' From then on stewards were no longer allowed to meet each other in 'company time', except in meetings with management. The deal had been implemented and participation and consultation were to be the rule, but they were the rule only within the context of the power of management – their right ('responsibilty') to manage in the interest of capital. ...

ChemCo managers know the value of the empty phrase, the nod and the wink, the pat on the back, and the occasional kick in the balls. And the most skilled of them put all this together in a highly professional performance. A performance so good that it appears real. A performance that is directed towards the *hegemony* of capital; the dominance of a particular view of things over all others. For these men are dealers in ideology.

The chemical plants at Riverside are small, as are most plants in the industry. Not small in terms of the capital employed but, compared to, say, the massed workforces that characterize parts of the engineering industry, small in numbers of men. Despite the fact that managers have been pushed off the plants into the admin. block, then, it is still possible, relatively speaking, for them to 'know their men.' And it's important that they do – precisely because so much capital is at stake. The 'professionals' know this and they devote a lot of their time to the 'personal' side of things. They know too that trade unionism has become a necessity; that it is better to 'have it in' and clearly established along agreed lines rather than be involved in perpetual arguments about a 'closed shop', 'non-union workers' and so on. They accept trade unionism and a lot of them will say that they 'agree with it' – providing it's 'properly set up'. It's part of the 'new approach' and they know that they need to give a lot of personal attention to the men's elected representatives – the shop stewards. The institutional-level relationships between company and union being fixed, what these men engage in at plant and site level – at an individual level – is manipulation. Here we find the 'old kidology' that the 'traditional foremen' talk of, revamped in the language of 'modern' human relations; a 'revolution in industrial relations' played out in the context of 'modern' manufacture.

It was just this relationship between the old and the new that had escaped Edward Blunsen and was to prove his undoing. 'Young', 'vigorous', 'clear-headed', 'profit conscious', 'scientifically trained', most certainly 'talented' and 'ambitious' and 'competitive', he was – in some ways – everything the rulers of this society are apt to bemoan British managers are not. Crystal clear where he wanted to go – workers reported that he'd told them he wanted to get on the Main Board – he still, however, hadn't got the style right. He might have got away with his abrasiveness in a small, up-and-coming cut-throat operation. But not at ChemCo. ChemCo plant managers *don't* thrust their power in workers' faces. They try *not* to let the iron fist behind the velvet glove show, and they certainly don't tell workers that 'a man with a good manager doesn't need a union.' Riverside managers play it 'firm but fair'. They push and jostle workers and stewards, they 'jump on them' – but their overall strategy is to seek to enmesh workers, to bring about a situation where they don't have to be *driven*. While they might *think* of workers in the language of engineering they also go to great lengths to relate to them 'personally'.

Sammy Bell, the group manager at Riverside, is perhaps the best of 'the professionals' on the site. Every month, for example, he makes a 'CO's visit' to each shift. It takes place at the same time every month, everyone knows he's coming and everyone's prepared for him. He knows this too. For him, though, it's a way of 'making them jump' and 'keeping them on their toes.' But this is just one side of Sammy Bell. He can play the hard man; march around issuing instructions to his supervisors, spotting things which shouldn't be there and things which are missing; losing his temper. Yet in his office – particularly in his regular meetings with 'my shop stewards' – he's much more amenable and accommodating. 'A lovely cuddly teddy bear' is how his secretary describes him. And while the stewards don't take their loyalty to him this far there is no doubt that they *are* loyal to him; that they like the way he is with them and that they look forward to the morning they spend with him each month, in his office discussing 'problems'.

Experienced managers know that 'the office' is their territory. Desks, chairs, secretaries, coffee (and biscuits), telephone calls: these are all part of their world – not the world of the shop floor. And they know how to use this world against shop stewards. Many shop stewards have been overwhelmed by, and sucked into, the world of the office; edged along by managers who tell them how much more 'reasonable' they are than the 'average worker we employ.' And those who resist such talk, try to push a different point of view, find 'their flow' cut off at key moments by telephone calls or by secretaries with letters to be signed. Sammy Bell was the master of the office. Other managers told us repeatedly of how inexperienced shop stewards go to see him with a grievance and come out of his office – having got nowhere – 'full of smiles'. They smile fondly as they tell you this. And they smile even more when they talk about the way he 'takes the stewards on his knee' – taking them out to dinner after the odd meeting and buying them drinks at Christmas. For them Sammy Bell is the supreme artist. They watch him and if they're wise they try to learn from him.

Colin Brown, for example, says that he's 'learned a lot from watching Sammy', and he's Riverside's system-thinker *par excellence*. For him 'the system' matters; NWA was 'an important step in the right direction.' He reads avidly from the pages of the new psycho-social theory books. He talks – endlessly so it seems – about the new 'new philosophy'; the 'problems of motivation'; the 'new role of the trade unions'. But Brown – like the rest of the managers – has a job to do and in his performance of this job there is no doubting that he has a very astute assessment of what is needed to keep himself – and ChemCo – at an advantage. The men who work on his plants tell you that 'he always tries it on – always.' There's 'a lot of spoof in him', they say. And Brown delights in his 'spoof'.

Every man is born to do something and my function in life is to manage and I've just got to manage. I think this is a problem that most managers have failed to get to grips with. Now take an example. As far as I can see any man who takes on the job of shop steward wants his ego boosting. But you've got to boost his ego in the proper manner.

Now if I get a bit of trouble – now take an example, perhaps of a serious case of a man who has been perpetually late. Now, I'm the manager, and it's my function to manage. It's my function to discipline this particular man. But I have to deal with the steward. So, what do I do? I take the shop steward aside and I tell him that in half an hour's time this man Smith is going to walk into this room. That I'm going to stamp and bang the table and tell him that I'm going to put him out on the road.

Then I'll say to the shop steward, 'and what *you* can do will be to intervene at this time. Make a case for the man. And we'll agree to let the man off with a caution.'

Now the man comes in and I bang the table and the steward says, 'Come on, Mr Brown. Couldn't you give him one more chance?' I relent. The shop steward gets out of the meeting with the man and says to him, 'I've got you off this bloody time but don't expect me to do it again.' You see, the shop steward gets his ego boosted. He gets what he wants and I get what I want. That's what good management is about.

It's Brown's function to manage. Like the rest of them he does 'bang the table', and occasionally he does make threats to put workers out on the road, but his main strategy is to get the steward to work *with* him. This is what the new stress on psycho-sociology is for. 'Democratic leadership,' he told us once, 'is the only way. But you'll know that, won't you? Psychologists have proved it with children.' Well, there are 'children' and adult workers, and there's 'democracy' and democracy. In Riverside's democratic family there's no doubt who plays the role of understanding parent.

Equally there is no doubt that in their practice of the 'new industrial relations' Riverside managers are involved in what is often a cynical relationship with the people they are dealing with. To put it at its hardest, they are involved in the manipulation of other people. This is a problem for people (like us) who try to understand them and people (like Riverside workers) who have to deal with them, for the defining feature of manipulation is precisely that it isn't declared for what it is. Self-deception and bad faith are structured in. So much so that it is often extremely difficult to separate the appearance from the reality – the shadow from the substance. Difficult, one suspects, for them too. For while these men recognize – and are critical of – the manipulation which goes on at the higher levels of the management structure (Jack Thompson's 'gentle form of corruption') they draw back from recognizing it in themselves. For them it's a 'game'; more a matter of 'being good with people'. . . .

It is possible to argue that Riverside is an exceptional case. Several things might point to this. The fact that the site employed a 'green' labour force with only a limited experience of large-scale factory production; the separation of the workforce from the national union, which negotiates wages on its behalf; the introduction of the check-off arrangement; the blocking of the development of the shop steward committee; the *extent* to which the workers were exposed to management's way of looking at things. All these things taken together create immense handicaps for any sustained opposition to management's strategies within the factory. But perhaps they aren't as exceptional as they might seem. ChemCo chose its Riverside site with some care and it has chosen others like it. So have other multinationals. The NWA deal was no coincidence either; it was formulated carefully over a period of several years. Riverside is neither an exception nor a coincidence because giant corporations like ChemCo are in the business of creating the very conditions that exist on that site. In particular the way in which the Company systematically restructured its 'labour relations' points to a *general tendency* within big business. This tendency involves a clear attempt to deal with and incorporate trade unionism – to encourage trade union membership amongst the workforce; to grant special facilities to trade union representatives and officials; and all this to the end of *subjecting the labour force to a degree of order, regulation and control.*

The experience at Riverside can tell us a lot about this strategy; about the day-to-day practices of managers which take place within its ambit. It also points to some of the contradictions involved. The value of trade unionism to management lies in its (apparent) independence from capital. An independence which comes from the fact that trade unions 'represent the workers.' In as far as this independence is real it can create real problems for management. At Riverside the Friday meetings were an example of this. On the other hand where the union becomes seen to be simply another tool of management it can lose all claims to represent, speak for, and commit the people who are central to the whole thing – the workers on the factory floor. The antagonism which management's sponsorship of shop stewards created is again indicative of this.

So 'incorporation' is no simple process and the function of management in large corporations like ChemCo is to *manage* the contradictions; at all costs 'to prevent the system from running out of *control.*' In this task it had a lot going for it, because it is clear that the factory is wrapped in the hegemony of a capitalist ideology. An ideology which finds it expression not just (or even most importantly) in managers mouthing the company line but in the whole fabric of day-to-day activity in the plant. The task of the working class is to break free of this.

NOTES AND REFERENCES

1 An additional potential source of division within the workforce is that of skin colour. During our visits to the Riverside site we heard enough 'private talk' to convince us that a deal of racial prejudice existed there. But while we heard many stories of serious fights between blacks and whites during the early days of the site, we were aware of no such overt racial conflict between 1970 and 1973. In the Zap and Zap X packing areas black and white men performed the same jobs and worked alongside each other. Their shared, common situation dominated any prejudice or cultural difference that might serve as a serious source of division. At Riverside prejudice was a much less severe obstacle to united action than the plant and shift system.

2 C. Sofer, *Men in Mid-Career: A Study of British Managers and Technical Specialists*, Cambridge University Press, 1970, pp. 164–7.

Planning, Strategy and Capitalist Crisis

Ernest Mandel

Clausewitz once made a comparison between war and trade and saw in victorious battle an analogy to successful exchange. In late capitalism, or at least in its vocabulary and ideology, the relationship between military science and economic practice is inverted: one now speaks of big companies planning their strategy.[1] It is a fact that in the age of monopoly capitalism there can no longer be any question of selling the available range of commodities produced at top speed with maximum profit. In conditions of monopolistic competition short-term profit maximization is a completely senseless goal.[2] Company strategy aims at *long-term profit maximization*, in which factors such as domination of the market, share of the market, brand familiarity, future ability to meet demand, safeguarding of opportunities for innovation, i.e. for growth, become more important than the selling price which can be obtained immediately or the profit margin which this represents.[3] The decisive factor here is not by any means disposal over all the relevant information. On the contrary: the necessity of making strategic decisions – in the final analysis the *compulsion* for internal planning in the enterprise – expresses precisely the *uncertainty* which is inherent in every economic decision in a market economy of commodity production. What makes planning possible is thus not the fact that today it is easier than ever before to collect a maximum quantity of data on matters outside the enterprise. What makes planning possible is the *actual control* that the capitalist has over the means of production and the labourers in his enterprise, and over the capital which in the event may be accumulated outside the enterprise.[4]

Inside the enterprise or company there is no exchange of commodities. Profitability considerations in no way determine whether a larger or smaller number of bodies, as opposed to engines or chassis, are produced within an automobile corporation.[5] Within the company labour is directly socialized in the sense that the overall plan of the company – the production of x cars per week, per month or per year – directly determines the output of the various factories, workshops and conveyor belts. The investment activity in these various factories or workshops of the same company is determined centrally and not by the directors of the individual plants. Within the company, therefore, planning is genuine.

Such planning can, of course, fail to achieve its strategic objectives; it is nevertheless real planning. There is a difference between a situation in which 5 per cent of an output of 1 million cars cannot be sold because of a sudden slump in demand, and a situation where with an output of 1 million car bodies and engines, 50,000 cars cannot be assembled because production of chassis has been inadequate. In the first case, circumstances outside the enterprise – whether or not these were foreseeable is another question – have an adverse effect on a planned objective. The second case is one of bad planning. The precise coordination of all the factors under the actual control of the individual company is objectively possible and only a matter of good planning. The precise coordination of all the factors inside and outside the enterprise, on which long-term profit maximization ultimately depends, is by contrast impossible, because the company cannot – or cannot fully – control the factors outside the enterprise. There is thus a clear distinction between *planning* with the enterprise (or company) and *programming* of the economy as a whole. . . .

Economic programming in late capitalism . . . in contrast to economic planning within industrial companies today (or within society tomorrow after the overthrow of the capitalist mode of production) cannot do more than merely coordinate the independent production prospects of the companies,[6] which are based in the final analysis on the commodity character of production – that is, on the private ownership of the means of production and the private character of the labour expended in the different companies. Such programming is thus irrevocably beset by two crucial elements of uncertainty.

In the first place, it is based on investment plans and expectations which are mostly nothing more than projections, corrected with certain variables, of *past* tendencies of development. If there is a sudden alteration in the market situation or an unexpected change in the relation between demand and supply; if a new product unexpectedly comes on to the market and threatens the 'planned', i.e. expected demand for a certain product produced by a company; if there is a sudden recession or if the cycle unexpectedly moves to 'overstrain', then companies may be forced to make abrupt alterations in their investment plans either by reducing them radically (i.e. postponing them) or by increasing them suddenly, i.e. accelerating them. Moreover, these companies can err by making false appraisals of the market situation, sales trends or business cycle; they are then obliged to re-adapt their plans to economic reality all the more drastically because belatedly.

In the second place, different units of capital are nominally coordinated in economic programming, which in this context do not have common, but *different interests*. All large companies, of course, have a common interest in knowing the investment plans of their most important supply and customer companies. In the last resort, this is the objective basis for the exchange of information underlying late capitalist economic programming. But these companies do not want this information so that they can *adapt* themselves to it; on the contrary, they want it in order to calculate their own private profit maximization as effectively as possible, and so ultimately in order to *combat* the plans of their competitors as effectively as possible. Competition and private ownership therefore means that precisely *because* there has been an exchange of information, coordination between different investment projects is liable not to function, because of the temptation precisely to use the plans of a competing firm to outlap it and force it to retreat. The coordination of the plans of private companies therefore inevitably implies both actual coordination and the negation of any coordination.

The fundamental uncertainty of late capitalist economic programming – in reality, the projection of future overall economic developments by a coordination of the investment plans provided by individual companies[7] – is the basis of its *forecast*-character, as opposed to the *goal*-character of a socialist planned economy. Those who construct these forecasts do not possess the economic power, i.e. the control over the means of production, to see that these forecasts are realized. It is characteristic in this context that the only means at the disposal of late capitalist economic programmers for the correction of actual development when they deviate from predictions, is State intervention in the economy – a change in goverment policy on money, credit, taxes, foreign trade or public investment activity. The limits of such government policy will be dealt with in a later context.

One of the greatest weaknesses of Shonfield's interpretation of late capitalism lies in its confusion of the fundamental difference between capitalist economic programming and post-capitalist economic planning. Shonfield cites the exception of US agriculture, where government agencies lay down the areas to be cultivated and even the quantities to be produced – with what success is another matter. He does not seem to see the difference between such practices and a loose 'consensus' among companies, where private control over the means of production is predominant. Such a consensus is always limited by efforts to compete, in other words by the constraint towards the separate maximization of profit on the part of each competitor. It is at the very least surprising that Shonfield, who views the above-average growth of international trade as one of the main causes of the long post-war boom, can exclude international competition from his analysis of the trend towards economic programming which is specific to late capitalism, and overlook the fact that integration into the world economy and international competition create even more hurdles for effective national economic programming.[8]

There is undoubtedly a certain reciprocal effect, of a both technical and economic character between planning of production and accumulation within individual companies and programming of the economy as a whole. The need to plan and calculate exactly within the enterprise, determined by the reduction in the turnover-time of fixed capital, creates the technical tools and interest for a much more precise registration of economic data, which can also be applied to the overall economy. This progress vastly increases the technical potential of effective socialist planning, compared with the techniques at man's disposal, say, in the year 1918 or 1929.

On the other hand, however, the basic economic uncertainty inherent in late capitalist programming must also have profound effects on the application of exact planning techniques within companies. Years of calculations and experiments, gigantic outlays on research and development may have to be thrown overboard at a stroke because of vicissitudes on the market or decisions by rival firms over which a company has no control and about which it can do nothing. Major errors in forecasting belong to the same category. Public programming centres have up to now repeatedly made such mistakes, sometimes with substantial boomerang results, such as the intensification of cyclical disequilibrium instead of the anticyclical effect expected.[9] Wide annual fluctuations in the volume of private

451

investments similarly fall into this category. Economic programming and increased State intervention in the economy have by no means caused these fluctuations to disappear; they continue to be a decisive feature of the capitalist mode of production and its cyclical development. In France, the very country which has an 'exemplary planned economy', these fluctuations have been particularly prominent:

Annual Rate of Increase of Gross Capital Formation in France[10]

1954:	12·4%	1959:	5·7%	1964:	9·6%
1955:	9·3%	1960:	16·2%	1965:	4·3%
1956:	21·0%	1961:	2·3%	1966:	9·3%
1957:	5·5%	1962:	11·6%	1967:	5·6%
1958:	7·3%	1963:	3·2%	1968:	7·4%
				1969:	10·3%

While the effect of economic programming is always uncertain and sometimes positively 'slap-dash', the calculations of so-called 'social programming' are of the utmost importance for late capitalism. The shortened turnover-time of fixed capital compels companies to plan and calculate costs with precision. But the exact planning of costs also implies the exact planning of wage costs. The exact planning of wage costs in turn presupposes the emancipation of the price of the commodity of labour-power from the fluctuations of demand and supply on the so-called labour market. It implies a tendency towards the long-range advance planning of these wage costs.

The simplest method of achieving this is a system of long-term binding collective agreements which eliminate all uncertainty concerning wage costs in ensuing years. But in a normal late-capitalist parliamentary democracy, in which there is a minimum freedom of development for the workers' movement and the class struggle, this solution cannot be enforced in the long run and has in practice proved a failure.[11] For one thing, during the 'long wave with an undertone of expansion' after the Second World War, the general tendency on the labour market was towards an increasing shortage of labour-power in a growing number of countries, so that agreements of this kind came to conflict with the laws of the market. They represented an attempt to cheat the workers of the chances of wage increases afforded by a relatively advantageous market situation. This inevitably became clear to a growing number of workers through experience (possibilities of changing jobs, payments above the agreements by employers, and sometimes enticements to other jobs). In the long run, even a trade-union movement which was only partially responsive to pressure from below could not escape the repercussions of these empirical discoveries by its membership. The impossibility of exact wage planning of a 'voluntary' nature between employers and trade unions thus became increasingly clear, and gave way to a tendency for state mediation. 'Government incomes policy' or 'concerted action', i.e. the proclamation of wage-growth rates binding on 'both sides of industry' has increasingly replaced purely contractual long-term agreements.

But the same laws and forces which doomed long-term collective agreements to failure, likewise condemn 'government incomes policies'. Wage earners have not been slow to discover that a bourgeois State is fully capable of planning and controlling wages or wage increases, but is incapable of keeping a similar rein on increases in the price of commodities or in the income of other social classes, first and foremost of capitalists and capitalist enterprises. 'Government incomes policies' have thus proved to be mere 'policing of wages' – in other words, an attempt artificially to restrict wage increases, and nothing more.[12] Wage earners have consequently defended themselves against this particular method of cheating them just as they had against voluntary self-restraint by trade unions; they have typically sought, by pressure on the trade unions and by 'unofficial strikes' or by a combination of both, at least to adjust the sale of the commodity of labour-power to the conditions of the labour market when these were relatively advantageous to the sellers, and not only when they were disadvantageous to them.

The medium and long-term planning of wage costs needed by large companies in the age of late capitalism thus calls for measures by the bourgeois State going far beyond the voluntary self-restraint of the trade unions or a 'government incomes policy' relying on the co-operation of the trade union bureaucracy. For a minimum degree of efficacy there must further be a legal restriction on the level of wages and the bargaining freedom of the unions, and a legal limitation of the right to strike. If a shortage of labour-power, i.e. a situation of actual full employment, which is not propitious to big capital, can be avoided, and the industrial reserve army at the same time be reconstituted, then the measures just mentioned will in actual fact have a certain temporary effect, as was indeed the case in the USA from the time of the passing of the Taft-Hartley Act until the mid-1960s.

There would then be an intensification of the integration, already incipient in the age of classical imperialism, of the trade-union apparatuses into the state.[13] In this case, the wage-earners increasingly lose all interest in paying their dues to an apparatus which does continual damage to their everyday interests, and the mass basis of trade unions declines. Since, however, the bourgeois class does not want to punish but to reward the trade union apparatus for integrating itself in this way, loss of membership dues must be neutralized or compensated. The logical outcome of the whole process is thus ultimately compulsory collection of dues by the employer at the source, i.e. compulsory membership of the unions. We would then see the public transformation of free trade unions into state trade unions, the conversion of union dues into taxes and the transformation of the trade union apparatus into a specific department of the government bureaucracy, whose special job would be to 'administer' the commodity labour-power, just as other departments of the State machine administer buildings, planes or railways.[14] Since, however, wage earners would by no means simply accept such a process and would interpose new private or 'illegal' mediators between the sellers and buyers of the commodity of labour-power in order to obtain the highest possible price for the sellers, such a system of state unions would be unthinkable without a major increase in passive and active repression – in other words, a substantial limitation, not only of the right to strike, but also of the freedom of association, assembly, demonstration and publication.[15] Hence the trend towards the elimination of the *struggle* between the buyer and the seller of the commodity of labour-power in the determination of the price of this commodity must ultimately culminate in a decisive limitation or abolition of basic democratic freedoms, i.e. the coercive system of a 'strong state'.

If, however, the trade unions, pressed by a membership increasingly acting on its own initiative and re-creating union democracy, successfully escape further integration into the bourgeois state apparatus and revert to resolute defence of the direct interests of the wage earners, they can shatter not only the exact planning of costs and wage costs within large companies but also any possibility of indicative economic planning by bourgeois governments. The trade unions must then increasingly come into collision not only with individual companies and enterprises, not only with employers' federations, but also with governments and the bourgeois state apparatus. For the growing extent to which the interests of large companies are intertwined with government policies on money, finance and trade is among the characteristics of late capitalism. The collision will then grow inexorably into a test of strength between the workers on the one hand and the bourgeois class of the bourgeois state on the other, for capital must again attempt as far as possible to restrict or suppress the activity of workers' organizations – this time also of the 'official' trade unions – which threaten its basic interests. In this scenario too, therefore, the whole process would end in a growing limitation of the right to strike and of the freedoms of association, assembly, demonstration and publication – *if* capital were to triumph.

Employers attempt on their part to turn to their own advantage the consequences of the temporary disappearance of the industrial reserve army, which is of such importance in the alteration of the relationship of forces between the seller and buyer of the commodity of labour-power. Techniques such as job evaluation, Measured Time Work, Method-Time-Measurement and the like[16] are designed to reserve the *collective* sale of the commodity of labour-power (which is the justification for the existence of the trade unions) by individualizing wages, in other words by atomizing wage earners once more and reintroducing competition into their ranks. The success or failure of such attempts, however, is in turn mainly dependent on the current relationship of forces between capital and labour.[17]

The combination of the trend towards the reduction of the turnover-time of fixed capital and the trend towards the limitation of the bargaining freedom of the trade unions clarifies a more general law: *the inherent constraint in late capitalism to increase systematic control over all elements of the processes of production, circulation and reproduction*, a systematic control which is impossible without growing regimentation of the economic and social life as a whole. This law has one of its mainsprings in the mighty concentration of economic power in the hands of a few dozen large companies and financial groups in each country, and of a few hundred large companies and financial groups in the totality of all the capitalist states. The pressure of this gigantic concentration of economic power towards a similar concentration of social and political power was described by Rudolf Hilferding even before the First World War as a characteristic feature of the whole epoch of imperialism and monopoly capitalism. In the conclusion to his book *Das Finanzkapital* he wrote: 'Economic power simultaneously means political power. Domination over the economy at the same time assures control over the means of state coercion. The greater the concentration in the economic sphere, the more unlimited will be the domination of big capital over the state. The resultant tight integration of all the state's instruments of action appears as the highest development of its power, the state as the invincible instrument for the maintenance of economic domination. At the same time, however, the conquest of political power thereby appears as the precondition of economic liberation.'[18]

But in the late capitalist phase still further driving forces are associated with this general tendency. The trend towards exact planning of costs and indicative economic programming, which we have described above, necessitates much close control not only over the level of wages or wage costs but over all elements of the reproduction of capital: 'programmed' research and innovation; organized search for raw materials; planned design of new machines; remote-controlled and planned reproduction of skilled labour-power; guided workers' consumption; a predetermined share for private consumption in the national income or the Gross National Product, and so on. Yet since this whole development is itself an objective education for the proletariat, teaching it to carry the class struggle beyond the enterprise to the overall economic and hence political level, care must be taken that the vast array of facts, which has been collected by empirical research for the specific purposes of the late capitalist bourgeoisie and the late capitalist state, either does not reach the workers at all or does so only in fragmentary, ideological and mystified form, veiling the actual conditions of class domination and exploitation. For this reason, the late capitalist State's function of general organization, regimentation and standardization must be extended to the whole superstructure, and specifically to the sphere of ideology, with the permanent aim of attenuating the class-consciousness of the proletariat. ...

The tendency towards thorough planning and organization within the companies or enterprises of late capitalism necessarily repercusses on the structure of the bourgeois class and the nature of economic administration itself. The constraint to adopt exact planning and calculation within enterprises and companies and to make maximum economies in constant capital, leads to the introduction of more refined and scientific *methods of organization* by late capitalist monopolies.[19] A far more technicized division of labour now replaces the old factory hierarchy. This gives rise to the illusion that bureaucratization of the *administration* of a company is equivalent to an actual bureaucratization of the *function of capital* – in other words, to an ever-increasing delegation of control over the means of production to an expanding army of managers, directors, engineers and 'bosses' large and small.[20]

The reality by no means corresponds to this appearance. The radical technicization and rationalization of the administration of enterprises and companies represents a dialectical unity of two opposite processes – the growing *delegation* of the power to decide questions of detail on the one hand, and the growing *concentration* of the power to decide questions crucial for the expansion of capital on the other. Organizationally and technically, this finds expression in the 'multi-divisional' corporation[21] and in the compulsion to subordinate the delegation of authority more rigorously than ever before to considerations of the overall profitability of the corporation.[22] The tendency for the direction of the 'immediate process of production' to be technically separated from the process of the accumulation of capital, a tendency which first emerged with the appearance of joint-stock companies and was briefly described by Marx and further reviewed by Engels, becomes more widespread in the age of late capitalism.[23] Actual productive technology, or scientific research in the laboratory, market research, advertising and distribution, can achieve a large degree of autonomy. But the ultimate determinant of decision in any company is profitability – in other words, the valorization of the total mass of accumulated capital. If this valorization is insufficient, then the whole of a corporation's programme of production, research, advertising and distribution may be thrown overboard, without the major shareholders who dominate the administrative board ever submitting themselves to the 'specialist knowledge' of the engineers, laboratory workers and market researchers. Indeed, the company may even be sold, temporarily closed down or finally dissolved without any of all these 'managers', technical experts, and controllers of detail ever being able to do anything about it. The unity of the delegation of power to decide ques-

457

tions of detail and the concentration of power to decide questions concerning the valorization of capital thus forms a unity of opposites, in which the defining relationship of capital, i.e. the capacity to dispose of the largest amounts of capital, is the ultimate arbiter. The mistake of those who argue the thesis of the 'bureaucratization' of corporations or the dominance of the 'technostructure' lies in the fact that they confuse the technical articulation of the exercise of power with its economic foundation – the actual sources of this power.

The questionable character of the whole notion of the 'manager' becomes evident when the problem of the relative financial independence of large corporations in a period of accelerated growth, with a high rate of self-financing, is confused with the problem of the alleged conflict of interests between the big bourgeois who own shares and company administrators. The increase in the rate of corporation self-financing as compared since the Second World War is a fact – as is the cyclical limitation of it. This has nothing to do with a conflict of interests between managers and large shareholders – who, after all, are much more interested in increasing the value of their shares than in raising dividends. It can hardly be denied today that these large shareholders further continue to dominate the American economy[24] – even if they do not normally need to interfere with the day-to-day running of companies. On the other hand, it is necessary to remember that in a capitalist social order, in which only property – the ownership of capital – guarantees income and power in the long run, managers themselves are extremely interested in acquiring property in shares. Indeed, this is precisely the way in which top managers climb up the social ladder into the ruling class of capital owners itself. The technique of purchasing optional shares, for example, is an important means to this end. When this device was called into question by fiscal technicalities in the USA, its function had to be fulfilled by other means.[25]

The real consequences of the reduced turnover-time of fixed capital, of the accelerated obsolescence of machinery and of the corresponding increase in the importance of intellectual labour in the capitalist mode of production is a shift in the emphasis of the activity of the major owners of capital. *In the age of freely competitive capitalism, this emphasis lay principally in the immediate sphere of production, and in the age of classical imperialism in the sphere of accumulation (the dominance of financial capital); today, in the age of late capitalism, it lies in the sphere of reproduction.*[26]

The spheres of both production and accumulation have become largely technicized and self-regulating. Objective scientific rules enable these proceses to run more or less 'smoothly'. During the 'long wave with an undertone of expansion' from 1940–65 it was customary for large monopolies to finance investments through prices, without the aid of bank credits. It is for this general reason that powers of detailed decision can be delegated to specialists, for they only need to ensure trouble-free operation of already predetermined processes.[27] The crucial area for the future and fortune of monopolistic and oligopolistic corporations lies in the *selection* and not in the running of these processes – in other words, *in the decision as to what, where and how production will take place*, or still more precisely, *where and how extended reproduction will proceed. Precisely because* accelerated technological innovation, accelerated obsolescence of the material means of production, and reduced turnover-time of fixed capital create *greater uncertainty* in the sphere of reproduction than was the case in the age of classical imperialism or classical monopoly capitalism, the options made in this sphere constitute the *really strategic* decisions which determine the life or death of corporations and also to a great extent the overall tendencies of the economy. The real masters of capital, the large shareholders of corporations, industrial magnates and financial groups, reserve such decisions for themselves without any delegation whatsoever.[28]

Ultimately, the impossibility of a genuine coordination between the economic plans of the different private companies is not due – as bourgeois economists claim[29] – to the uncertainty and discontinuity of technical progress, but to the fact that behaviour which is rational for individual companies *can* lead and periodically *must* lead to irrational results for the economy as a whole. Maximization of the yield of the economy as a whole cannot be simply the sum of the profit maximization of industrial companies. It is not the discontinuity of technical progress as such, but the discontinuity of technical progress within private companies governed by private maximization of profits – i.e. private property and commodity circulation – which is responsible for the insuperable instability and discontinuity of economic development in the capitalist mode of production.

In this sense the contradiction characteristic of late capitalism, between the constraint to plan within the company and the incapacity to move beyond 'indicative' economic programming in the overall context of the economy, is only a more acute expression of the general contradiction, which Marx and Engels showed to be inherent in capitalism, between the planned organization of *parts* of the economic process (production within the factory, disposal within the company, and so on) and the anarchy of the economy as a whole, dominated by the law of value: 'The contradiction between socialized production and capitalistic appropriation now presents itself as an *antagonism between the organization of the production in the individual workshop and the anarchy of production in society generally.*'[30] *This contradiction between the rationality of the parts and the irrationality of the whole ... reaches its apogee in the epoch of late capitalism.*

NOTES AND REFERENCES

1 Heckmann, op cit., p. 42. Bemarl, Bonhoeffer and Strigel, op. cit., p. 30. See also such titles as H. Igor Ansoff (ed.), *Business Strategy*; Alfred D. Chandler, *Strategy and Structure*; and the like.
2 One of the basic errors in Galbraith's *The New Industrial State* (London, 1969) is that he ignores the distinction between short- and long-term maximization of profits.
3 Gordon Yewdall (ed.), *Management Decision Making*, London, 1969, p. 91f.; Bemerl, Bonhoeffer and Strigel, op. cit., p. 34: 'Market expectations and considerations of profitability [exercise] the greatest influence on the long-term planning of enterprises'.
4 'Part of the information needed refers to processes and conditions within the enterprise. The extent to which these are available and the enterprise thereby becomes transparent is largely determinable by the management of the enterprise itself.' Bemerl, Bonhoeffer and Strigel, op. cit., p. 32. The availability of the data depends of course on the control over the means of production, and not the other way round.
5 It may occur that 'profitability calculations' are made within the corporation or within the factory for individual departments. These are then used to measure the relative

efficiency of the management of this department. See, for instance, A. J. Merrett, 'Incomes, Taxation, Managerial Effectiveness and Planning', in B. W. Denning (ed.), *Corporate Long Range Planning*, pp. 90–1. It is a matter, however, of fictitious or simulated profitability, since these departments do not possess independent capital, and the investments in them do not depend on 'profitability' but on the overall strategic plan of the corporation.

6 'The guiding principle of planning (in France) is to integrate the sum of these interdependent effects by extending the typical behaviour of the iron and steel producer as regards his supplies and outlets, to the whole economy. The instrument for market research on a national scale in the *Tableau économique* devised by François Quesnay, revised by Leontief and adapted for France by Gruson. The procedure is that of concerted consultation within modernization commissions.... A coordination of this kind can operate indirectly through the influence of the dominant industrial groups.... It is to their mutual advantage that a confrontation of the forecasts and decisions of the private sector should take place in a public context.' Pierre Massé, *Le Plan ou l'Anti-Hasard*, Paris, 1965, p. 173.

7 'Individual firms, having made separate market studies may find that the state of the market in respect to both the supply of inputs and the demand for outputs does not warrant any expansion of the firm. This assessment may be fully correct within that framework, but if a respected planning body sets up a target for, say, 10 per cent expansion, it may be easily attained both individually and collectively, except, of course, for the external sector.... The Japanese plan "forecasts" how the private sector and the public sector *would behave* if each business and government department carried out extensive research studies at both micro- and macro-levels considering all important economic factors and potentialities both at home and abroad, and after that proceeded to optimize its behaviour. Thus the plans are forecasts of what the optimal behaviour of the Japanese economy as a whole and in parts would be. ... Briefly, in Japan the execution or implementation of the plan rests solely on the 'announcement effect" of the plan, and the Economic Planning Agency acts as a consultant, and not as a director.' K. Bieda, op. cit., pp. 57, 59–60.

8 Andrew Shonfield, *Modern Capitalism*, Oxford, 1969, pp.

231–2, 255–7, 299–300.

9 'There was the plan in 1962 that the economy would grow at 4 per cent, but what happened? The economy did not grow at 4 per cent and this resulted in too much capital equipment in electric power, steel making and in many other industries.' Denning (ed.), op. cit., p. 197. For the mistaken forecasts of Swedish economic programmes, see Holger Heide. *Langfristige Wirtschaftsplanung in Schweden*, Tübingen, 1965.

10 Data up to 1963; *Rapport sur les Comptes de la Nation de 1963*; from 1964 onwards, in productive branches only, Mairesse, op. cit., p. 52.

11 The tendency towards long-term wage agreements has been reversed in the USA, West Germany, Belgium and other countries.

12 Bauchet admits that French trade union leaders restricted wage increases, while at the same time the official price index was falsified; the government was not in a position to control the rise in prices, and there was no mention either of controlling undistributed company profits, so that there was by no means an 'equal sacrifice by all', Pierre Bauchet, *La Planification Française*, Paris, 1966, pp. 320–1. We would add : the result was May 1968.

13 Trotsky analysed the growing tendency in capitalism for the unions to be integrated into the bourgeois state as early as 1940; see 'Trade Unions in the Epoch of Imperialist Decay' in *Leon Trotsky on the Trade Unions*, New York, 1969.

14 The so-called 'vertical trade unions' in Spain are a classic example of such a function of the 'trade union apparatus'.

15 The 'Industrial Relations Act', forced through the British Parliament by the Conservative government of 1970–4, made it illegal for unauthorized persons, which includes newspapers, to call for a strike.

16 See, for example, *Leistungslohn-systeme*, Zurich, 1970; Bernard Meier, *Solaires Systématique de Rendement*, Lucerne, 1968; and the contributions of Hans Mayr, Nat Weinberg and Hans Pornschlegel in *Automation – Risiko und Chance*, vol. II, Frankfurt, 1965.

17 See, among others, Tony Cliff, *The Employers' Offensive*, London, 1970. Antonio Lettieri analyses the conditions which led to the abolition of job evaluation in the most recent labour agreement (concluded in 1971) in the Italian state steel trust Italsider: Antonio Lettieri in *Problemi del Socialismo*, no. 49.

18 Rudolf Hilferding, *Das Finanzkapital*, p. 476.
19 Pollock, op. cit., p. 282f.; Reuss, op. cit., pp. 48–51; William H. Whyte, *The Organization Man*, London, 1960, and so on.
20 This theory of the 'bureaucratization' of capital, which has remained fashionable for the past forty years, from the standard work by Berle and Means (*The Modern Corporation and Private Property*, New York, 1933) through Burnham's *The Managerial Revolution* to Galbraith's *The New Industrial State*, is dealt with in greater detail in Chapter 17 of the present work. [*Late Capitalism*].
21 See, among others, Alfred D. Chandler, *Strategy and Structure*, New York, 1961.
22 'The fundamental problem of modern management is the control (effectively the planning) of profitability in large companies, given that such companies are, under modern conditions, subject to extremely powerful forces whose ultimate effect is towards the disintegration of central control over corporate profitability, with the result that the company becomes (or remains) a largely uncontrolled and inefficient confederation of conflicting power blocks and functional interests.' Merrett, op. cit., p. 89.
23 Marx, *Capital*, vol. 3. pp. 380, 514–26; Friedrich Engels, *Socialism, Utopian and Scientific* in Marx and Engels, *Selected Works*, pp. 427–8.
24 Domhoff confirms that 1 per cent of American adults owned more than 75 per cent of all company shares in 1960 – a higher proportion than in 1922 or 1929 (when it was 61·5 per cent). A Senate Commission has even reckoned that 0·2 per cent of US households control two-thirds of all such shares: William Domhoff, *Who Rules America?*, New York, 1967, p. 45. In 1960, the boardroom directors of 141 out of 232 large corporations possessed enough shares to control their concerns (p. 49). See also Ferdinand Lundberg, *The Rich and the Super-Rich*, New York, 1968, who likewise sharply attacks the notion of any managerial supremacy.
25 For this, see Arch Patton, 'Are Stock Options Dead?', *Harvard Business Review*, September–October 1970; and Shorey Peterson, in *The Quarterly Journal of Economics*, February 1965, p. 18.
26 'A recent report gave the observations of over forty of America's professional industrial managers on management in nine intensely industrialized countries of Europe. They visited hundreds of industrial enterprises. . . . They found too

many instances where top managers . . . failed to realize that their primary function is to plan for the future', OEEC, *Problems of Business Management*, Paris, 1954, cited in Goodman, op. cit., pp. 188–9.

27 Heckmann, op. cit., pp. 85–8. See also Merrett, 'Incomes, Taxation, Management Effectiveness and Planning' in B. W. Denning (ed.), *Corporate Long-Range Planning*, pp. 89–90.

28 Heckmann, op. cit., p. 63, distinguishes between the first two phases of long-term planning by enterprises (establishment of enterprise objectives and 'optimal competitive strategy') and the third and fourth phase (formulation of a programme of action and testing and revising the plans). The first two fall within the competence of 'top management'. The third and fourth can no longer be controlled by the top management of the firm alone, even if they take all final decisions.

29 See our discussion of this thesis in *Marxist Economic Theory*, pp. 373–6.

30 Friedrich Engels, *Socialism, Utopian and Scientific* in Marx and Engels, *Selected Works*, p. 423.

Acknowledgements

For kind permission to reprint published texts in this book, the Editor would like to thank the following publishers and copyright-holders:

Penguin Books Ltd, Harmondsworth, for 'The Labour Process and Valorization' and 'The Factory' from Karl Marx, *Capital: a Critique of Political Economy*, vol. 1, tr. Ben Fowkes (Penguin Books in association with *New Left Review*, 1976), pp. 283–304 and 544–50: edition and notes © *New Left Review* 1976, translation © Ben Fowkes 1976; and for 'Piecework and "Looting"' from Miklos Haraszti, *A Worker in a Worker's State*, tr. Michael Wright (Penguin Books in association with *New Left Review*, 1977), pp. 35–52: translation © Michael Wright 1977, selection © *New Left Review* 1977.

Pluto Press Ltd, London, for ' "Chibaro": Forced Mine Labour in Southern Rhodesia, 1903–12' from Charles van Onselen, *Chibaro* (1976), pp. 91–114.

New Left Books, London, for 'Labour and the State in Nazi Germany' and 'Planning, Strategy and Capitalist Crisis' from Ernest Mandel, *Late Capitalism* (1975), pp. 157–62 and 232–47.

New Left Review, London, for Stephen Castles and Godula Kosack, 'The Function of Labour Immigration in Western European Capitalism', *New Left Review*, 73 (May/June 1973), pp. 3–18.

The University of Chicago Press, Illinois, for 'Migrant Labor in South Africa and the United States' from Michael Burawoy, 'The Functions and Reproduction of Migrant Labor', *American Journal of Sociology*, vol. 81, no. 5 (March 1976), pp. 1051–87.

Routledge and Kegan Paul Ltd, London, for 'Education and the Long Shadow of Work' from Samuel Bowles and Herbert Gintis, *Schooling in Capitalist America* (1976), pp. 125–33; for ' "ChemCo", Bureaucratic Control and Psycho-Sociology in England in the early 1970s' from Theo Nichols and Huw Benyon, *Living with Capitalism* (1977), pp. 109–30; and for

'The Proletarianisation of the Employees' from Guglielmo Carchedi, *On the Identification of Social Classes* (1977), pp. 188–93.

Saxon House, Farnborough, for 'Working Class Kids and Working Class Jobs' from Paul Willis, *Learning to Labour* (1977), pp. 52–9.

Union for Radical Political Economics, Massachusetts, for 'A Marxist View of Ownership and Control' from Michel de Vroey, 'The Separation of Ownership and Control in Large Corporations', *Review of Radical Political Economics*, vol. 7, no. 5 (summer 1975), pp. 1–10, © *Review of Radical Political Economics* 1975.

Stephen Marglin for 'The Origins and Functions of Hierarchy in Capitalist Production' from Stephen Marglin, 'What Do Bosses Do? The Origins and Functions of Hierarchy in Capitalist Production', *Review of Radical Political Economics*, vol. 6, no. 2 (summer 1974), pp. 44–52, © Stephen Marglin 1974.

Monthly Review Press, London, for 'The Transformation of Office Work' from Harry Braverman, *Labor and Monopoly Capital* (1974), pp. 319–48, © Harry Braverman 1974.

Harvester Press, Hassocks, for 'The Meaning of "Job Enrichment"' from Michel Bosquet, *Capitalism in Crisis and Everyday Life* (1977), pp. 92–101.

The Editor and publishers are grateful to the authors of the following previously unpublished texts for permission to print them here:

'A Political Economy of the Family in Capitalism: Women, Reproduction and Wage Labour' © Jackie West 1980.

'The "Lump" in the UK Construction Industry' © Terry Austrin 1980.

'UK Productivity Dealing in the 1960s' © Martyn Nightingale 1980.

'Monopoly Capitalism and the Impact of Taylorism: Notes on Lenin, Gramsci, Braverman and Sohn-Rethel' © Tony Elger and Bill Schwarz 1980.

'Participation: the Pattern and its Significance' © Harvie Ramsay 1980.

'Fear Stuff, Sweet Stuff and Evil Stuff: Management's Defenses against Unionization in the South' © Donald F. Roy 1980.

'Italy's FIAT in Turin in the 1950s' © Hilary Partridge 1980.

Author Index

467

Subject Index

Fontana Paperbacks

Fontana is a leading paperback publisher of fiction and non-fiction, with authors ranging from Alistair MacLean, Agatha Christie and Desmond Bagley to Solzhenitsyn and Pasternak, from Gerald Durrell and Joy Adamson to the famous Modern Masters series.

In addition to a wide-ranging collection of internationally popular writers of fiction, Fontana also has an outstanding reputation for history, natural history, military history, psychology, psychiatry, politics, economics, religion and the social sciences.

All Fontana books are available at your bookshop or newsagent; or can be ordered direct. Just fill in the form and list the titles you want.

FONTANA BOOKS, Cash Sales Department, G.P.O. Box 29, Douglas, Isle of Man, British Isles. Please send purchase price, plus 8p per book. Customers outside the U.K. send purchase price, plus 10p per book. Cheque, postal or money order. No currency.

NAME (Block letters)

ADDRESS